ILLINOIS

Ohio River

KENTUCKY

D0425755

Cumberland
Mountain

Clinch R.

Middlesboro
Cumberland Gap

Tennessee River

Clinton
Oak Ridge
Knoxville
Maryville

Nashville

Cumberland
Plateau

Great Smoky
Athens Mountains
(N.P)

NORTH CAROLINA

SOUTH CAROLINA

Mississippi R.

Memphis

TENNESSEE

Chattanooga
Cleveland

Tennessee River

'Black Bottom'
'Goodall Boyville'

Atlanta

MISSISSIPPI

Birmingham

Talladega
Nat. Forest

GEORGIA

Tuscaloosa

Eutaw
Epes

Montgomery

Meridian

Jackson

ALABAMA

W

E

Lake Ponchartrain

Mobile

FLORIDA

Tallahassee

Pensacola

S

New
Orleans

Gulf of
Mexico

- - - Route of journey

IN THE
DEEP SOUTH

IN THE
DEEP SOUTH

Roy Kerridge

London
MICHAEL JOSEPH

MICHAEL JOSEPH LTD
Published by the Penguin Group
27 Wrights Lane, London W8 5TZ, England
Viking Penguin Inc., 40 West 23rd Street, New York, New York 10010, USA
Penguin Books Australia Ltd, Ringwood, Victoria, Australia
Penguin Books Canada Ltd, 2801 John Street, Markham, Ontario, Canada
L3R 1B4
Penguin Books (NZ) Ltd, 182–190 Wairau Road, Auckland 10, New Zealand

Penguin Books Ltd, Registered Offices: Harmondsworth, Middlesex, England

First published 1989

Copyright © Roy Kerridge 1989

Printed and bound in Great Britain by
Butler & Tanner, Frome, Somerset
Set in Linotron Ehrhardt by
Cambrian Typesetters, Frimley, Surrey

A CIP catalogue record for this book is available from the British Library

ISBN 0 7181 3140 1

For Jeremy Lewis and Family

AUTHOR'S NOTE

All the names of people and places mentioned in Chapters Eight and Nine are fictitious. Other fictitious names in this book are Desita, Celestine, Dulaney, Blues Boy Benjamen, Barrington-Wranglestone, Surreal and Nicolette. The Plaza Toro and Morrell House are fictitious hotel names.

CONTENTS

ACKNOWLEDGEMENTS

I would like to thank the following individuals for their kind help and encouragement: Mr and Mrs Segal; John Davey; Wayne and Jennifer Packer; Lola Wigan and John; Mrs Celia Henderson; Geoffrey Hellman; Marcus Warren; Michael Wharton; Mr Chisholm; Festus Okoh; Butch Willis of Lake Charles; Thomas Duncan of Cleveland, Tennessee; Steve Goldstein; Lena Morgan and George Gawrieh of the G.Q. Fashion Shop, 209, E. Broad Street, Texarkana; Sheri and all at Bowen's Restaurant, Arkadelphia; Lin Blackmon of Texarkana; Kevin Kell; Beverly Gianna of New Orleans; the Ace Team II; Pocahontas II; Irena and Jane of the Knighton Chip Shop; Sally Vaughan, Melanie Whitehouse and Alison Evans of Knighton; Jean Campbell of Cleveland, Tennessee; and all at the Old Mansion House, Knighton, Radnorshire.

I would like to thank Wolf Stephenson of Malaco Records, Jackson, Mississippi, for permission to quote a few lines from 'Down Home Blues' by Z.Z. Hill and from 'You've Got a Chance' by the Jackson Southernaires. I would also like to thank the following executives at Malaco: Roy Wooten, Thomisene Anderson, Tom Easley, David R. Curry Jnr and Melvin Williams, for all their kindness.

In conclusion, I would like to acknowledge my debt to two books which inspired my voyage: *Lost Highway* by Peter Guralnick (David R. Godine, publisher, Boston, U.S.A.) and *Through America by Rocking Chair* by Ronald Searle and Alex Atkinson (Perpetua Books, London).

CHAPTER ONE

Way Down Yonder

EVER SINCE I was five years old, I have loved the American South. Snug in our little flat at the bottom of Harrow Hill, just outside London, my mother would read wonderful stories to my brother Martin and me. Tales of Uncle Remus, collected by Joel Chandler Harris from a hundred Negro cabins, held us enthralled. I knew that Uncle Remus must be a real person, and I longed to meet him. His humorous brand of English seemed a superior tongue to that spoken outside in the unending winter of the ration-bound 1940s. Brer Rabbit, the trickster hero of his tales, became my hero and I have something mischievous about me yet.

My grandparents had a piano, and on the piano reposed the *Fireside Book of American Folksongs*; floral patterns on the cover and bright pictures within. Here were songs of cowboys, hillbillies, slaves and warriors of either side in the American Civil War. Negro spirituals, as sung by my mother's own hero, Paul Robeson, had a great appeal for me.

At Sudbury Infants' School I became famous for my Brer Rabbit stories, a precocious Uncle Remus in my own right. I would stand in front of the class and tell and act the stories, jumping from spot to spot as I became first a fox, then a rabbit. One story, which involved a tug of war between Brer Bear and Brer Terrapin, made a most successful show, as I leaned back grunting with strain, hauling on an imaginary rope.

Mr Evans, the bald-headed, bull-necked headmaster of the Juniors, put an end to these displays.

'This boy is a mental case. He thinks he is a rabbit,' he snorted.

I could bear this disappointment, as my next hero became Huckleberry Finn. Many children and adults find Huck hard going, as Twain's masterpiece is written in slang. Uncle Remus had attuned my ears to Southern English, and I raced down the Mississippi with Huck and Jim and asked for more. This I received, in the form of *Tom Sawyer Abroad*, a little-known tale discovered by my mother, one involving an heroic balloon flight across the Sahara Desert.

Hopping to and from school, I saw not suburban dwellings with privet hedges but red dirt lanes between fields of goober peas, bounded by wooden split-rail fences. Smoke curled from the clay chimney of Uncle Remus's cabin at the edge of the piney woods. Along the rolling lanes Brer Rabbit and Brer Wolf pranced by on their hind legs, greeting one another with elaborate politeness, one ready to run, the other to pounce. By now I would be home, ready for a glass of Tizer and the *Mickey Mouse Comic* where Brer Rabbit's adventures were retold.

When I was a little older, I recall my mother angrily reading a book review in *Soviet Literature* magazine. This was heresy, for we were a Communist family, our 'official' dream country not the American South but Soviet Russia. Here the two dreamlands collided, for my mother did not agree with the Russian critic's appraisal of *God's Little Acre*, a novel by Erskine Caldwell. According to *Soviet Literature*, working men just did not behave like Erskine Caldwell's Southern characters.

Perhaps that book review was the sharp end of the scissors that cut the Party Line in our home. I do not know. Erskine Caldwell's stories of 'poor white' life lasted me well into my teens, and the lurid pictures on the paperback covers greatly impressed the boys at my secondary school. By now we were Communists no longer. In between wanting to be a zoo keeper and an artist for the *Beano*, I yearned to be a collector of traditional songs, like Alan Lomax. Songs of the South, recorded by Lomax, became favourites in our family. My mother told me of brave Lomax's adventures in the Appalachians, where he was stabbed by the jealous hillbilly husband of an aged crone whose song he was recording: 'Oh Lovely Appearance of Death'.

Paul Robeson had been a Communist, and Alan Lomax a lonesome fellow traveller. Somehow it was felt by atheist English Communists that the great spirituals did not count as hymns to God, but were the slaves' counterpart of revolutionary songs in praise of Russia and the Workers of the World. Living a hundred years ago, and denied access to Soviet Literature, the slaves had clothed their longing for a Workers' State in Biblical language. So it was 'all right' to listen to Robeson. Traditional songs became Communist if called 'folk songs'.

As my childhood Communism fell away, so the Lure of the South grew stronger. I had tried hard to like Soviet Russia, but its many glories had always been difficult for me to love. There was a Children's Train, where even the driver was a boy, recipient of many points for good behaviour in the Pioneers. Then there was a funfair, and while at Sudbury I pictured myself married to a Communist Chinese girl with glasses and walking round the Moscow funfair without actually going on anything. For I did not like trains or funfairs very much, and the political side of the Soviet Union had passed me by in blessed incomprehensibility. So I was glad to escape from Russia.

Away from my mother's influence, staying at Hove with my grandparents, I left school under a cloud and fell under the spell of Lonnie Donegan. A nasal-voiced Glaswegian singer, popular at the time, the late 1950s, Donegan was a disciple of Alan Lomax. Lonnie Donegan's songs evoked a dream South he too had never seen. We appeared to live in the same mental world. In a dream, I floated around the coffee bars of Brighton, seeing teddy boys in bootlace ties as Mississippi gamblers and old lags from Lewes Gaol as fugitives from the Georgia chain gang.

I remember my doubt and anguish when Donegan recorded 'My Old Man's a Dustman', a Cockney song far removed from his usual Southern fare. Was this the beginning of the end? If so, it was the end for both of us, for gradually the very English teddy boys and the Sussex poachers who ended up in Lewes became more real than imaginary Southerners. Through the mist, they swam into focus, and I found that I was living in England for the first time in my life.

Delighted with England, once I had noticed my native land, I remained a faithful patriot, yet never lost my Old Alliance with the South. Libraries were scanned for all that was Southern, and over the years I revelled in *Black Boy* by Richard Wright, the *American Notes* of Charles Dickens, and the heartrending memoirs of Fanny Kemble, an English lady imprisoned by marriage in the Big House of a Georgia cotton plantation. Much against her American husband's will, she stretched forth a hand to help the starveling, ragged slaves who appealed to her in anguish.

These books are critical of the American South, the last two filled with pity for the Negroes held in bondage. Perhaps my early allegiance to a land where all was supposedly perfect (Soviet Russia) made the imperfect world of the South all the more attractive.

One day, at Brighton fishmarket, an open space beside the shingly beach, I heard an open-air Negro church service, where spirituals were chanted to hand-clapping and cries of 'Yes, Lord! That's true, amen.'

'Are you Americans?' I asked one of the Sisters, a big lady with her head tied in a bandana.

'No, we are from the West Indies.'

So before long, back in London, I began attending a West Indian church whose elderly Jamaican pastor spoke just like Uncle Remus. 'Care' was 'keer', 'card' was 'kyard' and 'going' became 'gwine'. I saw that my former belief in a Workers' State had been a longing for Heaven clothed in Communist language. Every year the Church of God of Prophecy went down to Brighton for their National Convention. One year Bishop McCalla addressed us there. He was organising a trip to the

church headquarters at Cleveland, Tennessee, and convention-goers
were encouraged to put their names down. Would Brer Roy like to go?

Would he! This was the chance I had been waiting for. And so, along
with hundreds of West Indians and Black British youth, I visited the
American South. I listened to Kentucky bluegrass music, heard gospel
songs in a Negro church and eavesdropped as rugged farmers from North
Carolina told 'mule jokes'. All too soon it was time to go. My eleven-day
visit had shown me that Uncle Remus notwithstanding, there was no
place for me in an America where the motor car ruled all. A non-driver, I
detest motorways and modern hotels, preferring old towns and public
transport. America was moving away from my ideals, yet traces of the Old
South remained. Would I ever return?

In 1986 the opportunity to return presented itself (thanks to a publisher)
and I was overjoyed.

My companion on my aeroplane flight (a boat ride to America
unfortunately being out of the question) was none other than Booker T.
Washington. He spoke to me eloquently from the pages of his book *Up
From Slavery*. Published over sixty years ago, the great Negro educator's
moving autobiography made a useful guide to the modern South. Two
years earlier, my mother had found the same pocket volume to be equally
valuable a key to Rhodesia-Zimbabwe.

My hatred of air travel ended the moment I stepped into the small
aircraft that would take me from the American North to New Orleans.
One look at the relaxed, comfortable, badly-dressed, swag-bellied
passengers, and all my cares seemed to melt away. These people were
Southerners! Some were coloured and some were white, yet all seemed
mercifully free from Northern sophistication. Until then I had not
realised how little I could get on with Northerners, or Yankees. Their
accents seemed harsh, their much-loved politics a matter of setting a
President up with cheers only to pull him down with jeers. A separate
nation, the complacent Southerners flying home to Dixie clearly didn't
give a tinker's cuss about world affairs, and very soothing I found it.
Waves of anxiety rolled from my mind.

Down the plane swooped, a black shadow moving across eerie white
skeleton forests growing from brown swamp waters. All at once we were
over blue Lake Ponchartrain, a vast inland sea where a white snake-
necked egret flew upwards from the reeds. At the airport, we were met by
a free white mini-bus or 'shuttle'.

'Welcome to New Orleans!' the coloured driver beamed. He drove us
'downtown' to the radio jazz music of Count Basie and Ella Fitzgerald.
My dream was becoming reality; memories of teds and poachers faded
away, and I was in New Orleans from whence my journey around the

South would begin. Armed only with Booker T. Washington, the works of Southern writer Zora Neale Hurston, and my ability to draw unicorns and sing 'My Old Man's a Dustman', I was on my way.

New Orleans seemed a shabby long-drawn-out town, yet in the motorway-suburbs I was entranced to see green banana trees growing in flowerless bungalow gardens, palm leaves spilling over roadside walls. A tropical sun still blazed in October. Two by two, the other passengers dismounted at their skyscraper hotels, greeting each modern monstrosity with cries of gladness.

'Y.M.C.A.!' shouted the driver, and I stepped blinking into the American South.

CHAPTER TWO

In New Orleans

I DRAGGED MY BAG to the steps of the Y.M.C.A., a flat-fronted building
that faced the large roundabout of Lee Circle. Dark-skinned men were
sitting on the steps, speaking rapidly in what seemed to be French. They
leaned slightly aside as I staggered past and lurched slowly to the
Reception desk. Instead of my usual plastic bag, I was travelling heavy,
with innumerable pairs of socks. At the desk, I blurted out my tale to a
quiet Reception clerk. A middle-aged one-armed man in blue shirt and
spectacles, he listened calmly and drily, but said nothing.

'Can you hear me?' I asked at length.

'You keep talking, I'm listening,' he replied, and gave me a key.

'Your room's on Floor Nine,' he said. 'If you want breakfast, ask at the
desk for a ticket – it'll be two dollars.'

I was aware of the American custom of separating bed and breakfast
into two expensive halves, so without complaining, I staggered into the
lift. Shabbily-dressed coloured men with moustaches stood round me,
this time apparently speaking in Spanish.

'I'm going to Floor Nine,' I told them conversationally.

'Floor Nine!' one of them repeated, and all laughed.

Floor Nine, when it arrived, was not as funny as all that. A brown dingy
corridor with many zigzags, it contained rows of wooden doors and a
shower room. My room, when I found it, was so hot and so squalid that
my heart sank. I had decided on a fourteen-dollar-a-night room – should
I have joined the aristocracy in the twenty-dollar rooms? The room, dark,
brown and musty like the rest of the Y.M.C.A., contained a small bed, a
wardrobe cupboard, a table, chair and writing lamp. Only the absence of a
washbasin outwardly distinguished it from the room in the Liverpool
Y.M.C.A. where I had once spent three happy months. Yet the dirty
curtains with their brown tide-mark, the cockroach poison on the floor

and the lively half-inch cockroaches scuttling about everywhere were very different from anything seen in England. The heat drenched me with sweat, and, after unpacking, I pulled the chair over to an air conditioning machine that nestled below the window.

After I had pushed several buttons, the machine gave a shudder and a roar, liquid sloshed about inside somewhere, and a thin stream of cool air began to emerge from a grating. I huddled over the machine as in English lodgings I had huddled over an electric fire.

Would I ever be able to leave the air conditioning machine without collapsing? Gloomily, I foresaw a week spent crouching in a chair, the pitiless sun waiting outside to slay me. Outside my window there was a very interesting view. Lawns, flowers and seats ringed an immense white column, on top of which stood Robert E. Lee, the great Southern commander of the Civil War forces or Confederate Army. Sternly, almost angrily, he stood with stone arms folded as he surveyed St Charles' Avenue. This avenue converged from narrow streets behind the Y.M.C.A. out into a wide thoroughfare leading uphill away from my window. Vagrant-looking men sat comfortably on the seats. Every now and then, a single-decker tram, shaped like an old-fashioned railway carriage, trundled along the roadway lines and vanished up the hill. Above flat roof tops, a golden dome and church spire gleamed, and traffic poured along an overpass. If only I could go out!

At last, I tore myself away from the life-giving air machine, took a small carrier bag out of my big bag, and set out to explore the Y.M.C.A. I refreshed myself at a drinking fountain, only to see a cockroach emerge hesitantly from the spout after I had finished. Had I been drinking pure cockroach? The staircase was locked, so I took the lift. This time it was empty. I grew to like the Y.M.C.A. lift, its dull red colour a nice change from the prevailing brown. Its mirrors were so arranged that I could see the front and back of my head alternatively, in a long vista stretching to a Looking Glass horizon, and so keep an eye on the progress of my bald patch.

Between Floor Nine and the ground floor were office rooms, a launderette and telephone booths where young black men could be found curled up asleep like dormice. Middle-aged women, well-mannered but tired-looking, hauled trolleys of clean towels from room to room and made the beds. There was no lounge or reading room, but outside, in the New Building next door, there was a gym, a blue swimming pool and a cafeteria.

The gleaming white New Building was a contrast to the old. All over America, I was told, Y.M.C.A.s had become places for sport and for exercise, particularly for weightlifting. I was lucky to be in New Orleans, as in most other American towns the accommodation side of Y.M.C.A.

life had been abolished. Money and resources had been poured into the gymnasiums, attracting not footloose young people at large in strange cities but well-dressed, health-conscious youngsters who lived locally.

Behind glass windows, in an airy carpeted hall, I saw what must have been one of the best equipped gymnasiums in the world. Huge weightlifting machines, gleaming with polish, were in constant use, pistons moving and weights hauling up and down as huge beefcake males sweated and strained, watched admiringly through the glass by their plump girlfriends. It looked as if the Harlem Globetrotters had run amok in the Science Museum at South Kensington, in the hall where boys press buttons to activate mysterious engines. Some of the Y.M.C.A. devices resembled ancient instruments of torture – the rack, the press and the thumbscrew. A frowning white girl pedalled furiously on a stationary bicycle.

On the wall hung a bright oil painting of a girl in shorts standing beside an oak tree, hung with pictures of athletes. 'Spirit of the Next Hero, by George Rodrigue,' the inscription read, 'on Loan from Tharp-Southerner Funeral Homes.'

So that was where all that healthiness got you! Could healthiness be a racket, promoted by greedy undertakers? Even the Y.M.C.A. café, a narrow empty room, had a hygienic carrot-juicy feeling to it. Here, climbing up the wall, I found a dear little green anole lizard with staring eyes and a white belly. He looked as if he were lost, so I caught him and released him in a bush outside, his skin soft and clammy to my touch.

At the café counter, hemmed in by arty trellis work, stood a round-faced, serious-looking coloured girl, who asked me what I wanted. I ordered strawberries and ice cream.

'I'm going to Chef's College,' she told me in a soft, slow voice, as she sliced the frozen strawberries into sections and, with a catering scholar's concentration, arranged them in a pattern on my plate. 'I'd like to study in Switzerland, as I got relations there. My name's Avis – what's yours?'

Taking a floppy white hat from my bag, I eventually said goodbye to Avis and ventured outside. The hot air sent me reeling for a moment, but drew me on with promise of tropical mystery and adventure. By walking slowly and keeping on the shady side of the street, I found I could move around New Orleans at will. Across the street, a tall rambling nineteenth-century office block was now the Institute of the Contemporary Arts. A glimpse inside showed that Art was just as Contemporary and inscrutable in New Orleans as in London. Outside, I saw a little coloured girl sitting on the steps. She watched entranced as a gigantic two-inch cockroach, his wings folded loosely beneath his brown shiny tail coat, strutted importantly along the pavement.

'Shall I kill him?' I asked.

'No, don't do that,' she smiled.

Then I went back to Floor Nine and admired the air conditioner as I waited for sunset. My view of St Charles' Avenue was impeded by a concrete barrier of circular patterns, like a gigantic fireguard that covered the whole front of the building. Between this safeguard and the rows of windows on my floor ran a long ledge heaped up with rubbish and pigeon droppings, iron bars preventing intruders from walking along it from room to room. Each floor had a similar unsavoury balcony, with barriers against burglary or suicide, but no way of removing cast-out rags, bottles, papers, tins and filth. I wondered if acrobatic rats could climb up there, and I closed the window.

Dusk fell, and I went out again, this time to walk in a circle around Lee Circle.

'Can you spare me a quarter?' a stout man on a bench enquired.

Below the great Lee pillar, two young rats danced across my path and vanished into a shrubbery. I returned to the air conditioned coolth of the gymnasium for a while, and then set out to explore the dark, narrow end of St Charles' Avenue, a street which obviously led to the town centre. Steamy, exciting and alluring, the night air of New Orleans was beyond mugginess and like nothing I had ever experienced. I admired the narrow pavements of red brick and white mortar, and at every narrow side street I waited impatiently for the bright white lettering to change from 'Don't Walk' to 'Walk'. I had no idea if it were safe to walk outdoors in New Orleans or not. Still, the sign said 'Walk'.

Square Spanish buildings alternated with nineteenth-century shops and offices, cheap hotels ('Rooms'), tiny dark cafés and pubs. In the Irish fashion, these were known as 'bars' and bore the owner's name rather than a painted swinging sign. I found a workmen's café and went in.

Here the freezing blast of a Siberian air conditioner hit me head on. I gamely pressed on and mounted a stool by the counter. Young staff dashed to and fro, all very busy, and a chef sizzled hamburgers a foot from where I was sitting. A girl with a narrow-eyed 'closed' face scooped up a shovel of ice and gave me a glass of water. All Southerners, I found, sloshed masses of crushed ice into soft drinks, hard drinks and lemon tea. A moment later a youth with an ironic ex-hippie look about him and a straw boater on his head took my order of corned beef and cabbage. A hot lump of yellow cornbread with a pat of butter and a dish of coleslaw came with the enormous meal, a white cabbage covering my whole plate. Afterwards, over a hot delicious peach pie and a mug of coffee, I relaxed and looked about me.

I was in a long narrow room, with settle chairs and tables by the window. The menu was chalked up on a board at one end of the room, a girl with a cash register sat at the other. I was sitting in the midst of big men, mostly lorry drivers, who lined the long counter on bar stools or sat in groups at the tables, talking loudly. Another eating room opened up behind the blackboard, and behind the cash register, narrow wooden steps led upstairs.

From a juke box in a corner, overloaded with country and western records, a Southern voice yowled the strange story of 'the day the squirrel went beserk in the First Saints' Baptist Church' as customers tapped their feet.

Most of the customers were white workmen, dressed casually, their bellies hanging out and hairy chests exposed. Young men had a hippie scrag-end look about them while older drivers looked like ageing teds. They seemed a pleasant bunch, with a slightly self-conscious air of 'toughness' about them. Coloured men moved and chatted easily with the others. Near the blackboard, a circle of huge, fierce men in bulging shirts sat, talking of 'truck' journeys they had made. ('Truck' in America means 'lorry', while railway trucks seem to be called 'railroad boxcars'.) These men were dominated by a huge, dark-skinned truculent 'trucker' with sunken eyes and a tall Brylcream-sleek hairstyle. He looked sarcastically at the few coloured customers. Perhaps he was a Red Indian.

'First thing I know, he pulled out two pistols,' I heard him saying.

At the next table, sitting low in a high settle, a black driver in a peaked cap looked fondly across the table at his little boy. 'Now you're old enough to travel with me *any* place,' he said. The boy's eyes shone, but he preserved a self-important 'grown-up' demeanour.

At the pay-desk, I gave the young lady a five-dollar note instead of a one dollar. They looked very similar.

'Not everyone's honest like me,' she explained. 'There's only one thing to do. Learn!'

And my change tumbled out of a chute into a metal cup.

Before returning to the Y.M.C.A., I decided to visit a pub. This I did with some trepidation, fearful that the landlord would laugh at me. A square, Spanish-looking building, the pub stood apart from its neighbours. Inside, I found myself in a long, dark, dingy hall full of hairy slob-like men in vests or open-necked shirts. Tropical climates may have had an adverse effect on some men of Northern ancestry. Certainly, the customers looked affable but extremely ugly, particularly one with a face like a cauliflower. Two plain-looking girls in jeans danced slowly with one another to the tune of a country and western record apparently called 'The Arsehole Song'. Fortunately the landlord, a tall man in bright red braces, seemed an agreeable soul.

'Could I have half a lager, please?' I asked him nervously.

'A lager!' he replied, with respect in his voice. 'Well, sir, if you're a serious beer drinker I can recommend an Irish bar in the French Quarter called Ryan's. There you can get Irish and European drinks such as lager. Don't go in the main bar at the front, as that'll cost you an arm and a leg, but take the small door at the side. Meanwhile, I'll be glad to serve you a beer. One "Bud", that'll be one dollar.'

Obligingly, he cracked the top off a small cold tin, with drops of water on it.

A fast tune swirled from the juke box, and one of the two girls grabbed the arm of a nervous-looking coloured man with glasses and dragged him to the floor for a lewd dance. I drank up my tin and left.

From a corridor window at the Y.M.C.A. I looked out on a Mersey-like view of old store houses standing among modern blocks, with the Mississippi bridge on the horizon. I decided that New Orleans resembled Liverpool in more ways than one. Both were crumbling, ruined ports with Y.M.C.A.s. New Orleanian iron balconies flourished in Liverpool's Rodney Street, and both cities looked back to a Golden Age of slavery. New Orleans, like Liverpool, had supposedly 'gone broke', bedevilled with strikes, the falling price of Louisiana oil and the cost of hosting an extravagant World Fair. None the less, like Liverpool, it seemed a fascinating city. I pored over a city newspaper given away in the Y.M.C.A. lobby, in which the woes of New Orleans were belied by a myriad advertisements for song, dance and entertainment – 'Blind Sam Myers at the Maple Leaf.'

Next morning at breakfast I was served not by Avis but by a sullen Chinese girl. As I ate my toast and 'grits' (maize porridge known in Southern Africa as 'sazda') a disconsolate and heavily-pregnant girl of Spanish appearance approached me.

'Could you buy me breakfast?' she asked. 'I have no money at all. The Y.M.C.A. man is letting me stay here for free because my husband is in prison and I am having a baby. My husband tried to stow away from Costa Rica. I do not like it here, but I cannot go out as the streets are too dangerous.'

I gave her my toast and then set off with a map to find the Greyhound Bus Station. There are no double-decker buses in America, and long distance coaches are known as 'buses'. The train and bus stations were merged, and I soon found myself in a large shiny-polished hall where black families sat in rows, their children playing about their feet, as they waited for a loudspeaker to announce the time of their ride. After I had made my enquiries, I wandered round the souvenir shop. Small Confederate flags were for sale.

The Confederate or Southern flag, far prettier than the Star Spangled Banner, consists of a wide blue cross on a red background, scattered with silver stars. It appeared on badges and ashtrays in the souvenir shop, along with slogans such as, 'Lee Surrendered – I didn't' and 'Forget? Never!'

'This is Dixie!' a Reception clerk had greeted me on my previous visit to the South. Only Unreconstructed white Southerners appeared to use the term 'Dixie'. As far as I could see, Southern Negroes good-humouredly ignored the Confederate-patriotism of their white neighbours. 'Reconstruction' is the name given to the period just after the Civil War, when Northern troops guaranteed the power nominally given to newly-elected Negro mayors and politicians. White Southerners had chafed under the short-lived Negro and Yankee rule. Almost all white Southerners, I was to find, were Unreconstructed, their ire vented not upon black people but on Northern humbug.

Despite the Dixie souvenirs offered for sale, there were few white people in the bus-and-train station. One of them, a short sad-looking fat man approached me and recommended trips I could make. We were standing below a large wall-map of United States railway lines.

'So y'all from England!' he said. 'I live at Waverley, Mississippi, and I'm mighty interested in the boys' choirs you have in England. I collect records of the Westminster Boys' Choir – beautiful! Those soaring voices! I collect all kinds of "ethnic" music, in particular polkas and country dances.'

'Oh, fancy! In Hove, where I went to school, a lot of Polish people had settled. They had polka dances, with saxophones, in the Polonia Hotel.'

'I'd love to see that, I sure would. They should have let all the Poles into England instead of those Commonwealth people who do nothing but make trouble. At least the Poles are Caucasian.'

'I suppose they are,' I said. My grandfather, for one, was a Pole who was not only 'Caucasian' but positively Russian. He was born in the part of Poland that had belonged to the Tsarist Empire. Since that Empire has gone, not even the Caucasians are truly Caucasian any more.

I did not share these thoughts with the man from Waverley. Instead, I brushed my way through the sardonic gang of taxi drivers clustered at the Greyhound entrance, and slowly made my way through heat-struck streets to the Y.M.C.A. Back in my room, I had a pleasant surprise. A draught of cooling air greeted me, for the maid had given me fresh soap, a clean towel and had hit the right button on the air conditioner. From then on, I kept the noisy machine on by day and night, and within two days I felt acclimatised to the South.

'Y'all should take the St Charles streetcar up to Carrollton,' Avis told me. 'They got beautiful houses up there, where the rich people live. They call it the Garden City.'

She spoke wistfully, and pointed up St Charles' Avenue, for we had met on the street outside the Y.M.C.A. I didn't think that I was yet sophisticated enough to take a streetcar. The brusque-looking drivers demanded the exact fares, for one thing. So I walked for a while along the pleasant green lawn between the streetcar tracks.

On my right, I noticed a huge stone building, a Masonic Temple. I went over to have a look, and saw a grave middle-aged man enter. Over his grey hair he wore a strangely shaped bright blue fez with gold lettering on it.

'Ancient Arabic Order of the Nobles of the Mystic Shrine,' I read, as I peered through the glass inner doors at strange Oriental insignia in glass cases. I knocked and entered at a small side door. Here, in a well-appointed library and office, a bearded young man with glasses greeted me in surprise.

'Do you mean to say you've never heard of the Shriners!' he exclaimed, handing me a sheet of literature. 'We're somewhat akin to the Freemasons. It's an Ancient Order we have here, sir. You're welcome to look around the lobby, but the Great Hall is locked at the moment.'

He led me through the office, opened a panelled doorway, and I found myself in an echoing parquet-floored hallway. Most of the Mystic Shrine seemed agreeably late Victorian, with astounding lapses into Arabian Knighthood. The emblem of the Shriners was a scimitar supporting the Islamic crescent. Shriners seemed to flirt with Islam's outer forms while remaining Masons who were probably Christians or Jews in other spheres of their lives. Peeping into the Great Hall, I saw, or thought I saw, a throne surmounted by miniature minarets.

Cloaks, tasselled fezzes of red, yellow and green, together with mystic shields and staffs hung in the museum-like glass cases. I learned that the Shriners began in New York, at a restaurant called Knickerbocker Cottage. There, in 1870, a festive group of Freemasons decided to start a new Order, one inspired by an actor-Mason named Billy Florence. Florence had attended an Arabian-style banquet in Paris, hence the Arabic touch.

From this convivial beginning, Shriners had apparently spread to a number of American, Canadian and Mexican cities.

I had heard of the American passion for grandiose Lodges, but had never realised before how seriously such ritualism was taken. The New Orleans temple had been built in 1885. Shriners all seemed to command titles – knights, nobles and potentates. I admired a silver cup donated by Noble Joe Weinerdorfer. Dressing-up may have been the original impetus for Shrinery, but now the Order had become famed for its many excellent hospitals for crippled children and for the victims of severe burns. Later I was to see Shriner clowns selling balloons and tickets to the Shriner circus, a well-attended event, attracting queues of mothers with children. Profits went toward the hospitals, where in a National Health-less country, the poor were treated free of charge.

'Out of the ludicrous cometh forth good,' I spoke aloud as I left the Shrine deep in thought. I was to repeat this remark many times during my Southern trip, and it could well stand as an epigraph for America itself.

Thankfully, I saw few crippled children in New Orleans, but I was to see many adult cripples during my wanderings. The Vietnam War has a lengthy aftermath. Now I understood why English councillors go around erecting 'facilities for the disabled' everywhere. They are simply copying America.

British 'whizz kids' often make trips to America to study the Future, which they believe lives there. Whatever differences they see are noted down, regardless of reason, and then applied to Britain in the name of Efficiency. Greyhound buses, I was to learn, have 'smoked' (or tinted) windows to keep out the Southern sun. That explained why so many English long-distance coaches now have dark windows to make England's gloomy weather seem even gloomier!

Poring over my map, I decided to go to Water Street and find the birthplace of my heroine, the gospel singer Mahalia Jackson. I meandered among crumbling warehouses towards the Mississippi Bridge. Both the bridge and the Mississippi seemed inaccessible from the Y.M.C.A. Grass and weeds grew from derelict sites. Wandering here and there, I came to a ruined church, just off Girod Street. Known as St Joseph's Altar, the remaining white columns had been tidied up into a park, a very Liverpool touch. Like Liverpool, New Orleans was a country in itself, bearing as little relation to the rest of the South as Liverpool does to England. A jolly moustachioed face on a St Joseph's column made me smile.

Somewhere between Lee Circle and the Bridge, I noticed another small square bar with a name painted on the front: 'Captain Monday's'. Another sign in the small window read 'Reggae Tonite'. Reggae! Did Rastas and Jamaicanery flourish in New Orleans as in London? I decided to return that night and find out.

As for Water Street, it didn't seem to be where the map said it should be. No statue of Mahalia could be seen, only a strange raised building that blocked my view of the elusive Mississippi River. It was called 'Riverwalk'. A long line of well-dressed coloured people, husbands and wives, were walking up to it.

'Pardon me, do you know how I could get to Water Street?' I asked their leader.

A tall businessman-type with glasses, he frowned down at me in the haughty disdain I had come to associate with a certain type of Jamaican. Another minute and he might have sucked his teeth: 'Tsst!'

'No, I don't, but we're all strangers here from Washington D.C.,' he replied, and marched grumpily on.

Northerners! That explained their rudeness. I stopped a white office-worker and repeated my question.

'That part of Water Street was pulled down when they made the World Fair,' he explained. 'Then when the Fair was over, they made it into Riverwalk, the indoor shopping mall. You ought to visit that, while you're here.'

Instead, I made my way in the shade of the great warehouses towards the Y.M.C.A. and visited the Civil War Museum behind it. I climbed the red sandstone steps, paid two dollars and found myself in a long shady hall with dark timbers criss-crossing the ceiling. In England such a building would have been erected by a Duke for the benefit of the villagers. Cricket club dinners and Christmas pantos would have been held there. In New Orleans it was a shrine with a polished wooden floor, a cannon in the doorway. It was a memorial to the great Southern tragedy, the War Between the States.

At the far end of the room, above a raised altar-like platform, a stained glass window cast soft colours over the dark wooden walls and furniture. The picture in the window showed Gustav Beauregard in an heroic pose. A dashing Southern general, Beauregard had become a King Billy figure to the Men of Dixie Who Never Forgot. Again and again his picture appeared around the long museum-room, a noble figure on a galloping horse, sword held upraised to defend Southern chivalry. Beauregard, in fact, had become the epitome of a Southern Gentleman.

'The forebears of Gustav Beauregard walked with kings. Scion of ancient and honourable French and Welsh families, he traced his ancestry to the year 1290', read one inscription.

A handsome man with a black moustache and 'sideburns', Beauregard had fired the first shot on Fort Sumter in 1861. It was the fatal shot that began the Civil War. In case later commentators should be tempted to call Beauregard a fathead for doing this, the label below one of the pictures made it clear that he was acting under orders when he fired. Beauregard survived the war and died peacefully in New Orleans in 1893. He seems to have been a brave and honourable man.

In the cult of Beauregard and Southern Gentlemanliness could be seen the yearning of white Southerners for an aristocracy of passionate young blades willing to die for their loves, their country on the battlefield or their mistress on the duelling ground. White-moustached old colonels with roguish blue eyes were first cousins to similar old titled colonels in the mansions of the English shires. Norman blood seemed as potent here as in those shires of Old England. The Civil War, to judge by the museum, seemed to be a matter of Gentlemen versus Upstarts, and slavery played no part in it at all. Parallels with the English Civil War seemed easy to find.

In the corridors beside the main hall of the museum hung rows of paintings by artists far too young to have known the Civil War or the nineteenth century. These showed Southern chivalry in all its facets, from firing cannons to bidding farewell to fan-clutching Southern belles in ruffed dresses. Some of the pictures were excellent, others a bit too chocolate-boxy. Below them, old photographs, watercans, pistols and watches, recovered from the dead, showed that the real Civil War was muddier and less comfortable than the romancers imagined. The real life mementoes recalled English war museum relics of Flanders.

Nowhere in my travels around the South was I to see anyone remotely resembling the Civil War Museum's idea of a Southern gentleman. The most aristocratic features I saw were on Negroes, some of whom wore gloves, waistcoats, white moustaches and craggy white eyebrows, together with an air of elaborate politeness. A corner of the Museum showed posters advertising runaway slaves, the modern caption expressing horror that such an institution as slavery should ever have existed. Then I noticed another theme in the Museum's mythology – the devil Butler, the dark opposition to Beauregard and the forces of light.

New Orleans fell to the Union (Northern) troops in 1862. For the remainder of the war, the city was governed by General 'Beast' Butler, apparently the most unpopular man who ever walked the face of the earth. He had hanged a man for tearing down the Northern flag from the Mint building, and then turned his wrath to the loyal ladies of New Orleans who 'insulted' Northern soldiers. (The museum caption put the word 'insulted' into inverted commas, as if to say that it was impossible *really* to insult such creatures.) 'Beast' Butler responded by making a law that said that women who annoyed his soldiers, no matter their birth or breeding, would be treated as common prostitutes plying their trade. At this, Palmerston in England was shocked. No wonder that Butler's name changed from that of mere 'Beast' to 'Hyena'. I admired a drawing of the man depicted as a nightmarish hyena ravening over an open grave.

Looking back at the museum draped with its Confederate flags, I showed the elderly lady at the door some of the photographs I had brought from England. These showed the men and women of the Sealed Knot, the society that re-enacts the English Civil War in full costume, but minus the bullets. She leaned over a counter piled with Confederate souvenirs and examined the Cavaliers approvingly.

'Slavery was wrong, and our General Robert E. Lee spoke out against it long before the War Between the States. Our terrible war was not really to do with slavery at all,' she said. 'It was a matter of standing up for States' Rights and not being bullied. Did you know that the very word "Dixie" began in New Orleans? The smallest French coin in this city was a "dix", nicknamed a "dixie". So when we became American, the dixie was still in circulation, and folk called New Orleans "dixie-land". Later it got shortened to "dixie" and became the name of the whole South.'

I left the Civil War Museum feeling that I better understood the South. How I would have felt if I had been a white Southerner in the 1860s I cannot say, but I now felt a decided sympathy for the diehard Confederates of the 1980s. America still supplied the world with jargon, humbug, modern art, psychiatry, psychology, feminism, computerism and expert claptrappery of every description. Only the South, proud and backward-looking, stood apart. If the Confederate flag stood not for slavery but for the South *now*, the country against the town, tradition against progress, then I too could learn to wave it with pride.

If there's one flag I prefer to the Confederate flag, it's the Union Jack. If only the rebels of 1776 had *lost* the War of American Independence! American slaves may then have been freed at the same time as those of the West Indies, and just as peacefully. Slavery was abolished in the British Empire in 1834, without war or loss of life. Former slave owners received compensation. Of course, if America had been British, the South might then have seceded from *Britain*. But I think not, for the Museum had shown me the friendship felt by Southern gentlemen for their English counterparts. Moreover, in the 1830s, the cotton plantation economy had not yet become fully established.

Musing on 'might have beens', I returned to the Y.M.C.A., keeping always in the shade. Bathed in air conditioning, I went to sleep in my room.

Rising after dark, I prepared to go out, in some excitement. For all I knew, New Orleans could be crawling with robbers and murderers. I shall never forget that night, how I walked along moonlit streets giving a wide berth to the black pools of shadow in the doorways of garages and warehouses. Whenever I passed the opening of an alley, I veered off into the middle of the road. Now I know New Orleans better, I look back on my cowardliness and laugh.

By this means, veering, jumping and giving berth, I finally reached the doorway of Captain Monday's. A group of young coloured men stood around the door. One, clad in a natty green-and-white uniform, sat on a chair in the middle of the pavement. He wore his hair in the 'bubbles' style known in England as a 'wet look' or 'curly perm'. 'There is a four-dollar cover charge, sir,' he said, with great respect.

Inside, I found myself not in a reggae club, but a sophisticated nightclub. Sleek young couples, white and black, sat at little tables waiting for the show to begin. When the music started, only the white people danced.

A ratty-haired Rasta with a Mississippi drawl sang a Jamaican song in praise of 'ganja' (marijuana), but no one was smoking the weed. American reggae seemed hesitant, a music that had not yet found itself. Sticks and a rattling calabash knocked out a bayou rhythm that had only the faintest Jamaican echoes. From the keyboard, a thin young lady sang in Frenchified tones. Dodging the shadows instead of the sunshine, I returned to my room, where the switched-on light sent the cockroaches scattering wildly.

By the following morning, I felt ready to explore the centre of New Orleans, and so set off along St Charles' Avenue, past the workmen's café to regions unknown. A large resigned-looking crowd of shabbily-dressed coloured people, men and women of respectable appearance, had gathered outside a building on the opposite side of the road. 'Unemployment Office', the sign read. I crossed the road and went in, noting a man lying asleep in a nearby doorway. The queue went round the walls and ended up on rows of plastic chairs, whose occupants were waiting for their names to be called out. No one spoke. I noticed two or three white people amid the throng. Staff sat at desks not far away, looking far more bright and friendly than English Job Centre people. I walked round the side of the desks and asked for the manager. A smart coloured girl rose from her typewriter and led me to the office of a cheerful white man with glasses.

'An English writer, hey?' he beamed, when I had introduced myself. 'We get a lot of your television programmes here!'

We discussed television programmes and the 'Andy Capp' cartoon strip. I asked him about the New Orleans dole, and he took me to another room and gave me some pamphlets.

'This is an Unemployment Insurance office,' he explained. 'The people who come here have worked before, and had insurance deducted from their wages. Now, if they can prove they're out of work through no fault of their own, they can draw two hundred dollars a week.'

'That's very good!' I said.

'Yes, it is! This is a separate programme from Relief, you see.'

'I see. One more question – why is virtually everybody here a black person?'

'Well, it's because they're poor, ignorant and unskilled. Many of them have come from the country and can't read or write too well. If there's been crop picking, their parents might have taken them out of school. It's the same in your country, I guess. The black people get the jobs like maids, bellhops and doormen.'

'Um, they don't, actually . . .'

Just then, a young man with a beard came in. 'There's a crazy woman in your office and she won't go away,' he told the manager.

'Get rid of her, I'm busy.'

'I can't, she says it's only you she wants to see.'

'It's not Louisiana Hannah, is it?' he asked with a groan. 'Hey, you're not kidding me, are you?'

'Yes, I am,' admitted the newcomer.

A well-dressed woman sailed smiling into the room, and the manager gave a happy cry of 'Hey, *baby*!' as he renewed a dear old acquaintanceship. I left, unnoticed, and later studied the pamphlets he had given me. They resembled old Labour Exchange tracts, with pictures to help the reader. You received no dole if you left a job of your own accord or got the sack. A great deal of space was devoted to explaining the type of conduct to avoid if you didn't want to get the sack: 'Drunk or drugged at work, refusal to obey orders, wearing of outlandish clothes, going on strike, inability to do work.'

It was that last one that got me every time, back in my own working days.

Of course, I didn't know the black people of New Orleans very well, but I felt a trifle hurt on their behalf by the manager's description. It seemed strange that so many Englishmen and white Americans have ignored the *mystic* qualities of the African diaspora. Everyone is ready to swoon over an Indian guru, but an old coloured lady who receives commandments from angels or converses with God is assumed by most outsiders to be 'mental'. Yet among her family and friends, she may be a priestess. If Heaven is real, as I believe, then why cannot African ancestors peep over the edge and speak to their children?

In his novel, *Arrow of God*, the Biafran novelist Chinua Achebe describes the day-to-day life of a West African fetish priest in charge of a sacred python. A Mississippi seeress, Fannie Bell Chapman, had a strange affinity with rattlesnakes as a girl. When her parents killed her reptile friends, she began to have Christian visions and composed divinely inspired gospel songs. Several years earlier, the Florida writer Zora Neale Hurston also played with the local snakes, went on to have visions and finally wrote books about Negro life. So if some black people in America seem to live in a world of their own, it may be because they are otherworldly. You wouldn't expect St Cuthbert to work in a car factory, or Joan of Arc to be an efficient secretary.

I walked on in the oppressive sun, and suddenly felt relief. I looked up and saw that I had reached a beautiful square, Lafayette. Dark and mysterious, it seemed a forest grove of ilex, magnolia and other dark-leaved trees, set down as an island of shade among shining white skyscrapers. For now I was in the prosperous business section of New Orleans. Lorry-driving loafers had been completely replaced by crisp short-haired bright young men in suits. Drawn by the magic spell of

Lafayette Square to the old grey fountain in the centre, I seemed far away from the dimly-glimpsed business world. A stage in an open corner of the square announced lunch-time concerts in aid of the needy – 'Snooks Eaglin, guitarist.' America may have no Welfare State, but there is no shortage of charity. Revelling in the shade and the jungle view of branches above, I came across a thin coloured woman in a headshawl. She scanned the ground keenly, then swooped to pick up a small object and put it in a bag.

'What are you looking for?' I asked her.

'Pecans!' she answered. 'My, ain't you heard of pecans? When I picked enough, I'm going to make me a pecan pie. Look, they're a kind of nut. This here is a pecan tree. You try one – don't go and eat the shell, now, mind.'

'Oh, it's quite nice. It looks a bit like an acorn.'

'Uh huh. Well, I sure hope you enjoy yourself here in New Orleans.' She gave me a long compassionate look. 'My, youse a *long* way from home. Here's my number, you call me if you needs any help. My name is Catherine Duronalacy.'

'My, that sounds French.'

'It *is* French,' she replied with dignity, and went on picking up pecans.

Walking on, I recognised one of the grandiose hotels I had seen from the airport bus. Crossing a road carefully at a green light, I pressed on, as St Charles' Avenue grew darker and narrower, the buildings framed by fire escapes and occasionally by ironwork trellises. All of a sudden I stepped out on to the wide pavement of Canal Street and found myself in a bursting metropolis. Huge shops and brisk, well-dressed crowds were everywhere. Coaches bore the mysterious indicator-sign 'Elysian Fields' in computerised writing. Neon signs flashed on and off. There was no sign of a canal, and I later learned that one had been filled in, no doubt adding to the width of the great street. A strip of pavement ran along the middle of the road, with gaps for the streetcar lines. Skyscrapers towered above the grand nineteenth-century shops. One bore a huge red neon slogan mounted on its high roof: 'American Bank'. Like a country bumpkin, I wandered along, gaping.

Soon I came across an old bearded coloured man sitting in a folding chair and writing Bible texts on a pad in swirling, ornate lettering. His face was pitted with black marks.

'I sell these texts in the French Quarter over yonder,' he explained. 'Of course mah real love is classical music.'

What did he mean, 'French Quarter'? Everywhere I heard the phrase. I crossed the road to find out. A bald, middle-aged coloured man, who exuded melancholy from every pore, looked at me for some time, and then spoke.

'Please help me, sir,' he said. 'Why, *Ah'm* so hungry Ah just don't know what to *do* for somethin' to eat.'

I helped the poor man. Another buoyant, cheerful man with a small black pipe saw this and breezed over, a coloured Ukridge.

'Hi, my name is Percy Thomas!' he announced. 'So you're an Englishman! My, my! I was in England in '66, I had a good friend who opened a club there. No, I don't remember his name. What I'd like you to do is this. Just give me some money for pipe tobacco. I'll pay you back when I get my relief cheque. In fact you don't need to *pay* me no money, just run across the street there and buy some pipe tobacco and bring it back to me right here.'

I turned down Percy Thomas's request. From the other side of the road I had seen a black tunnel of a street that looked as if it led into a land of mystery. It reminded me of the magic cave-like entrance to the Regency Canal from Limehouse Dock in London. Wandering up and down Canal Street, I discovered a similar dark sidestreet. *All* the sidestreets were dark and looked as if they led into the Casbah.

I chose one of them, walked along for several yards, then stared in happy wonderment as the twentieth century faded away. I had discovered the French Quarter.

CHAPTER THREE

In Jackson Square

So THIS WAS the French Quarter! For the next two hours I roamed through streets of enchantment, where banana trees grew in old red brick fountain-courtyards and shops and the windows above them hung enmeshed in a spiders' web of ironwork arabesques. Balconies were surrounded by black cages barred in wrought-iron pictures and patterns, and trailing ferns hung from baskets above my head. By the bay windows of old hotels that faced the pavement, gas flames were flickering in glass-lanterns. Alleys led to former slave quarters. I stood in art or poster shops trying in vain to imagine early morning in the old days, the slaves awakened by a shout, their day's work beginning as buckets of water were dashed across the grey flagstones.

Here were Royal Street, Bourbon Street and Burgundy Street, and by wandering down Dumaine Street where giant cacti grew on a flat roof top, I reached the wide thoroughfare of Rampart Street and the Louis Armstrong Park. Observing that this was the limit of the French Quarter, I turned round and walked back into the narrow maze once more. Sidestreets in the Quarter consisted of old plank houses painted in light colours, usually pale green, the New Orleans plank-house colour. These dwellings had slanty roofs and were raised from the ground by brick pillars. Steps led up to one or two front doors, and tall wooden shuttered windows sometimes gave a glimpse through a crack of surprising opulence within.

Although many of these houses were exactly the same as those of the Negro streets a few miles further out, their inhabitants were nearly all well-to-do white people. A Preservation Society guarded the French Quarter from modernisation and decay. The buildings of the main streets, such as gracious Royal Street, were originally French but later improved by the Spanish, the story of New Orleans itself. France had sold the colony to Spain, and following the terrible fire of 1788, the Quarter rose again in lazy luxurious hacienda style. Then, France bought the country back in 1803 and sold it to the United States within days, to finance Napoleon's conquests in Europe. Slave blacksmiths, disciples of the lame African smith-god Legba, worked by night fashioning ever more intricate screens, balconies and curtains of iron lace. Money raised in this way, after their unpaid slave work had been done, could buy their freedom. Legba's typical smith-god limp later gave rise to comic devil stories of Old Nick hobbling on one foot and one hoof.

'Step it up, Jackson, step it up!' a buggy driver cried to his mule, as a big-wheeled Surrey with a Fringe on Top rattled by, filled with gaping tourists. Antique shops whose old interiors housed a thousand treasures stood next door to the cheapest, most vulgar souvenir shops imaginable, hung with smuttily-inscribed T-shirts. French-style restaurants where elegant homosexual waiters flitted between basket-weave chairs alternated with sleazy pubs or with hat shops where the dyed egret plumes of Monsieur's latest creations nodded gently to the whirr of an overhead fan's propeller blades. Such was the French Quarter of New Orleans. No working people or families with children lived here. Ghosts of bygone slaves may have screamed and chaffed at one another in alleyways and rooms marked 'Upper Slave Quarter' and 'Lower Slave Quarter', but the modern-day Spirit of the Quarter whispered, 'Spend! Spend! Spend!'

Unreal, almost an hallucination, the French Quarter seemed not so much a tourist trap as a tourist maze, where I walked a-mazed for hours. This was no film set, people still lived in the pink, palm-fringed houses, yet even the Negro dustmen who leaped on to the back of their moving cart did so with histrionic and ballet-like flourishes. The French Quarter was just the French Quarter, and that is all that could be said. When businesslike Americans brought an uncalled-for reality to New Orleans, they shunned the seductive Quarter and built a new city of commerce on the other side of Canal Street. That was where I had been staying, in the Y.M.C.A. Commerce had gone tatty and run to seed, yet within the French Quarter not the worst vulgarities and profanities of tourism had harmed the spellbound streets of brick, plaster and cypress wood. Iron pillars along the kerbsides supported the shelter-giving balconies above, so the Quarter rested, at ground level, in a soothing shade.

Royal, the loveliest of Streets, boasted the hotel with the Corn Stalk Gate, pointed out by guides. Made of cast iron at a foundry in the 1830s, the gate and nearby fence sprouted railings cast as twining stalks of maize, painted in bright natural colours. Nearby, the musty shelves of a secondhand bookshop lured me further and further into its foxed and yellowing depths. Pralines, hot pecan-bagels, wafted a sweet scent from the shady cafés. Alleyways and archways led into slave courtyards whose tragic spell had been exorcised. In England I would have assumed the narrow two-storey brick buildings to have been converted stables in a miniature mews.

A gently-spoken white man, with a delightful sing-song accent, emerged from a wooden sidestreet-house leading a long-legged yellow puppy on a string. Neighbours stopped to admire his pet, and he sang its praises.

'Yes, that's the sweetest little dog. He's got an eye infection 'cos his previous owners didn't *treat* him right.'

In a dream, I nearly bumped into one of the 'young black males' who nowadays form so potent a demonology for many white Americans and Englishmen. 'Excuse me, sir, your money's hanging right out of your pocket. Do take care of yourself,' he advised.

It was true, for my meagre wad of dollars, seeing that I was defying all the rules of the French Quarter by not spending them, seemed determined to lose themselves. I tucked them further in, then produced a coin for a huddled coloured woman in a headshawl, whose skeletal features stared poignantly from a doorway, her cry for alms a scarcely audible whisper. A mad-eyed white woman in a Death's Head hood and long dress that clung to her like a shroud stopped me and offered to sell me a magic bead.

I turned away, and saw, from the corner of one eye, a white figure with outstretched arms. It was a statue of Jesus, beckoning amid dark magnolia leaves at the rear of a great church. A grey, intriguing alley ran along one side of the church. I wandered down it, and stepped out into bold sunlight. The church was the Saint Louis Cathedral and I was in Jackson Square.

A wide stone-flagged promenade separated the tall, narrow cathedral from the square itself. Rows of seats in the centre of this open space were occupied both by families listening to music and by some of the many street musicians themselves. Banana and other palm trees, flitted upon by giant orange butterflies, hung over the iron railings of the square. Beyond them, in the square's centre, a bronze Andrew Jackson, American hero of the Battle of New Orleans, sat high on a bronze charger. Along each side of the square, in the shadow of eighteenth-century shops, artists sat selling their wares. Some painted portraits on the spot, others offered Louisiana swamp scenes painted in bright colours on pieces of roofing slate. I don't wish to boast (well, I do, really) but I am a pioneer of slate illustration, a craft which began in North Wales.

Pausing to glance incredulously at an old blues singer who played a washtub bass, I entered the cathedral, a white French building with three blue-slated spires. Below the central and tallest spire was a large clock which could be seen from across the square. The bell which boomed the hours had, I later learned, been baptised when first cast, as if it were an infant. Though pleasant inside, with murals, gold paint and many decorations, the Roman Catholic cathedral seemed surprisingly small to my English eyes. On either side of it stood two almost identical buildings of grey stone, with a cloister-like archway-arcade in front of each. These were the Cabildo, where the Louisiana Purchase by America had been signed, and the Presbytère. Former holy buildings, they later became seats of law and government, and are now both museums. Square and cathedral had been built by aristocratic French settlers in the 1720s.

Having seen all this, and admired the woodcut in the Cabildo that showed the all-Negro government of Louisiana during the Reconstruction era, I turned my attention to the musicians. The old bearded blues singer, who thrummed a string tied to a broom handle stuck through a hole in an inverted metal washtub, had began the 'St Louis Blues', a fitting melody with which to serenade the St Louis cathedral. However, after a line or two, he slid easily into a blues of his own about a 'no good woman' who 'wouldn't do this – and wouldn't do that.' A bunch of cowbells, tied up in red ribbon, sprouted from the top of the broom handle. He was accompanied by a swarthy man in dark glasses, who might have been Louisiana-French or Spanish, yet who played guitar in the blues style of the 1930s.

A little further away, on a bench, sat a big coloured man who played an enormous black tuba which looked as if it had been made of cast iron by an enterprising boilermaker. Serpent-like, it wrapped itself around him and presented an open red loudspeaker-like maw that blew sweet jazzy tunes over its owner's head. Over the red paint inside the tuba's mouth had been painted the owner's name, Mark Tuba Smith.

'Mark Tuba is my real name I was christened with,' the musician told me. 'I only took up the tuba after that. Been playing outdoors in the Quarter since I was seven years old.'

He had a round, innocent face with a gentle expression, eager to please, and wore a peaked cap with a vent at the back in fashionable style. As I wandered the square, first one and then another friend of his, all coloured men, came and sat by his side and played drum, jazzy trumpet or saxophone. Their music followed me as I crossed the square and stood staring across the road at the high artificial banks that formed the Mississippi levee. A railway line, used by goods trains who announced their coming by a mournful siren blast, ran parallel to the motor road, Decatur Street. 'Jax', read the scarlet neon sign atop a magnificently weird Gothic building, newly painted and restored. Before me, in a patient row, stood the high-wheeled buggies with fringes on top. Jovial drivers held folded whips and tried to induce passing holidaymakers to take a ride.

A black school crocodile-danced by, the eight-year-old boys accepting the drivers' invitations at once. Some appeared ready to hop up on the seats, whereupon a woman teacher pushed them briskly away. 'They ain't going on *no* ride!' she announced firmly.

It was then that I noticed that the patient animals who stood in the shafts wearing blinkers and fancy hats were not horses, but mules. This was such a novelty to me that without further ado, I jumped into a buggy. The seats now being filled, the black driver gave a cry of delight and we were away, on a tour of the French Quarter.

'Hi, my name's Hawkins, and this yere mule's name is Jackson!' announced the driver. Jackson wore a red hat with feathers. He was a brown mule with wayward ears. 'Jackson's the onliest mule in New *Or*-leans who knows how to stop at a red light. Let's go, Jackson! On the left we have the Jax Beer building, now used as shops, but once a major brewery. They had a big strike in '74 and never re-opened.'

Pausing correctly at the lights without being told, Jackson took a right turn and soon we were jogging through the same narrow balconied streets that I had explored earlier.

'There was a big fire here in the slave quarters one year,' Hawkins continued. 'Marie Laveau the voodoo queen was behind it all. She was a terrible woman! The slave hants [ghosts] are still there, people reckon. One slave woman ran out with her baby, up and down, distracted, till she dropped her baby and the flames devoured both of 'em. Step it up, Jackson, step it up!'

We emerged from the French Quarter into a road of wooden Negro homes on brick pillars, facing the pavement. Jackson 'stepped it up' towards the levee, pausing to allow his master to point out the 'original streetcar named Desire', enshrined behind protective railings. 'Desire' was a place name I had seen on coach indicators. Back at Decatur Street we swung into the Quarter again, and trotted alongside a lengthy covered market built to resemble an overstretched Greek temple.

'This yere's the French Market – see those pumpkins! Whoa, Jackson! Well, we been round the corner and we been round the bend. Rest a while, Jackson, 'cause this is the end.'

And so it was, for we were back at Jackson Square. I was surprised to hear open references to slavery, for my West Indian acquaintances in London regard this as a taboo subject. Alighting, I came face to face with one of the hazards of Jackson Square, a frightful mime artist who moved jerkily and stared at me with inane clown's eyes from a white pancaked face. A box at his feet lay half full of coins. I blame Marcel Marceau. Inscrutable as the mime artist himself, I hung my plastic bag on his fingertips, for he had now frozen into immobility. Then I counted my money, removed my bag and trotted off rapidly. My spare change would be spent on a more worthy cause. I gave it to a tall shades-wearing saxophone player who weaved his instrument and his shoulders around as the school party I had seen earlier danced wildly, the teacher looking on.

A boy of school age ran up to me and said, 'Hey, your clothes look neat, but your shoes look beat! Shoe shine, shoe shine!'

Much as I like the New Orleans habit of speaking in rhyme, I passed him by and searched the cathedral-front for Mark Tuba Smith. But he was nowhere to be found. So I sat on a bench and examined the photographs I had brought from England. What would New Orleanians make of coloured photographs of Africans, West Indians and relatives of mine in England?

Before going to America I had met a cello-playing girl from Boston, named Sue Savage, who had married an Englishman and gone to live in Georgia. Her husband had promised to put me up and give me a taste of small town life.

'It's so absurd back in Goodall County, half our neighbours belong to the Klan, and yet they've integrated the schools,' she told me. 'Most of the white people took their children out of the county school and sent them to private schools, rather than let them mix with blacks! I ask you! Now, if you stay with Anthony, and get friendly with the local blacks, don't show them your family photos or let them know your stepfather was a black. If you do, they'll look down on you as a defective white man. Now I must rush, to fetch my Joanie. I have to catch a train to Cambridge where she's a day girl at a private school. I couldn't let her get educated in Georgia with all those rednecks.'

While I was musing over this, and looking at the photos, I heard a musical note sing out. A very spirited girl in a huge Napoleon hat, a pink frilly blouse and a South Sea Island skirt of red, white and blue strips of paper, had set up a portable keyboard and begun to play a jazzy rhythm. She danced on the spot as she played, her expressive hazel eyes shining in good humour with a touch of defiance, her high cheek bones smeared in rouge for comic effect.

> 'The buzzard gave the monkey a ride on his back,
> He flew so crazy till he lost his hat.'

When she had finished this song, she sang 'Five Foot Two, Eyes of Blue'. Passers-by smiled and dropped money into her box. A flute lay on the ground by her side and a man asked her if she could play it. She unfolded a camp chair and sat and played tunes with a French feeling to them.

'Would you like to see my photographs of England?' I asked.

'I sure would! I'm glad y'all like my singing. I do old songs and brand new songs like "Five Foot Two".'

'What sort of songs do you like to sing for yourself?'

'Gospel songs! Listen to this.'

Standing and swaying slightly, she sang the beautiful spiritual, 'I'll Fly Away', giving a blues inflection to the lyrics. Some of the loveliest of Southern spirituals are of white hillbilly origin. Old Negro spiritual songs, called Jubilee Songs by the singers, usually have *two* meanings, freedom in Heaven and freedom from slavery on earth. In the Year of Jubilee (Leviticus 25:10) the slaves must be set free. Jubilee Songs are not quite political songs in disguise, for the slaves were Christians and desired *both* freedoms. A hillbilly song with only *one* meaning, such as 'I'll Fly Away', is not very African, yet Desita made it so.

'Yes, that's my name, Desita Marie. Pleased to meet you, Roy. I likes to sing my church songs with feeling. Now in the Church I go to sometimes, as the choir march in, they sings like *this*: "I'm looking for a mira-*call*! I'm expecting the impossi-*bull*." They do it slow, but I like to jazz it up straight out, an' sing it fast and really step out! Them old Sisters look at me and go like they sucking a sour lemon. Later on, when the spirit hits 'em, they go jazz it up too! Times are, the whole church is rocking for the Lord! I like the Catholic church, where they chant and you answer.'

I showed her some photographs of the Mount Zion Spiritual Baptist Church of London, in their brightly coloured robes and turbans. This is a magic church that is considered 'not quite right' by orthodox West Indian standards. The sourpuss old Sisters of Desita's church would be shocked to see blindfolded men and women dancing to drumbeats while candles flickered.

'Oh, oh! I never realised there were black people in England! Oh, oh! I thought Africans and West Indians wore grass skirts or went around dressed in sacks.'

'Don't let them hear you say that!'

'Ooh-wee! I can see that's a funny church. The regular churches don't like that! Eh, là bas! There's black people here would like to dress like that, but they don't have the courage! You know, we have churches like that, but we keep it secret. I wish we could be so flamboyant!'

A white woman with a pleasant smile walked by, wearing a floral dress.

'That's a pretty dress you have, lady!' Desita called out. 'I'd like lots of pretty dresses. Hi, there!'

A coloured man looked up and gave her a nod, then followed a family party who were walking through the square.

'See that man who passed by?' Desita confided in me. 'He knows – he has the Power. There's a Madam Brown three blocks away. She has her own church and you can put money on the altar "for to get things done." Now she looks kind of like the Sisters in your photographs.' She riffled through the pictures, picking out the most respected Zionist priestesses with unerring accuracy.

'That's a holy lady . . . that's a ritual . . . that's a powerful holy lady, and so is that.'

'Yes, these are good people,' I told her. 'They do magic rituals, but only for good. Bad rituals are called "obeah" or "oby". What are they called here?'

Desita shot a fearful glance over her shoulder in case the Devil was there, and whispered, 'Hoodoo. When I was only seventeen, I got myself in the power of a Madam who operated a funny church, like in your pictures,' she told me. 'I was only a young girl. This really sweet boy came along, and I liked him. So I told the Madam, and she said, "No. I had a dream, and the dream told me he's a bad man, he's not right for you." So I went on ahead and met another boy, but it was the same thing, "No, he's no good for you." You see what I mean, she was trying to keep me for herself. By now I was gettin' horny as hell, so when the third boy came along, I took him anyway. Madam didn't like that. So she took me in her church, an' got me to dance so the Spirit was on me.'

Desita threw her head back in imitation of the trance-like Holy Rock and jerked her body to and fro.

'Well, I fainted, an' when I came round, I was so weak, I could hardly *crawl* home to my bed. The Madam said I should have a Holy Bath, but I didn't like the idea of her bathing me naked. So she told me to pee into garlic, and then rub my hands in it, like washing in garlic. I done that, but I could see she was beginning to take over my nature. You know, I believe she was trying to take possession of my head. She'd order me, say, "Come yere! Over yere! Do this!" So I started on ignoring her. Finally she said to me, "When I die, you will take over my work." She's alive yet to this day. I pay her no mind, but oh man, when she takes out her gris-gris bag! I cain't abide that.'

'They don't have gris-gris bags in England,' I said. 'I've been to see a woman called Mrs Keet. All the Jamaican oby men go to her, and she has all kind of oils and roots, John the Conquer – '

'High John the Conqueror! That's powerful.'

'Well, Mrs Keet keeps all her spells in a black chest, and she opens it out, so you can pick one. She's a white woman.'

'My Madam's black, but it sure sound like the same thing. There's a woman near here that has the Power, she don't never change. She's old now, but they say she looked the same a hundred years ago and a hundred years before that. Another man I done seed, he went into a trance an' his face changed, took on features of all different people as they possessed him, even an Indian guru. (Hi, lady, that's a lovely dress!) Now, let me see the pictures of your family. My, my, my! When I was a young girl, I thought it would be a grand thing to marry a white man. But I s'pose you has to stay on your own side. Just like the people in the church you showed me, I like to put on a blindfold, when in need of special prayer, all alone in my room.'

'This is a picture of my brother, Musa,' I said. 'He was a very dreamy boy, and he loved snakes. He wrote stories about snakes eating people, and he had lots of pet snakes. Now he's grown up, he works as an architect. And this is a photo of a painting a Japanese lady did of me. It shows me surrounded by my tame rats. I keep pet rats, you know, and they crawl all over me.'

'These pictures seem so exciting. I'll call you King Rat. You know, the rat is special. Anywhere you go, a rat can be there.'

At that moment, a fine car drove into the square, and an aged nun, perhaps from the nearby Ursuline Convent, was helped out by younger nuns, who began carefully to walk her towards the door of the cathedral. Desita gave a cry of wistful ecstasy.

'Oh, look, that's a really holy old lady, that Holy Mother. I'd do anything, if only I had the courage to kiss her hand.'

I took Desita's own hand and led her firmly to the procession. 'Pardon me, but my friend would like to kiss your hand,' I said to the elderly Mother Superior.

'God bless you, my child,' the Holy Mother whispered, as Desita curtseyed and then took the skinny freckled hand and kissed it. Borne by her attendants, the old lady vanished into the St Louis Cathedral.

In high elation, Desita returned to her keyboard, but the incident had excited her so much that her words got muddled, and she gave the buzzard a ride on the monkey's back by mistake. She whanged away in a different key, sang 'Roll, Jordan, Roll', and then picked up a tasselled stick, shook her tasselled skirt, tipped her Napoleon's hat at an angle and was off again.

'Your mama can grind, your mama can switch!
Your mama ain't nothing but a low down – oop! Wang dang doodle!
We're gonna have a wang dang doodle, a wang dang doodle tonight!
Roy will be there, letting down his hair – Wang dang doodle tonight!'

Actually I have precious little hair to let down. Desita's expression as she shot a hand over her mouth, rolled her eyes and said 'oop!' was a study in comicality. All of a sudden, the sky grew black, and in a moment the rain teemed down. My new friend hurriedly pulled her portable keyboard under the shelter of the Cabildo. Again and again, the black sky flashed into brilliant blue, electric-white crinkly lines rushing across it or cracks rending it in two. Five minutes later, the storm was spent, and resolved itself in warm drizzling rain. Desita told me that it was against the law to sing or play too near the Cabildo. Nevertheless, the tall, lean saxophone player, surrounded by the jumping, shouting black children who danced around him, retreated under the arches and played on. This shocked Desita.

'He's not allowed to go there!' she exclaimed. 'That ain't right! He *knows* he's not allowed to go there. That's like holy ground. You know, they took the slaves right off the Mississippi, and *took* 'em there to the Cabildo in chains and the white planters'd be here, all ready. They was forcing their mouths open, poking 'em, prodding 'em. My grandmother remembered slavery – she died aged one hundred and four. My, but she grew hateful before she died. All our family was what we call *house niggers*!'

Desita looked earnestly and beseechingly into my eyes, as if what she was saying was of great importance.

'Yes, we was all house niggers! We waited at table, we cleaned the house, served meals and held doors open. We was never abused and never worked in the fields under the lash. The white people was very kind to us. My father, the same. He was a house nigger. He worked right here in New Orleans, as a doorman in a *ho*-tel, same thing, opening doors. I felt real proud to see him. One time he worked as a waiter in a real fine *ho*-tel, an' he dressed beautifully! A white shirt-front with a ruffle, you know. Real neat. We never worked out of doors, on my daddy's side o' the family anyways.

'Our family had long blonde hair once, my grandmother told me. The Master at the Big House, he was our dad. My grandmother's mammy, that had the children, she acted as a wet nurse for the Master's right children, the legal ones. (She done mid-wiving too.) But the Master's children by his white wife looked just like we-all. He was scared that he'd get 'em mixed up. So what he done, he had our hair washed in cow pee. After that, it turned dark and nappy and stayed like that ever since. It was the cow pee.

'You ever hear of the Alligator Man? Well, back in slavery times, the swamps and marshes was full of alligators. You have 'em in your country?'

'No, the climate's not right for them,' I explained.

'Well, those slaves that was bad, and tried to run away, the alligators would eat them. And there was a man who lived in the swamp called the Alligator Man. He would eat people! Any children went too near the swamp, he would eat them. Even the Master's children, blonde hair and blue eyes; if they strayed near the swamp, he would eat them. So I think that's how come the people do the Alligator Dance, to please the Alligator Man. They still do some rituals in those little villages by the river in Louisiana.

'Well, matter o' fact, I've seen it done, 'cos we lived out in the country when I was at school. One man puts on an alligator skin, the big head draped over his own head, the back and tail hangin' over his back. Someone got a drum. Then we does the Alligator Dance!'

Desita suddenly crouched and grew reptilian, her hands outspread to make her fingers look webbed, her eyes staring. As if to an African drum rhythm she sway-danced, moving her body slowly up and down in honour of a crocodile god.

'It worked, too!' she shouted cheerfully, the spell broken. 'The crops never failed, and we got plenty fish. My ma would kill a chicken at the start of the Alligator Dance, by swinging it round and round by the head like a lariat, and then letting it loose to run and die. Other times a man would hold the chicken, stretch out its neck and bite through.'

As Desita and I spoke, we kept doubling up in laughter and staggering backwards, hands on our knees. Passers-by smiled curiously and seemed to wonder what we were talking about. A lady asked if she could take Desita's photograph. At once, Desita threw an arm around me and posed with the other arm outspread.

'You're fine, but I want *her*,' the photographer said hastily, so I backed away.

'Now, in Louisiana, we'd pick peas, cucumbers, all kinds of things, working for Mr *Prime*. That's who our boss was, Mr Prime.' She paused to look into my eyes once more, evidently attaching great importance to her boss's name.

'Now Mr Prime had a daughter, we called her Texas Ray. And the time came, we was told to go to the white girls' high school. An' at this school, the white girls could step and march, be cheerleaders an' twirl batons and we could do none of that. So Texas Ray said, "I'll teach you," and she did. Finally we could throw batons up like any of them! All thanks to Texas Ray. That was when I was working for Mr Prime.

'After I left school, an' after I got out of the Madam's spell, I went and got married. But I done it too young. My first husband was awful, uggh! But the husband I got now is good to me. He drinks, but not too much. You know, men get drinkin' together sometimes. When my husband and his friends have a few drinks an' they go out, they always throw a glass over the floor behind the door and say, "That's for Black Hawk!" You see, Black Hawk was a great Indian chief, and his spirit lives on.'

At that moment, I glanced up and saw an extraordinary sight. Two black steamboat chimneys were cruising serenely along behind the high bank known as the Mississippi levee. The serrated edges of the chimney funnels were familiar to me from many pictures of the Mark Twain days. Behind the levee, another world awaited – a great river churned by paddle steamers. Desita, meanwhile, was commenting favourably on the pictures of my family ('He's got good hair.'). She asked how my mother had met my Nigerian stepfather.

'He was standing on a soap box, giving a speech,' I replied. 'There's a part of London where you can get up and say anything you like. I think it's because in the old days people stood on platforms there and made last speeches before they were hanged. Of course, they don't hang them now.'

'Say anything you like?' repeated Desita, her eyes shining. 'Can you cuss?'

'Certainly! A friend of my stepfather used to go there every week and cuss white people.'

This was too much for Desita, who doubled up and danced forwards and backwards, hooting with laughter. So did I (a very defective white man) and we staggered with mirth up and down in front of the Cabildo.

'I have to leave y'all now, 'cos I sing in Bourbon Street,' she gasped at length. We had been talking for two hours. 'It's been a spiritual experience, talking to you, really spiritual. My children are grown up now, so I think I'm gonna open a Root shop and do spiritual medicine. But I'm never doing nothing bad, not like that "obeah" you told me about. I know I have to face Jesus at the judgment seat to account for my sins. I know what I'm going to do, I'm gonna go up to my room tonight and put on my blindfold. You will be here tomorrow, won't you?'

But I wasn't, and I never saw Desita again.

Musing on our conversation, I sat on a bench and looked at the Mississippi for the first time. Wide, brown and gloomy, it flowed through a land of scrubby forests. Boats chugged to and fro, but I saw no more paddle steamers. The walkway on top of the levee, an artificial bank raised to prevent a flood, was tussocky and neglected-looking, paved with planks pressed down into the earth. Steps leading back to Jackson Square finally beckoned. I was to find that the Mississippi grew more romantic upstream, where cotton barges, lashed together, were pushed down the river by tugboats.

The pathos of much of Desita's speech made me reflective. So America resembled Jamaica, where, according to my sister, lightness of skin among Negroes stood for social prestige. This attitude must have begun with a misplaced emulation of white masters. In both countries admiration now stops at light-skinned coloured people with loose floppy curls. Such an appearance is admired as 'good-looking' and socially superior, but a wholly white person is judged differently. Far from being considered the pinnacle of human godliness, he or she can be seen as a figure of fun. Desita's entry into the bewildering world of football cheerleaders and pom pom girls at 'the white high school' must have been the result of the famed integration of schools in the sixties. If so, it hardly seemed worth it. A vivacious young girl in looks, she must have resembled the person in her story, who never aged. Her free use of the word 'nigger' surprised me, but I remembered my friend Priscilla Blackman of Trinidad, when she first came to England, would shout cheerfully at her children: 'Come on, all you little niggers!'

When acclimatised to England, she nevermore used that word.

Jax's Brewery, now a department store, was so glittering and opulent, a place of red paint and fancy mirrors, that I felt both out of place and invisible inside it. Lifts like glass diving bells swung to and from the high ceiling on sturdy cables. Leaving Jax's and the Mississippi, I plunged back into the French Quarter. Here I found a shop that was more to my taste – Barrister's African Carving Shop. Here the incomparable carved treasures of West Africa were on display. Soon the owner and I were chatting away like old Africa hands, although I have never been to Africa and I'm not sure if he had, either. He employed collectors who travelled from village to bush village, buying old carvings.

'That figure looks like an African in a colonial policeman's uniform,' I commented.

'Yes, that style we call "transitional", though it's transitional to what? Transitional to nothing! When the carvings ceased to be sacred, they flourished for a while as ornaments or comments on a changing world. Then carving ceased altogether. The old gods saw it coming – look how doomed they look, they knew their time had come. When they were believed in, men would not part with their carvings for any price! But now, the white man gone, many Africans are feeling their way back to paganism. Some are finding their way through a veil of Hinduism. Carvings of many-armed gods, based on Indian art, are now appearing. My collectors tell me these are the strangest things imaginable. But nobody will sell them, they'd rather die, for the new carvings are more sacred to them than the old.'

In Britain, Celtic art, changed by Christianity, reappeared after the Romans had gone. It was not that the Romans, in their later days, were cruel and oppressed the art out of people. On the contrary, they were admired, and native British matters seemed too barbaric and old-fashioned to pursue while the Romans were there.

Blue dusk now enveloped the French Quarter, and I wandered down a sidestreet of wooden houses, gazing at the chimney swifts who were wheeling appropriately around the chimneys. A man who looked like a ragged grizzled prospector stopped me and asked me the way to Ursuline Street. I said I didn't know, although I'd seen it somewhere.

'English, hey? I've lost my broad A, but I come from Wandsworth, London!' he cackled. 'Be careful of these streets after dark, hear?'

Palms grew on flat roofs, and doors opened straight on to the road, with no front gardens. Coloured youths clutching musical instruments marched towards Jackson Square with an air of exaltation. They were led by a fourteen-year-old tuba player, a Mark Tuba Smith of the future. I followed them for a little way, then paused at a doorway marked 'Pat O'Brien's'. It seemed a beautiful building, once a Spanish theatre, so I walked along the usual corridor entrance to the courtyard. To my right I noticed a girl seated at the piano below an enormous tilted mirror.

I found myself in an outdoor bar and restaurant crowded with fashionable white people sitting at metal circular tables. Palm trees grew from corners of the exquisite courtyard, and steps led up to a fountain, where water swirled above a suspended basin. Hidden lights changed the plumes of liquid into red, green and violet. Most amazing of all, a fire burned in the midst of the giant suspended bowl, water surrounding the leaping flames. A waiter brought me a scarlet liquid in a tall glass, a Hurricane. What it contained I know not, but I grew sleepier and sleepier as I sat there among barbaric splendour, gazing at a Spanish wall of bright chestnut, laced over with iron balconies and fringed by palms. Waiters in green livery held trays of Hurricanes and mint juleps aloft on the fingers of one hand, as they weaved their elegant way between the tables. A hurricane had destroyed New Orleans in 1722, but these were a different kind, and merely sent me to sleep.

It was dark when I awoke, and the tables sang with chatter from the Southern Bright Young Things. 'Hi, how ya *doin*'?' was repeated a hundred times.

'How many stitches ya get?' was an interesting variant. 'He was so drunk last night, he fell over and hit his head.'

Admiring female eyes shone at the modest hero, who wore a bandage. At last I tore myself away from my wonderful discovery, the French Quarter, and reached Canal Street once more. A tiny, starveling child in a flimsy vest touted for his unpleasant-looking shoe-shining father, and a cripple in a wheelchair played mournful tunes on a saxophone while his friends looked on. In a doorway, a big husky young man lay sprawled out on the ground trying to sleep. Another husky young man, also a Negro, began to jeer at him, and walked off to a barrage of cuss-words. I crossed the road, and waited for a bus. None came. A prim coloured girl looked askance at a shabbily-dressed man who was drinking from a bottle concealed in a brown paper bag. Finding that the street leading off into darkness was St Charles' Avenue, I walked down it towards the Y.M.C.A.

At an unfamiliar-seeming corner, I asked an old coloured lady at another bus stop if I were going the right way.

'This is St Charles,' she said, 'but what are you *doin*'? You're walking at *night*? Well, Lord have mercy!'

'The Lord's spared me so far,' I pointed out, 'so perhaps He'll let me get home tonight.' And I was right. There seemed to be nothing to fear in New Orleans but poverty.

Desita was nowhere to be seen the next time I went to Jackson Square. The boys' jazz band, the same one I had seen marching through the twilit streets, was blowing away lustily, playing a sacred marching tune. Proudly, the young drummer biffed out a sprightly rhythm, his instrument hung round his neck.

'Over in the Gloryland!' the cornet player announced with a flourish.

I walked around the square, and at the corner of Decatur Street stopped in surprise. Another young lady, her eyes starting from her head, loudly sang a gospel song, jigging from one foot to the other, a cardboard box on the ground before her.

> 'Jesus on the mainline! He can give you anything you want!
> Anything you want, anything you want!
> He can give you anything you want!'

I applauded, so she sang 'Take My Hand, Precious Lord' with all the frills, trills and flourishes.

'This is my church, the United Church of Christ in Miro Street,' she told me, producing a card. 'We've got a Bible Study Class tomorrow night, y'all welcome.'

'I'll try and make it,' I said. 'I love to hear gospel music. What do they sing in your church when they have a baptising?'

'Why, they sing: "Wade in the *wa*ter! Wade in the *wa*ter! God's gonna trouble the wa-a-ater." '

We talked for a while, and I found that she was more sophisticated than Desita, with the unnerving 'zany, bubbling humour' I had come to associate with white show-business American girls. In fact, she had been in show business at one time, and had also 'taught school'. It was now her ambition to be a gospel singer.

'My name is Celestine,' she told me, 'and I was brought up Catholic, a Creole. That means we spoke French when I was small, and they say we're better than other black folks. I never knew any gospel songs till I growed up. Now my husband Dulaney, he's a real Southern Baptist, an' he's teaching 'em to me.'

'Ain't no church in Miro, that I knows of,' a bull-necked white taxi driver told me next day, as we cruised around neat, tree-lined streets of pale green plank houses with people sitting on the steps just as East Enders used to do. It was a Negro neighbourhood, named after a former Spanish governor. Finally, he leaned out and asked an old bald man where the church was. The man said it was in the school, pointing at a huge, ugly red-brick monument to the 1930s. So to the school I went, finding the right entrance with difficulty.

Inside, I saw pictures on the walls; shelves stacked with books, toys; desks crammed closely together; a fish tank and all the signs of a well-equipped English primary school.

'Be Proud of What You Are', a poster exhorted me as I entered. The picture showed a wild-eyed black militant in beard and moustache. Few children there could be proud of owning a moustache. Stepping into a large polished hall, I met a surprised woman in purple slacks who appeared to be in charge of a small playgroup. Perhaps made over-proud by the poster, the children looked rather sneering, I thought. When I explained my mission, the woman teacher's sour expression vanished, and with great kindness, she showed me to the very door of the church, two streets away. A young assistant with long black hair held the fort while she was gone.

A smart building, the church stood at the top of a sloping lawn, its glass doors open. I announced myself to a young man at the entrance, and he welcomed me effusively. I found myself in an airy corridor, among young churchgoers of great sophistication, all dressed to the nines. Unlike the West Indian-type church I had expected, the members were not sharply divided from 'the world', but could wear make-up. In their spare time, they could smoke and drink within reason, and even sing the blues. An office door opened, and a tall, young, bespectacled Pastor appeared. He shook my hand over and over again, and I soon found myself in a comfortable pew awaiting the Bible Study. The church was luxuriously appointed, with wooden panelling, a stage and an organ.

'We have here with us from England a young man who belongs to the Church of England!' the pastor introduced me. I beamed foolishly. 'Yes, that beloved Church of England from which our church has sprung. The old original church, the Church of England! One day, my brethren, there will be one United Church again!'

Everyone looked at me with interest. Crumple-faced old people, the Bible Students slouched almost irritably in their pews, many of the women wearing trousers. I had long wondered if the strict Pentecostal churches beloved of West Indians in England would benefit by relaxing their 'no this and no that' rules. The fervent, intensely religious passion that pervades such churches was wholly absent here. Church seemed a mere social occasion, though a pleasant one, where uplifting sentiments could be heard.

Briskly, the pastor set about catechising the old people. He was a slender, light-skinned man of faintly Jewish appearance.

'I ain't rightly got around to reading that yet,' a man with grizzled eyebrows and a white moustache protested.

Full of zip and zim, the pastor then launched into a brief sermon, accusing everybody there of complacency and selfishness. He spoke in a calm, measured tone with an air of great deliberation.

'You think of yourselves as a Christian church. But let me tell y'all one thing. Everybody talkin' 'bout Heaven ain't going to Heaven. There's even a *song* of that name. You are a boogewah church!' ('That's right!') 'You don't help your poor neighbours, just 'cos your poor neighbours are not as respectable as you are. You carry gossip around. Don't you know, whenever there's talk of a new prospective pastor, one of you will *steal away* and go see what colour he is! You know how all year you prepare a costume and look forward to sitting on a float in Mardi Gras throwing out *bookoo* money? There you sit, all dressed up, throwing out them trinkets. How would you feel if one o' those people gathered up all the trinkets you threw out and turned up at your house askin' you to exchange those trinkets for food or money? You like to give away trinkets, why don't you like to give away money? Jesus said we must give *all* to the poor and follow Him!'

'But where do I draw the line, pastor?' the eyebrow-man interrupted.

'Brother Bartholomew, I don't want you to give away your hard-earned money to any ol' rascal. I see young bucks beggin' who should be *made* to work or go to prison. An' I see people in prison who some might say deserve the e-lectric chair. Just use your common judgment.'

'Thank you, pastor.'

That ended the Bible Study. A nervous lady in blue, introduced as Sister Elizabeth, walked up and down the aisles handing out leaflets.

To my stunned astonishment, my leaflet read 'Vote Aquarium'. It appeared that if Mayor Barthelamy, the black Mayor of New Orleans, were re-elected, he would build a huge aquarium in part of the disused docks. Elizabeth gave a talk, complete with slides, to show the benefit a beautiful aquarium would bring to New Orleans. It would be paid for partly by private investment, partly by public funds, and it would create jobs. The Aquarium would be run by the Audubon Zoo, and the Zoo paid for itself, the cages endowed by business firms. And so on.

I was thunderstruck. This was *politics in the church*, a shocking sin in the eyes of most West Indian churchgoers. Martin Luther King-style politics in church has had an honourable history in the South, dating from slavery camp-meetings where Father Abraham could be God or Lincoln, the Promised Land both Heaven and the North. But mundane day-to-day politics in church seemed a blasphemy to my West Indian-attuned sensibilities. Perhaps the extra politics brought in by Martin Luther King had not been an unmixed blessing, but had politicised a godly people.

'Any questions?' simpered the pastor nervously. He clearly supported the Aquarium party himself.

Everyone began to shout angrily at once. Nobody wanted an Aquarium, all remembered the failure of the World Fair, which they blamed on the Mayor.

'That's hardly fair . . .' faltered the pastor nervously. I felt sorry for him.

'We want money spent on schools!' a woman roared.

'Why don't banks give loans to black people?'

'How will it help our race?'

'Hold on, pastor, I've got something to say,' announced Brother Bartholomew. 'Now, this is a situation of serious negativity of the interim segation of the situation.'

Everyone looked awe-struck at this wisdom, so he rose to his feet and continued: 'We want Black Power to overcome White Power! We are an ethnic minority. How can this aquarium help us as an ethnic group?'

As an ethnic group, I reflected, it would help them to see a lot of fish. I remembered taking Brother Brown, an aged member of a West Indian Church in England, to see an aquarium. Too feeble to speak, he tottered along, holding my arm. At a tank of coral fishes, he paused for a long time, then suddenly spoke in a strange croaking voice: 'See the wonders that God has made!' A week later, he was repatriated to Barbados to save hospital expense in England. Listening to the angry condemnations of tropical fish, I could well imagine a sensitive child in New Orleans being shouted at by his family for wasting his time observing the habits of sea creatures when he should have been studying to be a doctor or a lawyer.

'We black people don't need aquariums,' Brother Bartholomew continued. 'We know the jobs that we'll get – punching tickets and mopping floors! Why is everything done for tourists? Everything new is always in the French Quarter! What has the Audubon Zoo done for black people? When did you last go to the zoo?'

'Yesterday morning, with a party of schoolchildren,' Elizabeth replied. The pastor had fled.

'Yes, but you had a free pass.'

I stood up and came to Elizabeth's defence. 'Please don't murder me, people, but I'm a tourist, and I'd love to see an aquarium. I would certainly pay to see it. An aquarium is not only educational, but spiritual, showing God's creation. Now, the study of fish can be a career in itself, for natural history is an honourable profession. A young person might begin just sweeping up, and go on to be a world expert on fish. Thank you.'

I sat down again, to polite applause. The pastor reappeared and pronounced the final prayer, or Benediction. People who had been shouting about Black Power rushed to shake my hand and urged me to return.

'I'm a seaman, and I've been to Liverpool,' one man said. 'My name's Curly.'

'What's you real name, Curly?' someone asked.

'That *is* my real name.'

Celestine ran over to me, agile in a red track suit, and I persuaded her to give me a lift back to the Y.M.C.A. in her car.

'People are excited, 'cos the city is broke and no one knows what to do,' she explained. 'It's the fault of high-up people who want money – we should start petitions. Our pastor is such a good man! He is so blunt and so arrogant! He really woke our eyes up to things.'

Outside the Y.M.C.A. she sat in the parked car and told me of her ambition to be a professional gospel-singer, her eyes shining with enthusiasm.

'When I was a little girl, I would be in the mirror – that's Southern talk for "look in the mirror" – and just imagine myself singing in front of all those peoples. I'd put newspapers round my neck to act as mink.'

Later that evening, I sat on my stool in the workmen's café, musing on all I had heard and seen. A gospel music church with politics in it! I had never been so amazed since the day I first visited a Welsh pit village and saw a working man in a cloth cap reading *The Daily Worker*. In England, it is the blues people, the dancing, drinking, weed-smoking reggae fans, who are often mixed up in politics. Bringing left-wing politics into West Indian-run churches is a dream beloved of the Brent Black Power crowd, who follow American black politics. Paul Boateng is trying to bring it about, modelling himself on the Rev. Jesse Jackson. All that has been achieved so far is the disruption of the Mount Zion Spiritual Baptist Church. The church's foremost priestess, bewildered by grants, allowed herself to become a well-rehearsed 'plant' in the audience of a political meeting. She then found that she had agreed to turn her church into a Community Centre. Squabbles over grant money split the church, and now the formerly powerful and Godly priestess sits miserably in her Community Centre and makes wonky baskets out of piles of used lollipop-sticks. 'Go Down, Moses' is sung no more.

Sadly, I picked at my blueberry pie with a fork, since Americans have not yet invented the dessert spoon. How could Brother Bartholomew degrade himself by talking meaninglessly about 'negations of segations' and Black Power? Uneasily, I felt I was being watched.

A young blond-haired white man with pale contemptuous eyes, rocking tipsily on his stool, sat grinning and sneering at me, singing along with the juke box: 'Bad to the Bone'.

When people sing 'Bad to the Bone', be careful. I had put on a white shirt and tie for church, and these made me look conspicuous among the lorry drivers.

'What do you know of pulimanary psychosis?' he suddenly asked me. 'Should crawfish have the vote?'

'White Power!' boomed the Red Indian teddy boy from his corner.

I fled.

CHAPTER FOUR

Down Home Blues

DAY AFTER DAY, I felt drawn to the unreal beauty of the French Quarter. There, in Père Antoine's elegant restaurant, the door open to Royal Street, I would sit in style and eat Creole Bread and Butter Pudding with rum sauce. It was not long before I discovered Bourbon Street.

The first time I walked down Bourbon Street at night I could hardly believe my eyes. Crowds of people were surging along, mostly young white men in an uproarious, excited mood. Neon lights, souvenir shops, strip clubs and massage parlours suggested a second Soho. One club was advertised by a waxwork pair of ladies' feet, with high-heeled toes pointing upwards, going in and out of an upstairs window like a demented cuckoo clock. Touts stood, Soho-style, inviting passers-by to attend female-impersonation strip shows. In the midst of all this gaudily-advertised vice, respectable jazz clubs were sending trumpet solos tooting out into the night. Live music, jazz, soul and country and western could be heard coming from four directions at every corner. Coloured people, in twos and threes, seemed to enjoy the raucous pageant of Bourbon Street as much as did the tourists. I assumed that they were locals, as they paused at the open doors of the soul music clubs and waved to friends or relations in the bands.

The sex shows were doing less well than the musical pubs. Their audiences seemed to be entirely white, for most of the black men strolling up and down were accompanied by wives or girlfriends. I found a fascinating museum based on Ripley's 'Believe It or Not' newspaper strip. A similar museum used to flourish at Blackpool. Talking of Blackpool, Bourbon Street was surprisingly free of pin-table arcades, miniature funfairs or mechanical rides for children. The 'Believe It or Not' museum contained a most unusual waxwork show, including a spectacular

Chamber of Horrors with special graveyard effects. The part of this show that I found most interesting were the Mardi Gras exhibits, showing waxwork Zulu Kings and Indian Chiefs in their elaborate velvet, ermine, and feather costumes with giant gauze butterfly wings and every kind of flamboyant finery.

By the same psychological quirk that had caused Desita's husband to throw a drink on the ground *not* for the African Earth Mother but for the Red Indian Black Hawk, the Mardi Gras masqueraders had adopted West African pagan dances and regalia yet called themselves Wild Indians or Indian Chiefs. The West African past had been reinterpreted, and now lived on in Red Indian or Zulu guise. In just the same way, Sussex Bonfire Society Parades have *their* Zulus, (as in the past they have had minstrels and chimney sweeps) to justify the English pagan habit of blacking up for pre-Christian fertility rites.

I roamed up and down Bourbon Street, pausing at doorways to sample the three musical staples, Jazz, Country and Western and Soul. All three styles have originated in the American South. Nearly all the jazz bands consisted of prosperous-looking white people, with an occasional grey woolly head among them. Jazz joints were by far the most expensive and respectable places. Most of the musicians seemed to be educated middle-aged Yankees, Englishmen, Dutchmen and Swedes. In England their music would be called 'Trad Jazz', but here it was known as 'Dixieland'. Mark Tuba Smith and his friends, together with most coloured jazzmen, played out of doors for coins thrown into cardboard boxes. Jazz had begun with scuffling musicians who played at the funeral parades for which New Orleans is still famous. It has come a long way since then, though Mark Tuba Smith still played at funerals, and the white jazzmen of Bourbon Street took a pride in playing only old-time music.

Country and western music often alternated with soul music in the slightly cheaper places. None of these latter-day music halls charged an admission fee, but once in, I found that the invisible fee had been spread around on the price of drinks. Both these types of Southern music are now well known all over the world. 'Country and western' is the music of the rural White South. 'Soul' is the catch-all title for the popular music of the Black South and the city 'black quarters' of the North. Most such music consists of standardised love songs, but a tiny ember of traditional hillbilly music remains in country and an ember of Negro blues remains in soul. Sometimes the embers start glowing, sending up sparks, then flames, then lying low again for a while. Heat from these age-old yet living embers keeps the whole Southern popular music business warm and alive.

Outside Papa Joe's in Bourbon Street, I paused, standing amongst an earnest crowd of coloured people who could not afford to go in. Neither could I, so I sat on a hydrant and listened. Evidently something good was going to happen. On the stage inside, curly-permed youths were twanging guitars or lashing at drums, while a young lady with glossy black hair screeched in familiar pop style.

Suddenly the guitar notes grew longer, and soared with a Hawaiian tone as the young lady began to sing the 'Down Home Blues'. This song was, I found, the anthem of the rhythm and blues crowd throughout the South. It was always used to introduce a medley of blues songs. Excitement inside the club and out on the pavement intensified, as the blues rolled on. Like their sacred brother, the spiritual, the blues has several meanings. Songs about dancing abound in sexual metaphors, some subtle, some less so. Even the bawdiest, silliest songs possess a strange, moaning, yearning sense of tragedy when sung in the eerie Southern blues voice.

'I want you to roll me, baby, like you roll a wagon wheel,' the girl wailed.

'I can't roll like that!' shouted a fat white man from the audience, with surprising candour.

'Oh yes you kin,' the singer answered, making the lines a part of her song. 'No matter how much you roll me, you know how good it makes me feel.'

'Going up, going down, anyway you wanna let it roll,' the girl continued, then stopped in mid-sway and looked straight at me. 'You outside, come on in, you got me doing what you wanna – Baby, what you want me to do?'

I walked back towards Canal Street, and decided that next day I would change a traveller's cheque and go to Papa Joe's. So the blues still attract the coloured people of the South! In England, where blues are a bohemian intellectual music, the myth has arisen that among American Negroes the blues are dead. This myth is insisted on vehemently, and seems linked to colour prejudice, the modern Negro soundly berated for his dreadful taste in music. Only noble white students can sing the blues, the torch handed down to them by the great black men of the Golden Past. Tchah! Or as a Jamaican might say, Cho!

Why should the blues mean so much to me? They seem linked in my mind to the English aristocracy. As a teenager, in the fifties, I listened to 1930s blues and read 1930s P.G. Wodehouse stories. I felt that the best things in life, the two traditions that once typified England and America, had vanished just before my time. When I see a white Georgian manor house standing in its own park, waves and waves of pleasure seem to pour over me. A similar ecstasy overtakes me when I hear blues, as the blues people of the South were quick to notice and comment on. 'You like that, huh?'

Later in life, I found that both country house life in England and the blues in America are alive, if at a low ebb. Blues, to my mind, are the Great American Achievement, a tradition that links the New World to the Old, for blues came from West Africa as work songs. African rhythms and the garbled half-understood words of Scottish and Irish ditties sung by cruel overseers came together in the minds of lowly slaves and a truly Southern art was born.

When I left the fire hydrant outside Papa Joe's it had grown dark, and the crowds were thickening. Outside a jazz club door I saw a small boy tap dancing in time to the music, his hat (for tips) waving in his hand. Further on, near Canal Street, the crowd had parted and formed a circle in which fervent boys and coloured teenagers tap danced feverishly, eyes gleaming in concentration.

'I fix metal plates on the heels and toes,' a boy told me, as he bent his knees and hurled his body into a frenzied jitterbugging heel-castanetting rhythm. A youth of fourteen spun a polished bicycle wheel on his head, faster and faster, and a frowning, intensely serious boy of eight out-danced and out-limber-legged his older rivals. He even persuaded a laughing white tourist girl to dance with him, before pressing round the crowd with his cardboard money box. Did his parents know he was there?

In the morning I collected fifty dollars from a bank where most of the staff were coloured, then headed for Bourbon Street once more. Music there went on all day, and I took my seat in Papa Joe's. A debonair curly-permed soul singer and his band came on. Most of the other customers were coloured, including a jolly table full of round-faced girls with one young man. After a while, the singer broke into a rasping 'Down Home Blues', and it was a delight to see the way the girls, eyes shining, bodies bouncing and arms waving, enjoyed the blues medley that followed. I roamed up to Jackson Square, looked at the river then stepped down to Bourbon Street once more. But long before I arrived, I could hear the strange electrifying cry of the blues, louder, stronger and more insistent than ever. Trailing the blues-shouting to its source, I found myself in a large, almost-empty club, with rows of wooden tables and chairs, a bar and a stage. High on a rostrum, like a pastor, a beaming, sweaty brown man was playing the blues on a keyboard, helped by a drum machine. He wore rings and a neck medallion, and he sported a curly perm.

'B.B. Benjamen at the Rising Sun', a yellow poster proclaimed on the wall behind him. He roared:

> 'I want you to leave, leave my woman alone,
> Lea-e-eave, leave my woman alone!
> 'Cos I love that woman like a bulldog loves a bone.'

A depraved-looking hollow-eyed barman, a blond youth of no more than twenty, dried glasses in an ironic manner, while the sparse customers, white and drunk or black and sober, listened to B.B. intensely. When B.B. had finished singing, I congratulated him and requested an interview.

'So you like my singing, huh? All them pretty women sure give you the blues! Well, B.B. ain't my name, you know, it stands for Blues Boy, like in Blues Boy King. B.B. King, he's my main man, him and Otis Redding. Other singers I like are Sam Cooke and a blues singer called Johnny Taylor. I was born in Texas, but I spent most of my boyhood in the country fifteen miles out of New Orleans. My mother died when I was small, so I was brought up by my grandmother. I liked her, but then I went to an aunt, and her husband was too strict. I couldn't live there! So, I ran away from home in my early teens, an' took up music. I'm thirty-six now, and been playing music ever since. Got my own band, when I can get 'em together. I've been on tour with Zee Zee Hill, the creator of the song "Down Home Blues". At thirteen I had to be a *man*.'

Very eager to please the public, smiling effusively, big Blues Boy Benjamen urged everyone out in the street to come in and have a drink and listen to some good music. I slipped out and soon found myself at a similar musical pub, the Krazy Korner.

'Joan Magee and the Foundation Band' were advertised.

A waiter performed a St Vitus jitterbugging dance in the doorway, and crowds of white youngsters milled around holding drinks. At one point, a group of bare-armed moustachioed young men and scarlet-faced tipsy women performed a conga dance around the room. On stage, an all-black rhythm and blues band poured music out into the night – drums, saxophones, a trumpet and an amplified blues guitar. Solemn black people crowded around the open windows, wide-eyed, drinking in the blues. Two of them danced and swayed slowly to the music. A few turned out their pockets and managed to get in, making one expensive drink last the evening. Still outside, a mother crouched on the pavement holding her little daughter on her knee. Apparently the myth that coloured people hurl their bodies about, sing and leap around all the time, like manic minstrels, is not only believed in by B.B.C. television producers in England but by white Southerners in New Orleans. It was the blind leading the blind, for the doormen played up to this prejudice by jitterbugging, and the ribald tourists felt bound to show that they could outdo the coloured race by jumping and yelling. When country and western music came on, the white tourists invariably calmed down and became their normal well-mannered selves.

As the guitarist played the introduction to 'Down Home Blues', Miss Joan Duvalle Magee, a serene, self-possessed and portly woman, stepped down from a bar stool and sailed effortlessly towards her microphone.

'Down home blues, lord, down home blues!
Play me some of them down home blues . . .'

When Southerners go north to work in Detroit or Chicago they refer to
the South as 'Down Home', just as West Indians in England refer to their
native islands as 'Back Home'.

'Every day, every day I have the blues,' Joan Magee sang on.

After a song about an organ grinder, she ended her show by singing
'Respect', a modern rhumba-blues, saxophone notes spiralling away and
liquid notes pouring from the guitar.

'Honey, I've no time for an interview, but I'll tell you this, they're gonna
put me in a movie called *No Mercy*,' she told me.

I finished my orange juice and shuffled Y.M.C.A.-wards through the
crowds. At the doorway of another pub, the After Hours, a hillbilly trio
played from a high pulpit overlooking the bar. One of them sawed frantic
jigs on an electric fiddle, and sang a square dance ditty, 'Cotton Eyed
Joe'. The fiddler was a wild, hairy looking man. He played so well and so
quickly that the slick-haired clean-shaven guitarist could only stare in
frank admiration.

Near Canal Street, where the real world began, I caught a glimpse of a
guitarist sitting on the bonnet of a taxi in a dark, narrow sidestreet. I
hurried over, and found the musician to be a taxi driver who was giving a
private concert to a friend, between fares. His friend was a pipe-sucking
prosperous black man in a tweed jacket and a black beret, a man whose
eyes flashed in admiration as the blues twanged from the acoustic guitar.
The driver sang with a sad, questioning, poignant lilt.

'Will I survive?
Will I survi-i-ive,
Teaching my baby how to drive?'

'He makes up all his own songs while he's cab drivin',' the pipe-man
told me.

Concluding his song about a hair-raising driving lesson, the Singing
Cabbie began another one, about his life spent racing to and from the
International Airport in search of custom. I can only remember snatches
of this story in song, with its swinging chorus: 'There must be a better
way!'

'. . . I hit a tack and got a flat!
Well, I heard on the grapevine, they said the airport's moving.
I drove my cab on out there and I thought my luck's improving.
I ran into heavy traffic and before I got through,
A Speedway cop pulled up and said "I'd like to speak to you . . ." '

'Do it in rock and roll!' the driver's friend suggested admiringly.

'No, I want to do it blues,' the musician insisted. Despite the comic words to his songs, he seemed to take his craft very seriously.

'Rock and roll is still blues! You could make it big! Look at Johnny Copeland!' his friend urged.

'No, I'd rather write songs for someone else to sing.'

At this point, I interrupted the two men and asked if I could put the Singing Cabbie in a book. Both friends were thunderstruck, and their cosy chatting mood ended instantly.

'My name is Mem Dennis Shannon, cab driver, and I've lived in New Orleans all my life,' the driver stated, as if giving an alibi in a police station. He held up his cab driver's badge with his photograph stuck to it.

'He's very good at singing,' the pipe-man told me, helpfully.

I felt ashamed, and left them to pick up the threads of the ruined concert.

Avis at the Y.M.C.A. had urged me to go and see the Riverwalk shopping centre down by the levee. Strolling up and down this glossy mile-long arcade overlooking the Mississippi is a favourite pastime of New Orleanians. So I strolled along Canal Street, past the Hilton and other ugly hotels, and found the entrance to the Riverwalk between an equestrian statue and the booking office of the good ship *Cotton Blossom*. A middle-aged woman with vivid brown eyes, black hair and a French appearance showed me the way.

'I'm called Josephine, and I'm a Creole,' she told me.

'Does that mean you're part French?' I enquired.

'Part French, part Spanish and part Indian! Oh yes! Don't know what tribe, though. New Orleans is in a bad way right now. I have a dressmaking job three days a week, but I need extra work, maybe weekends. So I'm going to try in the Mall. I'm a widow-woman, you see.'

'Mall' appeared to mean shopping arcade or shopping centre. The title 'Creole' appears to have been transferred, on the whole, to French-speaking Roman Catholic Negro citizens of New Orleans. Originally the term was applied to Frenchified white people such as Josephine.

We chatted away until we entered the imposing Mall, a shiny glittering arcade of shops and stalls, with an outside walkway attached, above the Mississippi. Giant white paddle steamers churned by, the decks alive with tourists. Leaving my Creole companion behind, I hurried on and found that the Mall climbed steadily upwards, with stairs and escalators provided.

As I was browsing around, I heard a bell ring, and a girl's voice loudly shouted, 'It's Fudge Time!'

At a nearby counter, I found that four very jolly coloured girls in aprons, helped by a morose aproned youth, were making and selling fudge with great rapidity. They poured the delicious-smelling brown fudge from a cauldron on to a four-foot metal plate, ladling it about with a silver spade. The youth then cut the cooling fudge into small portions, some of which became free samples for lucky customers such as myself. Finally the girls lined up, tapped their feet in gospel-singing style, swayed their arms and sang a paean to the glories of fudge. It went to the tune of a pop song, 'When Will I Be Loved?'

> 'When I find a new fudge that I want for mi-ine,
> It always breaks my diet in two, it happens every time!
>   I've been cheated
>   And mistreated!
> When will I eat fudge?'

After which they all fell about laughing. I was reminded strongly of London girls in Black British churches, and wondered if any of my talented friends 'Back Home' in England will ever be discovered and used by commerce.

The Riverwalk led out on to the streets leading to Lee Circle and the Y.M.C.A. However, I doubled back on my tracks, as I thought I ought to ride on a riverboat before I left New Orleans.

And so I did. Sitting on a red seat on the top deck of the *Cotton Blossom*, said to be a 'paddle steamer with a real tail drive powered by a diesel engine', I sailed up the muddy Mississippi towards Audubon Park and the Audubon Zoo. A loudspeaker commented on everything in sight – long, low cotton wharves, now used for cleaning services, and two huge dirty cargo boats, one Yugoslavian and one registered in Liberia. Both flew the Stars and Stripes out of courtesy. The sun beat down, so I put on my white floppy hat and looked up at the smokeless chimney of the *Cotton Blossom*.

From the landing stage at Audubon Park, I walked across a heat-struck meadow towards the entrance of the zoo. Birds sang sweetly in the young trees and big flapping red butterflies flitted above my head. A young coloured girl took my entrance money. The ice-cream selling and ticket-punching jobs at the zoo were done by older schoolchildren in their holiday time.

A flowery jungle of banana trees and artificial rockwork, Audubon Zoo is Paradise. I walked through an aviary where parakeets of brilliant colour clung chattering to the palm leaves overhead. In a large enclosure nearby, the only pack of Southern red wolves in captivity prowled up and down, visible through a glass window in a jungle of bamboo. They looked not unlike ordinary wolves to me. A traveller once told me that wild wolves he had seen in Turkey were smaller and differently marked to wolves he had seen in Finland.

Living in a hot climate can do funny things to a wolf, and indeed to a bear, for the grizzly bears of Mexico are said to be small, scrawny animals compared to their neighbours in North America.

A bronze statue of Audubon, the nineteenth-century artist, naturalist and sportsman who had lived in New Orleans, looked out over his park. Audubon had shot most of the creatures he painted, propped the bodies up on wires and then sketched them. As a result his animal heads are very well painted, but the limp back legs often hang down lifelessly. The backgrounds to his paintings, usually provided by his son, give us a fascinating glimpse of pioneer landscapes. When I was a boy, these backgrounds had fascinated me, as they so much resembled the opening scenes of a vintage Barney Bear cartoon – a forest, a farm with a criss-cross fence and a log cabin where the hero dwells. Some of Audubon's animal paintings were on show in the Presbytère at Jackson Square. Like most artists, Audubon was a bit dotty, and liked to hint that he was the Dauphin, the rightful heir to the throne of France. In this he resembled the King who, together with his equally bogus friend, the Duke, shared Huckleberry Finn's raft on the Mississippi.

Behind Audubon's back, squirrels were romping around the trunks of a grove of mature evergreen oak trees. To my wonderment, I saw that the branches of these trees were hung with thick grey strands of Spanish moss, dangling like tattered curtains in a haunted house. For years I had yearned to see such moss, which to me epitomised the South. Instead of being woolly as I had imagined, the moss was fibrous and crumbled into crinkly segments in my hand. The squirrels seemed smaller and thinner than English grey squirrels, with an extra tint of russet in their fur. Brilliant blue jays with flecks of white on their long tails swooped from tree to tree. A ruined Greek temple at the far end of the grove decorated a beautiful neo-Classical pool for seals and sea lions, who skimmed through the clear waters or climbed on to platforms of granite boulders.

Nearby a hippopotamus snorted in the depth of a deep muddied pond. A path twisted through the banana trees from one enchanted glade to another, homes of lively and unusual monkeys. Each monkey jungle was separated from the path by a water-filled moat that replenished itself from artificial waterfalls. Black howler monkeys from the Amazon forests shook the branches and gave tongue in strange ventriloquial gibberings that no doubt could be heard across the Mississippi. White plumed guereza monkeys from East Africa leaped across the green grass, their long silky white mantles flying like cloaks pinned to their black furry limbs. Baby guerezas, like black and white squirrels with monkey heads, romped beside their parents, looking up at their mothers with dark liquid eyes. In England, all these monkeys would have to spend half their lives indoors in glass-fronted hothouses.

Human families wandered happily from glade to glade, the piping comments of the small children reminding me of the old 'Our Gang' films. White people and coloured people spoke in the same delightful Southern tones, the Negro speech a little faster, but all the remarks showing a lively sense of fun. Happy families may be the same everywhere, but that makes them none the less delightful to meet.

'Yeah, you can't get me *now*, you ol' snake, you!' a boy taunted an inscrutable serpent through a glass barrier. This was heard on the other side of the zoo, where a maze of red-brick farm-style buildings housed a large selection of animals. Children could crawl down a tunnel and emerge in the middle of a prairie dog town, staring at the surprised ground-squirrels from a giant prairie dog hole enclosed in a large glass bubble. Tunnelling rodents of the Texas plains, prairie 'dogs' get their name from their yapping cry, not from their appearance.

A tunnel through a banana forest led me to a tub of water at the bottom of which sat a fat coypu rat, like a tubby white-whiskered otter. Two charming girls of fifteen were sitting beside the coypu. One of them lifted it up and the other tickled its tummy. The coypu seemed to enjoy this treatment, in a non-demonstrative blasé manner.

'It's a nutria,' one of the girls explained, as other zoo-goers approached. This is the name by which the coypu rat is known in the fur trade. Apparently, a hurricane had released hundreds of the large water rodents from a fur farm into the Louisiana swamps. There they bred and now seem very popular, hunted for their pelts by the Cajun people who live in the wilderness. In England, the coypu (or nutria) also escaped into the Broads, the swamps of East Anglia, but in our country the beast is hated. A body of men and women known as Coypu Control go out every day in boats with one object in mind – exterminating the coypu. Killing is apparently the most effective means of controlling them. Until dead, a coypu can be quite uncontrollable. At least so say the proud members of the Coypu Control, that dedicated band who set out in bitter cold before the dawn and ceaselessly patrol the waterways of Norfolk to make sure our land is a fit country for non-coypus to live in.

I prefer the American approach. A housewife stopped to pet the coypu and told the girls that she once had a tame nutria which had lived in the house like a dog. However, it began taking longer and longer walks outside on its own, and the neighbours complained. So with many regrets, she had let it go.

'Look at that big old neutral there,' a Negro father told his admiring children.

'We're Junior Keepers,' one of the girls told me. 'A man from the zoo came to our High School and asked for volunteers. Not many are chosen, so we're very lucky.'

An Indian elephant with a resplendent Oriental howdah and carpet over its back plodded round a small field carrying a load of happy children. Their father looked on fondly. It was the first time I had seen an elephant standing beneath palm trees. Turning its dark grey face towards me, the pachyderm stared into the middle-horizon, its look of wisdom enhanced by having two brows, or brain bulges, instead of one.

But no doubt the finest exhibit of the Audubon Zoo was the Louisiana Swamp. A wooden platform had been raised above a chain of lakes and pools surrounded by reeds and trees dripping with Spanish moss. Cajun fiddle music swirled from a loudspeaker and swamp animals cavorted among old-time Cajun artefacts – floating cabins, punts and fish traps. Black bears roamed among the palms, and pumas (or mountain lions) paced within yards of a shaggy Houma Indian hut made of reeds. Light, fluffy flame-coloured foxes leaped from log to log.

On the other side of the walkway, big alligators swam, half submerged, cutting a swathe through the duckweed. Alligators live within a few miles of the city itself, and these long grey reptiles in their vast playground may not have known that they were in captivity. One on the far bank, however, suddenly flew into a rage when a keeper had put the fish-bucket away. Roaring loudly and gaping horribly, it lashed its tail at him. It seemed odd to look over a log balcony and see a cruising 'gator cast knowing eyes at all and sundry. How different from most zoos, where alligators sit motionless in small heated tanks and passers-by refuse to believe that they are alive! A cypress tree grew from the edge of the swamp, its roots running under the water, and protruding like a row of periscopes. Such roots are known as cypress 'knees'.

After enjoying a spicy crawfish pie in a log cabin café, I strolled on to the aquarium, where local people were making knowledgeable comments on the creatures on display – redfish, alligator gar, big-headed snapping terrapins and baby 'gators. These swim like fish, darting, wriggling and waving their tails from side to side, arms and legs pinned back to their sides like fins.

Outside, a Negro father pointed out to his son the long-nosed gar fish which continually rose to the surface and then vanished into the depths once more.

'Gar must breathe air,' he said solemnly.

Some scuttling armadillos, a cross between pigs and woodlice, failed to impress a woman who told her husband that she had seen bigger armadillos squashed on the road.

Near the zoo exit, I admired the leopards in their bamboo forest, then stopped transfixed by the deer enclosure. For in the park outside, dimly glimpsed through a hedge and a fence, a team of black men were chopping away overgrown thorny bushes, swinging machete-like tools in unison. As they worked they sang, a loud, unearthly, rhythmic roar, full of mystery – the Birth of the Blues. Try as I might, I could not understand a word.

'Tee na na na, tee na na!' the leader chanted.

'Wah!' the men responded in chorus, then roared almost angrily as they chopped.

It seemed to make the work easier, for they were hacking bushes down at a tremendous rate. Perhaps they were singing in French. I ran out of the zoo to take a closer look, but another wall separated us. Disappointed, I glanced around the parkland and saw, to my surprise, a bus standing at a bus stop. I sprinted over, and was told by the driver that he was going near Lee Circle Y.M.C.A. 'by way of Magazine'.

Sitting by the window, I admired spacious, leafy Magazine Street, a lengthy continuation of Decatur Street. Many of the fine wooden houses seemed to be antique shops. Dusk began to fall, and Magazine seemed vibrant and exciting. (The word 'street' is seldom used in American speech – Regent Street, say, would become 'Regent'.) Black people stood talking and laughing outside their houses and crowded on to the bus at each stop, heading for Canal Street or the French Quarter for an evening out. Others simply rode for a few stops on Magazine itself. Some of the elderly white people on the bus pulled long faces. In fact, their faces grew longer and longer as more and more coloured passengers embarked. It seemed that the notorious colour prejudice of the South had dwindled to a ludicrously transparent snobbery.

'I usually get the tram car, 'cos it goes the *other* way,' a woman told her equally disapproving husband.

All the coloured passengers were models of politeness, but one very old lady, perhaps remembering the bad old days, faltered at the idea of sitting beside me in case I didn't like it. By now, the bus being full, the alternative for her was standing, so I guided her gently into a sitting position. Churches, antique shops, a 'Gin Mill' and more wooden houses sped by, and soon I was back at the Y.M.C.A.

It was now my last day in New Orleans, so I set out to explore Magazine Street from the other end. After searching for a while amid the rubble of a half-completed flyover, I found it. It was a magnificent street of fine wooden houses of varying size, from snug cabins raised from the ground on corner stones to middle-sized mansions with white Grecian columns. Palm trees grew between the houses, and bits of extra house seemed to have been added to the original plank buildings, stuck on the roof or halfway along a wall.

Crazy steps led up to doors or second-storey porches. Some of the houses were run-down with flaking paint, but all well worth restoring. Dark pubs called 'lounges' were lit by gleaming juke boxes.

Children played merrily in the street, and men in dark glasses, moustaches and peaked caps sat on barbershop steps and gossiped idly, sharing cigarettes. I saw a few white people, looking very much at ease. Dark-leaved ilex and magnolia trees spread their boughs over sloping roofs, and the warm red brick of an old Baptist church contrasted well with the surrounding shades.

Rusty wire netting surrounded the grim playground of a thoroughly decrepit 1930ish school, but nearby, as if to compensate, stood a fine mansion behind a gate of ornate ironwork. This was the St Vincent's Infant Home, evidently an orphanage, for the metal alms box outside was inscribed 'Pity the Poor Little Orphans'. Another call on my purse came from two disconsolate boys of fifteen or so, who glumly asked me for fifteen cents and just as dourly received it. They were standing outside a tiny, dark, overcrowded corner shop, run by a Chinaman. As most of the passers-by and householders reminded me of West Indians in an English town, it seemed odd to see no Pakistanis. Perhaps Chinese from Formosa took their place, with Spanish-looking Costa Ricans doing duty for the Irish and supporting the Catholic churches.

Three big clompy girls stolped up the steps into the Orphans' Home, looking very like the oafish, insensitive girls who sometimes work as Care Attendants at Homes in England. Pity the poor orphans! Meanwhile, in the dirty little corner shop, a small boy earnestly purchased a mouth organ. A large dusty, second-hand record shop was filled from end to end with soul records, including blues. Houses gave way to closely packed dingy shops, under ironwork balconies of surprising ugliness. This was no French Quarter, but a lived-in neighbourhood, a bit shoddy but full of lively children.

One of the shops, Delta Books, seemed to be shut. An arrow pointed to a bell, so I rang and was admitted. A pleasant-faced young white man of bohemian appearance introduced himself as David and told me to go ahead and browse. It turned out to be a socialist bookshop, just such a one as might be found in a West Indian district in England. But in the South, revolutionaries are frowned on, and David had to be careful. It was a long time since I had seen so many books by Lenin, his silhouette on a score of covers. Nearly everything else concerned Albania. There were Albanian political books, Albanian tourist guides, Albanian toys, records and peasant crafts.

'You seem to like Albania,' I hazarded.

'Yes, I believe that true socialism only exists in Albania,' said David. 'The Party that calls itself Communist deviated a long time ago.'

He had heard of Ken Livingstone and other prominent Labourites of

England and referred to them as Social Democrats. David seemed a kindly man, and much of the literature that he and his friends produced was about the plight of black victims of the police and of the Ku Klux Klan. Most of the casual shootings and killings I read about had the ring of truth. I had seen New Orleans policemen with guns and two-handled clubs. Some seemed decent enough, but a few looked capable of anything. But many of the nastiest-looking policemen I had seen had been coloured. In the force, all men were brothers. Aware of this seeming anomaly, for to the revolutionaries, 'blacks' represented the faultless proletariat, the writers had got round it by labelling such police as 'Uncle Toms'. Once so labelled, that was the end of them. Instead of calling for police reform, the Delta writers assumed that only a violent revolution and the overthrow of the entire American Constitution could help matters. It seemed a drastic remedy.

'Someone shot my window out a few weeks ago,' David told me. 'I just had to replace it, as the police told me when I opened this shop that I would get no help from them. There are very few bookshops, and very few reading people at all in New Orleans, compared to, say, San Francisco, a city of about the same size.'

I didn't mind, as the South made up in folklore what it lacked in booklore, but David looked rather sad. To cheer him up I bought the autobiography of Black Hawk, the Red Indian chief, as taken down and translated by an Indian agent in the 1830s. Desita, the Jackson Square singer, had given me an interest in the old chief.

Before David let me out and re-locked his shop, I asked him why so many people in New Orleans slept out of doors every night.

'That's right, twenty years ago, only alcoholics and drug addicts slept out of doors in this city. Now it's able-bodied men. Homeless people from all over America come here in the fall, as you can sleep outdoors here without freezing. Coupled with that, the city has a high illiteracy rate.'

I didn't say so, but I felt that I would rather be illiterate than read his books about Albania. I bade David a good-natured farewell.

Further on, Magazine Street grew exclusive and posh, a glossy Magazine. Many of the Spanish-styled houses were for sale, and the antique shops had few customers. The district was 'going down', I was told, because of the Project. A Project in New Orleans means a Council Estate. So I hurried to Josephine Street, expecting to see a little bit of England.

The pace of life quickened in Josephine Street, where wooden cabins both worthy and unworthy of Uncle Remus faced the narrow pavement. Children scampered around, and young people played loud radios. It was very cheerful. Some of the householders were Costa Ricans, a trifle slatternly-looking. No one gave me a second glance. As for the Project, a row of grey flats with courtyards between them, it resembled a group of English 1930ish council tenements. It was hard to believe that it was new. Every door and window oozed life, and sparkle-eyed youngsters yelled greetings to one another. Stout, good-humoured old ladies struggled gamely along with washing and shopping bags. At the corner of the Project, I was struck by a tropical-looking Roman Catholic church of barbarous beauty, surrounded by palms. Project life, I imagine, must have its compensations.

Back at Magazine Street, I entered a café at hazard, the Hamburger Grill. Only the serving-lady, a buxom blonde, was white. Everyone seemed interested in my accent, so I told the lady that I came from England. For my part, I was fascinated by the juke box, which was full of blues records, some over thirty years old. Imagine finding such treasures in a workmen's café in England!

As I sat at one of the tables and solemnly ate a hamburger, the other customers looked at me with innocent curiosity. I moved over to the counter, sat up on a stool, ordered a coffee and looked about me.

My nearest neighbour was a very old thin and crinkled-up man who wore a yellow construction helmet. He was making rather a messy job of eating a salad, probably because he lacked teeth. 'Ah'm from Texas, an' Ah been workin' on the oil fields,' he told me, between mouthfuls.

At that moment, a big jovial man in a red-peaked cap bounced in from the kitchen. 'So you're from England!' he boomed heartily. 'My name's Larry, an' I'm the owner o' this place. England, hey? I was born in British Honduras! Have you met Princess Di?'

'No, but I've seen her,' I said truthfully. 'So you're British, like me! Well, well.'

'That's *right*! I left British Honduras when I was young an' worked in Spanish Honduras for a while. Then I came here to the States. I been to England and Scotland on vacation, and I been to Italy and seen the Pope! That was something! I'm a Catholic, you know. Over there in Rome, when I was there, they were digging big marble columns out of the ground. One place I long to go, where I never been, is Rio de Janeiro for the Carnival.'

At that moment, a tall, slim tough-looking young lady in a blue cap and jeans summoned Larry and began to whisper some news to him. Her hair was straightened into a fringe that stuck out over her forehead. 'I ain't instigating nothing – it's she that was instigating!' she insisted fiercely, her large eyes flashing.

I rose to leave, having enjoyed two free coffees. From my pocket I pulled some English coins and showed them to Larry and his friend. They seemed so interested that I ended up by dividing the coins between them. The young lady examined her pennies and tuppenny bits as if they were rare doubloons.

'That's about the same as a cent in your money, madam,' I explained.

'Don't call me madam! My name is Jessie!' she exclaimed proudly. 'Jessie Bee, that's my name. I sure am pleased to have met you.'

By now it was dark outside, and Larry called me back from the door. 'There are burglars on the street outside come from the Project right behind this building,' he said gravely. 'Also, there's no cops on the street 'cos the city is in a state of crisis like New York used to be. Let me put you on the bus.'

I waved goodbye to Larry as the bus pulled away. Near the Y.M.C.A. I looked out of the window and saw what seemed to be a dead man lying on his back in the road. Four policemen kneeled around him, feeling for a bullet or a heartbeat. None of the passengers took much interest. For all their fearsome weaponry, the New Orleans police had their uses. (Unless, of course, they had shot the man in the first place.)

CHAPTER FIVE

Five Days on the Road

A T LAST THE time came to leave New Orleans. On a rainy morning my coach pulled out of the Greyhound Bus Station and set off towards the state of Mississippi. I had bought a Greyhound ticket in London which allowed me to travel anywhere I liked for five days. So I planned my journey to the Smoky Mountains of Tennessee in five half-days of travel. A huge coach with a built-in toilet at the rear, my Greyhound was silver with a red and blue streak. Over frightful grey flyovers it roared, where tottering Negro shacks stood amid forests of concrete pillars.

One of the city's famous cemeteries could be seen from the road, the tombs in marble rows, the dead raised above the surface of the ground to prevent their being washed away in the muddy slurry of a Mississippi flood. A monstrous Dome of Discovery, the Superdome, flashed by and disappeared from view. Most New Orleanians seemed proud of this modern building. Regional patriotism, in America as in England, is linked to football and the Superdome covers an indoor arena where the Saints football team challenges all comers. Now the coach sped across huge Lake Ponchartrain, along a narrow bridge with the ocean-like lake stretching to the horizon on either side. Stalks of reed poked out of the shallows as the further shore came into view. Weird forests of dead trees with steep-sided creeks between them gave way to palms and evergreens around scattered houses. Soon the Southern countryside resolved itself into a scraggy, ragged and forlorn mixture of secondary forest and pine plantation. Half-grown 'lolly pines', fanned out at the top like monkey puzzle trees, were growing along the ridges.

Scrubby forest and lolly pines, typical Southern scenery, cover the farms and cotton plantations of a former age. Cotton-picking machinery can only be used where land is reasonably flat. Sharecropping no longer takes place, and the wilderness has returned. Although there is a commercial reason for this, one concerning saw mills, wood pulping factories and the paper industry, the return to the forest seems to satisfy the Pioneer who is so close to the surface in the Southern white man. A gun, a dog and plenty of deer in the woods – that is the Southerner's dream. I had not yet reached this conclusion on the day I left New Orleans, and I marvelled to see such ragged desolation side-by-side with a Spaghetti Junction of roads on stilts, and roadside signs of every kind that flashed beside my window.

Few white people travel by Greyhound, and on this particular coach none of the travellers felt like talking. Most of them dozed or sat deep in thought. I looked out of the window, noting a well-managed farm here and there among the pines. One estate, where cattle grazed in oak-studded Capability Brown parkland, looked as if it had been founded in slavery days. My destination that day was Meridian, Mississippi. Just before the coach reached Meridian, the forest grew taller. I seemed to be among genuine wildwood; soaring, rolling vistas of oaks, beeches and pines, with white splintered dead trees here and there poking out of the foliage. A cardinal bird flew by, a flash of bright crimson against the green. Above the tree tops, a red tailed hawk, large as a Welsh buzzard, soared from one look-out post to another. Four wild turkeys on the grass verge scrambled towards the forest as the coach passed by and I caught a vivid glimpse of their bald red heads and lustrous pangolin-scale feathers. Then the coach pulled in to Meridian, and I was left standing bewildered beside my bag.

What happened next was a foretaste of all my Southern travels. I asked the ticket-man in the busy little Greyhound office to phone for a taxi, and the taxi took me to an ultra-modern hotel on a traffic island surrounded by motorways. This hotel was miles out of town, ringed by impassable roads and impossible to escape from except by another taxi. Roadside shops, hotels, garages, restaurants and the modernistic arcades known as 'malls' have all-but abolished the American small town. The original remnants of town, the only bits worth seeing, would always be known as 'downtown', or 'the business sector'. Offices would often remain there as a relic of the glorious times known as 'pre-mall days'. Sometimes there would be a smart residential district known as 'uptown'. There would be no buses, for everyone was expected to own a car. Some black men had no cars, but they could hitch rides from other black men. Such is the pit that America has dug for itself.

To my surprise, my hotel, the Best Western, had a coloured manager. He was a worried-looking man in glasses who treated me cautiously. After I had been assigned my room, a big red-faced man in a cowboy hat rolled up and cheerfully hit the Reception bell. The manager at once relaxed, and the pair of them were soon chattering rapidly away in what I assumed to be the local Mississippi accent. My bedroom, which was to be duplicated in every modernistic hotel on a traffic island that I stayed in, was huge and had brown curtains drawn open or closed by strings. Lamps were scattered here and there, a long chest of drawers contained stacks of brochures, and coat hangers dangled from a gleaming rail near the bathroom door. In the bathroom, ten towels of assorted sizes were poked into tight-fitting racks. The smallest towels, pocket-handkerchief size, had to do duty as flannels. Americans have not yet invented the flannel. And there was a television.

In a way, such hotels are quite soothing. This one had no dining room, and I was advised to use the café next door. To my mortification, I found that motorways hemmed me in and prevented me from visiting a funfair only half a mile away or from finding a path into the woods. In the dark, I walked beneath towering black trees in the hotel grounds, listening to the cicada chorus of a Southern night.

In the morning I took a taxi to uptown Meridian and the Jimmy Rodgers Museum. Meridian is the birthplace of Jimmy Rodgers (1897–1933), a country and western singer noted for his songs about trains and hoboes. He was known as the Singing Brakeman, a brakeman being a type of railway policeman whose job it was to catch 'freight-jumping hoboes' (or goods train stowaways) and punish them. So there was a contrast between Rodgers' daytime job and his after-hours singing, when he played a guitar and sang of the Romance of Rail and the carefree life of a hobo. I see myself as a kindred spirit to Rodgers, for in my days as a lavatory attendant in Sussex I was supposed to expel tramps from the cubicles, but instead listened to their stories and ended up writing their praises.

A large station-like building, the museum contained Rodgers' guitar, his peaked cap, and a great many bits and pieces of obsolete railway equipment. The lady at the door told me that many of Rodgers' songs had been written by his sister-in-law, Elsie McWilliams. Her photograph was hanging on the wall – an unlikely source for so many tough he-man ballads of bar-room brawls and prison cells. In his day, the twenties and thirties, Jimmy Rodgers conquered the South, a Singing Sensation. Many of his songs, including those he claimed to have written, were straightforward traditional Negro blues. Since his day, whenever country and western ballad singing is beginning to grow bland and tedious, it receives an injection of blues from the Negro side of music, and at once perks up again. Even the banjo, the typical hillbilly instrument, is borrowed from the coloured man. Two musical traditions exist in the South, with criss-cross currents between them. Rodgers' innovation, a startling one, was to yodel like a Swiss mountaineer, making his voice a second instrument between verses of blues.

Outside the museum, I admired a statue of Rodgers, a man cut down in his prime by T.B. Nearby, on small strips of track, stood railway engines and carriages of the Singing Brakeman's day. One of the achievements of the motor car in its victory against American tradition, romance and decency, is to have caused the train, even the electric train, to vanish from American life. Later I was to meet a middle-aged country and western guitarist, a computer operator by day, who had *never ridden on a train*.

I traced vanished, uprooted railway tracks here and there in the park. Blue jays swooped from tree to tree, and gardeners swung their hoes in unison.

Suddenly, by the roots of a big tree, I saw a chipmunk! I had never seen one in the wild before, so I ran towards the little animal, who jumped into a hole, flipping up his tail so that I could see the red underside. I waited for a moment and his striped head appeared. When he saw I was still there, he gave a squeak of surprise and vanished. Running around nearby, the grey squirrels were more wary than those in English parks. No wonder – the Southerners eat them!

The museum lady kindly phoned for a taxi, and a woman driver took me through Meridian town centre, where I saw a Confederate soldier a-top a high monument and a fine-looking museum and art gallery. But I had no time to linger if I was to catch my coach.

'My father worked for the railroad, and he knew Jimmy Rodgers well,' my driver told me.

Luggage was being loaded on to the coach when I arrived. Many of the tall black men, with high cheekbones, looked aristocratic and disdainful. One elderly dandy wore a new forties-style hat and a pearl-grey suit with a waistcoat. Women resembled haughty teeth-sucking Jamaicans, and one ordered me peremptorily to open a door. A weight machine by the door interpreted dreams. Only a few standard dreams were in stock, on the dial, and I hadn't had any of them. I took my seat and we were off, Alabama bound.

By the roadside, mile upon mile a thick green porridge of kudzu vine covered the woods along the verges. Strange bunches of smothered trees seemed to have been drowned by kudzu, for tree-shapes could be discerned beneath the bright green covering of vines. Strange black holes, doors and windows, had been left between the glob, making mystery caves amid the thirty-foot high heapings of kudzu. Although the vine had grown up from the ground, it looked as if it had been dropped on to everything by a giant syrup spoon. The leaves were not really sticky, but they did look as if they had flowed over everything in a kudzu tide.

Kudzu, I learned, came from Japan and was introduced to the South in the thirties by the Tennessee Valley Authority, a work-making scheme much praised at the time. The vine was supposed to be an 'earth stabiliser', popular at a time when men feared dust bowls. No one knew it was also a tree-killer. Apparently, it dies away in the winter but returns in the spring.

Stopping at various halts, the coach soon filled up, the women passengers making friends, laughing and joking, but directing blank or cool looks in my direction. However, after I had praised a particularly enchanting baby, the atmosphere improved.

'Her name's Letitia, but I call her Li'l Bit,' the mother smiled.

Alabama, from the roadside, seemed a land of continual woodland, sometimes scraggy and half-open, sometimes deep forest. The barrier of kudzu along the edges of woods made them seem impenetrable. Most Greyhound Bus Stations were little more than sheds.

Deep in the forest, we came to the village of Epes, a scattering of Negro cabins beneath the trees. It could have been a pioneer settlement of Africans, with raw patches of newly-cleared ground and the wooden cabins brown and unpainted. A dark-skinned woman stared suspiciously from an equally dark doorway, a washerwoman's white bandana on her head. Passengers climbed in and out at Epes, and the next stop was Eutaw, a big town. Here the coach passed a school whose playground was a metal cage, not very large, with a roof of wire mesh. Tall dark-skinned youths leaped energetically inside, throwing balls into baskets.

We crossed the wide Tombigbee River and the narrower wilder Black Warrior, and then pulled in at Tuscaloosa. There a taxi driver took me to the Ramada, a modernistic hostel on a traffic island.

'They closed the last downtown hotel just two weeks before you got here,' the taxi driver told me. He was a very smartly-dressed coloured man. 'You sure have been unlucky, sir.'

Most town centres seemed to have decrepit, recently-closed hotels near the bus stations. Tuscaloosa appeared a smart town of wide streets and white buildings. I noticed the First African Baptist Church with a 'historic building' plaque outside, and then we were on the motorway (or 'interstate highway').

'Come back in a couple of hours and take me back to town,' I told the beaming driver, who had begun to tell me his life story. 'What's your name, sir please?' (Two can play at the 'sir' game.)

'My name's Snoddy, Pastor Amos Snoddy, for I am a servant of the Lord,' the driver told me.

I told him my name, and we shook hands. After a wash and a nap, I went out to the traffic island and waited for Pastor Snoddy. He soon arrived, accompanied by a bright-looking thirteen-year-old boy.

'This here's my godson Darren, he's come to stay with me, all the way from Chicago,' Pastor Snoddy explained, as he drove rapidly into town. 'I'm a Pentecostal minister, and I was called to come here from Chicago.

The Lord called me to drive a cab, too! I have had a miracle in my life; it happened this way. I woke up one night and I could feel the Lord directing me to take pen and paper. So I took 'em, an' I was writing all night, writing in the Spirit. I didn't know *what* I was writing. When I finished an' I read what I written, I was surprised, I tell you! I had wrote all about the life to come, after death, with certain proof. Yes, I was mighty glad to see that writing. Now there are four kind o' bad houses in Tuscaloosa, where I try an' carry the word o' the Lord. There's houses for bootleggin', drug peddlin', prostitution an' gambling. They lets me go in the county jail to evangelise, an' one man found the Lord who came out after serving fourteen years.'

'What does "bootlegging" mean?' I asked the Pastor.

'Well, Roy, over here it's prohibited to sell liquor on a Sunday. So folks make their own whiskey on Saturday an' sell it at parties on Sunday.'

He parked his taxi in front of a run-down garage. Coloured men were pottering about everywhere, with oily rags dangling from the pockets of their overalls. Pastor Snoddy seemed loath to let me go, so I let Darren draw pictures on my notepad for a while. He handed the book back to me, full of stylised drawings and scribblings in the 'hip hop' style that had originated in New York. Coloured boys in London draw, or spray graffiti, in exactly the same way. Darren, I was moved to see, had written my name in various graffiti styles.

'What do you want to do when you're grown up?' I asked him.

'I don't know, but I wish I could go back to Chicago.'

'I'll be right here when you want to go back, Roy,' said the Pastor. He seemed to take great pleasure in using my first name. 'It certainly is a pleasure to find y'all so congenial.'

I walked round the town in the growing dusk, admiring the many fine churches with white columns that enhanced the spacious, leafy streets. The First Episcopal and the First Baptist churches were particularly grand, their histories engraved on notice boards outside. 'First' churches, like the First National Banks so beloved of cartoonists, are simply the first churches of their sort to be built since the Pioneers came. Most of Tuscaloosa's First Churches dated from the early years of the nineteenth century.

Behind the imposing courthouse, as if tacked on, stood the huge County Jail, a square building which opened straight on to the street. In Britain there would have been a grim wall around it, with occasional gates where notices would proclaim that it was illegal to smuggle gifts into prison. A university town, Tuscaloosa had fairly intelligent magazines in the shops, a small theatre and a Chinese Restaurant. The white people seemed well-mannered and pleasant, but with an English reserve that made them hard to speak to without an introduction. In the Mandarin

Restaurant, the owner told me of his visit to Northampton in England, to stay with Chinese relatives.

Back at Pastor Snoddy's garage, with its red neon Texaco sign, I found the Pastor and two other men poking about in the innards of the taxi. The Pastor waved a greasy hand and told me I would have to wait for a while. As he worked, he proudly shouted introductions, again using Christian names with emphasis.

'Roy, this here's my brother Sam.'

Sam, a bespectacled man, shot me a worried glance from the bowels of the car.

'He's an Englishman!' Pastor Snoddy whispered to him dramatically.

Leaning there against a crumbling garage wall on a warm autumn evening, watching Sam and the others working and cracking jokes, I felt that this indeed was American small-town life at its best. Young black couples, arm in arm, drifted to and from the coffee stall nearby. 'Spend black dollars' read a sign in the garage window. Muffled explosions in the distance, I was told, came from the university. The students were letting off 'firecrackers' (bangers) to celebrate a football match.

In the morning, my coach left for Birmingham, Alabama. Pastor Snoddy and his repaired taxi got me to the bus station on time.

'Me and my wife was up all night talkin' 'bout England!' he told me excitedly. 'I believe the Lord is going to call me to go to England next.'

Soon the great coach drew out, and I admired the mansion-like university buildings. Crowds lined the streets and there was evidently going to be a parade. Goodbye, Tuscaloosa and hello, Birmingham.

At Birmingham coach station, I felt moved at the sight of an old country Negro with a foolish smile stumble around in a daze as he emerged into the big city. A very capable, sophisticated girl, evidently his daughter, appeared from nowhere and swooped down on him, leading him away by the hand. He gave her a doting glance of admiration. In the souvenir shop, peaked caps were on sale with this slogan: 'My Wife: Yes. My dog: Maybe. My Gun: Never.' It seemed to be a Southerner's protest against laws prohibiting domestic firearms.

A tall black driver with a shut-off 'closed' face, a mask between himself and the white people he clearly disliked, whisked me to a modernistic hotel. We sped through concrete canyons with no redeeming features and emerged *not* on a traffic island but beside a wooded hill close to yet another university. Furthermore, this hotel had balconies with railings, whence I admired the view of classical-looking buildings rising from the trees. One of them appeared to have a column, topped by an immense figure of a man holding a beacon, sprouting from its roof. I vowed to reach this strange building and find out who the man with the torch could be.

First of all, however, I went to a nearby workmen's café, a pleasant place where my meal time was spent listening to a rough, wild-looking Negro who was urging a white man to apply for a job that was going. A merry-faced youngster, the white man seemed content to stay where he was, serving in a café. But the other insisted, and wrote the name of the job down on a paper napkin.

After roaming the serene suburban streets for a while, I found a road that seemed to lead in the right direction, and set off. On the way, I found a public library that looked almost exactly the same as an English library. American children's libraries, however, are usually better than English ones, as they have kept their old books from the forties and fifties.

To my surprise, the statue and the column detached themselves from the university building as I approached. They had been standing behind it, further up the forested slopes. Where the trees began, a man drove out of his garage, then stopped to give me a lift. Thanks to this act of kindness, I could reach the column in time, before the pay desk closed. Apparently the column contained a lift with a wonderful view from the top.

'It's called the Vulcan Statue,' the man explained, as I scrambled out.

A jolly dark-haired girl in jeans took my money and gave me a guide book to Vulcan.

'To save walking all round the car park, y'all can squeeze through a hole in the fence,' she advised me. She demonstrated by darting out of her kiosk, wriggling in and out of a gap in the railings and then taking her place at the pay window once more. So I squeezed too, and so reached Vulcan by a short cut. A souvenir shop and indoor lift had been built around the base of the great column.

Excruciating verses had been inscribed on a nearby tablet. I looked up at Vulcan, and the gigantic figure, at closer quarters, seemed ungainly and grotesque. He was a thickset man, this Vulcan, with a huge shaggy bearded head. The original Vulcan, the son of Zeus, was a smith-god like the African Legba and the Saxon Wealand, and had a gammy leg. This Vulcan, I learned, symbolised Industry and had one arm nearly twice as long as the other. Whether it was the arm that raked in the profits or the arm that handed out the wages, I could not tell.

According to the guide book, the Birmingham Vulcan had a chequered career from the first. He had been made for the World Fair at St Louis in 1904, as the Birmingham exhibit. Made out of iron sections, his head had been put on back to front at first. Then the head was put right, but a hand went on back to front. When the good people of St Louis had had enough of this, Vulcan was brought back to Birmingham, the city in which he had been forged. He was 55 feet high, the world's biggest iron man, and his pedestal was 124 feet tall. The torch in his hand lit up at night – green if all was well, red if something horrible had occurred.

I sailed up in the lift with a chattering cargo of schoolgirls. A window showed us the woods behind growing smaller, and at last we stepped out on an enclosed observation platform just below Vulcan's feet. There was a superb view over rolling green forests to the tall, iron-bearing Red Mountains.

'Look, there's the Birmingham jail!' a girl cried from the other side of the platform, where the grey city of Birmingham stood revealed.

I retraced my steps to the pay kiosk, then looked back at Vulcan in the dusk. To my dismay, his torch shone red.

'There's been a traffic fatality,' the girl at the kiosk explained. 'Are you from England? Have you seen the Queen? Come into the kiosk, make yourself at home and tell me all about England.'

So I perched on a stool and gave a lecture on England.

'What happens at Halloween here?' I asked Cynthia Reid, for that was her name. 'Halloween is only now being reintroduced to England.'

'Well, children used to go from door to door in disguise, saying "Trick or Treat",' she explained. 'People give them sweets, and if they didn't the kids would play tricks on them. But now people give pennies, 'cos crazy sick people were going round giving out sweets with poison in 'em! Parents can't let kids run around at Halloween like they used to. Sometimes hospitals scan sweets for poison, most often people have their own private Halloween parties where they know everyone. The crazy people have kind of spoiled Halloween. That's not all they do – sometimes they buy pills at the drug store, put poison in 'em and put 'em back on the shelf.'

Changing the subject, I asked Cynthia if her ancestors had come from England.

'No, from Scotland! We have a fiddle in our family that's supposed to have been brought from Scotland by my great-grandfather when he came to America. It has a date on it, but I can't read it. Seventeen or eighteen something. I keep it safe under my bed. I've also got my great-grandfather's fob watch. Some day I'd love to go to Britain. I've bought a raincoat in readiness!'

Cynthia phoned for a taxi, and I was soon back at the University Inn. My driver was a polite Nigerian youth of the Yoruba tribe. He was studying finance and accounts at the university, when not driving a taxi. At the hotel, I found that a dinner dance for the blind was taking place. Some of the guests were being led in by harnessed guide dogs.

* * *

My Fourth Day on the Road was to take me to Chattanooga, Tennessee, by way of Atlanta, Georgia. Young white working men on the coach, in peaked caps and moustaches, chatted uninhibitedly with coloured passengers. The conversations were all about football. It seemed as if the lowering of racial barriers in America presented a golden opportunity for young white men to find a new audience for their football-talk. Many of the Negroes themselves seemed fond of football.

I preferred to look out of the window, for we were now passing through dark, wild and haunting upland forests, peaks and valleys. This was Talladega National Forest, a new name for these ancient virgin woodlands of pine and aspen. Here, for a brief half-hour's ride, I could begin to visualise the America of the Red Indian. Such a chance did not occur again. I reflected that if I had not known American history, and had travelled with an open mind, I would certainly have supposed the Negro to have been the original American. Negro cabins looked indigenous to the Southern forests – white men's houses did not. Black people had the air of being rightful Americans, not transplanted Africans but a usurped race who had dwelled in the South long before the day of Columbus.

From Alabama to Georgia the earth in the farm tracks, gulches and rarely-seen ploughed fields was a beautiful, thick, paint-box red, mixed with orange. I could have been in Devon. Near Atlanta, the roadside adverts grew picturesque. Large signs seemed to sprout from the forest, supported above the trees and telegraph poles on tall pine stems driven into the wooded slopes. Atlanta seemed another grey, frightful city like Birmingham. The tops of the skyscrapers were hidden by mist, and a massive road-building scheme devastated the approach to the city.

I had to change here, so I waited outside the coach for my bag, which had been locked in the boot. Trolleys were hauled to and fro as luggage was collected. Greyhound porters seemed an agreeable body of men, and very eager to please. At every large coach station from New Orleans onwards I had heard the porters softly humming and singing to themselves, often in a high-pitched whine. Usually a popular soul song formed the basis of each hum, but it became progressively embellished with funny little quaverings of voice until it grew to fit its new owner. A porter at Atlanta seemed particularly good at this form of porterial half-singing. I recognised one phrase: 'Drifting on down the line.'

'That's a nice song you're singing – what's it called?' I asked, as I collected my bag.

His dreamy expression gave a jump of shock, then broke into a smile. 'Oh, that's just an old song I sing to make me be's happy when I'm feeling sad,' he replied.

Another coach took me from Atlanta to Chattanooga, where I found a modernistic hotel just next to the coach station. This was more like it!

The following morning I set out to explore Chattanooga without having to take a taxi.

I soon found a long shopping street and browsed along it, until I came to a wooden hoarding where a new building was going up. Here a tall moustachioed coloured man had set up an elaborate shoe-shine stand, with rows of cloths and polishes neatly tucked into a shelf. He kneeled on the pavement beside the stand and added the finishing touches to a mural painted on the fence. As he dabbed away, he chatted to a prosperous chipper-looking man in a tweed jacket, derby hat and pointed shoes.

'The music I like is old-time blues, Muddy Waters, Howling Wolf, them guys,' the painter was saying.

Those were names I had seen on the juke box at Larry's café in New Orleans. I looked at the picture in surprise. It showed a shoe-shine stand flanked by space rockets. Nearby was an excellent painting of a coloured boy shining a rich white man's shoes, while above his head hovered an angelic girl, half black and half white, the line going down her middle. Tears from Heaven fell across a brightly coloured background and surrounded a sentimental poem about runaway children.

I greeted them both, but as the artist shoe-shiner was busy, he handed me his card and continued painting a delicate white pair of skeleton feet. The card advertised the shoe-shine stand, a handyman service and a musical act, all under the name of 'Nigger On the Run'. It appeared that the artist had been denied a permanent shoe-shine stand, and moved here and there about the city.

'My name is Barrington-Wranglestone,' the well-dressed man told me. 'I am a political comedian. So you're from England! Well, I'm from Cleveland, Ohio, and I sure would like to go to England. Is there any prospects there for a black comedian?'

'Well, Lenny Henry's very popular,' I said dubiously. 'I doubt if anyone in England could understand jokes about American politicians.'

I thought hard, and realised that the only living American politician I had heard of was Ronald Reagan (later I remembered Edward Kennedy and Jesse Jackson). Barrington was a bit taken aback at my admission, but rallied and told me that he worked by linguistics.

'For instance, take the word "is". That's a joke in itself, as it contains letters found in the name of the Chief of Police,' he said, drawing me aside.

'If you walk a li'l piece further on you'll get to the Chattanooga Choo Choo in the old railroad station,' the Chattanooga Shoe-Shine Boy said, looking up for a moment. 'Across the road there you'll see my partner at my other stand. This here picture on the fence is a portrait of my other stand; it's a real strange-lookin' stand, y'all can't miss it.'

Barrington-Wranglestone spoke rapidly, peering into my face all the while. None of his ramblings made sense, and I realised that the poor man was mad. Drunk on words, he talked faster and faster, confidence draining out of his face. After a few yards of walking and talking, his appearance had completely altered. A stunned, self-pitying little boy's face stared out of the big man's frame, his well-cut clothes seeming for a moment to be hanging loosely on a dressed-up child. He seemed to be thinking: 'Something terrible has happened to me, but I don't know what it is.'

'What does the word mean, "infractions"?' I asked.

'Yeah, I said right now there's no infractions on the street, meaning shootings and killings!'

'I should think not! Er – were you in Vietnam, by the way?'

'No, I did my military service in Alaska. I do hope I can work up a new act and make a new start in England. Do you think I can? Right now I stay at the Mission for free, get all my meals there. I never been married, I should o' stayed with my mother, 'cos I got no money. Maybe I can phone her for my bus fare home.'

It was a long walk to the railway station, and the town scenery grew ever more decrepit. We passed a small park where old men sat tightly packed on to benches, and workmen scrubbed graffiti from a wall. Then, just when I thought Chattanooga had collapsed in ruins, we came to a smart shopping arcade. I decided to go in and ask the way. My Greyhound would be leaving in an hour, and I wanted to see the trains and then hurry back. A tall shopping arcade youth in red livery took us outside again and pointed the way. Barrington swelled up at this encounter, and once more looked every inch the fine gentleman.

'What part of England are you from, sir?' the youth asked him deferentially, but he swept on.

We crossed a railway line and I saw a large red-brick Victorian station ahead, with a statue of a lion outside. (Americans use the word 'Victorian' too.) I was at a loss how to be rid of Barrington-Wranglestone, who talked in a never-ending 'stream of consciousness' and seemed quite unable to leave me, a Tennessee Old Man of the Sea. He was by now so footsore he was almost staggering, but he wouldn't give up. Since we were speaking on equal terms, man to man, I could scarcely give him a dollar and tell him to go away. So he came into the station with me and looked at the trains.

Hiltons, the hotel people, had bought the station when passenger trains in Chattanooga had come to an end. They had made a splendid restoration, with Covent Garden-style shops where booking offices had been, and lanterns everywhere. Every last scrap of ironwork had been painted in bright colours. Tubs of bright flowers stood on the rails, near polished buffers. Pullman cars, rows of elegant carriages with steps up to the doors, had been made into miniature hotels, complete with beds and dining rooms. I wished I could have stayed in one. They reminded me of the long-lost Brighton Belle in England, a palace of a train. Each carriage had a name, such as 'Wabash Cannonball Club Car', well worth the half-crown extra fare.

Near the luxury Pullman cars stood the Chattanooga Choo Choo, so-called, a magnificent Western engine with a cowcatcher and an eccentric smokestack chimney. It was painted bright red and yellow, rather childish colours for so distinguished an old gentleman of a train. The copperwork was gleaming. Once serving an important line that linked North and South, the Chattanooga Choo Choo trains have long been celebrated in song and story. Now, in the person of this old Western veteran, they had reached the end of the line.

Barrington still talked, and I was near the end of my tether. When I paused to buy some stamps, he began to charm a waitress from the nearby restaurant, resuming his confident gentleman personality. So I took him into the restaurant, where the station interior, with its magnificent domed ceiling, had been filled with tables, chairs, palms, buffets and scurrying waitresses.

'I'm in a hurry,' I told Barrington, 'so how would it be if I bought you a meal here, paid in advance and left you in possession of it!'

Barrington, who was probably as sick of me as I was of him, seemed to think this was a very good idea indeed. So as I left, I had the gratification of seeing him sit down to an enormous meal with a look on his face that clearly said: 'So dreams do come true!'

Free! Free! I felt as light as air, so happy was I to be free from Barrington's oppressive personality. I danced across the railway lines outside the station, where goods trains still ran. A wild, gaunt black man was staggering along these tracks – presumably a drunk hobo.

Across the street, I noticed the shoe-shine stand I had been told about. This stand, fringed by model spaceships, the original of the artist's paintings, was extremely weird. Somewhere on the large model, covered in misspelled poems, was a place to put your feet. A shabby, broken-down old coach was parked nearby. A big man with a black cowboy hat and a grizzled beard, the shoe-shiner looked at me enigmatically through dark glasses. His hat band was made out of grizzly bear claws.

In a hurry, I sprinted on and hailed the first shoe-shine man. He had finished his picture and was now in a more talkative frame of mind.

'You saw that old bus, huh? Next time you come round here, that bus gonna look like a steamer! We're gonna make it look like a brand new ocean liner.'

He asked if there were black people in England, so I told him about the Africans who stowed away on ships in the early fifties and the West Indian immigrants who came afterwards.

'Adventurers!' he said with relish at the thought of the African stowaways. 'My partner's from the Caribbean – one o' those islands near Florida. Bemiddy, I think. I play guitar and he plays drums. We've invented this music that's half blues and half reggae. We calls it Reggae Rock.'

Despite all this gossip, I caught my Greyhound and ended my Fifth Day on the Road at Cleveland, Tennessee near the Smokies. Feeling quite road-weary, I dragged my bag from the Greyhound shed and looked around. I was on a very large traffic island indeed, one of the all-in 'truck-driver' islands invented by the Americans. Adverts on high posts stood everywhere, and hotels and garish restaurants were dotted about amid parked lorries. Tall lolly pines looked down from a high ridge across the road. At my comfortable airy room in the Days Inn I sank on the bed exhausted. My Greyhound ticket was used up, and I would stay here for a while.

CHAPTER SIX

Bible Belt

.

I LIKED THE DAYS Inn at Cleveland, Tennessee. My door and picture-window faced one of the balconies that ran right around the hotel on every floor. Many Southern hotels are built on this attractive plan, rather like unusually light, airy and well-fitted council flats in England. Girls wheeled trolleys of fresh towels from door to door at all hours. Here the staff were all white. For the most part they were unsophisticated country girls with blue eyes, tow hair and lean faces, who looked as if they had just come down from the mountains. The television in my room showed non-stop country and western singing, jangling guitars and swirling fiddles. There was no dining room, but a jug of free coffee stood on a heater in the cosy Reception room. A black coffee is all the breakfast I need, so I would sit and sip and read verses from the Bible, for a large copy of the Book was prominently displayed.

On my first morning, the Reception girl was a sturdy, frizzy-haired young woman with a strong hillbilly accent. A friendly soul, she sat by her switchboard shelling pecan nuts, the bowl jammed between her knees, a basket of okra pods by her side. As she worked, she sang loudly.

'Mind your own business! Mind your own business!
'Cos when you mind your own business, you won't be minding mine!'

A Waffle House and a Steak House in the lorry park meant that I would be able to eat near the hotel, but to see the more interesting sights of Cleveland, I would have once more to be dependent on taxis. Just across the road from my hotel, fir trees grew from a high ridge. It was a fine day, so I thought I would go for a walk in the woods.

As Americans have given up walking, footpaths through the woods have mostly vanished. However, I soon found a broad muddy track through the trees, where men had been laying pipes. The soil was not as red as in

Alabama – it seemed to be sticky clay. A mourning dove, similar to our collared dove, flew by. After a while, I reached a churned-up mountain of mud, and was able to gain a bird's eye view of Cleveland. The town lay in a bowl far below the towering blue heights of the Smoky Mountains. Very soon, I came out of the woods and found myself in an exclusive housing estate. Each wooden dwelling stood a long way from its neighbour, set among dark trees. The suburban Southerner's ideal seemed to be the Pioneer in his wilderness log cabin. Trees, not flowers, surrounded the Southern Dream House.

These were wealthy pioneers, I decided. Many of the delightful giant-sized wooden cabins had artificial wells on their lawns, with wooden buckets beside them. Porches were liberally sprinkled with swings and rocking chairs, and the dark pines brooded over all. Three-storey cabins the size of rectories, the planks stained dark brown, made delightful homes. As yet I had seen no people. Suddenly I saw a notice: 'Neighborhood Watch. Please Look Out for Suspicious Behavior.'

Quickly I retraced my steps for I knew very well what constituted suspicious behaviour in America. Walking about! I dived back into the forest like a deer, and as I did so, a police car swung around the corner, three lights flashing from the roof. Looking back fearfully, I made for the hotel.

In the Steak House, the waitresses seemed excited by my accent, yet too reserved to question me closely about England. Instead they hovered around asking if I wanted mustard, sauce or pepper, and listening to my polite responses. My accent is a lower-middle-class whine, acquired at grammar school and suitable for a tax inspector. The misguided waitresses evidently thought that I spoke like an English gentleman. Their own soft Southern tones, each word a drop of pure mountain honey, transformed my meal into a mutual admiration society.

Travelling by taxi, I was soon on my way to the Tabernacle of the Church of God of Prophecy. On the way, I noticed several Jodrell Bank radar devices on suburban lawns, and asked the driver what they were for.

'Them's for cable television,' he answered shortly, in his gravel voice. He was a big grizzled, bull-necked man, and very tough looking. 'I'm not from these parts at all. I'm from Florida, an' I wish I was there right now, fishing for trout, bass and bluegill. Not to mention alligators.'

'How do you catch alligators?' I asked. I also wished to know what bluegill were, but didn't like to press my luck.

'You got to shoot 'em right above the eyes, where the brain is; that kills 'em. You eats the tail. It's real good sliced up, all white meat; tastes like frog legs. Plenty bears in the woods round here. I shot my first bear when I was fourteen. Weighed five hundred pounds, had to go get a pick-up truck to fetch it home to skin it, cook it. I never did care for the taste – too greasy. A bear is nothing but a dog. It's got a dog's head, you know.'

Cleveland, Tennessee, is the place where the Bible Belt tightens up, and we passed a church at every corner. Whether in old downtown Cleveland or in the endless roadside suburbs, every fourth building seemed to be a church.

'Here's the Tabernacle,' the driver said, pulling in beside a gigantic auditorium surrounded by white office blocks. I paid him and set out to look for my friend, Sis Janie Sanders.

I had met Janie Sanders four years earlier, when I had accompanied a party of West Indians and Black British youngsters to Cleveland. We were there to attend the Assembly, the Convention of the World-wide Church of God of Prophecy, held in the Tabernacle. In our hotel, the Holiday Inn, we slept two in a bed, four in a room. Unfortunately, the man who shared my bed, a big Jamaican deacon, became suspicious of me. Why did I keep going for walks in the forest on my own? He slept with a knife under his pillow, and when our other room-mates remonstrated with him, he said, 'I always carry a knife, ever since an incident in Birmingham with a white man.'

In the end, we became friendly enough, in a guarded way. He could not understand my interest in Nature, yet when a tiny ruby-throated hummingbird flew forwards and back around the flowers by our window, he too gave it a grudging smile. I had met Janie Sanders in a Cleveland restaurant, where we sat at the same table. She was a tough, humorous, vinegary and common-sensical coloured lady who cleaned the floors in the bookshop and offices adjoining the Tabernacle.

As the convention season was over, the Tabernacle was closed, so I browsed around the bookshop and remembered those heady days of 1982. From its hillbilly tongue-talking Pentecostalist beginnings at the turn of the century, the Church of God has spread all over the world. West Indian members send clothes to their brethren in West Africa and Botswanaland, receiving fervent letters of thanks. ('Now we can be baptised as we have other dry clothes to change into.') In America, most of the members are white farmers and country people. Outside the U.S.A. the majority of members are West Indians from Britain and the Caribbean.

Some West Indians felt the loss of the British Empire very badly, as being British had given them an important and honoured place in the world. In my opinion, the Church of God of Prophecy serves as a substitute Empire. A white man, heir of A. J. Tomlinson the Founder, is always at the head of the church. All his subjects throughout the world are spoken of as a happy brotherhood, regardless of race, colour but not Creed. All receive the same literature wherever they are, and have the same church ceremonies, with military music, parades and a great deal of flag-waving. The church flag: crimson, purple, white and blue, is held in great solemnity. God is above all. Within these broad guidelines, the folklore of the various West Indian islands and other countries creeps in and is allowed fairly free expression. Instead of a District Officer, England has a National Overseer set above several West Indian District Overseers.

The English National Overseer, so far, has always been a white American. Brother White, the English Overseer in 1982, had been a kindly father to his people. Even if, as could happen in the Church of God as in the former British Empire, the man in charge was a rotter, the Caribbean subjects would still feel safe and privileged to be under his care. At Conventions, shaking hands with the Overseer is a long-looked-forward-to treat. A world-wide network of Negro churches where God is worshipped with heartrending passion, sincerity and a love of truth is held together by a jovial old Tomlinson in Cleveland, Tennessee.

I found Janie emptying ashtrays in the office, and she 'studied me hard' with her ironic brown eyes before she recognised me.

'Why don't y'all come to *my* church?' she enquired, when 'how do you dos' were over. 'I go to Pleasant Grove Baptist Church, I only *work* here. We'd be mighty pleased to see you at Pleasant Grove. Here's where it's at.'

I pocketed the address, and went over to the Main Office, hoping for an interview with the head of the Church, M. A. Tomlinson, the Founder's son. On the wall behind the Enquiries desk was a huge bright mural showing the original Tomlinson, resplendent in a business suit. He kneeled on a Smoky Mountain hill, while Christ in a Heavenly vision told him to found the Church.

'Sorry, M. A. Tomlinson is unavailable,' I was told. 'However, we are shortly going to hold a service in the Upper Room. You are more than welcome to attend.'

I did so, and found the sing-song prayers of the white Southerners and the calm, reasoned sermon to be unexpectedly soothing. Then a Brother from El Salvador announced that guerrillas had burned down three churches in his country. Six Christians had been killed.

In pensive frame of mind, I tried to walk back to the Days Inn. I was not sure if I could remember the way. There was no pavement, so I walked along the verge, cars hurtling by ceaselessly. Sometimes they stopped at traffic lights, strung across the road on a cable.

My mind went back to my first visit to Cleveland. On the plane at Gatwick, I had met my first white Southerners, an elderly couple who looked out on the rain with indignation.

'Before I left, I prayed to God to give the people of London good weather, and here it is raining!' the woman had complained in a tone of outrage. What did He think He was playing at?

'Well, this isn't London, it's the country outside,' I had soothed her.
'Oh, I see. Maybe the farmers here need the rain.'

What kind of people were these, who dared to order God about? I named them Mr and Mrs Canute.

At Assembly-time, early September, the Tabernacle had been a crowded gospel circus, with speeches, balloons, waving placards, pom pom girls, cheerleaders and brass bands going full tilt from morning to night. Ministers from every State and half the nations of the world had shouted their sermons.

'I come from the prairies of North Dakota,' a minister had introduced himself. 'Last year we had exceptionally bad snow. I've never seen such snow – ah! And all the snow drifts was covered in dead deer and antelopes. And when they cut open them dead deer and antelopes – ah! – they found their stomachs was full. They starved, but their stomachs was full, 'cos they done eaten dry grass with no nutriment in it. Now isn't that like some of us in the church today – ah? We dig in the snow of erroneous doctrine and just swallow up the first thing we can find. And then we wonder why our souls are sick – ah!'

The South Florida Mass Choir, led by a big deep-voiced man who resembled Paul Robeson, sang 'This old time religion sometimes makes me shout'. On cue, a Negro minister from Kansas took the microphone.

'I'm from the new black church in Kansas City! We calls it a black church 'cos it has predominantly black members. Shall we all say "amen"?'

Everyone said amen. This preacher resembled Lenny Henry's spoof minister, the Rev. Nat West. Every three sentences would be punctuated by a chant-on-demand. It became particularly absurd when he began to speak about a Pentecostal college.

'One of the college features is a post-graduate course,' he announced. 'Everyone say "post-graduate course".'

'Post-graduate course!' echoed from thousands of throats.

Honk! A car speeding by woke me up to reality. I was very lost, but the countryside was interesting. Tall sedge-like grass surrounded a stream that ran parallel to the road. Beyond the stream lay a wooded marsh, a between-the-roads patch of wild country. Clouds of red-winged black-birds filled the air, settling over three tree-top roosts like starlings. Red as the patches on their wings, the setting sun glowed through the branches. I crossed the stream at a bridge, and looked down to see a large ginger cat sitting on a boulder staring hard at the water, clearly ready to scoop out a fish. Little Tennessee warblers flitted from bush to bush beside the water.

Now I found myself in an empty suburban street of plank houses raised over huge cellars, with open hedgeless lawns and towering firs. Seeing a floodlit patch of light in the darkening sky, I came across a school where two teams of fourteen-year-olds played English football, to loud cheers. A nearby Health Home with a well-equipped gym proved my salvation, as the kindly office girl phoned up a taxi for me.

Rugged, lean and leering, the taxi driver looked like a fighting man. 'Ah got many friends,' he told me, 'but Ah got 'em the hard way and Ah take keer to *keep* 'em! This is one of the meanest towns in Tennessee. Shooting and killing every night! You take keer now, hear?'

So I entered the Waffle House near my hotel in a wary frame of mind. The other customers *did* look a bit 'mean', particularly a man in a black cowboy hat. However, as I settled down to my waffle, these fears vanished. In Birmingham, Alabama, a waffle had been a pancake with syrup. Here it was a first course, with meat. In England, it's my conversation.

'Hey, cowboy, you're not messin', sure!' the blue-jeaned waitress responded to a sally made by the man in the black hat.

A group of lorry drivers discussed squirrel-hunting animatedly. 'Them woods is a squirrel paradise!' a lank-haired young man proclaimed.

After my waking-up cup of coffee next morning, I ordered another taxi and asked the driver if he would take me on a tour of the Smoky Mountains.

'What do you want to see, exactly?' he asked. He was a young man, perhaps in his thirties, with a bright, intelligent face, brown eyes and a frayed ginger moustache. On his head, he wore a hunter's cap.

'Wild forest scenery and, if possible, a Red Indian,' I replied.

'Well, I can promise you the last item,' he said. 'I'm eighty-five per cent Cherokee Indian myself. My grandfather, who's eighty-seven, now he's pure Cherokee. He speaks in Cherokee most of the time, all about his time on the Trail of Tears. My father speaks Cherokee too, but I never took no interest in it. There's a Scottish side o' the family too – our name is McCulloch and I'm Billy McCulloch. I was always more curious about how the Cherokee became Scottish. Round these parts, the two people are nearly the same.'

'I don't know about that, but your grandfather *couldn't* have gone on the Trail of Tears. It took place in 1838.'

'Well, it must o' been his dad, then. I never *could* understand Cherokee! There was some talk of an arranged marriage for me, Cherokee-style, but I got out of that. My own marriage broke up, but I got two good-looking boys.'

Here he showed me a photograph of two blond youngsters with their father's alert features.

'Look Scottish, don't they?' he commented with pride. 'This is Joshua, and that's Noah. I always *said* if I had children, I'd give 'em Bible names. I live on my own in Cleveland now, in a sleeping room. That's what you English call a bedsitting-room.'

'How did you know that?'

'I *been* to England. I was in the navy, and we went to Plymouth. I've got a very high regard for the British serviceman, and thought England was just fine. When I was on leave, I hitchhiked into Dorset and came across a family o' Romany gypsies, the Lovells. I stayed with them for a while, an' we became best o' friends. One o' them tattooed my arm for me – look! Then I was sent to the Lebanon and I was shot in the knee. I was real sore about that, 'cos I been slightly lame ever since, and the Navy couldn't use me – I got invalided out. So here I am, driving a cab. Now, if we're gonna go on this Smoky Mountain trip, we better go back to the office and check up with the boss. I'd be really happy if we could go, as driving round the Smokies is what I like doing best! Most of my fares are just pickin' some feller up and settin' him down about two miles away. When I was a boy, even if we had no money, Dad would drive us round the woods for a treat. Gas was cheap in those days.'

Very soon, I was sitting in a large dingy taxi office, part of a small garage in downtown Cleveland. The proprietor was an immensely stout man, stout in a way only achieved by Americans, and he sat wedged into his desk trying to contact his other drivers on the radio. He liked the idea of a Smoky Mountain tour very much, and wanted to come too, saying that he knew where all the best places were. But as all the drivers were busy, only Billy and I set out for the Smokies that day.

Sitting in the taxi office, deep in a broken-down easy chair, I relished this glimpse into small-town America. Everything was musty and dusty, and life moved at an easy pace. One of the drivers, to my surprise, handed me a torn scrap of paper with my own name and address on it. He had driven me around when I had last been in Cleveland, at the Church of God Assembly.

'Good Heavens, is it you!' I cried, shaking hands.

I remembered that he had told me of his time in Vietnam and had asked me if it were true, as his pastor had stated, that England was the most sinful country in the world.

Another driver, a gnarled veteran in glasses, told me that he had been stationed in England as a G.I. near Tewkesbury, 'on that Number Seven river'. Apparently he thought that all the rivers in England were numbered, as some streets are in America, and that the Severn was the Number Seven. A bent old lady, her white hair permed, hobbled slowly towards the paraffin fire in the middle of the room. She was the proprietor's mother. Standing over the portable fire, she lifted her faded skirt, revealing scabby knees and stood warming herself in stolid ecstasy. A fee was agreed upon, and Billy and I set out.

As we left Cleveland, I mused on the age-old attraction between Red Indians and Gypsies. Levi Smith of Ipswich had once entertained me in his caravan with tales of an Indian who came to Essex with a Wild West Show and endeared himself to the Smith tribe by his way with horses. I had read of a Barnardo boy, taken by the Welfare of his day from the gypsies and sent to Canada as a farm servant. He had run away, joined a tribe of forest Indians and married a squaw, who henpecked him cruelly. Charles Dickens, in his *American Notes*, likens the broken-down pauperised Indians he meets to gypsies.

The 'Trail of Tears', I should explain, was the result of a strikingly modern, twentieth-century-style notion; that of displacing thousands of people of an unpopular race (Red Indian) and sending them on foot, often in chains, to a distant 'homeland' where most of them would perish. Not the Russians, not the South Africans did this deed, but the white Americans, when they declared that all Red Indians should live west of the Mississippi in the 'Indian Nation'. Imagine if Indians were to regard the Russians, Irish, Norwegians, Spaniards and English as a 'White Nation' and then were to force them to walk from their various homes to (say) Nicaragua, leaving their dead by the wayside. Then you may realise why the enforced trek of many Indian nations to Oklahoma in the 1830s now goes by the name of the Trail of Tears. Later, the Indian Nation shrank into a few reservations. Some of the Cherokee found their way back to their native forests, where fugitives had remained throughout the Troubles.

Most famous of the Cherokee spokesmen of those days was Chief John Ross, another Cherokee Scotsman! Back in England, I delved among books and found that many Scotsmen who had sided with Britain in the War of Independence in 1776 had fled to the mountains when defeated. There they joined the Cherokee, already a Christian tribe. And so a new people were forged of whom Billy McCulloch was one. He was a better talker than any white American I had met so far, and he gave me the key to white Southern conversation. From henceforth I would talk about hunting, shooting and natural history. It was a strange thought to reflect upon later, that the racial ideas of some white people had sent others (the Scots) to their doom, 'reclassified' as Red Indians.

'We'll go to Maryville first,' Billy said happily, on holiday from the dusty office.

Leaving the motorways to the juggernaut lorries and Greyhound coaches, he took a narrow road among green fields. Brown tobacco leaves hung up to dry in the doorways of grey barns and plank outhouses.

'This is a prejudiced town,' he said cheerfully, as he sped past a collection of shacks.

'Who are they prejudiced against?'

'Everyone! Strangers!' he cried, sailing on.

We passed delightful villages of plank houses with rocking chair porches, and I saw one old-time log cabin, the logs painted dark blue and the chinks white. Split logs criss-crossed at each corner of the dwelling.

'The farmer here used to keep a herd of buffalo,' he said, slowing down for a look. 'Nope, he must o' sold them.'

Buffalo (or bison) are now extinct in the Smokies, but, according to Billy, plenty of wild animals remain.

'People round here go after bears with pit-bulls, Rottweilers and dogs like that, but very few bear hunts are allowed. We have bears here, grey foxes, red foxes, racoons, wild hogs, bobcats – me and Dad ran over a bobcat once. We looked up and saw this dear little bobcat kitten coming down the hill. So we reared it, an' it made a good pet, very tame. When it was grown, I gave it to a zoo.'

A bobcat is the hillbilly version of a Spanish lynx, a red, stump-tailed, tassel-eared, black-spotted cat-animal. Billy slowed down once more to show me poison ivy on a tree, as I had told him that this dreaded plant doesn't grow in England.

'We got beavers, an' every now and then, a mountain lion gets reported. Wolves are all gone, I'm glad to say. Me and Dad hunted a grey fox for two days. Then we let it go – it was just for sport. Wonderful to crouch among the trees at night, passing the whiskey bottle round and picking out your own dog's song when they start baying after that old grey fox! That's a fox that can climb a tree! Skunks here come right up to you and spray you. I had a de-fumed skunk once – good pet. We got poisonous snakes here – rattlesnakes and copperheads. Feller killed a rattlesnake near here, seven feet long.'

I thought of the mountain lion, or puma, the great yellow cat that haunts the East coast of America, appearing like a ghost in country where it had long been supposed extinct, and then vanishing once more. How strange that the puma should haunt England in the same way, when it has never lived here in the wild! Yet reports of 'mysterious sightings' appear every day, and puma rumours abound all over Britain. Just another strange example of the way that Britain follows America in ways that would once have seemed impossible.

'What's a pit-bull?' I asked Billy, as his car began to climb among woods of blue spruce.

'Well, a pit-bull is like a bull terrier specially bred for dog fighting. Dog fighting with pit-bulls is a big thing among black people all over the South, I reckon. The dog homes where they give you a stray dog for free don't even deal in pit-bulls! When they did, black people would come in crowds from miles around, each one pleading for that pit-bull. The dogs tear each other up, hanging on with those big jaws and that bull neck, and all the fellers whooping and betting money! It's not legal, but they do it. Cock-fighting, now, that's legal. Feller near here breeds game cocks.'

Three dogs, all of different sizes and colours, scrambled out of the way of Billy's car and stood at the edge of the dark forest staring at us. One of them had a collar on. I had seen such wayside dogs from the Greyhound, but I had thought that a master could not be far away.

'No, people just dump their dogs; pedigrees too,' Billy said. 'Now they're breeding with coyotes and running in packs. But mostly they just stand by the road staring at people, hoping for a master. Lots get killed that way.'

I remembered having seen a dead beagle and a Shetland sheepdog, left squashed in the road like hedgehogs. (America doesn't have hedgehogs, but I did see a run-over porcupine.)

'A farmer found a cave somewhere round here, all full of blind fish and all kind o' creatures,' Billy continued. 'Talking of creatures, you ever tasted turtle meat? Lovely white meat – I love to eat it! Now this is the foothills, where we are now. See that land, where they're building houses? All that used to be our farm. That's where I lived as a boy, up here in the forests. I was heartbroken when Dad had to sell up. But we still got a piece o' land down there, where the woods begin. See that old wooden house? That's where my pap – that is, my grandfather – lives now. Used to be he stayed on the reservation. No, he ain't in, or his car would be there right now. He's probably off courtin' his girlfriend. We tease Pap about her, you know. We say, "If there's not enough McCulloch family now, you're fixing to make some more!"

'See that field there! Me an' Dad ploughed that field, an' we turned up stone arrow heads by the score, even a stone axe blade. It makes me wonder 'bout the Indians who used to live there before. We've suffered more than the blacks, you know! But the black people are all right. Lots of cafés won't serve them in Cleveland.'

'Oh! Now I remember, there were no black people in the Steak House, it was all white families with children.'

'Yeah? Well, I used to go to a black juju lady down at Cleveland one time, and have my fortune told. A lot o' the black people round here go in for juju – that's what they call it. This lady has a sign outside her house, readin' "Fortunes told, Palms Read, Spells Cast." But the folks there run her out of town. Now what I like is that black music called Blues. There's a couple o' fellers at Cleveland, one plays the banjo, one plays the harmonica, an' they go round the clubs playing blues. But the best blues is at the clubs in Chicago, only you can't go in them without a black friend goes with you. I been up there and heard it.

'Some years ago, the roads round here weren't safe 'cos of the Hell's Angels. You don't see 'em now, they've become like the Mafia, doing organised crime behind closed doors; that's since they've grown up and settled down. It's like the Teamsters' Union, that's run by Mafia drug peddlers. You ever see the like o' those trees. Those are red maple – look at those colours! We're getting high up in the Smokies now. There used to be rhododendron jungles here, but they cleared 'em out. Still got Laurel Hells, though. That's when laurel run wild takes over an' spreads across the mountain. People have got lost in those, wandered for days, even died. See that old rascal flying over there? That's a brown hawk.'

Now we were within the boundaries of the Smoky Mountain National Park, the foothills left behind. Our road twisted round the mountainside, past precipices which Billy called 'drop offs' and through green virgin forest only just starting to turn. Soon the trees would form a dazzling display of crimson and yellow. Beech saplings grew from rocky ledges, and below us, among gigantic oaks, the Smoky Mountain River splashed over polished boulders. Pines and broad-leafed trees grew together, the broad leaves very broad indeed. Oak leaves of familiar English shape could here be eight inches long or more. These Appalachian oaks were known as 'white oaks', because of their pale bark. I was reminded of the mountain woodlands of Wales, seen through a magnifying glass.

'See that!' called Billy, and I caught a glimpse of a big fat short-eared rabbit busily munching grass on the verge. 'That's a whistle pig! Set a dog on that and it'll put up one heck of a fight!'

Looking back, I saw that the brown animal, with its expressive black eyes, was the rodent known in English zoos as the woodchuck.

'We'll look at this church, if you like,' suggested Billy, and parked beside a grey wooden church standing on its own amid the oaks.

'Primitive Baptist Church', proclaimed a National Park-type notice, but it was clear when we looked at it that the church had not been a place of worship for years. Billy refused to look at the graveyard, so we drove on. A little later, we passed another half-hidden deserted church, taken over by the National Park. No settlements seemed to exist near the deserted churches.

Our road grew level, and Billy swung out of the forest into wide farm meadows, with open birch woods on the slopes around. Horses swished their tails as they grazed, separated from the road by 'stack fences' of split logs resting on criss-cross posts.

'Whistle pigs everywhere! I love to see 'em!' cried Billy happily.

And indeed the distant shapes of woodchucks, black in the heat haze, could be seen chasing each other round the meadows, lolloping low to the ground, their short bushy tails bouncing behind them. Others sat upright in the long grass on sentinel duty, ready to whistle if anyone approached. Two pretty girls sat in the grass side by side, winning an appreciative glance from Billy.

For now we were in a holidaymakers' paradise, surrounded by healthy young people straight from a *National Geographic* Coca-Cola advert of the 1950s – all glowing pink cheeks and lumber shirts. Youths in shorts half dismounted from their bicycles as they consulted maps. Cars were parked here and there, and happy families were sitting beside their picnic baskets.

It was pleasant to be among such innocence, but I had a perverse yearning for another Smoky Mountains of pre-National Park days. I wished to see fanatical bearded men springing from their knees as they prayed curses on their neighbours, reaching for their shotguns and blasting away at our fleeing car with cries of 'Dagnabbed revenooers!' Such mountains called for mountain men, grim, Calvinistic, taking their vices and virtues to extremes.

Billy swung around the far side of the meadows and slowed down to let me look at the weathered grey farmhouse cabins, the top-heavy barns and the smokehouses for meat or tobacco. At each farmhouse gate, a National Park sign proclaimed the farmer's name, usually a Biblical one. Black empty windows stared back at me in reproach.

'Ain't that nice!' said Billy in a tone of scathing irony. 'They've run all the farmers off from here, but put their names up to remember 'em by!'

He went on to tell me that a thriving mountain community had lived and worshipped here until quite recently. Then the National Park authorities had compulsorily purchased their farms and homes, leaving only the meadows on a lease system, with a great many rules for the commuting farmers to abide by. After putting up a futile fight, the men of the forest realised that they were beaten, took the money and left. A friend of Billy's had tried to hang on, and we went in search of him.

'Nope, he's gone, too!' Billy said disgustedly. Holidaymakers were walking round his farm gawking at things. We walked and gawked too. The cabin was open for anyone to enter, swept and clean but empty of furniture. Across the road, I admired the sad emptiness of the grey top-heavy barn which looked uselessly out over the meadows. Wooden pens for animals stood inside the great doorway, and a ladder reached up through a trap door to the enormous loft.

The barn roof, a triumph of the carpenter's art, spread out far beyond the wooden walls that supported it, a mushroom-top on a stem. Space under the eaves had a floor added, to form a part of the ingenious loft. Notices here and there explained what we were looking at.

It seemed so stupid as to be past belief, yet very American in the Northern, Yankee sense. The Smoky Mountain farmers had been evicted from their Smoky Mountain farms so that the public could see how the Smoky Mountain farmers lived! Houses of God no more, their churches stood empty, a reproach on modern America. Smiling happily, modern America took photographs. We left in a hurry.

'Kermit Caughrin's gone too, I see,' said Billy, pointing to a farm with the winsome notice: 'Kermit Caughrin's Place.' His sloping field of wooden beehives in rows remained, but the bees had vanished. 'Old Kermit was famous for his bees,' Billy observed.

Two hikers, in shorts and holiday pilgrim staffs, stood at the edge of a young beech wood staring at something. We stared too, and I saw two deer, greyish-brown and white, move disdainfully away beneath the dappled trees. These were white-tailed deer, each the size of an English fallow deer.

On our way back to Cleveland, Billy drove alongside a vast expanse of water, surrounded by loops of roadway with neatly shaved lawns between the concrete.

'This used to be the Tennessee River Valley, where my Cherokee ancestors lived and farmed for centuries,' he said. 'Now look at it! The Tennessee Valley Authority went an' made the Norris Dam and flooded out the farms. Seems like a poor farmer can't win. You see that brick tower sticking out o' the water? That there's the top of a silo. That's my old church I used to attend, stuck way over there on the other side. Now what I'm looking for is the Sequoyah Birthplace Museum. See, this Sequoyah was a famous Cherokee in the old days. They named a giant tree after him. His house used to be around here, but someone burnt it down. Didn't like Indians or didn't like tourists, I reckon. The authorities kind of hushed it up, and they went and built a museum on the same site. It's supposed to be owned by the tribe, but the staff are all white.'

The museum, when we found it, proved to be a modernistic library-like building by the shores of the blue lake. Large portraits of Sequoyah (1776–1843) lined the walls, showing him to be a wise, humorous, pipe-smoking man. In the pictures, he wore his own version of white man's dress, with a bright bandana and a turban. Sequoyah's achievement was the creation of a Cherokee alphabet, completed in 1821. Although he had been suspected of witchcraft while he was transforming Cherokee into a written language, his tribe quickly saw the advantage of the new system, when it was completed. For it is the lack of the written word that marks a man as a 'savage', fair game for any literate intruder. Lack of a title deed has led to the loss of a kingdom. Sequoyah invented his own letters, each corresponding to a Cherokee sound. Who knows, if the Trail of Tears had not been taken, and the spirit of the Cherokee destroyed, we might now have a fine literature at our disposal.

Known as one of the Five Civilised Tribes, the Cherokee used to live in neat, stockaded villages. Their thatched huts resembled pioneer cabins. By the time the Cherokee of the Smokies had become half-Scottish, they lived amicably amid white people in identical cabins. Christianity and metal-work were taken up eagerly as soon as they had become known to the tribe. All this counted for nothing to Andrew Jackson, the cruel enforcer of the Trail of Tears. This is the same General Jackson who fought the British at the Battle of New Orleans, with the help of Red Indian troops, and was rewarded by having Jackson Square named after him. Billy and I gleaned all these facts as we walked from showcase to showcase.

In the souvenir shop, I admired the work of modern Cherokees, who had painted bright landscapes on to the blades of saws.

'My sister does that – she's always painting on saws,' Billy commented.

Outside the museum, a green mound with a plaque on it attracted our attention. Apparently, when the lake had been made, the remains of 196 Indians had been found. Possibly they had been killed in an early skirmish with white people. Now all of them had been buried in a heap, the mound planted over with grass.

'I wonder what it was really like when only the Cherokee lived here,' Billy said. We looked around and saw modernity everywhere.

'Perhaps if you came here in the very early morning when the lake is hidden by mist, you might have some idea,' I said. 'Now we'd better go back, as I promised a friend I'd call at the Pleasant Grove Baptist Church tonight.'

Billy showed me the wooden house where the juju lady used to live, and then drove me to a Baptist church, a beautiful white building that resembled the better class of Greek temple. Pleasant-looking white families strolled up the steps, and I jumped out and asked if this were Pleasant Grove.

'No, you want the *black* Baptist church,' a smartly-dressed man told me with a polite smile. He seemed to be admiring my accent. 'That's a long ways out of town – just follow that road. There should be someone there – every church in the nation has a meeting on Wednesday night.'

A difference of style in worship divides churches of the same denomination into 'black' and 'white', as much as does prejudice. In England, where West Indians and Black British don't like to refer to colour, they speak of 'country and western gospel music' and 'soul gospel music' and everyone knows what they mean.

'This must be the church I'm meant to call at,' I told Billy at last, after we had driven through industrial wastelands, under bridges and out to the edge of town.

'Yep, that sign says "Pleasant Grove". But in this country, if you say "call" it means "phone someone". You call on a phone and you visit a place. I've enjoyed meeting you, an' if you come to Tennessee again, you can visit at *my* place. Here's the ad-dress.'

I shook hands with Billy and sneaked into church, for the service had already begun. Entering by a side door, I found myself in a whitewashed meeting room where a small congregation sat around a large table, heads bowed in prayer. Those heads soon bobbed up again in surprise, as Sis Janie Sanders silently motioned me towards a chair. Big Pastor Robinson smiled a greeting, and I could see I was among sympathetic people. All were plainly dressed, and the women wore no lipstick.

Prayers were spoken aloud in turn around the table, each in a sing-song voice, while the rest of the congregation filled in the gaps with cries of 'Amen!', 'That's the truth!' and deep heart-felt moans. I had never heard moans like these in a West Indian or West African church, but I had heard them on a record by Fannie Bell Chapman, the old Mississippi holy woman.

Simply written down, each moan would be a prosaic 'Ahh-*umm*!' Perhaps the Cherokee alphabet can do a church moan better justice, for between the eerie 'Ah' and the 'Um' could be felt all the passion and tragedy of Negro life in the South from the Middle Passage onwards.

'*Ahh-umm*! Oh yes, Lord, that's the truth!'

'Massa Jesus, help us, Lord!'

'Now I will continue with the Bible Study,' the pastor declared. His young son sat by his side, regarding his father with bright-eyed innocent admiration. 'Now, I believe, as I understands it from the Bible, that Love is not natural to mankind. Love has to be taught.'

'Oh no, Pastor!' a young woman broke in. 'When you hold a little baby, an' it looks up at you, that's Love. That *is* Love!'

'Ain't nobody taught the baby,' someone pointed out.

'Well, maybe we need to discuss that a little further,' the pastor acknowledged. 'However, it's coming up to choir practice time, and the members are just arriving now. All those who want, move into the main body of the church.'

We rose to our feet, and everyone shook my hand. I was struck by the appearance of one of the men, who wore blue denim that matched his blue eyes. I had never seen a coloured man with blue eyes before. As if reading my mind, the bearded Brother told me that he was not an American but came from the West Indies.

'Oh, I've got West Indian friends in England!' I exclaimed.

'Yeah, but I'm not Jamaican!' he said hastily. 'I'm from Bermuda, a lot further north. We're the last British colony!'

I slapped him on the back, as congratulations seemed to be called for. The pastor could not stay, but before he left he asked me into his study and took my address. Although the church was a modern construction, his study would have done credit to an Anglican vicar, for it was full of books and looked very cosy.

Meanwhile, an organ pealed, Sis Janie Sanders and the other choir members took their places on the rostrum, facing a vast row of pews, and I took a seat near the front. An Italianate, fussy man, the choirmaster, took great pains in rehearsing his charges. His small son Mark moved restlessly among the pews while the singing was going on.

Most of the choir were elderly, and bore a strong resemblance to a Church of England choir in a remote country parish. Two of the white-haired ladies and one old gentleman in particular had the kindly appearance, restrained enthusiasm and polite manners of distressed gentlefolk who have devoted their lives to a village church. First of all, with many false starts, they practised two songs from sheet music, 'Unclouded Day' and 'I Am In No Ways Tired'. Finally, without any written music, they sang with a new and fervent spirit.

> 'I'll be all right
> Some day.
> I'll be all right
> Some day.
> I know, I really know
> That I'll be all ri-i-ght
> Some day.'

When the song was over, Sis Janie Sanders found me a lift, and left me in a young couple's 'pick-up-truck' with many goodbyes. 'Now I'm goin' home to do my ironing,' she said.

'I've been all over the Smoky Mountains today,' I told the elegant young woman by my side, 'but I never saw a bear! I would have liked to have seen one, as they don't have bears in England.'

'No bears in England!' she cried, amazed. 'What have you got, kangaroos?'

'No, that's Australia you're thinking of. England used to have bears, but it's such a small island that there isn't room for them and people too.'

'England *small?* If England is small, then where's Great Britain? Is England near Africa?'

The poor young couple's heads were whirling with my explanations about England and Britain by the time I reached the Days Inn. I tried to entice them into the Steak House, but they demurred. So I bade them farewell, with all my best wishes to Pleasant Grove. Later I remembered Billy McCulloch telling me about places that refused to serve Negroes. He told me that most black people felt nervous going in somewhere new, in case somebody refused to serve them.

I sat down to my steak and listened to the hunting stories told by big men at tables all around me.

Suddenly someone said 'The game warden's here! No bear-hunting tonight!'

Back in my bedroom at the Days Inn, I reflected on my long day, the sad strains of an old slavery song running through my sleepy head.

> I'll wear a crown
> Some day.
> I'll wear a crow-own
> Some day.
> I know, I really do believe
> I'll wear a crow-o-own
> Some day.

CHAPTER SEVEN

Nuclear Families

AT KNOXVILLE COACH station, near Cleveland, Tennessee, I met Mr Vaden. A polite, gently spoken man in late middle age, he had kindly offered to put me up for the weekend. He lived at a place called Oak Ridge, not very far away. I had heard of Oak Ridge only in connection with the Oak Ridge Boys, a group of country and western harmony singers. Somehow I imagined Oak Ridge as a line of oak trees, growing along the top of a ridge facing the mountains. Between each pair of trees a young man would stand singing.

'Do you know the Oak Ridge Boys?' I asked my host.

'Oh no, they're from a different Oak Ridge. Oak Ridge, Tennessee, is the place where they first split the atom. I have spent most of my life in the atomic energy industry. Oak Ridge is a relatively new community, built around the scientific research stations.'

Oh dear! This was decidedly un-Kerridgean territory. Nevertheless, my host drove into a beautiful suburban street set among high trees. Some of them were oaks.

'We own a few acres of woodland behind the house,' Mr Vaden said, as he pulled into his driveway. Mrs Vaden welcomed me at the door, along with her long-time friend and guest, Lady Lever. I was among polite society indeed. In a country house in Berkshire I had long ago enjoyed tea with Sir Christopher Lever, the eminent naturalist, and his vivacious young dark-haired wife from Tennessee. On that occasion, the conversation had centred on frogs, but a chain of circumstances had led to my invitation to Oak Ridge. Sir Christopher had remained in his study in Berkshire where he was busily writing *The Naturalised Birds of the World*. Lady Lever was revisiting childhood haunts.

My room looked out on to the woods through thick mosquito netting. Beautiful red leaves, I was told, belonged to a young dogwood tree.

Coffee was served in the conservatory. Through the conservatory window, I watched a dear little white-breasted nuthatch, halfway between a titmouse and a tiny woodpecker, run along the side of a tree, then hop on to a suspended feeding box with a flutter of slate-blue wings.

Apparently, an Englishman was a novelty at Oak Ridge, and the Vadens had invited guests over to dinner that night to meet me. While they were preparing the meal, I roamed among the beautiful woods behind their house, feeling that I had shrunk to a pigmy. The leaves and soaring boughs were so enormous! Perhaps when England had boasted virgin forests, the oaks and beeches grew as large as they do today in Tennessee. Could Robin Hood's greenwood have looked as lovely as this, a bright blue sky peeping through gaps in the high foliage?

Around the dining table that evening, the guests included a big bearded young man who spoke about hunting all the time, a comforting reminder of the South I had left behind. Another guest was Carson Brewer, author of several books about the Smoky Mountains. Now was the bow-hunting season, and the Vadens' daughter and several of her friends were deep in the woods stalking deer with bows and arrows. The deer-shooting season would begin a few weeks later. Ginseng roots, I learned, grew deep in the woods of the Smokies, and the men who collected them for sale to the aphrodisiac-minded Orient were known as ginseng hunters. So hunting talk was general. The sports page of the local paper was taken up by hunting news.

'Huh!' woofed the bearded young man whenever I told him anything about England. This bear-like utterance expressed not scepticism, but deep interest. I grew to know it well, for it proved to be a white Southern trait. Carson Brewer told me of the time he had met a she-bear with two cubs while walking in the forest.

'She was on the path in front of me, so I stopped and waited,' he said. 'She moved into the woods and put her cubs up a tree, so I walked on. Then I turned round, and there was the mother bear galloping after me! I picked up a big stick and rushed at her, shouting with all my might! This surprised her, and she turned round and fled!'

Many of the company were atomic energy people; Lady Lever came from a Tennessee Valley Authority dam-building background and Carson Brewer was connected with the National Park.

They all took atom-splitting, dam-building and National Parkism very seriously. I took my cue from the company, and tried to be as polite and well-mannered as possible. However, all three occupations fill me with disquiet: I don't mind atom *bombs* so much, as at least they scare the Russians, but I am very much against using atomic energy for peaceful purposes. After all, why harm your own side? There may be more to dam-building than flooding out farmers and creating artificial jobs; and

National Parks may have other uses beside ruining farmers in America and pastoralists in Africa. They may be as regrettable a necessity as the National Trust in England – the museumisation of a country which would otherwise be destroyed in a less attractive way.

Next morning, Mr Vaden took me on a tour of the radioactive research stations of Oak Ridge. We didn't go inside them, but merely admired them from various vantage points, for my host felt very proud of this scientific settlement.

'Look, there's the Senior Centre for old people, and there's the bowling green,' he said. 'We're a very happy community. I've no time for protestors, no time at all. After all, atoms split all the time on the sun.'

'Yes, but people don't live on the sun,' I demurred.

'Now I'll show you the public library. I have to change a book myself, so it's no trouble.'

It was a well-stocked library, built in the Oak Ridge Atomic style, a long, low, flat-roofed brick building with large windows. The various research establishments looked similar, but larger, with wire fences around them. Among the newspaper-readers, I was struck by the ludicrously tranquil face of a Red Indian (or so he appeared to be). He was not smoking a peace pipe, but reading a magazine called *Changing Times*.

'Are there many Indians around here?' I asked Mr Vaden.

'No, but we did know a Cherokee man who married a girl from India itself,' he said. 'By some genetic quirk, the children had curly hair. Very attractive children.'

He drove me to the top of a hill, and I looked down on the scattered and ultra-hygienic-looking radioactive buildings. Canada geese and swans paddled serenely on a large lake, to the delight of passing scientists.

'The buildings are separated one from another in case of an explosion,' my host explained in a quiet, thoughtful voice. 'There was a lot of opposition to the Oak Ridge scheme from the local farmers at one time. Of course the farmers have all been bought out now.'

We drove across the calm blue Clinch River, where a solitary heron stood silhouetted on a branch overhanging the water. A warning sign by the road showed a white-tailed buck in mid-jump.

'There was a little fuss not long ago when it was found that radioactive material had leaked into the river and been drunk by the deer,' Mr Vaden said, as he swung the car round and headed for home. The woods were fenced off with a notice that read 'No Entrance to Hunters'. Deer meat was not yet safe.

On the way back, we passed an empty church used by the farmers in pre-atomic days. Later, Mr Vaden pointed out his own church, a modern flat-roofed Presbyterian edifice known affectionately as Fort Calvin.

That evening, Mrs Vaden and Lady Lever went to a women's meeting of some sort, so Mr Vaden took me out to a restaurant. There he greeted several friends, mostly middle-aged couples. I found that eating out was an American pastime, particularly among the middle class. Not that 'class' in America corresponds to anything we have in England. Mr and Mrs Vaden and their friends reminded me of well-to-do English Northerners, from Lancaster or Harrogate, with working-class great-grandparents and with 'refined' Northern accents. Americans make much of English class distinctions, while forgetting about American race distinctions. Curiously enough, at the same time that American county schools for black and for white were merging, the early sixties, English schools for the working and middle classes were also being forcibly combined. Can you spot the fallacy in this comparison? It is that skin colour remains constant, while a person's class can be changed. Grammar schools changed working-class children into middle-class adults. Even without grammar schools, an adaptable Englishman or woman can change class many times in a lifetime and still remain the same person.

Mr Vaden told me of holidays he had spent in England. He had been horrified at some of the prices he had been charged, and wondered if all Englishmen were honest.

'No, of course they're not,' I explained. 'Many people think that Americans are so rich that it's almost a moral duty to rob them.'

My host reeled back, shocked and hurt, as he called the waitress and paid the bill. I had been talking about the nastiest type of Englishman. Some of these nasty types literally rob Americans by jostling them in the Underground and snatching their wallets. Perhaps there ought to be a Kindness to Americans in England Society.

The following morning, we all went to a Champagne Brunch. This appeared to be an established custom among the gentle atomic families of Oak Ridge. Champagne and a kind of High Breakfast (as in High Tea) were served at eleven in the morning, the guests invited by telephone.

Murmuring politely, and shaking hands with all and sundry, I found myself in the most expensively furnished open-plan house I had seen in a long while. With its gleaming yet folksy wooden fittings and ornaments, it was a dazzling combination of pioneer, aristocratic and modernistic styles. We sat down at a table covered in glassware and exquisitely folded napkins. I can't remember now if he was the host or not, but the most interesting person there was a merry round-faced Jewish man with spectacles. His wife persuaded him to tell his war story. He had served in the U.S. Air Force and had baled out of a damaged plane over Yugoslavia. There he and the rest of the crew had lived among the partisans in the mountains. Their families in America, told that they were 'missing', had feared the worst. Finally they were met by the Russian 'liberators' at the end of the war. The Russian captain gave them a banquet, with many vodka toasts, until the American colonel tried to toast Chiang Kai-shek. At this, the Russian smashed his glass in a rage, a new twist on the old Tsarist officer style of toasting.

'We were in London a short while ago,' he told me, 'and we went to an Elizabethan banquet. Everything had been fixed up for us – it was an educational vacation, with classes on the British way of life. "Bawdy serving wenches", we were promised. The whole thing was phoney as hell! Then we had a seminar on the British class system. We learned about the working class, the middle class and the upper class. How do you people stand it?'

'I don't know,' I said, surprised. 'I'm middle class, myself.'

Soon I realised that he and no doubt most Americans did not realise that people can change class in England, learning new accents in the process. The phrase 'class system' is misleading, as it suggests that someone is in control, and that the vague generalisation of class describes a Hindu style *caste* system.

'Well, our teacher told us that Britishers like having a class, as it gives them a sense of security, a position in the scheme of things. Then we had a coffee break. We were all in this room, absolutely bemused, looking round till we found coffee and tea urns behind a counter. So we went round there and began helping ourselves. A woman burst in and began absolutely to *scream* at us. We were terrified!'

'Was she a West Indian?' I asked.

'I guess so; she was a black lady. Well, that night in our hotel I tried to reason it out. I thought, perhaps she feels it's her *place* as a member of the working class to serve us with tea or coffee. So next day, I went up to her and said, "Excuse me, Madam Coffee Server, but could I have a cup of coffee, please?" And she served me, friendly as pie! We became the best of friends! We used to poke each other playfully.'

Poor Americans! I had never realised before how alien they must feel in England. What my friend had mistaken for a class problem was actually a coffee problem. In America, I found, coffee is usually free, like water, and you help yourself. Even where coffee has to be paid for, you still help yourself. In England, you have to buy coffee and tea in a café, and they are poured out for you. Only a robber would go behind the counter in a café if he didn't work there. The outraged Jamaican lady had found, as she thought, a gang of American desperadoes stealing her tea and coffee!

Among the Vadens and their friends, I felt part of America the continent, rather than of the South. At the Brunch, I heard casual reminiscences of childhood holidays in Venezuela! Before I moved on, my hosts kindly offered to drive me up into the Kentucky mountains to see the Cumberland Gap. At this historic site, in the late eighteenth century,

Daniel Boone had opened up an old Indian trail through the mountain forests, hitherto thought by pioneers to be impenetrable. Later, the armies of North and South had camped in turns at this wild Cumberland Mountain pass. Both found it an uncomfortable posting. History and romance should be found a-plenty at the Cumberland Gap, and I was in great excitement as the four of us set out. There was another reason for my interest, which those old enough to remember the 'skiffle craze' might appreciate.

It was the day of a great football match between Alabama and Tennessee, and many cars we passed bore stickers urging us to 'Hate 'Bama'. In America, gangs of murderous thugs are unknown at football matches (unless you count the players) and the word 'Hate' can be used lightly. Mr Vaden bravely pretended not to care for football, but I noticed that he kept switching on the radio to see how the game was going. Lovers of classical music, both Vadens and Lady Lever constantly poured scorn on the country music beloved of most Tennesseeans. I half-heartedly agreed with them. Most country music is fairly undistinguished these days. They particularly disliked an entertainer called Cousin Minnie Pearl, who acted the part of an old-fashioned hillbilly lady, and cracked corny jokes on television. However, I quite liked her jokes: 'Q: Pardon me, did you give me a funny look? A: Lady, you've got a funny look, but I didn't give it to you.'

Yellow stalks of maize in the fields bore witness to the summer's drought. Halloween was not far off, and enormous round orange pumpkins with thick broken-off stalks lay in boxes for sale by the roadside. Life-size dummy ghosts and witches stood propped against chairs or posts on wooden porches. English Guy Fawkes dummies must be a vestige of this custom, 'Penny for the Guy' our 'Trick or Treat'.

Soon we were up in the wilds of the Cumberland Mountains, over the border of Tennessee into Kentucky. At one point we cut across a corner of Virginia. Forests covered the mountains, and now at last the frosts of autumn had begun to burnish the leaves. Sudden bursts of bright red or vivid orange appeared among the greenery. Dogwood and walnut trees combined crimson and yellow shades. Here and there a log cabin could be seen among the trees. However, some of the mountains tapered up to craggy blue crumbling peaks, with bare scars among the trees on their flanks. Poor-looking towns and derelict buildings by the roadside testified to a failing worked-out coal-mining industry.

'Open-cast mining has spoiled the forests here,' snorted Mr Vaden in disgust. 'That's why hydro-electric power wins my support – it stops coal mining. Atomic energy has great potential! It could solve the population explosion.'

I agreed there, of course.

The romance of the Kentucky mines has been put to music by one of the local country bards, Merle Travis. I was witnessing the end of an era. At the Champagne Brunch I had sat opposite a thin woman with penetrating eyes.

'My husband was a labour organiser for the coal mines,' she had told me. 'The Tennessee strip-mines were non-unionised until he came along. But the coal bosses tampered with his car to make him have an accident.'

In England, it is a safe rule to assume that trade unions are always in the wrong, but in America, the bosses apparently stoop to union-like tricks themselves.

A road sign pointed to the Cumberland Gap, and we swung off the main road and dived deep into a valley, along a narrow mountainside lane, a tunnel in the forest. We emerged into the sunlight to find ourselves at Cumberland Gap the town, rather than at the Gap itself. A forgotten town, off the tourist route, Cumberland Gap resembled an old Western cow town of the 1870s. There were no suburbs, and front doors of two-storey brick houses opened directly on to the narrow dusty road. At one corner, a tall man with long, thin, dangling yellow moustaches hiccupped, rocked and staggered, grasping at the corner of a dingy shop for support. Around this corner, the road led up to a sheer wall of mountain.

A young housewife, her head in a shawl, stepped from a car and began lifting her children out on to the road. Mr Vaden asked her for directions, for he wished to show me the Gap from the official tourist viewpoint.

She cheerfully showed him the road, adding, 'I used for to live here, but now I'm just come here to see my *grand*mother.'

Beside the driveway of the Cumberland Gap tourist centre grew the reddest tree I had ever seen. Branches and leaves formed an almost perfect circle, like a child's drawing of a tree, and the foliage blazed like fire. Mrs Vaden called it 'the Apple Tree', as it looked like a giant apple. Its proper name was the Scarlet Oak.

At the Centre, an 'interpretative film show' was announced, and our party hurried upstairs to the cinema room with murmurs of delight. The film showed hardy pioneers, represented by actors, struggling through the Cumberland Gap in the snow. It began as it ended, with a country and western song.

> 'I'm the Cumberland Gap,
> I'm the hope in the heart of your mind.'

I saw what Mr Vaden meant about country music. We then walked around the Centre looking at twigs and things, and reading the history of the Gap from panels around the walls. My impression, by the time I had finished, was a vivid one. I saw a tide of land-hungry people spreading

Westward by every means possible, even risking the hardships of the Cumberland Gap. This was Peasant Power, unhampered by the civilising restraints of feudalism and aristocracy, insatiable for more and yet more land, justifying its actions by a comparison with the Hebrew children ousting the Philistines from the Promised Land. A contrast indeed to the patient, suffering Negroes who used an earlier part of the same legend to sustain their hopes – 'Let My People Go'. Hardihood, courage and other virtues I could not deny the pioneers who crossed these mountains in ox wagons, led by guides such as Daniel Boone who could fight off Red Indian attacks. The red cattle who now grazed around the little town of Cumberland Gap far below may have been cousins of those pioneer oxen. In Sussex, red plough oxen gave way to the dairy breed of Sussex cattle a hundred years ago.

The British Empire, in Virginia, Africa, Australia and many other countries, has always had two separate ideas in its London-based 'mind'. One is to encourage British settlers and to look after their interests abroad, the other is to protect the indigenous people, and attempt to give them legal rights before they are expelled, enslaved or exterminated. Both ideas stem from benevolence, and both are somewhat incompatible. Government has usually been too far away to enforce its wishes.

'Go forth and prosper' is the first command to the pioneers.

'Hang on a minute, you are killing people and burning villages! Stop at once! Look here!' is the second command, usually an ineffectual bleat.

'You *told* us to go forth and prosper, and these savages are getting in our way,' is the pioneers' reply. 'We are out of your control now, the Old World is finished and the day is ours!'

A land rush is like a gold rush, and the prospectors in both cases are furious if a government tries to stand in their path. That government is almost sure to be overthrown. Boers in South Africa hitched up their own ox wagons and went on the Grand Trek rather than submit to feebly expressed British notions of fairness to Africans. Later, in Boer territory, British prospectors started a war against the government when a gold rush began in the middle of a state founded by a land rush! I am getting into a whirlpool of deep waters here, but my daily-growing knowledge of American history had, at the Cumberland Gap Centre, led me to a crucial question: Is America a mistake?

By now I had finished reading the autobiography of the Red Indian warrior Black Hawk (1767–1838). From it I had learned, to my happy surprise, of the affection the frontier Indians had held for the British. They did not mind white *protection* at all, and referred to British 'district officer'-type agents and traders as their Fathers. Before such friendly white men appeared, Black Hawk's great-grandfather (Na Na Ma Kee or

Thunder) had been told by the Great Spirit, in a dream, 'I am sending you a new Father.'

Under British rule, east of the Mississippi River, the Sauk tribe of Indians received credit for a year's supply of goods, and then lived by trapping furs for the white man. Unfortunately, no one appears to have introduced them to Christianity. No master of logic, Black Hawk began his book by stating how he and other warriors had completely wiped out various neighbouring tribes for sundry misdemeanours. Finally, tricked out of his land on the present Wisconsin–Illinois border, Black Hawk raised the *Union Jack* as his standard against the Americans. He befriended an Indian known as 'The Prophet', a man who mistakenly prophesied that the British would send troops to oust the Americans and protect the Indians. Black Hawk's village had been divided into lots and sold to white settlers; bovine, insensitive men who began digging and building over the Indians' farms when the Indians were still there, looking on aghast. As in Southern Rhodesia many years later, the ousted natives were labelled 'illegal squatters'. Troops were sent to chase them away, petitioned for in high indignation. The Black Hawk War lasted for fifteen weeks in 1832. Seventy white men were killed before the Sauk Indians surrendered.

Arrested, Black Hawk was taken to Washington to be shown the might of the white man. His memory of the cities a blur, the old warrior was particularly struck by the friendly, hard-working, kind-hearted hillbilly farmers whom he met on mountain roads near the Cumberland Gap. He was impressed at their resilience in these hills, and asked why all white Americans could not stay happily on farms such as these, instead of pressing Westward. He did not realise that a few generations earlier, the Appalachians had been the West. Grandparents of those hardy home-steaders had also fought with the Indians. Putting those days behind them, the kindly hill people whom Black Hawk met were as innocent of blood as are most modern Americans.

In the 1960s a popular hippie poster showed a smiling all-American family sitting down to a cereal breakfast, while deep in the earth below their suburban home lay the remains of slaughtered Indians. You were supposed to think that the family were hypocrites who did not deserve to live, or at least to live in America. But I was glad that the imaginary cartoon family were happy. Why should they be blamed for deeds done by long-ago ancestors? No, let them get on with their breakfast with a clear conscience.

America is a *fait accompli*.

Black Hawk's last words of advice to white people concerned 'the Negroes'. His opinion was asked as to the best method of getting clear of these people. No mental giant, his solution was to separate the men from the women, so that they couldn't breed, at least with one another. He then urged that any Negro women left over in this Great Division ought to be sent to the Indians, to work as slaves for the squaws. Poor Desita and other New Orleans devotees of the Black Hawk cult! How ill-founded their simple faith had proved to be! I was interested to note that it was slave-owning white Southerners who had asked Black Hawk his advice on how to 'get clear' of Negroes. King Cotton had not then begun to reign in earnest.

At last our tour of the Cumberland Gap Centre was over, and the Vadens, Lady Lever and myself went out to see the real thing. Narrow winding steps led upwards among the trees to a look-out point. We passed immense wooden spikes pointing outward from a long beam. I thought it must be a giant pioneer's harrow, but the strange object proved to be the remains of defences left behind by the Civil War. A wide concrete balcony fixed to the hill top gave us a splendid view over miles and miles of dark forested mountains.

A strange grey stack crowned one peak, as if the mountain had suddenly decided not to come to a point but to be Table Mountain instead. This was explained as the doings of the mining engineers. A great spoonful of mountain seemed to have been scooped neatly away by the Hand of God, allowing vistas of yet more mountains to be seen through the forested moon-curved valley. A dark line through the trees immediately below us showed the Wilderness Road cut by Daniel Boone in 1775, with the help of thirty axemen. Above this rose a towering escarpment. Crowds of tourists took photographs, and I met a man from Yorkshire. Such was the Cumberland Gap.

Near Middlesborough, Kentucky, we stopped at a restaurant. There seemed to be a lot of Yorkshire about, with a Harrogate, Tennessee, not far away. 'Heidi,' the waitress greeted us, with Swiss simplicity.

As we sped back to Oak Ridge at the end of the day, we passed green rounded hills, half in shadow, and wooden porches with limp Halloween dummies that looked *exactly* like guys. At the little town of Clinton, a 'Country Music Show' was advertised outside a cinema-like building. I noticed an unshaven man plodding along the side of the road, a huge bundle on his back and a guitar in his hand. Perhaps he would be famous one day. American flags on poles fluttered from lawns and suburban roofs, and soon we were back at Oak Ridge. The day had given me a valuable lesson in American history, and I had not the heart to tell my hosts that the whole excursion had been inspired by a Lonnie Donegan song, 'Cumberland Gap'.

After the gentle manners of the Nuclear Families of Oak Ridge, it was a shock suddenly to find myself at the Greyhound Bus Station at Knoxville, Tennessee.

'Greyhound buses are a different culture to the one we're used to,' kindly Mr Vaden explained, as he shook my hand in farewell. I was bound for Georgia, while Lady Lever was taking a plane to New York and returning to England by Cunard.

Quickly getting used to my own culture again, I put my bag into the Left Luggage office and set out to explore the town. I had an hour before the coach went. Across the open railway line, I found a sleepy, crumbling but very 'downtown America'-looking neighbourhood of old shops and dwellings. Leisurely downtown America is my delight, an antidote to the flashiness of the shopping malls. This was a black district, and a fat man sat snoozing on a chair in the doorway of a shop selling garden spades, a hat over his eyes. Out of work men sat chatting on a bench, and a poster on the wall advertised a saxophone player, 'A. C. Reed and The Spark Plugs'. Further into town, I admired a huge revolving globe, like a giant diamond on a column. It rotated slowly. Whenever a sunbeam hit one of the crystal patterns the beam was reversed and sent up again as a shaft of yellow light cutting through the blue Tennessee sky.

Apparently, the diamond globe had been left over from Knoxville's World Fair. The man who had organised the Fair was now languishing in prison. I retraced my steps to the railway line, waiting as an enormous goods train rumbled by, each orange truck (or boxcar) thirty feet in height, and with the word 'Southern' written on the side. I was pleased to see a 'caboose' at the end of the procession, a small back-truck with a rail for hoboes to hang on to.

Soon I was in a Greyhound heading South, past verges covered in goldenrod, a plant which (according to cartoons) makes you sneeze when you sniff it. Enormous supermarkets, called 'Piggly Wiggly', appeared here and there beside the road. Juggernaut lorries thundered by, their cabins connected to their huge loadbearing hindquarters by giant black coiled springs. Once I saw a row of them parked beside a shed marked 'Truck Wash'. At a lonely country stop, a wild-looking coloured girl got on with her belongings inside a black polythene sack slung over one shoulder. I changed coaches at Atlanta, Georgia.

A spirited country girl, very pink, with blue dungarees, boarded the next coach, talking to everybody and helping old people up the steps. She countered every 'Thank You' with a 'You're Welcome' in the Southern way. She had made friends with two tall merry-faced youths, one white and one coloured, and the three of them sat in the back seat laughing and talking.

'I'm going to Florida to see my boyfriend!' she said loudly. 'Whenever I phone him, it sounds like a girl is answering, but it's his little brother! Ha, ha – going to Florida!'

A moment later, however, she had doubts about the safety of her bag, locked up in the side of the coach. 'I hope no one takes my baggage, or they gonna be *gone*! No matter if they're a black man or a white man, a black woman or a white woman, they gonna be gone. I'm gonna get a .38 Special.'

'Yes, that's the best kind for shooting people,' the white boy agreed.

Just then, she spotted a group of coloured men on the pavement outside, passing round a whiskey bottle. 'Just look at them fellers outside passing that liquor around!' she exclaimed. 'Got it in a brown paper bag, too, to keep it cool. Hey, fellers! Pass some *my* way!'

For the rest of the journey through the hideous environs of Atlanta, which stretched on for at least forty miles, the three of them sang loud, jaunty country and western songs.

CHAPTER EIGHT

Small-Town Life

PASSENGERS, BOTH black and white, were lying asleep on the seats of the Greyhound coach as it rumbled through the Georgia night. After each stop, the driver would make the same announcement.

'Cigarette smoking only at the rear of the bus. No pipes and no marijuana. Thank you for riding with Greyhound.'

At last, at an obscure town in Goodall County, Georgia, it was my turn to dismount. I stood blinking beside my bag as the coach vanished into the darkness. Then I peered around inside the ticket shed, hoping to identify the man who was going to look after me. He was an Englishman named Anthony Savage, who had chosen this remote neck of the woods as a suitable spot in which to carry out his scientific research. I can't recall ever having met a scientist in England, apart from schoolteachers. So far, Southern-based scientists seemed to hold the monopoly on Southern hospitality.

A big bullet-headed man with deeply-set eyes and a curt, confident upper-class accent stood asking a coloured porter if anyone else had got off the coach. I approached him nervously, and he turned to bare his teeth in a welcome smile. He looked like a rich successful novelist or play-wright, frank and brutally truthful, who would stand no nonsense from any television man who might seek him out in Morocco or the South of France. However, it was too late to run away.

'You can stay three days!' he told me, as he drove into the forest. 'After that, I'm flying back to England to see Susan and the children.'

Susan, his wife, had eagerly fixed up this meeting. She it was who had warned me against appearing 'a defective white man'.

'What kind of research are you doing?' I ventured.

'Into the Aids virus! Fascinating subject! My secretary is in New York now, preparing to make a shock announcement on television. I expect to

have the television men besieging my office! Damn nuisance, as I've got
work to do!'

A scientific consultant, Anthony worked for himself, and could have
settled anywhere in America. He and his wife had taken a liking to the
little town of Goodall Boyville, set in the midst of the new Southern
scrub-forest that had grown over the cotton plantations.

'This is famous deer-hunting country now,' he told me. 'Bears have
come back, but you hardly ever see them except in the very early
morning. Mountain lions and I daresay wolves must be somewhere about.
Conservationists love to exaggerate how rare animals are, so as to get
protection laws. Most of all, though, these woods are full of marijuana
dealers. Just walk anywhere in the woods, and sooner or later you'll
stumble on somebody's marijuana crop and very likely get shot. This part
of Georgia is a centre for the drug traffic. Moonshiners and bootleggers
have evolved straight into drug dealers. We still have moonshiners, of
course. Another thing – watch out for rattlesnakes! The woods are full of
them. We've got a big one that lives under our house. He earns his keep
by eating the rats. Sometimes he comes out and suns himself, but I think
it's getting a little cold for that now.'

Now the headlights on his car had begun to pick out vast square white
houses made of boards. He swung into a hedgeless garden and parked
beside a palatial back door. The huge oddly-shaped frame house rested
on granite supports, and the steps up to the door seemed as if hewn from
enormous boulders. One side of the three-storey house was occupied by a
red-brick chimney piece. Most of the large houses of Goodall Boyville,
built in the mid-nineteenth century, resembled a log-cabin builder's idea
of a Palladian mansion.

Inside, I found myself in a spacious kitchen, with steps up to a long
hallway which led through the house to the front door. Rooms leading off
the hallway had high ceilings and bay windows. A staircase spiralled up to
a cock-eyed wooden ceiling that looked as though it belonged to a mill.
Sparsely but elegantly furnished, with a modern kitchen, the house was
also home for a querulous feather-bitten grey parrot who flew freely
around, always returning to his cage. Doorways opened on to steps, as if
the house had been built on several levels. I put my bag in my room, and
joined my host in the kitchen for a light repast.

'I'll show you where everything is in the kitchen, and then it's up to
you!' he said. 'I've got three children, so I've no patience with anyone who
can't fend for themselves.'

Curtly, he pointed out various inscrutable appliances. As I can't cook, I
resigned myself to living for three days without food. The lack of coffee in
the morning was a particular blow. Instead of drinking instant coffee, in
the civilised fashion, he used some kind of percolating device. I would

have thought that being a father would have *accustomed* a man to caring for the helpless and dependent, but Anthony Savage was made of sterner stuff.

'In the morning I'll show you my office, where I take calls and do my research,' he said. 'It's just an ordinary brick house near the centre of the town. People round here can't understand how I make a living! America is due for a rude awakening!'

'Why is that?'

'Aids! You'll see! My researches have already shown that Aids has become a heterosexual disease, striking both at men and women! But now my studies have taken me further! Aids is about to reach plague proportions! It's hard to put it into laymen's terms, but let's just say the virus will become vaporised! It will go into the air, and all you will need to do to catch Aids is simply breathe! You see the implications! Two-thirds of the Western world will be wiped out, just like that! It will be like myxomatosis, the disease that wiped out rabbits! You'll remember my words in five years time! I'll be safe here at Goodall Boyville, as I know what precautions to take! I can tell *you* what to do, if you like.'

'No thanks, I'd rather not think about it.'

'Like the governments, ha ha, who will do nothing to protect themselves until too late! Come on, I'm driving you to see some friends of mine!'

'Isn't it a bit late?'

'I thought you wanted to see the South? If you don't see these people tonight you may never see them again!'

So off we went, out of town and into the woods once more. I had always known that scientists were like this, of course. We drove into a clearing, where cars were parked outside a dark windowless building that looked like a giant wooden shed.

'This is it! The American Legion Club, supposedly for war veterans, but actually a drinking club for all the white men round here,' my host explained. 'Drinking is scarcely legal in Goodall County and *this* place only stays open by a miracle. The manager is a great character, and a good friend of mine.'

Pink lights from a long bar beckoned across a dark, empty room. Big men, rough diamonds in peaked caps, sat on stools, arms slumped across the bar. All greeted Mr Savage with genial respect. A miniature Star Spangled Banner hung among the whiskey bottles above the slogan 'Be Proud of Your Flag'.

'Hello there, Mr Anthony,' the barman said, pronouncing the name with a soft 'th'. 'Another Englishman, huh? Pleased to meet you, too – my name's Moose Meadows. What'll it be?'

Mr Anthony had a whiskey, and I settled for Budweiser. A very agreeable man, big, broken-nosed, curly-haired and friendly, Moose Meadows towered over us, and talked about football and deer hunting. Although much older than the English scientist, he treated my host with great respect. Soon it became evident that he and several of the other Legionaries had placed their savings at Mr Anthony's disposal to invest on the Stock Exchange.

'I must thank you for that last tip you gave me,' Moose Meadows said. 'Looks like the money I gave you to fix it up has gone and doubled itself. I can't understand these things myself, so I'm mightily obliged to you for fixing it.'

'Quite!' the business-genius smirked crisply, then rattled off a lot of Stock Exchange gobbledygook. An honest person, Mr Anthony was not swindling these good men, but merely exercising his power and his will over them, chiefly for their advantage.

A rheumy-eyed young man, his face framed in black whiskers, his lumber-shirted tummy hanging over his belt, asked Anthony if it would be all right 'to come round your yard tomorrer afternoon when mah auto-part store's closed, to pick some o' your pecans?'

Mr Anthony thought, then nodded.

'That's a dandy pecan tree you got growin' at your place, Mr Anthony! Your friend from England, too? Hah, my name's Gene!'

I greeted Gene, and showed him some carefully selected photographs of England. At the first sight of a coloured face on a picture, he gave a great start, so I took them back. Moose Meadows, who had a deep, kindly voice, offered us each another drink on the house. Apparently, Mr Anthony avoided the company of other scientists, which is why he had decided to live at Goodall Boyville.

'None of the people here have the *least* idea of what goes on in my head!' Mr Anthony exulted, as we drove back to his house. 'For instance, most of them go to some church or other on Sundays, and they suppose I must go to a church somewhere too! They would be amazed if they knew my views on religion!'

'Why, what *are* your views?'

'The usual scientific opinions. People here don't know *anything*, anything at all!'

He looked almost as happy at this thought as he had done when imagining a world decimated by plague.

When I awoke in the morning, I found that Mr Anthony had gone to work. Watched by the suspicious parrot, I opened his enormous fridge and breakfasted on ice cream and Perrier water. Fending for myself has never been my strong point. Through the large kitchen window I looked out across a large untidy lawn, shaded by tall evergreen oaks and the famous pecan tree. Similar white plank houses could be seen through tree-lined avenues, along with a white-painted church spire. Like many Southern spires, it had not been built on top of a tower, but simply stuck on to the tallest point of the church roof, an outsize wooden spike. I seemed to be in a well-to-do neighbourhood.

A honk outside showed that Anthony was ready to show me round. He was very generous in his unnerving, larger-than-life manner. He showed me his office, outwardly an old run-down house, facing a dusty street. Inside, it was light and airy, bookshelves reaching to the ceiling and a jumble of papers and old coffee cups everywhere. Susan Savage painted in Grandma Moses style, and a portrait of their housekeeper's daughter hung on the wall, a wide-eyed coloured girl.

'She's more sophisticated than her mother, so she doesn't think being painted will steal her soul, she only has a feeling that it might,' Anthony said. 'She's supposed to have a sister with a rat's ear, as her mother had been frightened by a rat. That's about the level of education you can expect here.'

I put on my white floppy hat, and he led me into the town square. Huge, barn-like white dwellings led down to the square from various shady avenues. Away from the trees, the town of Goodall Boyville baked and shimmered in the sun. A few shack-like shops selling motor accessories faced an immense red sandstone Gothic fortress, actually the County Court. Its roof sprouted towers and balconies like a seaside hotel. Anthony led me round the side of the court, where I saw a modern post office, with a flag dangling outside, a newspaper office and a dusty road trailing off into the woods.

'That path leads to the swamp,' I was told. 'Come on, I want you to meet the editor of the *Boyville Bugle*.'

Office and printing press were combined at the *Bugle*, and a vast chaotic interior revealed itself as I stepped in from the heat. A hound and a puppy ran to meet me, both wagging their tails. Papers with typed or printed news items on them lay carelessly around the antiquated printing presses, with their big copper wheels and inky smells.

After introducing me to the editor, a tall bearded man, Anthony Savage left me for further investigations into the Aids virus.

'I'm afraid at this moment, the only news is buck-hunting,' the editor told me. 'Your visit to Georgia isn't strictly news. However, my junior reporter will give you all the help he can. That's him over there.'

I found the junior reporter holding up photographs of white-tailed deer, wondering which ones to print. An eager young man with spectacles, he said he could find me a great deal to write about. Picking up the phone, he rang up his mother, the headmistress of the local primary school (known in America as an 'elementary school').

'Hello, this is Hickory Pillow of the *Bugle*. May I speak to Dr Pillow, please?' he said.

Handing the phone to me, he allowed me to talk about my fact-finding mission, and I was invited to see the school. Then the obliging Hickory took me across the road to the court 'to meet my friend the judge'. As I left, I noticed the editor and a tall black man animatedly discussing deer-hunting.

It was dark and soothing inside the Victorian courthouse hall, with its shiny floor and old panelled doors leading to various offices. A white-haired old tax appraiser came out and shook my hand elaborately, sprinkling his conversation with 'sirs'.

'Hickory of the *Bugle* here!' said the intrepid youth, as he poked his head around an august-looking door. 'Michelle, I've got a visitor for you, all the way from England.'

'Hi, how ya *doing*?' smiled a pretty girl, rising from a desk.

'Probate Judge Michelle Wilkinson' read a name-plate near her typewriter.

'Are you really a judge, if you don't mind me asking?' I enquired.

'Sure am. Why?'

'Well, in England judges are mostly very old men in wigs.'

'Is that right? Gee, I'd like to go there, I sure would! Now, I'm a *pro*bate judge, I handle wills and so on. Go on, have a look around my office! There's books here going back to the State's beginnings – see, there's one marked "1803".'

Leatherbound with gold writing on their backs, the books looked most impressive.

'Hickory and me are old pals!' said the judge. 'He comes here to find out all the County gossip! If you want to see a lot of human interest, you ought to come here on Pleas Day. That's when every one pleads "Guilty" or "Not Guilty" in line, before being tried one by one.'

There were many differences between English and American law, it appeared. I had never known about conveyor-belt pleading before. Apparently the plea would be entered in a book before the case was tried, and (if the case was not too serious) the pleader could then go home and wait until the next court day for his trial. The distinction between barristers and solicitors didn't seem to exist – both were lumped together as 'lawyers', an official title instead of a slang name. It was all most baffling. Unluckily, Pleas Day coincided with the day chosen for my school visit, but if I arrived at the Court on time I could hear the first few Pleas and then rush off.

After telling Michelle all I knew about the English Royal family, I left along with Hickory. With a cheery wave, he dived back into his air-conditioned office. I decided to walk down to the swamp.

This at last was the South I had dreamed of, the red, dusty road rambling up and down through the woods from farm to farm. Soon the town of Goodall Boyville had been left behind. Butterflies, resembling English fritillaries and brimstones, fluttered around me. Black on the red road, my shadow looked up at me, far more Southern than I was, with its broad-brimmed hat. I felt like Uncle Remus in the Walt Disney film *Song of the South*, and began to sing 'Zippety doodah'.

A white-painted plank church stood by the road, its name roughly painted on a board over the door: 'Friendship'. Nearby, under the overhanging trees, small headstones poked from the tussocky grass, each with an inscription and a plastic flower. A car sent the dust swirling, and a large, cheerful black family tumbled out into a long one-storey house that faced the church.

Half a mile further on, the road dipped and crossed the swamp. Water poured beneath the pathway, through a drainpipe, and splashed and bubbled into a pool on the other side. Islands of young trees rose from the swamp. It was not a muddy place, but a clear lake full of trees, or a flooded forest. Luxuriant foliage spilled from earthy banks and hung over the water. Cicadas sang a perpetual metallic tune, and green grasshoppers leaped from one reed to another, under a sky of azure blue. I found a path, about a foot wide, that wandered off into the woods. So I wandered after it, but it led to nothing more romantic than a rubbish-dump.

Leaving the path, I scrambled between the trees for a few yards, then heard a crashing sound. I had startled a small herd of white-tailed deer. Flashing white hindquarters bounced away from me through the undergrowth, as the deer leaped like rabbits, their white tails standing straight upright all the while.

I returned to the main path, treading warily in case of snakes. Two cars passed me, the coloured drivers staring suspiciously, and then I reached the town square once more. I ran straight into Anthony Savage, who seemed pleased to see me. He stood alone in a ghost town, for nobody in Goodall Boyville ever walked in the streets.

'Jump in, I'll give you a drive,' he said, as he led the way to his car. 'So you've seen our swamp, and had a look at the woods? Those woods are full of the graves of Federal soldiers. There was a lot of shooting here during the Civil War, and they simply buried Northerners where they fell. No one here feels that they belong to the United States. During the last war, not a soul from Goodall Boyville got conscripted, the friendly postman saw to that.'

I was not sure that I believed everything that Anthony Savage said.

'I'll take you to see an old plantation, and then drop you at Black Bottom so you can look at the blacks,' he kindly offered. 'All the black people here live at Black Bottom, and always have done. Some are living in the same cabins that their ancestors lived in before the Civil War. You won't see much there today. It's on Friday and Saturday night that they all hang around in the street, shooting cocaine and smoking marijuana. Since cotton ended, they simply live on relief. They can live where they like, now, but none of them have ever left Black Bottom.'

By now, we were out of town, in a landscape of open fields where soya beans and maize had recently been harvested. Anthony took a farm road, across a cattle grid, and into a private estate.

'This is the plantation founded by Governor Jim Boy, who also founded our town back in 1850. He grew cotton, using free labour.'

Anthony sounded so approving as he used the word 'free', that I assumed that Governor Boy had employed free Negroes on his estate, and paid them wages. However . . .

'Yes, all Governor Boy's labour was free! He didn't have to spend a penny on slaves, but simply took convicts from the penitentiary and set them to work. A very astute man! Look there across the fields at those fine brick barns where he stored the cotton. He had his own steam railway that carried the cotton to the barns from every part of the estate. Look, there's one old wooden carriage left, under a tree. I think someone's been living in it. Here's the original Boy mansion! He built a white classical mansion after he'd made his fortune, but this is where he started out.'

Leaning this way and that way, the tall ramshackle plank house, weathered grey with age, seemed about to fall over.

'One or two rooms are still inhabited, round the back,' Anthony said. 'The new house? No, we can't see that – we'd run into the security guards. It's now the home of Hank Hutt, the millionaire country and western singer. He's bought the whole estate. However, a descendant of Governor Boy lives quite near me, in a house very like the plantation home. You'll see it as you come out of the Black Bottom.'

Now we drove along narrow red earth lanes through woods and over shuddering log bridges over the many streams or 'creeks'. Once a fox ran across the road in front of us. A long low creature, Brer Fox seemed to have shorter legs than his English cousin Reynard.

'You can drive for miles and never see another human being!' Anthony exulted. 'Won't it be wonderful when England is like this! It won't be long now! The new lethal spread of Aids will reduce the population to around five million. A nuclear holocaust might well take care of the rest. I look forward to the day when England is as lovely as Georgia.'

Just then his expression changed, from a blissful smile to an angry frown. 'Oh no! Damn! Damn! What a fool I've been! Look!'

He stopped suddenly and pointed at two delicate mourning doves sitting on a telegraph wire. Had the dove, the emblem of peace, caused him suddenly to see the error of his ways?

'It's open season for doves and I've left my shotgun at home!' he snapped, and drove on broodingly.

Anthony pointed out the present Boy dwelling, a Greek temple of a town house, with the American flag flying. Then he drove down a lane fringed by wooden cabins with porches and large cluttered gardens full of washing tubs and clothes lines. He greeted a skinny old lady with her head in a shawl who stared lugubriously over her garden gate. Curiously enough, every cabin had been creosoted a dark brown colour, whereas every white home in Goodall Boyville had been painted white. Even the houses kept to the colour line.

Black Bottom ended at the bottom of a hill, where the woods began. Anthony let me out at a long low barrack-like shed with boarded-up windows that stood in a clearing among the trees. It had been patched with many different sorts of wood and material. 'Lounge and Disco', the faded sign read.

'It's usually a Disco,' Anthony told me. 'They call it a Lounge when they have live music. It's amplified so loud when they play, on a Friday and Saturday, that you can hear the electric guitar, drums and harmonica all over town. Damn nuisance – we're trying to put a stop to it. See you later – I'm going back to the office now. My Secretary's speech on Aids, using notes that I prepared, will be shown nationwide from New York in a couple of hours. We can expect some action soon!'

Now quite cheered up, he drove off rapidly. I walked all round the padlocked Lounge and Disco, but saw no sign of life. I did not make a hit in the Black Bottom. All the black people had cars, however battered, and did not trust anyone who walked.

'What you doing, *walking?*' two youths shouted angrily from their car, which narrowly missed me. Other householders went indoors, scowling, as I approached. A middle-aged man returned my greeting politely, but still hurried indoors. The plastic carrier bag I always have with me might have enhanced my tramp-like aspect. Loud rhythm and blues music blared from the porch windows, where long slopes of roof joined wooden stakes fastened on to the plank porches. Each porch had a rocking chair. In a few minutes I was back among luxurious white homes near the First Baptist Church.

White nonconformist churches seem extremely rich in the South. The Baptists worshipped in style, their church a tall, pointed mansion whence tape-recorded bell-music rang out merrily on the hour. From my Greyhound, I had seen many Pentecostal Churches built like Roman villas, with Sunday Schools attached.

I let myself into Anthony's house and dined frugally on ice cream and Perrier water. There were no food shops or cafés in Goodall Boyville. The great man returned eventually and cooked himself a sizzling steak smothered in mouth-watering onions. No television reporters had arrived, but he had had several phone calls and seemed to be contented.

Wakened next morning by the parrot's baleful shrieks, I helped myself to ice cream and Perrier water and toddled down to Anthony's office, as instructed. I was very frightened of my host. He was alarmingly brisk and abrupt, tolerating no bumbling or dithering, and the proud owner of a pair of steely-grey eyes that stared straight into your soul. Then they laughed at what they found there, disappearing into creases. Most unnerving.

'Ah, there you are!' Anthony greeted me. 'Sleep well? Good! There's a do on at the Legion tonight – Moose Meadows will be expecting us. Meanwhile, I suggest you go down to the Sheriff's office, on your left, past the courthouse. He might let you interview him. I've met him once or twice – to my surprise, he seems incorruptible. Not like the old sheriff, whom I suspect of being a member of the Klan.'

My eyes roved around his office, library and laboratory. Vials, phials, bunsen burners and other occult devices of the necromancer's art lay scattered around the place.

'Do you keep Aids viruses on the premises?' I enquired.

'Oh no. Would you care for a drink? Let's see, I'm out of coffee. Have a glass of water. It will do you good in this heat.'

He gestured towards a ready-poured glass standing amid miscellaneous jumble on his desk. The glass was very dirty indeed. As I drank, my host looked keenly at me, as if this were some sort of a test. I knew that Aids, like snake poison, has to get into the bloodstream before it can kill. So I did not worry overmuch, and in fact the water cooled the mayhem that the ice cream and Perrier water had been getting up to inside me.

I found the Sheriff's office, a big square building, the front door high on the second storey, up an iron staircase. Scottish chieftains have built their castle fortresses on a similar plan. A typewriter was rattling in a small overcrowded room with 'Deputy' on the door. I knocked and entered.

A huge, bloated, bleary-eyed man in shirtsleeves, the Deputy read my credentials suspiciously, pausing now and again to spit into a paper cup. Without rising from his desk, he sent his secretary to find the Sheriff.

A moment later, I was shaking hands with a tall, personable, red-haired young man, wearing a shiny star on his blue shirt and a pistol at his hip.

'So, you're a friend of Mr An*tho*ny, hey, and you're writing a book? Well, I'm Sheriff Robert Terrell, and I'll give you all the help I can. I'm the law in Goodall County,' he added, tapping his star badge. 'We don't have no police or nothing. Why don't y'all step into my private office for a while.'

So I stepped, and found myself in a large, comfortable room full of confiscated rifles, stacked around the walls. A guitar lay in a corner, with a label attached: 'Evidence. Do *Not* Return to Owner Until Case is Adjudicated.' I sat looking at it while the Sheriff spoke into a phone, 'Yes, ma'am. No, ma'am.' Finally he put the phone down.

'It's about a dawg, and I ain't no dawg catcher. What do you want me to do, tell you about myself?' He seemed uneasy, almost nervous, obviously afraid of a 'hatchet job', just as any English policeman would have been. In his case, the matter was more serious, as he 'ran for office' like a councillor. If he were ridiculed in an American paper, no matter how unjustly, he could lose his job as Sheriff at the next election.

'I'm in politics. This here is a political office. We gets voted in or out every four years,' he told me. 'I'm in the middle now, with two years to go. You tell Mr Anthony I'm countin' on his vote. Well, before I was a Sheriff, I practised law and laid bricks for a living. Is that a trade in England, a brick-layer?'

'Yes, that's a trade. There are more brick houses than wooden ones in England. Do you know the term "hod carrier"?'

'Yes, we say that too! Seems just the same. Then I became a night club bouncer, and just before bein' elected Sheriff I was the security guard for Hank Hutt, the great country singer. Lived down there in his mansion, lookin' after his wife and children while he was on tour. They treated me real well, the Hank Hutts. Drugs is a problem here in Goodall County. We're often called out to destroy a marijuana patch someone has discovered. Anything else you want to know? Hey, why don't you come an' visit my *jail?*'

At this happy inspiration, Sheriff Terrell looked almost frisky. He was clearly very proud of his jail, which turned out to be housed on the ground floor of the same building. Prisoners were held there for short sentences only.

Pottering about in the open doorway of the jail was John Henry, a 'trusty' whose name was on a tag sewn to his shirt. He was a rake-thin bearded black man with narrowed eyes and a wide-brimmed hat. 'Everything's okay here, Sher'ff, just fine,' he murmured, hovering around.

'John Henry's one o' the local characters here in Goodall Boyville,' Sheriff Terrell said, genially. 'Now, have a good look, but don't talk to anyone.'

In the dim light I made out two cages, joined side by side. There was a solid wall between them, so that the two sets of prisoners could not see each other, but thick iron bars, criss-cross like gigantic mesh, encompassed them on every other side. Bars stretched from the floor to the ceiling, with a barred bird-cage door to each cell. Both cells were small, and crowded with a confusion of beds and odds and ends. Each held five men. In the first cell the men were coloured, in the second they were white. A very pink man in the second cell, clad only in his shorts, shouted 'Hey!' and beckoned me over to the bars. The Sheriff gave me a warming glance, so I ignored the shout. John Henry lounged over towards the bars, and the Sheriff hustled me outside.

'All these men have got *rights*,' he told me, importantly. 'We has to take 'em out and exercise 'em every so often. Well, I hope you've seen all you came for.'

'Er, yes, but I've just one question. Why are the white men and black men kept separately?'

'We cain't do that! That would be against the law.'

Smiling, he began to climb the steps towards his office.

'Well, why *are* they separated, then?'

'They just be's that way,' he said, gave a wave and vanished.

No doubt he was afraid of fights if the races were mixed in the prison. After all, outside in Goodall Boyville they lived separately, with separate drinking clubs and churches.

I went back to Mr Anthony's house and gave myself a treat. I discovered some bread and butter that I had not noticed before. Then I went for a walk along the swamp once more, finding that it led on to a prosperous farm and a lake beside the woods. A dog barked and I turned back. At the church named Friendship, I disturbed a white-tailed buck, which was cropping the grass around the graves. By now it was dusk, and the white tail that bounded away into the trees looked blue in the half-light.

I found Anthony Savage at home when I returned, and we immediately set out for the Legion Club.

'Those prisoners you saw used to live on the second floor, next to the Sheriff's office,' Anthony explained as he drove through the woods. 'They lived a free and easy life then, their rooms unlocked, strolling in and out as they pleased. Then someone complained on their behalf that they lacked air conditioning, and it was a "violation of rights" to deny it to them. So they had to be put in the cells, which are air conditioned. You should have heard the way those convicts swore! John Henry's an incipient convict, always doing thirty days, and he keeps me informed. Look, that's the school where you'll be going tomorrow. Dr Pillow, the principal, is an old fraud. She's not a doctor of anything! Nobody here knows anything at all, I mean *anything*!'

'Oh, um, I helped myself to bread and butter at your house earlier on. I hope you don't mind.'

'Oh!' he said loudly, with a jerk of surprise. He seemed to be biting his lips and trying to keep his temper. Now who did he remind me of, with his strange mixture of generosity and overbearing pride, his helpfulness and sudden temper, his delight in lording it over people he considered to be his mental inferiors?

'Colin MacInnes the novelist has been a great friend of mine since childhood,' Anthony suddenly remarked, as if mind-reading. I had been similarly terrified of MacInnes in that author's sixties heyday, when he had been a friend of my mother's. He too could not stand bumbling ditherers, and would explode with temper, only to relent a moment later.

'Now I hear that there's a MacInnes industry,' Anthony continued, 'but I'm not going to let my MacInnes drawings and letters be snapped up by those vultures. I saw a biography of Colin that looked more like a character assassination.'

That night, the Legion was full, for there was going to be a Veterans' Association meeting in the back room. We found a place at the bar, saying hello to Moose Meadows, Gene and other big men. The conversation, about a football team called the Georgia Bulldogs, was rather over my head. So to bide away the time, I took out my notepad and drew a cartoon picture of a bulldog. Gene looked over my shoulder and spluttered on his whiskey.

'Well, I'll be *hot damned*!' he said. 'Will you take a look at that? Show the lady what you done done!'

I tore out the page and handed it to a squat, merry little woman whose dress was looped round and round with artificial pearls.

'Can you draw a unicorn for my son?' a giant of a man in white hair and a peaked cap enquired.

Unicorns are what I draw best, so I rattled one off, to cries of 'Dang *me*! Did you see what I just seed?' and so on. Apparently no one else there could draw. From then on, I was kept busy, drawing unicorns for the excitable customers. Sheet after sheet of paper was passed into ham-like hands. After getting over his surprise, Anthony seemed pleased by my success, and sat smiling on his stool. He remained drinking at the bar while Emma, the pearl-covered girl, took my arm and waltzed me off to the buffet.

As an honorary member of the American Legion, I helped myself to a free plastic tray of beefburgers and cole slaw. We sat at a long wooden table among pleasant-faced Legionaries and their wives. A drum kit and a large American flag stood side by side on a stage, next to a polished dance floor.

'Mah name's Emma,' my companion said, looking at me with brown eyes that filled with sadness. 'I cain't find a job since I had my accident.'

Apparently someone had fallen asleep while driving, and had ploughed his car into the one driven by Emma's boyfriend, with Emma herself and her baby daughter in the back. All had been slightly injured. Emma's broken foot had not healed properly.

'I had to leave the sewing plant where I was at, 'cos my foot got tired working the pedal,' she explained.

'Oh, do you say "sewing plant"?' I asked. 'In England, we say "tailoring factory". Your job would be called "machinist". At one time nearly all the girls I knew in England seemed to be machinists. I used to work in a tailoring factory myself.'

' "Tailoring factory"! I declare! Is that what y'all calls it!' Emma exclaimed in wonder, forgetting her troubles.

Just then, the Veterans' meeting began, so I said goodbye to Emma and returned to the bar. There I found Anthony Savage outlining his future to an admiring Moose Meadows. 'A million dollars is not enough,' he was saying. 'I have my whole life planned out! I shall make two million dollars, keeping the money in my wife's name as I always do, and then I'll write a novel.'

'How can you say a million dollars isn't enough?' Moose enquired. 'I wouldn't even know what to do with *half* a million dollars.'

'You're not married, Moose! If you were, you'd know that a wife can spend upwards of twenty thousand dollars in a day, just buying clothes.'

'I don't believe it!' I said.

Moose looked from one Englishman to the other, as if wondering whom to believe. Anthony grew insistent, telling us that his wife Sue spent thousands every time she went to Paris.

'And you've put your money in her name!' I exclaimed. The unexpected beefburger was working its magic on my ice-cream saturated body. Someone had been feeding me meat!

'It's bad luck to plan your life out in public,' I continued. 'Rather than get richer and richer, you might lose everything and end up as a tramp wandering round in rags. Your wife could run off with the money.'

'Susan would never do that!'

'She might if I asked her.'

Moose seemed to be thoroughly enjoying this exchange. But poor Anthony looked so unbounced that I felt sorry for him and changed the subject.

Back at his house, he opened a wardrobe and showed me various black slinky items of female attire that he said were worth thousands. Then he cooked himself an enormous meal, but I had had my beefburger and I was content. Honour was satisfied.

Anthony seemed in a good temper in the morning. I rose early, and found him whistling to the parrot.

'Jump in the car; you're having breakfast with Moose Meadows,' he told me. He drove me to a roadside cabin-like café with a wooden porch, a lone building on a forest road amid green birch trees.

'Moose and all his friends from the Legion have breakfast here every day,' he told me. So Americans eat out even at breakfast time! 'He'll drive you back to town, and I'll meet you outside the courthouse at ten-thirty.'

Inside the little café, Moose and the others greeted me, then went on with their buck-hunting stories. A waitress served me with black coffee, buttered toast and bacon, eggs and hominy grits. This was luxury!

'I could tell he was in rut by the swelling around the neck,' Moose was saying, discussing a big buck he had seen.

Listening to the men, I learned that buck-hunting would begin on the following Saturday. Just as with fallow deer in England, the male white-tailed deer was never called a 'stag'. 'Doe days', when female deer could be shot, were announced sometimes. The hunters made camps deep in the woods, and skinned the deer that they shot. Some had their own private hunting lodges or huts. At night, the game warden would call at the camps to make sure that each man had shot no more than the permitted six animals. Night shooting with torches was illegal, and the warden would have to look out for this.

Breakfast over, the men drove off on their various ways.

'Come and see my pick-up truck,' Moose suggested. It was painted dark brown with a pattern of olive-green vines all over it. 'This is my hunter's truck,' the owner said proudly. 'It was painted white when I bought it, so I got a friend to camouflage it.'

I climbed in, and he drove me to his private stretch of woods, unlocking a log gate and then driving downhill along a rough track between pine trees. Then he stopped beside a log cabin. We climbed out, and I saw, between the trees, an enormous blue lake. Moose unlocked the cabin, which acted as his summer house, and contained a rather 'nouveau riche' lounge, complete with plaster ducks on the wall. He collected a loaf of bread and led me outside once more.

'This was once all forest and swamp,' Moose said, gesturing at the lake. 'Got a friend to bulldoze it for me, just over two years ago.'

I was surprised, as the view seemed one of unchanged primeval wilderness. I was to find that most American lakes are newly dug. In England, lake-making went out with Capability Brown, and we tend to think that all lakes are natural.

Mist rose in clouds from the still waters, and a blue heron flapped its way across the scene. Moose began to break off pieces of bread and throw them, and a beating of wings could be heard. Tame Muscovy ducks, his beloved pets, came flying towards him from the lake's furthest shore. These large birds were black, with white wing-tips. A few white farmyard ducks were with them, and a mother duck had made her nest underneath the cabin porch. Two floating plank jetties lay anchored to the steep wooded banks of the lake. Moose stepped out on to one of them, the ducks swimming beside him, and he threw them a goodly breakfast of bread and maize.

'That old white duck is blind in one eye,' he pointed out. 'I calls him Old Peg-Eye.'

When we had left the jetty, he removed the plank bridge from the shore, to prevent racoons from getting too near the birds and fish.

'We have all kinds of creatures here. Beavers, too – they're a pest. That was my duck jetty, now we'll go on my fish jetty.'

From this jetty, I could see bass and bream rising up to take the bread. All of a sudden, a delightful shoal of blue-striped cichlids, giant versions of the tropical fish sold in English pet shops, appeared in the clear lake water. Greedily, they snapped at the crumbs.

'Bluegill,' said Moose, with satisfaction. 'Now when the fish here are bigger and fatter, I'll start fishing and invite all my friends and family. I got eleven brothers, you know, but one died recently.'

On our way back to town, Moose sang the praises of the Savages. 'That Anthony and his wife Sue are the nicest folks I ever *did* see. I b'lieve they'd do most anything for you.'

At the courthouse, I said goodbye to Moose, and went inside to find Judge Wilkinson, her brow furrowed, surrounded by anxious black people whom she was helping. She showed me the way up to the public gallery and continued with her tasks. My stairway led me to an outdoor balcony overlooking the white houses of Goodall Boyville. Coloured families stood around talking, discussing their own fates or those of their loved ones. A pair of large doors opened on to the rear of the courtroom. I took a seat, and the black people followed my example, glancing around warily. They consisted of dumpy, cross-looking young women in slacks and tall, good-looking young men. The latter were usually accompanied by their mothers. A few white people were already seated.

Below us, on a raised podium or stage, hung the State Flag of Georgia, which resembled a Confederate flag. A large desk stood below it, with two small desks to one side for the Sheriff and the Deputy. Sheriff Terrell stood erect, looking around the court. The unpleasant Deputy waddled towards his desk, a pistol sticking out of the side of his trousers. An altar rail, so to speak, enclosed the rostrum, with large posts at the corners of the gate. Almost all the woodwork in the church-like court was painted sickly brown, as in the old chapel at Lincoln Prison. White columns, mounted on the slope of pews, held up the ceiling.

'Court rise!' somebody shouted, as the judge walked on to the stage and took his seat at the big desk.

'All right, ladies 'n gentlemen, you kin sit down now,' observed the judge mildly, as he poured himself out a cup of coffee. He seemed a pleasant, even-tempered old gentleman, strict but fair. In England he would be a magistrate, dressed in his everyday clothes.

All the people who had been charged with offences were sitting freely among their relatives in the gallery. As each name was called, the accused person would walk down the aisle to the stage and stand there, raising a hand as he or she pledged to be truthful with the simple answer, 'I do.' No Bible was used. Few non-Negroes had got into trouble. It seemed to me that the de-cottonisation of the South had made most rural Negroes redundant. They had not necessarily been 'framed', for the devil finds work for idle hands who have been laid off. However, the most popular crime was that of 'selling alcoholic beverages on a Sunday', which is not a crime at all in England.

First of all, a smartly-dressed woman pleaded Guilty to the above 'crime'. Her plea was entered in a book and for now she was allowed to go. Secondly, a fat man stood up and pleaded Not Guilty to writing a 'bad cheque'. Again, this would not be a crime in England. If it were, I would be in prison to this day; for a bad cheque did not mean a forgery but simply a cheque that had bounced. In England, of course, the bouncing cheque is the mainstay of many a domestic economy.

A tall dark-haired white man, very indignant, claimed that he was Not Guilty of wife-beating, drunkenness and assaulting an officer. His plea was gravely entered, and he left, slamming the door.

Next to plead Not Guilty was a tall, gangling, coloured youth. He had been accused of smoking marijuana. Unlike the other pleaders, he had no attorney lined up to defend him when his case was to be resumed. This disturbed the judge, and the following exchange took place.

JUDGE BANKS: Now young man, where do you work?

YOUNG MAN: Don't!

JUDGE (*sharply*): Why not?

YOUNG MAN: Got fired!

JUDGE: And what job was it that you were fired from?

YOUNG MAN: A cook.

JUDGE: Well, why don't you have an attorney?

THE BOY'S MOTHER (*rising from her seat at the back of the court and calling out to the judge in anguished tones*): He cain't! He cain't afford it!

JUDGE: Now, young man, don't you keep looking round the court like that! This is a court of law – you should show respect! I believe that your attitude needs adjusting. Are you indigent?

YOUNG MAN *shrugs*.

JUDGE: That means, 'Are you living in poverty?' If so, the state can furnish you with an attorney.

With that, the boy was allowed to leave, shuffling and surly, his arm gripped by that of his anxious mother.

Next, in rapid succession, came three Drunk on Sundays and a Bad Cheque, all Guilty. One of the Drunks was a white man. A very young-looking coloured boy, also with an anguished mother present, pleaded Not Guilty to shoplifting. It was now nearly time for me to meet Anthony Savage. I stayed for just one more Plea.

A tall, countrified white man in shirtsleeves pleaded Guilty to keeping his children home from school. He hung his head in shame. Remembering how much I had hated school as a boy, I warmed to this noble man. Perhaps he had a pressing mortgage on his farm, and needed his boys to help in the fields. I tiptoed out of the court, and met Anthony outside. He roared with laughter when I told him about the youth who had been asked if he were 'indigent'.

'Every black person in Goodall Boyville is on relief,' he said. 'They've all got money, but they kept quiet about it.'

'Oh. Whereabouts is the school, by the way?'

'I showed it to you yesterday!' he snapped, looking disgusted at my feather-headedness. We drove on in silence, and I dismounted at Goodall County Elementary School.

A long low brick building, the school resembled its English counterparts. Inside, I found a cheerful, busy atmosphere. Dr Pillow, the headmistress, greeted me in her tiny office. A defeated-looking lady, she gave a weary sigh and then told me a little about the school.

'Until 1955, every little town round here had a black school and a white school,' she said. 'In that year, this school was built for blacks, and all the black children of Goodall County were taken here in buses. Their old schools got closed down. After a time, the schools were told to integrate, and now there are more white children here than black. The school was greatly added to, with more facilities, at that time. We have a computer room with five computers. This being an elementary school, all the children of Goodall County come here from age five up till age eleven. Then they go on to the County High School. Each day begins with saluting the flag, then classes go on until lunch at twelve-thirty. At one o'clock, classes recommence, and at three-thirty the buses come to take the children home.'

'What about playtime?' I asked.

'You mean "recess"? Well, the Juniors don't have recess, but the Infants have play as a lesson. Kids nowadays have to be taught to play, I can't think why. We got swings an' slides an' stuff for them to learn the techniques of playing skills. That's it, really. You're mighty welcome to spend the day here with us, an' have lunch with the others.'

So saying, Dr Pillow took me to an English class of eleven-year-olds, and left me there. I sat in a corner and made notes, a cross between an inspector and a student on teaching-practice in an English school.

'Hi, my name's Ginger!' smiled the young teacher. 'So you're from England? Have you seen the Queen?'

Formalities out of the way, I observed a lesson on Action Verbs, Tenses and Subjects and Objects. I remembered this lesson from my own primary school days. In those days, we were taught Subjects and Predicates and so on at the age of nine. Now, I believe, grammar is scarcely taught at all in English state schools.

All the children looked good. Open-faced and well-mannered, they regarded me with interest. Hands went up as questions were answered, and all the desks were in traditional rows, facing a green blackboard. Notices on the wall must have been aimed at the coloured children: 'Don't hide your pride!' and 'Be happy about what you are.' This seemed to be a misguided attempt to cure the feeling of inferiority that so often saps Negro confidence all over the world. Being so obvious, the posters were merely embarrassing. If I were a black person in Goodall Boyville, I am not sure that I would be happy to be what I was.

I looked at the children's books, and was impressed by their joined-up handwriting. Their essays were not very coherent, but probably of the same standard as at a comparable English school in the 1980s. Just as in many English schools nowadays, History, Geography and Social Studies had all been merged into one subject. I looked at the exercise books concerned and found that Social Studies was not thinly-disguised Communism, as in England, but Civic Affairs, a useful subject. History began with Christopher Columbus. The Middle Ages in the Old World, and the civilisations that preceded it, were not taught at all. This explained American incredulity at anything that was not American. Western civilisation, to a Southerner at least, is something existential, only existing *now*, and somehow involving cars and Coca-Cola. If Americans understood the Middle Ages, they would realise that their way of life is in part an inheritance from the Old World, and so gain a better understanding of themselves, and of the world. Geography at Goodall County had almost been whittled into nothingness, but I was to find that excellent relief maps of America hung on most classroom walls. Plastic mountains sticking out of the paper looked most realistic and satisfactory to touch.

For a few minutes, I answered questions on England, all concerning the Royal Family. The plethora of Royal Weddings in recent years had been shown on American television, and symbolised England to everybody I met. Surely America will soon apply to join the Commonwealth!

Miss Ginger then took me to the Maths class, where the teacher was a young girl with black glossy hair. 'Hi, my name's Betty!' she greeted me.

Soon I felt just as bored as some of the children, for Maths is definitely not my subject. All the same, it seemed very simple Maths indeed, considering that the class were ten-year-olds. They were learning ordinary multiplication. Luckily, Betty soon told them to put their books away, as the English visitor was going to give them a talk about England. I found myself facing rows of eager children, black and white in equal numbers, and all looking forward to a Treat.

'First of all, let me say that I have *not* met the Queen,' I began. 'I have *seen* the Queen, but not spoken to her, as unless you are born into a rich country family, you are not likely to know the Queen to talk to. Yes?' – for a keen-faced white boy had put up his hand.

'Sir, what language do you talk at home?'

'English.' I answered promptly, trying not to bat an eyelid. 'Very many of you boys and girls had great-great-grandparents who came to America from England. That's why you speak English, just as I do.'

The children looked open-mouthed and almost stunned at this. Hadn't their kin always lived in Goodall County? How come they had come from England?

Warming to my work I continued. Throwing in a sop to their supposed patriotism, I told them that I had seen the *very steps* at Plymouth harbour where the Pilgrim Fathers had descended to their ship, the *Mayflower*. More stares of mystification. They could see that I expected them to look impressed, and some tried to assume the right expression. Betty looked embarrassed. She too seemed to be racking her brains to think of who the Pilgrim Fathers might be.

'Plymouth is in the West of England,' I went on. 'People there don't talk like me, they talk like this: "Arr, Jim lad! Don't tell I, tell 'ee! 'Ow be thy mangel wurzels?" '

This dramatic piece of over-acting and nonsensicality went down a storm at Goodall County. The children laughed, clapped and jumped up and down. Miss Betty seemed delighted. Success going to my head, I went on to improvise a Welsh accent, a Norfolk accent ('Who's that little ole boo-oy?') and a Cockney accent. To top it all off, I sang 'My Old Man's a Dustman'. This brought the house down. I was only halfway through the song when two coloured boys leaped to their feet and performed a wild devil-dance, flinging their knees and elbows about as their feet moved like magic on the spot. Their eyes grew huge, and they grinned wickedly. Faster and faster I sang, as the boys leaped and the class applauded. The words could have made very little sense to them.

'One day whilst in a café, he spilt a milkman's tea.
The milkman stood up angrily, and he was six foot three!
"I'm very, very sorry," my Dad cried in remorse.
And then 'e scarpered out of there and kicked the milkman's 'orse!'

All too soon, the bell rang. From then on, I was to take Goodall County by storm. First of all, however, it was lunchtime.

'I'm very fond of English music,' Miss Betty told me, as she led the way to the hall. To my chagrin, it turned out that she meant rock music, the bane of my life and the scourge of civilisation. Virtually all the teachers seemed to be young good-looking white girls. Perhaps they left the profession when they married.

Lunch had to be paid for at a till, just as in a café, without the English school weekly ritual of 'dinner money'. The meal came ready-served on a tray, along with cold tea or lemonade. I sat with the chattering girl teachers, while nearby the pupils sat at long tables, all with excellent and most un-English manners.

With great pride, Betty introduced me to the school's one remaining black teacher, a thin middle-aged man who appeared to be in a state of advanced terror. He gabbled something nervously, then sat on his own at a separate table, his back to us as he rapidly swallowed his food. His eyes did not focus, but each went its own way, and I gained the impression that he was mentally ill. Zora Neale Hurston, whose flawed autobiography, *Dust Tracks on a Road*, I was now reading, did not approve of integrated schools in the South. She thought that integration would throw excellent Negro teachers out of work. How far this has happened, I cannot say.

After lunch, I was to see a Remedial Class at work, then a Gifted Class, and finally I was to receive a guided tour of the school from the headmistress (or 'principal') Dr Pillow.

Nearly all the seven-year-olds in the Remedial Class were coloured. It was a small class, with nine coloured children and two white girls. Their teacher, Miss Wilma Snow, kept them hard at work. I sat at a table next to the class 'bad boy', a delightful rogue with rolling, expressive eyes. His name was Tyrone. Near him sat a girl in a long faded dress, her face screwed up in a mixture of perplexity, scorn and concentration. This seemed to be the class expression, for several of the boys wore it also. Their clothes were skimpy, and so were their badly-bound rags of school books. Many of the crop-haired boys had features rather like Kalahari Bushmen. Today's lesson was on 'compound words'. I had a feeling that Miss Snow had swotted it up the night before, but she went to work with a will. She made the children read a selection of words from a text book, then pick out a compound word.

Bright-eyed, giggling and naughty, they stumbled over the words, getting most of them right.

'Listen up!' Miss Snow warned them. 'One o' these words is a compound word and I'm not going on till one o' you gits it.'

'Junkyard!' said a big-eyed girl.

'That's very good, Chantelle,' said the teacher. 'Now tell the class what a junkyard is.'

'It's sump'n that smells bad. You throw all your junk there.'

Tyrone lay his head across one arm as if asleep, but put his hand up in the air as if he wanted something. His pencil needed sharpening. At once the scornful girl in the faded dress offered to sharpen it for him. She took the pencil with a grin, put it in a pencil grinder and ground the handle as noisily as she was able. Then she gave the pencil to Tyrone and sat down again with a flouncy Little Madam-type air. Tyrone leant across and stabbed her with the pencil.

'Tyrone!' shouted Miss Snow, as the girl indignantly rubbed her thigh and mouthed terrible cuss words.

'Yes, ma'am?'

'Tyrone, go and write your name on the board, sir!'

He danced over to the board, wriggling and chuckling.

'That's not funny, sir! Sit down, sir!' commanded Miss Snow.

Tyrone sat down, grumbling to himself. The next compound word was 'rattlesnake'. A thin girl in jeans picked this word out correctly, and was asked to tell the class what it meant.

'A rattlesnake, ma'am? It's sump'n that goes "sssss". He can strike at you!' – she mimed with her hand – 'Me 'n Linda found one once, ma'am, it was down by . . .'

'That's enough, madam!' Miss Snow stopped her.

That was the end of compound words. Reading disconnected passages from the text book came next. Each reader had to define a word that was underlined. The first such word was 'scold'.

'It's when someone busts out shoutin' at you!' a boy declared with great feeling.

The next word to be defined was 'trust'.

'It's if you be-*lieve* in someone,' a boy answered.

'I don't trust *no*-body but my Mom!' Tyrone called out.

'Tyrone!'

At this moment I put my own hand up and asked if I could give my talk on England now. Miss Snow agreed. Everyone looked at me. For a 'remedial' class, they seemed very bright. I tried to explain how Great Britain is a name that covers four different countries; England, Scotland, Ireland and Wales. Miss Snow seemed interested. The difference between England and Britain is almost impossible for an American to grasp, as any Scotsman congratulated by a tourist for having 'such lovely mountains in England' will testify.

'In Wales, nearly everyone is called Jones, Morgan, Hughes or Evans,' I said. 'So sometimes, when a village is full of Joneses, they call each one after his job. They say "Jones the Butcher", "Jones the Baker", and so on.

What's your second name?' I suddenly asked a very startled boy.

Oddly enough, it was a Welsh name, Thomas. I then asked him his father's job. Immediately, I wished I hadn't, in case the man was out of work.

'He works for the railroad,' the boy whispered, fearing some impending doom.

'Now if your dad lived in a Welsh village, they might call him Thomas the Train,' I said. This information pleased everyone, even the boy Thomas, so while I was on a winning streak, I launched into 'My Old Man's a Dustman'. Again the song was rapturously received.

'You sometimes hear songs like that in pubs, in England,' I said. 'I'm sorry, I mean "bars".'

But still the children looked blank.

'They don't know what "bars" are,' Miss Snow whispered. 'Their dads drink in illegal beer joints deep in the woods.' So I compromised with 'beer joints'. If I had been Gussie Fink-Nottle, at the Market Snodsbury Grammar School prize-giving, in the P.G. Wodehouse story, I could not have been more popular with my youthful audience. I asked for questions.

'Sir, are there fish in England?' was the first.

When I had dealt with that, one of the white girls asked me if I had seen the Queen. My answer led me on to a description of the Tower of London, Traitor's Gate, the head-chopping block and other marvels of the romantic past.

'I need an assistant here,' I proclaimed. 'Tyrone!'

A brilliant actor, young Tyrone endured my accusations of treachery against the person of Her Majesty, Elizabeth the First and went through the motions of being ferried by barge through the Traitor's Gate, up the steps and so to the block where the executioner awaited. I played executioner, a priest, and a soldier who rattled on a drum. Tyrone lay his head across the desk top, his eyes bulging. By now he may have thought it was real. I almost did so, too, but luckily I didn't have an axe.

'So, Tyrone, sirrah, how dare you commit foul acts of treachery against our noble Queen?' I roared, not quite sure who I was at the moment. I brought my arm down with a chopping gesture, and Tyrone winced, then stood up boldly and returned to his seat. He looked relieved, as if he had overcome Death. At that point the bell went. My next lesson was with the Gifted Class.

This class was taken by a pleasant-looking woman named Mrs Maxey, the wife of Goodall Boyville's Baptist Minister. A large class, it consisted almost entirely of white children, all well dressed and eager-looking. Only two eight-year-olds were coloured, a boy and a girl who sat together. The boy was very solemn, with strange amber eyes that gave him an otherworldly appearance. Again, the children seemed utterly astonished and perplexed to be told that many of their ancestors had come from England. All their questions concerned the Royal Family.

'What's your first name?' I asked a cheerful-looking boy with curly yellow hair.

'Sir, it's Brandon.'

'All right, Brandon, I'll show you what it's like when the Queen makes somebody a knight. She still does this nowadays, but we'll make it the olden days, so you can put on armour and ride off on a white charger. Kneel, sir! On one knee, that's right. Brandon, for the immense service you have done to this realm, by saving Goodall County school from being burned down, I shall dub thee knight.'

With a ruler, I tapped the boy's shoulders and head. 'Arise, Sir Brandon! Take this sword and use it to defend the realm against all enemies!'

Clutching the ruler, Sir Brandon returned to his seat amid cheers. I had not enjoyed myself so much for a long time, and only regretted beheading poor Tyrone instead of knighting him.

A child knocked and said that Dr Pillow the headmistress wanted to see me. Fortunately, I had not got into trouble. She merely wished to show me around the rest of the school.

'We have 850 children here from all over Goodall County,' she told me. 'There are handicraft classes for the less academic pupils.'

'How do you decide if a pupil is academic or not?'

'Ah. Well, the handicraft classes are so popular that even the *academic* children ask if they kin do them. Now, this here is our school shop, where the children can buy sweets with money they've earned themselves, makin' handicrafts. We have handicraft sales here. Handicrafts are made of wood, mostly.'

They seemed to be handy things to have. To my surprise, she led me into a long badly-lit corridor where 'the mentally handicapped children have their classes'.

'Oh! Perhaps that would be a good idea in England,' I said. 'As it is, normal children seldom see the mentally handicapped, who are pushed away into Homes.'

Mrs Pillow seemed to be as harassed by officialdom as any English headmistress. Her weary look suggested that the mentally handicapped might be the last straw. They had their own entrance to the school, I noticed. It may have been an 'official idea' to integrate them, following the so-called 'success' of Negro integration.

A bewildered little Mongol boy named Carson, a child of five, was trying to drink from a water fountain when we arrived. He then tried to find his own way back to his classroom, but couldn't. Luckily, an older child rescued him. I glanced through the glass windows on the doors of the mentally handicapped classes. Each class seemed a melee of Negro children jumping about on climbing frames.

'Why are nearly all the mentally handicapped black children?' I asked.

'Well, it's often very hard to tell if a child is mentally handicapped or just black,' came the reply. 'Um, that is to say, some of these black families have had no experience of school up till now; they had to stay home and pick crops, so they can't help their children as much as they'd like to. Now come outside and I'll show you something very typical of an American school.'

In the school yard stood twelve yellow long-snouted school buses in a row. According to Dr Pillow, each child was taken to a spot near its home, no matter how remote.

'Unfortunately, the High School children use the same buses, and they sometimes bully our children,' she added.

At that moment a bell rang, and the happy, joyous children of Goodall County ran from the school to their buses, laughing and shouting. Many of them waved to me, and thanked me for coming.

'Goodbye from Sir Brandon!' shouted that noble knight, as he rushed off.

I had to wait for Mrs Maxey who had promised me a lift back to Goodall Boyville in her pick-up truck. The teachers all had to attend a meeting on the Education of the Mentally Handicapped Child. Dr Pillow excused herself, and I took my seat in the classroom reserved for the meeting.

Soon I was joined by all the teachers, and a sallow, apologetic-looking moustachioed young man. He was the lecturer.

'Right now, if we want more money from the Department, we got to know all the latest terms for the mentally disordered,' he said frankly. 'There's L.D., that's Learning Disordered; then there's B.D., that's Behaviour Disordered. You all know that, I hope. It's important to use these initials right on the files and when you fill in forms.'

So if you were bad at your books you were Learning Disordered, and if you were naughty you were Behaviour Disordered. Such categorising was not a conscious plot to re-segregate the school, even if it worked out that way. In England, the children of West Indians are termed 'black' and are regarded as interchangeable with American 'blacks' for the purposes of sociological study. Using American documentation, it has been 'proved' again and again that such children 'underachieve', which is interpreted as meaning 'cannot learn'. Teachers in English 'inner-city' schools (translation: 'schools with coloured children') receive an extra bonus for their courage and daring, and swank to other teachers as if they were Stanley and Livingstone rolled into one. Here, at last, in America, the ideas that plague English education could be seen 'at source'.

In theory, it would not have surprised me if discarded, redundant descendants of slaves, living on relief in Black Bottoms all over the South, were a trifle stunted in intellect. But in my encounters with black people, I found there was no intellectual comparison between them and most working-class white Southerners. Full of imagination, able to picture any situation, the Negro seemed brighter by far, his speech full of lively imagery. White people, being reserved, may have had qualities that were not at once apparent. Articulacy was not one of them, but ability to read long, dull newspapers and to pass exams might well have been. The Negro and the White Man are like the Celt and the Saxon or even the Man and the Woman – a little bit different, but they certainly need each other!

Meanwhile, the lecturer droned on. Now he was talking about Re-Evals. Miss Betty leaned over and whispered to me that this meant the Re-Evaluation of the L.D.s and the B.D.s which took place every three years.

'Are there any questions?' the young man asked.

A young teacher with glasses put her hand up nervously. 'May I leave early, as I've got to meet someone?'

'It's okay, I think we've all learned enough,' was the genial reply, as handbags were gathered and a prim stampede to the door took place.

Mrs Maxey was so interested in my tales of England that she parked outside Anthony's house so that we could finish our conversation. I told her about the Romany gypsies.

'We have those here, too!' she said. 'When I was a girl I would see them shaving out of doors in the snow in front of their caravans. They would hang mirrors from the branches of the trees to shave in front of. Then off they would go, on down to Mexico and Central America for the winter, people would say. If one o' their number died while they were going South, they'd bury him by the road an' dig him up on their way North again, to take to their burial ground near Nashville, Tennessee.'

'Do you know what family they were?' I asked. 'Were they Lovells?'

She didn't know, so I went on to tell her of the way the gypsies, in fifteenth-century England, had put themselves under the protection of great lords, and taken the name of the noble family who shielded them from the wrath of cheated peasants. Lord Lovell, famed in balladry, no longer sits in the House of Lords, for his line has become extinct. But Gypsy Lovells are everywhere.

'That's just like our black people!' Mrs Maxey cried. 'When the slaves at Goodall Boyville were set free, they took the name of their old masters! Everyone here still knows who belongs to who, or who *would* belong to who if it weren't for that terrible War. When folks here talk about "the war", they mean the War Between the States. That's where all our history comes from. It was a terrible unjust war! That's why we're all Confederates here. Oh yes, I was saying about the black people. Well, there was a powerful landowner here one time, by name of Mr Savage. All his family are long gone from these parts, but his slaves, or their descendants, live all over the country. So when people round here saw Mr Anthony Savage's name all over the place, an' in the phone book, they straightaway concluded he must be a black man!'

Hmm. I wondered if Anthony Savage were an English relative of the old slaveowner, who had chosen to live in Goodall Boyville because of the family connection.

'Most people were very kind to their slaves – only a few were wicked,' Mrs Maxey continued. 'A slave could learn a trade and work on his own, after his master's work was done. He could earn money and even open a store downtown. Those Yankees had no right to do what they done. That's why "Yankee" is a terrible insult here, an' most people keep a Confederate flag indoors. But tell me more about England! I've heard all about your terrible class system! We don't have that here. For example, the principal of the High School is best of friends with the custodian – that's kind of like the head janitor. They go on picnics together. I don't believe that could happen in England.'

'No, there'd be a gulf between them,' I said.

'What people here like to do, is hunting,' Mrs Maxey went on to say. 'They prize their hunting dogs above everything. Why, my husband's the Baptist minister here, and a farmer came asking him for advice, saying "Can I sue my neighbour for killing my dog?" You see, his neighbour had gone an' put poison on his lettuce plants to kill the bugs. A rabbit had ate a lettuce an' died an' the dog went an' ate the dead rabbit. So the dog died too. My husband said it wasn't strictly the neighbour's fault. But the farmer said, "If that man had planted by the moon, as Nature intended, he wouldn't *need* to put poison on his lettuce 'cos it'd thrive anyways." Do people believe that in England?'

'I think they used to,' I said, a little unsure of my ground. I told Mrs Maxey a little about Celts, Romans, Saxons and Normans and then went in the house for my ice-cream supper, washed down with Perrier water. Mr Anthony came home in great excitement, and asked how my school visit had been. I told him how surprised I was to find that the children didn't know that their ancestors had not always lived in Georgia.

'No one here knows anything, anything at all!' the superman exulted. The thought obviously gave him enormous pleasure, and also justified his children's expensive education in England. 'Of course they have no pride in the Pilgrim Fathers! They see them as people in funny hats, a cartoon people that they see on television. Everybody here watches television from the minute they get back from work or school till it's time to go to bed. That's why the streets are always empty. It's a curious thing: although they don't believe anything unless they see it on television, they still think that what they see on the box is somehow not real. People here can't believe that I have no television! My housekeeper's daughter had never seen the sea until she went on a trip last year. She came back and said, "I never knew before that the sea was *real*." It's the same with men landing on the moon – deep down, the people here believe it never happened!'

University-educated Americans, Anthony went on to say, had only achieved a different kind of ignorance. They believed in the perfectibility of Man, particularly American Man, and thought that science and democracy could eliminate all human problems. Although Mr Anthony was probably right in some of his estimations, I didn't like his gloating attitude. He had no pity for a people doomed to live in the perpetual aftermath of a terrible Civil War. Moreover, he was as superstitious as any American, for he had enormous faith in computers, and measured a school by the number of computers it had.

'I'd *never* send my daughter to the County School,' he shuddered. 'Only five computers, you say? Even worse than I thought. That Dr Pillow is a phoney! I thought of sending Jemima there, but do you know what Dr Pillow told me? She said that a girl of six ought not to be learning Latin!'

'No teacher in a primary school in England knows a word of Latin, I'm sure,' I said. 'I imagine at Goodall County it's much the same. But surely you didn't burden your child's mind with Latin at the age of six? She'll have a breakdown, like John Stuart Mill.'

'Not only did she learn the rudiments of Latin at six, but she also studied the piano and 'cello,' he replied. 'I believe the mind should be driven to the furthest expanse of its powers.'

'Oh. Well, anyway, I have to leave tomorrow. Do you know how the Greyhound buses run?'

'The phone's in the hall!' he snapped, in his most abrupt tone.

Now what was I going to do? Would I never escape from this land of ice cream and Perrier water, with Aids clouds on the horizon? I got through to two different Greyhound offices, whose staff seemed bemused at my questions, perhaps not understanding my accent. I could make no sense of their replies. One of them began discussing landmarks I had never heard of, and asked me if the bus stopped at them. The other flatly said there was no bus, which I knew to be untrue. In order to meet my next contact, I had to travel hundreds of miles across the South to Jackson, Mississippi. Finally I drove my mind to the furthest expanse of its powers, and found a shuttle-bus service that ran from a Goodall County hotel to the airport at Atlanta, Georgia. It was rather expensive. From Atlanta airport, I would have to find my own way to Jackson, I knew not how. Anthony curtly agreed to drive me to the hotel, so I left it at that, and went to bed in an uneasy frame of mind.

Happily sitting in the comfortable shuttle-bus, I relaxed as mile upon mile separated me from Mr Anthony Savage, the Aids expert. Mrs Maxey, Moose Meadows, Tyrone and Sir Brandon had been pleasant companions, and I could never have met them without Anthony's help. So I tried to feel grateful. My present travelling-companions were two smartly-dressed elderly ladies. One of them came from New Orleans.

'The jazz musicians there are wonderful!' she enthused. 'They follow a funeral procession to the cemetery, playing sad tunes, and then on the way back they rejoice with happy music. And that's what jazz should be – happy music. The Negro church was right near my house when I was a girl.'

Both ladies talked about flowers, and I felt quite soothed by the time I arrived at Atlanta airport. From there I took a bus and then a Tube train, and finally arrived at the centre of Atlanta city. The Tube had either been free, or else I had evaded payment without knowing how. A city of shining skyscrapers, Atlanta seemed very rich, with smart black businessmen everywhere, exquisitely dressed. I came upon a Trailways coach station, a slightly cheaper rival of Greyhound. To my joy, I found that a coach could get me to Jackson, Mississippi, by midnight. If I could only find a place to stay I would be all right. Mrs Celia Henderson, a farmer's wife, would be meeting me at eleven on the following morning.

My coach did not leave for two hours, so I dragged my painfully heavy bag to a row of seats, and sat down. A very old man sat on one side of me, watching television in a lacklustre way. Each seat had a pay-telly attached to it.

'Georgia is boring!' he croaked, switching off his set. 'Whenever I get bored of Georgia, I go to London.'

On the other side of me sat a middle-aged man who wore a cowboy hat with a sprig of coloured feathers pinned on to it by a brooch in the shape of a lorry. Dark, expressive eyes looked at me from the sad face of a failure. He introduced himself, and shook my hand.

'How do, my name is Jerry Masten, an' I'm from Arkansas. I did work in sanitation, but now I've been to truck-driving school. So has my wife, and we're going to drive a truck together as partners. There's a scheme where the government loans you money to start a business, and the truck-driving company lets you have a truck and holds back some money till one day that truck is yours! Then you can travel all over these United States, an' you can choose destinations so you can visit your relatives. I'll probably end up seeing a good many states, even Alaska. If your partner is your wife, your business is bound to thrive. Now I'm just getting the bus down to Arkansas to pick up my truck.'

He proudly showed me photographs of his grandchildren, but could not remember all of their names. Strange how in England juggernaut lorries are cursed as pestilential objects that shake Tudor market towns to pieces. In America they become Trucks, a symbol of Americana. Truck drivers have taken over from cowboys as True Americans. They wear cowboy hats, and sing country and western songs about their trucks. My new friend Jerry Masten was captivated by the Romance of the Truck. I hoped he would not have a rude awakening.

We went to the cafeteria, where I put a record on at random on the video-jukebox.

'That's country. Thank you,' Jerry said simply.

A helpless man, like myself, Jerry shared my fears of missing the coach. However, we both boarded her safely. 'I'd like a window seat, so I can see America,' I told Jerry.

'I hear you, son! I hear you!' he cried, his patriot's face alight with happiness.

The woods of Georgia and Alabama were fiery with autumn leaves. Every time a lorry passed, Jerry would jump up and give a running commentary on it. He was bursting to be a driver.

'You have to stop every so often and weigh your load,' he told me. 'Inspectors look at it. Some bridges you cain't go over if you're over a certain weight.'

Jerry had to change coaches at Birmingham, Alabama, whereas I could stay where I was. So I shook his hand in farewell.

'See America!' he cried in parting.

Somewhere in Birmingham, our coach passed a Negro school where girls in red and yellow, clutching flags, performed a cheer dance to the tune of five enormous tubas. Young men blew lustily, and the tubas turned their gaping brass whale-mouths towards me. Heavily padded football players charged to and fro.

Later in Mississippi, the night woods looked frightening in the heavy rain. A crowd of young Texans boarded the bus, laughing and joking and playing the radio. The driver kept telling them to switch their radio off, but they always turned it on again a moment later.

'God I *hate* Alabama!' an elderly man exclaimed, to their amusement. 'I was in the hospital there at Tuscaloosa, and they didn't allow me to smoke more 'n six cigarettes a day.'

Brooding on man's inhumanity to man, the old man muttered to himself. The Texans laughed, then went on talking about how much they loved Texas. Arriving at Jackson, Mississippi, I tottered exhausted from the coach station, and was imperiously swept into a taxi and taken to the Ramada Inn.

This proved to be a beautiful hotel, with a stuffed grizzly bear towering over the leather armchairs in the Reception Lounge.

'Of course we've got a room,' smiled the glamorous coloured Reception-girl. 'My, so you're from England! Have you seen the Queen? You *have*? I saw the Queen riding in a carriage on T.V., but I wondered if it were really true.'

CHAPTER NINE

Plantation Life

RAIN POURED DOWN as I was waiting in the coach station for Mrs Celia Henderson to come and collect me. She and her husband owned a farm near the Mississippi, and that was all I knew about them. I presumed that they were devout Christians, as their address had been given to me by an acquaintance of mine, a Baptist minister from Aberystwyth. Every year, this Man of God left Wales on a missionary journey. While preaching in Mississippi he had been befriended by the Hendersons, who were Presbyterians, and they had invited him to stay. Now I too was to stay with them. Mrs Henderson was very late. She attended some kind of college in Jackson, and her farm was a long way away.

Meditating on my Baptist friend, I recalled one of his missionary stories from Africa, told to me in simple Welsh wonderment, without a smile.

'My missionary friend and I were sent out to preach the gospel to a village in Kenya that was so remote that I doubt if anyone from the government had ever been there. Ragged thatched hut roofs almost came down to the ground, and the doorways were black holes with chickens running in and out. The people belonged to the Luo tribe, and they were very friendly. They really wanted a church with lots of dressing up, ritual and parades, but we persuaded them against this. My friend knew how to speak their language.

'After we had got settled in our bungalow, we decided to teach the villagers how to use a latrine. The previous missionaries had dug one, complete with a wooden seat with holes in. But the villagers never used it, and just went anywhere in the bush. So we told them how healthy a latrine was.

' "He's talking about the Place of Evil," they began to whisper. They held it in superstitious dread, you see. Next morning we told everyone that we were going to use the latrine, to set an example. From behind huts and behind trees the men and women were timidly creeping after us and watching us.

' "They're going to the Place of Evil," we heard again and again.

'When we reached the latrine, we could see them hiding in the bushes watching us. So very deliberately we lowered our garments and sat down on the wooden bench. But a second later, we jumped up with a shriek! Clouds and clouds of black bats were flying out of the deep trench, buffeting against our bodies with their horrible wings and making the air hideous with their squeaking. So we went back to the village along with everyone else, and after that we used to go in the bush ourselves.'

Of course, this story has to be told in a pop-eyed Welsh accent. My reverie was broken as I looked up, and saw a tall, slim young woman in jeans, with long curly black hair and a very intense American expression on her fashion-model face. She looked as if she had just returned from an aerobics work-out or a karate class.

'Mr Roy Kerridge? Hi, I'm Celia Henderson.'

Rather nervous when driving through Jackson, a large and confusing city, Celia Henderson relaxed as we entered remote Beauregard County in the State of Mississippi. It was still raining steadily. Celia was as unlike a dumpy, apple-cheeked English farmer's wife as anyone I had seen, but she was an interesting person none the less.

'Are you going to write about the black people?' she enquired keenly. 'You're not a Liberal, are you?'

I assured her that I was not. American politics was not for me. 'Liberal' and 'Conservative' had different meanings over here. You could be an American Liberal and see no wrong in Negroes or Russian Communists. Or you could be an American Conservative and see no *good* in Negroes or Russian Communists. For someone such as myself, who disliked Russian Communists but liked most Negroes, there was no label.

'The black people here are all ruined!' Celia lamented, looking very upset. 'They used to have a system called a matriarchy, where men would come and go, but the family would have the same mother. It was different ethics from us, but it worked. Now it's all broken up! Children are having children, and everyone is apathetic! The Welfare cheques have ruined the black people. They've gotten very lazy. In fact, they've gotten so *arrogant*! In the shops, the young people just push you out of the way! Up in the mountains you get a better class of black people. They're more ambitious and pushy than these ones down here.'

'Er – what subject are you studying?' I asked, eager to change the subject.

'I'm going to seminars in Redemptive History,' she told me. 'That's a real interesting Christian subject, and my perfessor is such a clever mayun [man]! He's teaching us about history from the Creation to the first Adam; then the second part of the course takes us to the Second Adam, that's Our Lord. The third part, which we haven't started yet, shows the signs we can expect just before the Second Adam returns.'

It seemed more sensible than the courses that many wives and mothers go in for when they want to be 'fulfilled'. Streams of water were running across the windows of the car, making it difficult for me to see outside.

We seemed to have reached flat, low-lying country, though wooded hills could be seen on my left. Celia told me that her three eldest children were away at college, so I realised that she was yet another forty-year-old girl who looked like twenty. She and her husband would be going to a 'ball game' that night, but I would have her two youngest children for company.

'Oh, look at that turtle crossing the road!' she exclaimed, pointing at a dejected-looking tortoise. Her voice grew harsh, as she pointed out into the rain. 'That's a black subdivision, where they can buy land and build houses. That's a totally black school on the left, with black teachers, and the children leave unable to read or write. The black preachers are all in the pay of the Democrats – you see preachers riding round in great huge cars! Mind you, I don't like to see black people mistreated, you know, made to wait until everyone else is served. I always say, "You were first in the queue, go on ahead!" Some of the old people call a sixty-year-old black man a "boy". That's not right, but it's because, thanks to inbreeding, the black people are just like children. It's Martin Luther King I blame for what's gone wrong with our black people!'

At the mention of this dreaded name, she gritted her teeth for a moment, filled with suppressed rage. Then she went on: 'He's the one! That Martin Luther King brought politics into the black churches! Now the Democrats are spoiling the black people, promising more and more relief if they get voted in. Martin Luther King associated with Communists! Either he was dumb or else he was very clever, and *I* think he was very clever.'

I pondered on what I had heard. Negroes are unique as a race, inasmuch as so many of their white well-wishers are Communists or near-Communists. In fact, to most white people throughout the world, Negroes are a Communist cause, almost as if they were Russians. Colin MacInnes hit the nail on the head when (in his novel *Absolute Beginners*) he depicted a Marxist folklorist who believed that 'Mississippi jail songs are in praise of sputniks'. Being a Communist cause is a terrible burden on Negroes everywhere. When black people seek political solutions to their problems, and turn to white people for help, they often fall into the hands of Communists. Their initial adoration of the kind white people who are helping them often turns to disillusion, as the victims see themselves being used as dupes to further the interests of the Party and the Soviet Union. But to the white sympathisers, Negroes and the Communist Heaven are as one.

I think that Martin Luther King would have preferred his Civil Rights crusade to be wholly a Christian one, but in enlisting white support he *must* have had dealings with Communists or near-Communists. Unlike some South African leaders, he proved strong-minded enough to ride over this difficulty. For all I know, he may have used the Communists, a neat turning of the tables. There had always been a political undercurrent to Negro church life in America, ever since the age of the great spiritual songs. But Martin Luther King certainly *did* bring more politics into the Negro church, and after his untimely death, some Communist or Black Power ideas may have gained a foothold. Rascally preachers, however, often preside over saintly congregations.

'Black people now are just about worthless,' Celia Henderson was saying. Her tense face relaxed, as she swung into a private road among the open fields. 'But *our* black people are precious! They're not like the others. We brought one family, the Joneses, with us when we moved from our old farm in Louisiana. My husband had *their* house built, out of brick, before he even began on *our* house. Then the folk in one o' the cabins have the *sweetest* little cripple boy. I take him to church with me sometimes, 'cos *I* want him to be a preacher.'

By now, the rain had subsided to a low, steady drizzle. To my surprise, I found we were driving up a long straight concrete road between cotton fields. Cotton plants stretched on forever, stalks and stems dotted with white. Through the rainy haze, they looked like giant snowdrops.

'We've picked the cotton on the lower field,' Celia Henderson said. 'But most of our cotton is waiting for the second picking. The rain makes them grow extra shoots, and that's not good.'

Looking ahead, through the windscreen wipers, I saw that our road ran straight to the doors of an immense mansion of brick and wood, standing stark and upright in the centre of a plain of cotton. A new house, it had been built on the classic plan of a plantation Big House. Huge, white Grecian columns beside the front door supported a balcony porch that hung over the wide wooden rocking-chair porch below. Evidently the words 'farm' and 'farmer' were euphemisms for 'plantation' and 'plantation owner'. Mrs Henderson parked the car, and as we hurried in out of the rain, I caught a glimpse of a big, genial, practical-looking man looking at us from a doorway framed by stripped timbers.

My hostess led me through tall wooden doors, below high ceilings hung with chandeliers and through rooms whose walls were lined with books or hung with pictures of Civil War generals. Journey's end was a large, dark 'guest room', with two beautifully made-up four-poster beds. The posts on the beds were slender, and slightly rickety, but the overall impression was one of sombre splendour. I was reminded of the night I had once spent at a haunted castle in Scotland.

'I'll just leave you to freshen up a little, and then you can join us in the dining room,' Celia said.

I chose a bed, unpacked some of my belongings, then drew aside the heavy curtains and looked out of the window. Far away, a line of dark trees marked the boundary of the cotton fields, and near at hand stood a corner of the porch, a column and a rocking chair. Rain hissed down, and all of a sudden a blue flash of lightning exploded over the cotton rows. A moment later, thunder made the tall windows shake. I turned, and made my way through ghostly rooms towards a bright light and the sound of children's voices.

'This here is my husband, Meadow Henderson,' said Celia, darting forward to do the introductions. 'And these are our youngest two children, Alec and Emma.'

A big round-faced man, with short hair and enormous hands, Mr Henderson greeted me with a jovial smile and a handshake. He was the man I had glimpsed earlier. Then he had been in shirtsleeves, but now he was dressed up and on the point of going out.

'We're mighty glad to have you here!' he said sincerely. 'We're a Christian family, so you're in good hands. Celia and I are going out to the game now, but the children will show you where the ice box is at. I like guests who can fend for themselves and don't require no one to *do* nothing for them.'

Although he said this in great good nature, my heart sank at the thought of a renewed diet of ice cream and Perrier water. I needn't have worried, for in fact the Henderson family waited on me hand and foot.

'Hi there, sir,' the children greeted me in chorus.

Alec, the eight-year-old boy, was toothy, blond and full of eager friendliness. His thirteen-year-old sister Emma, a brunette, was dressed in an old-fashioned frock, with white ankle socks. Both children 'sirred' me so much that I felt that I was living in a Bertie Wooster and Jeeves story. At the same time, they both seemed to regard me as a delightful new playmate.

'Pam!' commanded Celia, just before she left. 'Fix our visitor some coffee and hot biscuits.'

'Yes, ma'am,' a soft dutiful voice replied. A slim coloured girl of seventeen, whom I had not noticed before, the maid Pam slipped quietly into the kitchen.

I made friends with the family dogs, a Pekinese and a Golden Labrador, who were showed off with pride by the two children.

'When did you learn to speak English?' Alec asked. 'Is England out of America?'

'He means "outside America",' Emma explained. She had heard of England.

I asked to see their school books, and was impressed by their neat well-written work. Later I found that Celia took great trouble to help them with their homework. My hostess was a complex character. There was more to her than mere colour prejudice. Everything that distinguishes the American South from the rest of the world began here, on the cotton plantation, and here were valuable lessons to be learned.

'Our maid Pam is real sweet,' said Emma. 'Her sister, Catrina, has got cancer. Isn't it sad? Mom and Dad took them here from Louisiana. Sometimes Dad has to take Catrina to hospital in the city. Pam doesn't usually eat with us, but I know you don't mind if she comes and listens to your English talk.'

Pam returned with hot scones, which the family referred to as 'biscuits'. Real biscuits were called 'crackers'. I showed a few carefully selected photographs and Pam looked very interested in the pictures of a West Indian church.

'I'm a Baptist,' she said. 'At our church, we baptise people in the river.'

'Do you have sticky frogs in England?' Alec asked. He pointed, and I saw a green tree frog clinging to the outside of the window, its pale tummy pressed against the glass. A moth flew by, and the frog gave a jump through the air, missed the insect and fastened on to the glass once more, with sucker-tipped fingers and toes. I was most impressed.

'The rain's stopped now, sir,' said Emma. 'Alec, why don't you show our visitor the cotton fields, and I'll help Pam with the washing up.'

'Thank you, Miss Emma,' Pam murmured appreciatively.

Alec frisked around me in happy excitement. We walked back along the concrete path that led through the cotton fields. It had rained so hard that the ditches at the side of the fields were full and brimming over, making our path resemble a causeway over a marsh. Snowballs dangled from the cotton plants, but I was too late in the season to see the mass of white so often shown in pictures of the Old South. Sapling trees had been planted in a long avenue beside our path, and loquacious, long-tailed mocking-birds swooped from tree to tree and out over the fields. Objects that slightly resembled rubbish skips were pointed out to me as 'pallets', used when picking the cotton.

'Won't the rain spoil the cotton?' I asked.

'It doesn't matter at all, as we've already picked our cotton in Louisiana,' Alec said.

A strong smell of polecat-ferret in one place had been made by a skunk, Alec told me. No wonder the early settlers had called the skunk by the name of an Old World animal, the polecat. Drops of rain began to fall once more, so we hurried back into the house, well pleased with our expedition. Alec seemed excited at having shown me the cotton and now offered to show me around the house. Emma came with him. Both children assured me that their parents wouldn't mind.

A long room halfway between a hallway and a wood-and-glass pioneer-style conservatory stretched along one side of the house, tall doorways leading from it into the state rooms. At the end of this gallery, a spiral staircase led up to the family bedrooms. Ferns in great jars grew in the conservatory, and a wooden table and some nearby shelves were decorated with old tin plates and miniature 'bales' of cotton from the fields outside. A large hand-carved and painted wooden decoy of a Canada goose was now used as an ornament. Upstairs, an outdoor balcony-porch ran right around the square-shaped house. There were four-poster beds in each bedroom.

'This is my father's office, sir,' Alec said respectfully. He showed me a room with stacks of paper lying on a large desk. I had seen a similar room in a landowner's house in Wales. 'All these papers show him how much his farmers are earning. He's a farmer, you see, sir, and he has lots of farmers working for him. Some of them are black and some of them are white.'

A small bird room housed a delightful white Cockatiel, which came out of its cage and waddled up and down the table, allowing us to stroke its soft dove-like feathers and tickle its crested head. In a nearby cage, bright finches hopped from perch to perch.

'Our momma can paint pictures,' Emma said proudly. 'This is her picture room. Look!'

I did, and saw a small room lit by a chandelier and cooled by a propeller-like ceiling-fan. All around the walls were bright oil paintings, full of vigour and expression. Apart from a study of black-and-yellow oriole birds clinging to a bough, every single painting showed a cotton plantation in slavery days. Happy slaves sang and danced outside their cabin doors. Others, smiling, singing and waving, worked waist-deep in a snowy sea of cotton. Mules pulled carts laden with cotton, like hay wagons. On the top of the mountains of cotton, happy barefoot slaves sat with legs dangling, enjoying the ride. No white people could be seen in any of the pictures. This was the white Southerners' Dream Time, a vision of the days before the War. It did not closely resemble a contemporary account by the Englishwoman Fanny Kemble, who portrayed slaves who could give their living descendants lessons in apathy and hopelessness. As a dream, Celia Henderson's vision was an attractive one, and I praised the pictures to Alec and Emma.

Now we descended to the cellar, where the children had a playroom. A very sturdy, thick-walled room, the playroom walls were decorated with prints and woodcuts of the Civil War.

'There's a map of the world!' Alec exclaimed, but it proved to be a map of *his* world, the State of Mississippi.

A row of pin-tables filled the room, looking incongruous beside the pictures. The television set had been built into a large wooden chest, and looked like an early pioneer model. Alec switched on and watched a programme about a successful black doctor who lived in suburban style along with his successful all-American black family. Again, no white people intruded on the idyll.

'Do black people really live in fine houses like that?' I asked.

'Oh no,' said Emma. 'It's only make-believe. Do you have black people in England? Are they bad? Ours are bad, they drink all the time. Not all, though – some go to church.'

I did not tell them of the black city gents I had seen in Atlanta, but left them to watch the show while I looked at the books in the great library, a room that adjoined my bedroom. Nearly all the books were about the Civil War, as seen from the Southerner's viewpoint. They ranged from scholarly works, to books of photographs, paintings and newspaper cuttings, down to Reader's Digest volumes of *Gone With The Wind*.

Mr Henderson had not in the least resembled a haughty Southern aristocrat. He looked like a bluff, hard-working farmer. Nevertheless, the slave-owning aristocrat seemed the ideal to which he and his wife aspired. This imaginary figure was no doubt held to be kind to his Negroes, as the Hendersons aspired to be. When present-day Negroes proved ungrateful and unslavelike, the Hendersons were discomfited. I returned to the kitchen, and found that Pam had prepared another meal for us.

Later, the children showed me some family photographs, with Pam looking keenly over their shoulders.

'Mom and Dad don't believe in Halloween, as we're Christians, sir,' Alec explained. 'So we have Reformation Day on the same day instead. That's Dad dressed up as Martin Luther.'

'Is that the Pope, the one he's chasing?' I asked, but Alec had never heard of the Pope. Pam read the captions aloud, and seemed at home in the world of letters. She had evidently left school able to read and write.

'This year we're having a Harvest Festival at Halloween,' said Emma. 'Our church has never had one before.'

It was now time for Emma's piano practice, so we all went upstairs to her music room. Pam, in her capacity of family friend, came along too. She carried herself with a gravity and dignity that would have done credit to a Jane Austen heroine.

To our admiration, Emma tinkled away at old-fashioned Southern hymns with titles such as 'Church In the Wildwood'. Then we played I-Spy, and I found that the children spied not by the first letter, as in England, but by colour – 'I Spy something brown.' Pam was quite good at the game. Next, I asked the children about their play-songs and skipping rhymes, but found them to be exactly like the English ones, even down to the ubiquitous 'lady with the alligator purse'. So I told stories learned from Mrs Brown, my Jamaican friend in London, and finally I sang 'My Old Man's a Dustman'. All too soon, Pam reminded the children that it was time to go to bed.

In the morning, I awoke at seven and heard Celia Henderson giving Pam the orders for the day. Much later, I tottered into the dining room, which opened on to the kitchen. Celia had already driven the children to their private school and returned. Meadow, her husband, was out looking at the cotton.

'I think it's too wet to pick cotton today,' Celia told me. 'Usually Meadow goes out on the cotton fields all day – he works so hard, we daren't disturb him, just make sure that he rests good when he comes home. He directs all the men out there working the cotton pickers. That's our machines – we call them "cotton pickers". Meadow can see all the right places to start picking – he was born to it. Whenever a cotton picker breaks down, Meadow leaves the driver right there and goes to fetch a spare part himself. The black people take the machines out to the fields and then just wait there. They call it "Waiting for the Man". None o' them will start working until Meadow's out there to direct them.

'Anyway, I think today's too wet, so Meadow should be back any minute. I told him he ought to drive you down to Vicksburg. The Union soldiers besieged that city, and the poor people were reduced to eating rats and cats.'

Meadow returned, changed into dry boots, and then genially offered to show me around the cotton country. 'What kind of things do you want to write about?' he asked, as he drove out of the plantation and on to the main road.

'Well, I'm very interested in wild animals,' I replied truthfully. 'When did they kill the last wolf around here, do you know?'

'No, I can't say by rights. We've still got a big old coyote I hear howling outside the house some nights. Just now, we're all of us feeling that we're living through Reconstruction. We're afraid it'll end up with the black man ruling over us. The Welfare system is destroying the black man. Politicians are subverting our black preachers here. You see, a politician will approach the preacher an' buy votes in a circumspect way. The preacher will say, "I need 25,000 dollars for my *campaign* money, if I'm to get folks to vote for you." So he gets the money, shares it out among his flock, an' they all vote for the man who paid it. But luckily, the Lord preserves many country churches, 'cos if their flocks are small the politician won't *bother* with 'em.

'In the old days, before Martin Luther King brought politics to the black people, the pastor of a black church'd have a daytime job. The church would do fund-raising by holding special events. Finally the pastor would go to the plantation owner and he'd help out with paint an' get the roof fixed, like I still do with some o' the country churches. But most o' the churches have gone over to politics.'

Wet-looking cotton fields, the ditches full of muddy water, stretched away across the flat country. The sun had come out now, and we saw two more tortoises crossing the road. With expressions of great caution, they pulled their little round heads into their yellow-and-black shells as the car sped by.

'Box turtles,' Mr Henderson said affably, taking care to miss them. In America, tortoises, turtles and terrapins are all referred to as 'turtles'.

On my left, Negro cabins and little white plank churches nestled at the edge of the woods, on the fringe of the hills. It was difficult to imagine political unrest in such a rural setting. On the other side of the road, cotton stretched on forever. Cotton 'haystacks', tightly packed oblong masses of white wool, fastened over with green tarpaulins, stood in lines of three or four beside the fields. They were called 'modules', Mr Henderson told me. Cotton trailers also stood here and there – roofless menagerie cages on wheels, with bits of cotton sticking to the bars. They were used for transporting the modules. Meadow stopped the car, picked up a loose piece of cotton from the side of the road and handed it to me. It was full of black seeds.

'I'm gonna show you a cotton gin in operation, if I can,' he told me. 'That's where they take all the seeds out.'

Green, ominous, metal dinosaur heads curving from tank-like bases were pointed out to me as cotton pickers. Other machines I saw parked among the fields proved to be combine harvesters for gathering soya beans and crushing machines for packing heaps of loose, picked cotton into modules. Now and again, a lorry would rumble by with a huge load of knobbly timber, symbol of the New South as it had been of the pre-cotton Pioneer South. Mr Henderson showed me a wood-pulping factory far away on the banks of the Mississippi, a distant silver gleam.

'The Mississippi River feeds thirty-nine states,' he told me knowledgeably. Then he reverted to his old fears, and repeated his wife's words about a 'matriarchy' that had 'broken down' leading to 'children having children'. These were clichés that I had heard on the television in one of my traffic-island hotels. One programme showed a fatuous 'concerned' white man lecturing classes of coloured children, earnest twelve-year-olds, and urging them not to be children that had children.

'No, sir, I ain't gon' have no children,' a small boy had solemnly assured him.

All was not well among the coloured people, I was sure, but when *had* it been well? Were the green dinosaur machines their doom or their deliverance?

'It's like the chicken and the egg,' Meadow told me. 'Did the tenant farmers leave for the Ford car factories in Detroit, or did the machines come in because the men had left?'

So saying, he left the road and turned down a muddy lane between the cotton fields.

'Beauregard Planting Co.' read a faded sign. Ramshackle wooden cabins faced the pathway, and the plantation office was merely a larger version of a cabin. A thin, anxious black man with a ragged moustache ran up to Mr Henderson's car window.

'Have you come to pay us, sir?' he asked.

'Sure have,' said Mr Henderson with a smile. He pulled out a pink cheque book and turned the pages, writing 'Two Hundred Dollars' on each one and then tearing it out.

'There's Little Joe and Charlie,' the man reminded him.

When everyone had been paid, the foreman clutching a wad of cheques, Mr Henderson wound up his window and drove on his way. Now we were travelling along narrow plantation roads. My host stopped at a grey, unpainted wooden building, with a porch and a dark interior.

'This is the old commissary store,' he told me, leading me inside. 'It was built long before the War Between the States, and right up till the end of sharecropping it supplied everything for the plantation. During the Depression, these stores minted their own money. We used to call that money "brozen".'

Inside the dark, barn-like shop, I saw an old black stove with a pipe snaking up the wall, a mule plough and other remnants of past times, now kept as souvenirs. After a chat with the present lugubrious proprietor, my host trotted to the door, pausing to show me some old metal P.O. Box Number safes.

'At one time, this was not only a general store, but a post office,' he explained. 'Instead o' just you and me, there'd be 150 customers in there, some years ago. My father owned 850 acres, and had fifty black people working for him. My farm here has 3,000 acres and I employ seven black people. That's why I think, without even having a war with the Yankees, slavery would have died away by itself, like tenant farming. There's a stigma to the name "tenant farmer", to this day.'

By tenant farmer, Mr Henderson seemed to mean 'sharecropper'. He drove on, the road winding between ploughed fields, the property of small independent farmers.

'How tenant farming worked is kind of like this – the white man would loan the tenant a plough and other things he needed for cotton farming, then give him credit at the store for his daily necessities,' my host continued. 'At the end of the season, the white man took the cotton and was s'posed to pay the tenant whatever was owing him. But as the tenants couldn't read or write, they'd nearly always get cheated. The white man would keep the money, an' say, "We broke even." Then he'd furnish 'em up for the next year, an' so on. Finally, though, times got so hard that the white man couldn't even make a profit when he was stealing! So tenant farming came to an end. The tenants each used to hold a few acres, and own a mule and a cow.'

Mr Henderson took his Christian belief seriously, and I understood the disapproval in which he held dishonest landowners. His employees drew wages, as I had seen, but were still tied to the soil, as they were provided with cabin homes that were free, or held at a nominal rent. Repairs were carried out at the estate's expense.

Pointing at a brick house with a garage attached, and a huge outhouse for 'hawgs', Mr Henderson told me that this was the home of a prosperous Negro farmer. Most of the country people, however, lived in dark but cosy-looking wooden cabins, usually on hilly ground. The long slope of shingled roof on the dwellings recalled my missionary friend's description of African huts whose thatch almost reached the ground. Larger than Irish cabins, these creosoted plank homes could contain up to three rooms apiece. Each one, however shed-like, had a shiny car outside. Wheeled cotton trailers at the doors showed the occupation of many of the men.

'I was asked to give a sermon at the black church over yonder,' Mr Henderson said. 'It's the only time I've been lost for words in church! The pastor gave me such a flowery build-up that I got confused and forgot what I was going to say. Most of the churches you see here are still Christian.'

I was entranced to see beautiful waterways stretching beside the road. Bald cypress trees, half pine, half mangrove, grew out of the water, their root-periscopes or knees poking out for yards around their sturdy trunks. Beautiful white egrets stood with delicate coiled necks among the rushes, an Audubon painting come to life. Swallows, looking like their English cousins, swooped and dipped. Branches lay in the shallow water. Each fallen bough held rows of large brown terrapins perched upon it, necks stretching around and clawed feet holding on tightly. As our car drew near, the terrapins let go and all fell head first into the water, 'kerblunkety blink!'

Mr Henderson called the tall egrets 'cranes' and the terrapins 'mud turtles'.

'We've got boocoodles of turtles here!' he told me. 'There was talk of putting alligators in the bayous to eat the turtles. These creeks are called bayous. They look like canals, but they're purely natural waterways.'

We crossed a bridge over a bayou, alarming a blue heron who flew up sharply, with a beating of purple wings. Then we entered an industrial-looking yard full of storehouses and corrugated iron buildings. Modules of cotton stood around everywhere, waiting to go in the gin.

'My cotton gin's more modern and better looking than this one,' Mr Henderson said, 'but it's not working today. The people here won't mind you looking round their gin. It's a Co-op, used by lots of farmers.'

So this was a cotton gin! Amazed, I looked at the strange, jagged zigzaggy factory, which pointed wonky arthritic fingers to the sky. How did it stand upright? The large towered building seemed to be made of patches of corrugated iron, all painted battleship grey. Lethargic black men, one with an Afro hairdo, leaned against a cotton module and watched us cynically. We got out of the car, and I gaped at an enormous elephant trunk hose, its nozzle over a foot in width, which moved around by itself, sucking up heaps of cotton. It was operated by a man sitting high up behind a glass screen, in a crane operator's seat.

A blonde office girl at a switchboard told us to go ahead and look at anything we liked. So in we went. High in the corrugated-iron cathedral roof, sheets and pulleys whirled around, and strange machines rolled to and fro, or pounded, crushed or bit at clouds of tormented cotton. Coloured people were moving rapidly about the floor, working very hard, but in sour ill-humour. None looked us in the eye.

A young woman swept vigorously with a straw broom, a disgusted expression on her face. Perhaps Martin Luther King had raised expectations in the cotton workers which had not been met. Did they yearn for the town, yet fear to leave the security of their cabins? I had no way of telling.

Huge metal square-edged pipes stretched from the floor to the ceiling, like crazy 'Z'-shaped columns. Cotton hurled through them with great force, on a round-the-gin journey to be de-seeded, washed and fluffed up. A carding-type machine, like a printing press with teeth, devoured the cotton as it clamped down again and again, moving with a steady roll. Below the rows of triumphant fangs, a glass panel showed cotton whirling around, the black seeds flung from the white fluff and ricocheting around like melon pips in a spin drier. Dickensian elephant-head devices nodded up and down, and I felt as if I had seen the entire Industrial Revolution in concentrated form. My mind whirling like the cotton, I tottered outside, feebly composing jokes about leaving the gin alone in future. It had been an impressive experience.

I climbed into the car and we moved on towards Vicksburg.

'That farmer's going broke ... that one's selling up,' Meadow Henderson said, pointing at land and houses belonging to white people. 'See, farmers don't like to talk about their troubles, but farming is in a bad way here. It's because o' the World Bank helping out Nigerians and others, lettin' them sell produce as they like, an' makin' up the money. That makes low prices, an' our farmers can't compete.'

We came out on to a main road, and around the next corner, there was the Mississippi River! Wide and shining, with trees on the far shore, it flowed on its way to Vicksburg and eventually to the Gulf of Mexico between the steep artificially raised banks on either side: the levee.

'That's a pretty sorry-looking gin,' Meadow said, pointing down the levee banks. 'It's an old one – prob'ly ran by steam when it was first built. See that old rusty funnel and that big paddle wheel sticking out of the water? That's all that's left o' the last paddle steamer used down here to take the cotton down the river, before they built the railroad.'

'Does any cotton travel down the river now?' I asked.

'Sure does, but we use barges. Now when people here talk about The Flood, they don't mean Noah. They are referring to the terrible flood of 1927. Before that time, we didn't have no national levee system. Each farmer banked up his own piece of levee as best as he could. But after that flood of '27, the Federal Government stepped in and had one mass levee made, strong an' high as could be, along both sides of the whole southern Mississippi. The testing time came in 1973, year of another big flood. Water came up to within six feet o' the levee top, but it held firm.'

As we neared Vicksburg, we passed fields of stacked timber and the factory chimneys of the 'Southern Pulping Co.' beside the river.

'Those logs are waiting to be sprayed,' Meadow Henderson told me. 'They used to soak logs in a millpond to kill parasites, but now there's so many, there ain't a millpond large enough. So they spray 'em.'

A desolate fish-dock greeted us as we entered Vicksburg. The landing stages seemed disused, but one or two warehouses, with shops outside, advertised 'Catfish'.

'This is Catfish Row,' I was told. 'It used to be a real flourishing fish market, with restaurants and everything. They say that the Mississippi Delta begins at the Peabody Hotel in Memphis and ends here at Catfish Row in Vicksburg.'

Mr Henderson drove on through 'downtown Vicksburg', a pleasant street of old shops that were being artily restored so as to compete with the new shopping malls. I hope that this plan will succeed. I have seen American civilisation and it is downtown.

'In England there are places where the whole town is downtown,' I said.

'Is that so? Well, over here, a man wants to live outside of a town, where he can be natural and grow vegetables. What's that? In England they grow *flowers*? Over here, that would be considered too much of a luxury.'

Although Vicksburg had suffered very badly in the Civil War, there were a few fine mansions left. One of the most elegant of these town houses had a sign outside reading 'Bed and Breakfast'. When I had spent a few days in the South in 1982, I had found two items of English civilisation sadly wanting – plastic carrier bags and Bed and Breakfast houses. Now America has discovered the plastic bag and it *thought* it had discovered the Bed and Breakfast. But it had got it wrong. Instead of being a tiny villa-style house in a row of similar houses, charging the cheapest price possible, the American Bed and Breakfast house was a huge antebellum mansion standing in its own grounds, with a nightly rate of one hundred dollars per person. What a mistake!

Mr Henderson drove me to the Vicksburg National Military Park, a grassy hill guarded by long black cannons. It was the site of the fort. Here he parked and sat in religious silence for a few moments, deeply moved. There was a beautiful view of the Mississippi River and its two bridges.

'General Grant, the Yankee leader, thought he could go straight into Vicksburg.' Meadow Henderson spoke in heartfelt tones. 'But he couldn't get past those cannons. The siege lasted for months, and when it was over, there was not a mouse alive in Vicksburg. When Vicksburg fell, the South was lost. The fourth of July, eighteen hunnerd and sixty-three. Oh, the war went on for another two years, but there was no hope after Vicksburg.'

So saying, Mr Henderson drove down to the levee and across the Mississippi Bridge. Here the great river looked far more romantic than it had done at New Orleans. My host showed me the point, along the tree-lined shore, where the Yazoo River joined the Mississippi. A boat chugged by, and passed under us, pulling a flotilla of covered barges, all lashed together like a huge log raft. They were full of cotton, perhaps bound for Manchester.

'Cotton still goes to Lancashire,' Mr Henderson said. 'The Liverpool Index is the world system for pricing cotton.'

I was surprised, as I had thought that the North of England, and Liverpool in particular, had been entirely ruined.

We were now on the far shore, at Mr Henderson's Louisiana estate. Treasure hunters with metal detectors were walking up and down a field of picked cotton, looking for relics of the War. The countryside looked melancholy. Perhaps it was haunted. An old brick silo stood in the middle of the field.

'Those treasure hunters asked my permission to go there,' my host said, saluting them from the car. 'They give me some of the things they find, but they're a bit of a nuisance. General Grant stayed in a house right there, between those trees, but it burnt down recently. This is where I started out, here in Louisiana. My Daddy began as a tenant, then bought his own land.'

In a short while the countryside took on a prosperous air, with cabins tucked beneath the trees and a large white antebellum house, with the usual Greek columns, standing at the top of a rise.

'That's the house where I was born,' Meadow said. 'When I found the farm here was failing, I went ahead and bought a richer farm and had our new house built. I didn't want the children to fall in love with the old house and spend all their lives trying to save it. It's rented out now – better that way. Those houses over there were built by Confederate soldiers who saw this place during the War and were smart enough to come back an' buy land here afterwards. See that mansion? It was moved up here on rollers when they built the levee on its previous site, back in '27.'

A red-tailed hawk swooped over the fields, and a moment later a car passed by, towing a pig along in an open trailer. Mr Henderson wheeled around and headed for home, this time taking a road that ran beside the Yazoo River.

'The Yazoo is almost at flood point now,' he said. 'See, the water has got behind the Yazoo levee and flooded the fields here. That's what we call a "backwater". Look there, at that big bull! It's a Hereford bull with a Charolais cow. That's 'bout the only place you can graze cattle round here – on top o' the levee, where the pasture is good.'

In a thoughtful mood, Meadow Henderson drove home along the old 'Sixty-One Highway'. Before long, he was on his own land once more, driving round corners, under trees and beside the cabins.

'These are the old sort of tenant farmer's house,' he remarked. 'I tore some of them down, an' built new ones. Now see that sorry-lookin' house with the broken window and everything just anyhow? The man there, a kindly good-hearted feller, gets paid exactly the same money as the man in that other house, with flowers an' chickens an' everything neat looking. Every year, the man in that sorry house breaks his window! Every year I have to mend it. Now why does one man break his window, and the other man keep his house decent-looking? It's a puzzle, whichever way you look at it. I can't understand it.'

Faced with the problem of human diversity, my host confessed himself baffled. The superior house was the home of the Joneses, Pam's family.

The head of the household was an elderly man named Casey Jones, Pam's grandfather.

'Casey Jones is the most honourable man I know!' said Mr Henderson gravely. 'That's the family I brought here from Louisiana. They used to work for some people that was cruel to them, but they're safe here.'

As we drove up to the Big House, Mr Henderson asked me what I thought would happen to the white people in South Africa. I could not say. If my host were comparing himself with a white South African, he may have been doing himself an injustice.

Indoors, the children ran to greet us, and Pam had prepared a supper of beefburgers and scrambled eggs. Celia Henderson had just returned from her college.

'Today we did Covenant Theology', she said. 'The Covenant is God's promise to supply a New Creation, as the first Creation warn't good enough.'

'I remember when *you* did the cookin' and prepared everything,' her husband chided her, jokingly.

Standing at the table with closed eyes, he said Grace, and then we all sat down.

'When I get to Heaven, I want to meet Christopher Columbus,' Alec said eagerly. 'I don't suppose I'll recognise him. How will I know him?'

'God will show him to you, I suppose,' said Emma.

On Saturday, Celia and Meadow Henderson left the children with Pam, and took me to see their neighbour, Mrs Epps. Her house lay in a small park screened from the road by trees, and I realised that I had been driven past it the day before.

'Mrs Epps is a wonderful old lady,' Celia told me fervently. 'Her great-grandfather bought this land off the Indians.'

Before calling at the house, we strolled around the gardens in wonderment. Apparently, at the right time of year, the place was ablaze with flowers. Mrs Epps and her daughter Emily were famed horticulturalists in flowerless Mississippi. For the first time in my life I saw persimmons, like shiny waxen oranges, growing on a tree.

'That's no good to eat until the frost hits it,' Mr Henderson said.

Large chunks of petrified wood were laid in a pattern around the roots of the 'simmon tree'. White peacocks strutted proudly across the lawns, and Canada geese swam on a lake surrounded by dark, enormous trees, evergreen oaks, pines and pecans.

'Those geese were reared here as tame, and then their wings were allowed to grow,' Meadow told me. 'Every spring they fly North, and each fall they come back here to the place where they were raised.'

I stopped to look curiously at a little brown volcano of earth in the middle of the lawn.

'That's made by fire ants,' Mr Henderson said. 'They can get all over you in seconds, biting way up your legs.'

I poked a stick into the ants' nest, and the insects rushed up it towards my hand. I hurled both stick and ants away. Two white gazebos stood on the green forest-glade lawn, ornate bandstand or Victorian birdcage-like summer houses. Mrs Epps's house was a tall compact white-columned dwelling, with large windows. A log cabin, made by pioneers, had been brought down from the hills and reassembled as an annexe to the Eppses' home. It had now been sold to another family, the Maxwells. Mr Henderson rang the Eppses' bell, and a cheerful white-haired lady answered the door. This was Mrs Epps's daughter, aged seventy.

We followed her into a large, luxurious front room, where her 106-year-old mother sat in a wheelchair. Mrs Epps was now both blind and deaf, but she realised that company had called and raised her head to murmur a greeting. We sat nursing coffee cups and making polite conversation with the daughter. After a time, the daughter Emily led us on a tour of the house, which was ornately furnished in a somewhat French fashion. The house formed an unfinished square with a courtyard in the centre, a truly delightful place of green banana trees growing around a fountain. French windows opened between white columns so foliated as to resemble palms.

Celia Henderson admired the morning room, where porcelain stood in cabinets below a crystal chandelier. 'What a perfect spot for a wedding!' she exclaimed. 'You must have lots of weddings here!'

To my surprise, I learned that in Mississippi, a minister could marry a couple anywhere, even in a private house. Weddings had indeed taken place in that room.

We then said goodbye to the Eppses and went to call on the Maxwells in their log cabin. Mr Henderson was a bit scornful of Jim Maxwell, as the latter lived off his wife's earnings as a successful hairdresser and a country and western gospel singer.

A lean greybeard, Jim Maxwell welcomed us into a very different sort of home. Huge beams of wood made us duck our heads, and the place was furnished as if it were a frontier museum. A broad axe, used by the pioneers, hung over the large open fireplace, and ox-yokes dangled from the ceiling, transformed into lamps.

'My Daddy used to plough with oxen, using them very yokes,' Jim said proudly. 'Jean's away right now, but this is her latest LP. That there is the harpsichord where she sits and practises her songs.'

Sheet music lay open at a grand old Southern hymn, 'Press On'. One of the cabin windows opened on to the Eppses' courtyard, banana leaves hanging like green curtains. A most un-frontier-like view.

Jim Maxwell proved a garrulous man, and it was some time before we could get back to the children. We found them with their school books spread over the dining-room table.

I looked at Emma's written work, which was of a high standard. The children referred to their private school as a 'grammar school'. Emma showed me a magazine which the children and staff produced every year. It was a 'glossy', like *Vogue*, and full of pictures of healthy, laughing young people, all white. Many of the pictures showed a 'Homecoming', which appeared to be a yearly show-cum-fancy-dress party put on by the school. It beat an English Open Day by a long way.

Alec was struggling with 'American History', then gave up and said he'd wait for his mother to help him.

'I'll tell you some English history while you're waiting,' I said. 'Have you heard of the Battle of Hastings, 1066, and the Norman Conquest of England?'

'No sir. Which side were the Yankees?'

'The Yankees don't come into it. Well, England had a king called Harold, and he was being invaded by two enemies, the Norwegians in the North and the Normans in the South.'

'The South lost!' he said tragically.

'I give up!' I said. 'Now you tell me some American history.'

At once he began with the tale of his hero, Christopher Columbus. No sooner was America discovered than we jumped straight into the Southern Dream Time of happy slaves picking cotton for their benevolent masters. Then came the Civil War, the cause of all evil and the foundation of the modern world. The End. Most adult white Southerners could not have done better, but it was a world-view that could not be shared by coloured people. White students at the newly-integrated University of Mississippi ('Old Miss') had been amazed, in all innocence, when black students had objected to their waving of the Confederate flag.

Celia Henderson returned from giving Pam her orders, and drew a chair close to Alec as she prepared to help him.

'Look, Momma, at this poster I've done for school!' cried Emma, holding up an enormous picture of a bearded Robert E. Lee standing beside a Confederate flag.

Later in the day, when the children were in bed, I went to the library and sat poring over the Hendersons' books. Celia came in to see if I needed anything. Her eyes fell on a picture on the wall, and they filled with tears.

'That's a terrible sight!' she sighed. The old print showed an auction block, and weeping slave families being torn apart and sold to different owners. 'The children do like your stories. I wonder if you would mind, after church tomorrow, going to Pam's house to say hello to her poor sister Catrina. No doubt the children told you about her. I know she would like it if you did go.'

Of course I agreed.

'Let me recommend you some books,' she said, turning to the shelves. 'I'm sure you'll like these paintings by W. A. Walker. They show life as it was before the War. And you *must* read this little book about an old slave called Esau. It's such a sweet, funny true-to-life story. Now if you'll excuse me, I must go to the kitchen and lend Pam a hayund [hand].'

The book of coloured plates by Walker was very interesting, and made no attempt to romanticise Negro life in slavery days. W. A. Walker seemed deeply moved by the pathos of old black men who had given their lives to slavery. Beside laden cotton-wagons manned by healthy young men, sage old Negroes in white beards tottered out their last days, their deeply-etched faces a study in stoicism, their melancholy eyes speaking with eloquence: 'How long?' Corn-cob pipes were clenched between their lips, and their clothes hung in oddly-stitched tatters, their ragged trousers all patch and no trouser. My only criticism was that Walker had given all his subjects bright pink lips. Other paintings of Negroes by Southern white artists in the same book were more realistic but less pathetic, and showed cheerful scenes of squabbling urchins.

Esau's tale was printed in a tiny cloth-bound book dated 1880. Purporting to be a series of letters, it told the story of one Major Tommy who had entrusted all his family silver to a slave named Esau, who drove it away in a mare and cart just before General Sherman's Yankee army arrived on the scene. But the Yankees missed the Tommy plantation, the War ended and fifteen years went by with no Esau and no silver. Major Tommy, believing Esau to have been murdered, advertised for the return of his silver. He was, of course, from an ancient aristocratic English family, and a medieval silver cup with a Latin inscription contained the Luck of the Tommys. According to tradition, whenever a Tommy got married, both bride and groom had to drink water from this cup. Now the Major's daughter was about to marry, but the silver was still missing! Hence his advertisement in a Southern paper.

Letters flooded back to the Major, all from people who had seen Esau. Apparently, the poor slave, who could neither read nor write, had spent ten years in search of his master, trying to get home again. Esau asked everyone he met if they knew Major Tommy. He had visited settlement after settlement, state after state, earning a living by preaching at churches and betting on horse races. The major's mare, Lightning, had given birth to a champion colt, Chain Lightning. Every time Esau described Major Tommy's estate he made it bigger and grander, adding an extra fountain to the one that played in the forecourt. No one recollected having seen any silver with Esau. According to one informant, Esau had finally abandoned his Quest and settled down with a mulatto woman near Birmingham, Alabama.

On the day of the Major's daughter's wedding to a Southern gentleman, a mighty hullabaloo broke out, and here came Esau, thundering into the Major's grounds on the same old cart, with cries of, 'Whoa, Chain Lightning!'

He dismounted, made his way to Major Tommy and asked in an elaborate stage whisper, 'Whar's Nancy?'

'Dead,' replied the surprised Major. Nancy had evidently been Esau's wife.

'Thank Heaven!' Esau cried piously, and produced a handsome new wife and a string of children from a convenient hiding place. He then tore the straw from his cart, produced the silver, and the lucky cup was delivered into the bride and groom's hands just in time.

'I know they say there's Freedom,' Esau announced to the Major, 'but I know that these here Birningham Yallerhammer niggers belong to you,' gesturing at his wife and children. 'That Confederate money you done gave me weren't no good, but I got seven hundred dollars here I won on Chain Lightning.'

'Keep it, Esau, keep it!' cried Major Tommy, embracing his old slave amidst tears of laughter. 'Those Birningham Yallerhammer niggers more than make up the difference!'

Here the story ended. Esau represented the type of Negro most loved and admired by the Southern white mystics who dreamed of the Dream Time. Like many saints, he had never really existed, but unlike most Good Examples he was funny as well as faithful, a New World Sam Weller. His infidelity to Nancy, treated as an amusing peccadillo, would have been deemed shocking if attributed to a white man. Musing on the many facets of the Southern character, I made my way to the kitchen for a cup of coffee before retiring to my four-poster bed.

Sunday was a sunny day, so I made my way to the front porch and chose a comfortable rocking chair from the row of eleven. Looking out on the white nodding heads of the cotton plants, I sat and rocked. All too soon, the call came to go to church. John Edward, a big clean-cut young man who always wore a tie and blazer, had come home from college and would be going with us. We travelled in two cars, and I had Celia at the wheel.

Outside the long, low, school-like Presbyterian Church, the car park was almost full. Well-dressed, good-looking, pleasant-faced white people greeted one another, the men crisp in short hair and ties, the women in white hats and summer frocks. At the crowded church doorway, Celia stopped to introduce me to her friends. 'This is Roy, he's a writer from England. I've just been telling him about the black people here, how *worthless* and *no-good* they are.'

And she stepped into Christ's house.

I followed and found myself in a corridor with a big poster on the wall: 'Heroes of the Reformation.' These heroes included Martin Luther and Oliver Cromwell, for the Reformation had been stretched to take in the Puritans of the seventeenth century. In a large, airy room, rows of pews faced a rostrum, and we were reunited with the rest of the family. After some prayers and songs, the minister rose from the table where he had been seated, and began to pace up and down. He was a peevish-looking man with glasses.

'I'd just like to say a few words,' he announced, 'concerning what deplorable sinners you all are. Your souls are cesspits of iniquity! That's all the more reason why you should revere authority! The Authorities are put there by God. They may be no good, they may be worse than you are, but respect them! It's God's will. Jesus never preached against slavery. He preached that you should be content with what you are. When people like Martin Luther King get up and preach civil unrest, that's not Christianity! I'm a Conservative, and I'm getting tired of these Liberals busting out all over preaching stuff that isn't even *in* God's word!'

With that he lost his temper altogether, and began to splutter with irritation. Apparently he objected to politics in the Negro churches. Composing himself, he launched into his original sermon, and told everyone at length what deplorable sinners they all were. Everyone looked pleased, for it seemed obvious that many of the congregation were of Scottish, or even Ulster Scottish, stock. Being told that they were damned and doomed soothed and delighted them, and gave them an appetite for dinner. Such is the Scottish character, and so it was here in Mississippi.

'Our freedom and our country is based on the Reformation!' the minister exclaimed. 'I don't see why anyone should be a Liberal,' he added petulantly. Then he compared the world below with a community of squatters living in the shadow of a big dam construction. The engineer gave them permission to stay there until the dam was ready, and then the valley would be flooded. It seemed an apt simile in a land where Tennessee Valley Authorities were allowed to run riot. When the dam was nearly ready, some of the people left, but others refused to go, saying it was their right to remain. So the water poured in and drowned the lot of them.

'My friends, we are here by Squatters' Rights!' he concluded his sermon. 'Any moment we may be asked to go.'

With that, there was a song and a prayer and we all left.

Outside, John Edward and all the other smart young college men and teenage schoolboys stood around talking about football, young ladies giggled and enchanting little children chased each other round and round, watched by fond mothers. Meadow Henderson, resplendent in a check blue, green, black and white jacket, jovially greeted his friends and neighbours.

'Hi, Jed, how ya *doin*'? Did you sell your timber? Did you get more than what you paid for it? That's good.'

His voice was drowned by the sound of a goods train, and a line of yellow trucks (or boxcars) chugged by on the nearby track. Each one bore the legend 'Illinois Central'.

'The South lost the War,' Alec repeated thoughtfully in the car on the way home.

That afternoon, I had a surprise when Emma asked me if I wanted to go for a drive.

'I'm allowed to drive, even though I'm thirteen, as long as I stay on our land,' she explained. Alec sat by her side, I climbed into the back of the car, and off we went. After driving for a few minutes she stopped and said, 'There's our stables.'

Near a storage shed filled to the roof with bales of cotton, the Henderson land changed in character to that of a Western ranch. Pastureland for horses adjoined a long building with a wide aisle between rows of pens, clean and smelling of fresh sawdust. Few of the horses were at home. I was reminded of an Antelope House at a zoo. Outside, the horses grazed quietly here and there, behind ranch-type fences. A sawdust circus ring was used for exercising them, I suppose by riding them round and round.

'Now I'll show you our dogs,' Emma said, pointing at a row of pens beneath some trees a hundred yards away. 'Jump in!'

To her astonishment, I insisted on walking the distance, and admired the Henderson beagles and gun-dogs. Then we drove back to the house, where Pam was waiting. In a pre-arranged manner, she took over the wheel.

'That's so we can drive on the highway,' Emma explained.

However, we were only on the highway for a few minutes, and then we crossed back into the shady lane where Negro cabins stood beneath the trees.

'Who lives here?' I asked, as Pam stopped outside a small, plain brick house, which resembled a miniature bungalow. Even as I spoke I recognised it as Casey Jones's home.

'*I* live here,' said Pam in a resolute do-or-die voice, and she led the way to the back door with the children following. I realised that Pam and the Hendersons had been afraid that I would wriggle out of entertaining the cripple girl Catrina. They little knew how much I had been looking forward to the visit.

Alec and Emma rushed happily into the dark little house, very much at home and delighted to be there. Mr Casey Jones rose up from a table where rhythm and blues music played on a transistor, and came to shake my hand, looking flustered. He was a tall shirtsleeved man who looked as if he had spent an active life, his ragged moustache and eyebrows grizzled white. On his head he wore a blue peaked cap.

'This here's another o' my granddaughters, Catrina,' he said, gesturing towards a settee. A wild, dark-skinned girl gave me a wide-eyed glance like a frightened animal. Her right leg had been amputated. Although only thirteen, she looked far more adult than Emma. I sat down beside her and began to tell her about England. She never spoke, but looked at me. Meanwhile, other members of the Jones family emerged from rooms enclosed within the small house by flimsy walls of plywood and veneer. The main room of the house, where I sat, was sparsely furnished and had a stark appearance. However, a modern, brightly-lit kitchen unit had been installed near the back door, which cheered the place up. A small boy appeared from one of the two back rooms, along with a jolly shiny-eyed round-faced young lady called Lily, who seemed quite at ease in my company. Finally a disdainful young lady emerged, who stood aloof in the kitchen unit holding her little baby, who was called Eric. I kept bounding from my seat to shake hands. Everyone except Eric's mother gathered round me admiringly, as if I were a rare pet. Emma and Alec stood smiling proudly, as if to say, 'I told you so!'

I formed the impression that Eric's mother did not like white people very much, so I went out of my way to praise the baby, until she relented and gave me a half-smile. By now I had used up my meagre knowledge of the English Royal Family and the legend of Robin Hood, so I picked up my plastic bag and produced a drawing pad and pencil. My unicorns caused great excitement, and at last Catrina began to talk.

'Draw an elephant,' she whispered.

I did so, and she gave a wicked, mischievous smile. She reminded me very much of a Trinidadian friend in England, also a mischievous girl.

'My, my, will you look at that!' Casey Jones said, studying a unicorn. 'Can you draw a racoon? I surely would be obliged if you could draw me a racoon. Can you draw a pit-bull?'

'These are creatures that they don't have in England, but I'll do my best,' I said.

Unicorns and google-eyed rabbits are my strongest suits, but I drew various creatures at the request of the vivacious Jones family. Catrina now was speaking softly, just as her sister Pam had done when I had first met her.

Finally, to top it all off, I sang 'My Old Man's a Dustman' to wild applause, and made a hasty exit. A future Alan Lomax will probably find the song alive and well in Mississippi, transformed into a blues, and wonder at the strangeness of the lyrics.

No one in England had ever appreciated me like this! They just tell me to shut up. Stage-struck and exhilarated I returned to the Big House, where Celia gave me gushing thanks for my 'trouble'. Much more trouble of that sort and I would become unbearable to live with.

'Don't misunderstand me when I say that Welfare's spoiling the black people,' Mr Henderson said thoughtfully. 'I'm not in favour of starving folks to death as an aid to social reform. There has to be some Relief for the poor. Only thing, it's come about, through gerrymandering politics, that Welfare money is seen as the *only* cure for what's wrong with black folks. At one time, the politicians elected to give the black people loans to buy farms. Gettin' farms for nothing, they just squandered them away. While *other* black folks, who worked for their farms, became real good hill farmers. It's the hill black people make the best farmers. There's more white people in the hills than black, while down here in the Delta it's fifty-fifty.'

He seemed to imply that Negroes in the hills took on 'white ways' from their neighbours, for he went on to say that the Delta needed a 'black middle class'. This view has become something of a cliché, even if true, and has found its way into the race relations jargon of England.

'When a man is well-to-do and middle class, he doesn't want a revolution!' Mr Henderson concluded heartily. I was surprised, as in England those are the only people who *do* want a revolution.

This was to be my last night in the Henderson house, a place of happy memories. As I prepared for bed, a letter slipped under my door. It was a goodbye note from Emma and enclosed a photograph of the whole Henderson family.

In the morning, I said goodbye to the family and to Pam. Mr Henderson stood with eyes closed and boomed out a prayer for my safe journey. Then he drove me to Vicksburg, where I was to catch a Greyhound going South to Natchez, Mississippi.

We stopped at an out-of-the-way café in Vicksburg and he led me round to the back. There, in a little yard, I saw logs lying beside old black ovens. The air smelled strongly of charcoal.

'Most places by the road just do fast food,' Meadow Henderson told me. 'They don't have the leisure to barbecue properly, with charcoal. Unless you knew this place, you'd go right by it. The man deserved to prosper – he started off selling barbecued sandwiches from a stall. Now all the farmers come here when they go to Vicksburg.'

Inside, he greeted a friend ('How's crops?') and then we sat down to a delicious meal. We had slices of hot beef in barbecue sauce, barbecue beans, corn on the cob, hot garlic bread and slices of pickled cucumber. For pudding, we each had a big slice of pecan pie, like a treacle tart with nuts on. Then he saw me to my coach.

So ended my stay on the cotton plantation. It is to the cotton plantation that American black people should go if they are in search of their 'roots'. Here, on bloodstained soil, Negro America was forged; beaten into shape. West Africa's forest mysteries are unlikely to be revealed to the casual visitor, and would frighten him if they were. No, let American 'black origins' be sought for amidst the fields of whitest cotton. Here the chants of the slaves gradually evolved into the soul of America, the blues.

What was Mr Henderson's place in this Southern story? Was he as much a victim of slavery as any of the coloured folk? Born to be a plantation owner and to inherit some fairly preposterous views, he had succeeded in making a triumph out of these disabilities. As he himself might have said of his employee, Mr Casey Jones, Meadow Henderson was one of the most honourable men that I had ever met.

My coach travelled on through the South, away from the cotton lands and back to the kudzu-vine-encrusted woodlands. Black caves opened among trees bowed down by kudzu, and small creeks were transformed into kudzu-tunnels. Now and again, strange tropical waterways could be glimpsed between canyons of towering kudzu. In one of them, I saw a man fishing from a flat-bottomed boat. It would have been interesting to penetrate the kudzu and wade along the waterways in a pair of knee-high boots, fending off snakes and mosquitos. One day somebody is sure to do so, and to write a book entitled *My Life in the Kudzu Hell*.

Soon we came to the town of Port Gibson, heralded by a signpost: 'Too Beautiful to Burn'. Port Gibson had escaped the fate of Vicksburg, where the people had borne the brunt of Northern wrath, and its buildings had been spared. Most interesting of those visible from the roadside was a church whose spire was topped by an enormous gold hand, shining in the sun. One giant gold finger pointed upwards.

On the fringes of Fayette, the coach passed a 'council estate', rows of roughly-made shed-like buildings. A sign, reading 'Martin Luther King Apartments', showed the people for whom they were designated. Fayette seemed in turmoil. The courthouse, once a fine-looking Victorian building, was a newly burnt-out shell. No white people could be seen in this town, a place where bombings and murders had been carried out by white opponents of integrated schools. Black citizens milled around looking wild and distracted. Some laughed, others waved their arms in the air and shouted. At the time, I thought a riot or a Klan atrocity might have take place, but all I learned afterwards was that the courthouse had mysteriously burst into flame on the previous night, when nobody was inside it.

The straight featureless highway lured me into a doze, and then I was at Natchez, sitting beside my bag and looking round for an antique dealer named Jimmy Guercio. He had been recommended to me by an English friend as being brimful of Southern hospitality.

CHAPTER TEN

Natchez and Jackson, Mississippi

A BOYISH MAN, with expressive brown eyes and a neat beard, Jimmy Guercio greeted me as if we had been friends for life. Soon we were speeding towards his house through streets so beautiful they made me gasp. I knew that Natchez had been spared the worst horrors of the Civil War, but I had not known of the mansions which the wealthy slave-owners had built in the town. We passed 'Dunleith', a vision of cool white columns peeping between dark ilex trees, then we slowed down as we entered streets of delightful plank houses, painted white or pink. Front porches faced the pavement, and brick slave quarters could be glimpsed here and there amid the foliage of back gardens.

'Are you a Mexican?' I asked Jimmy, rather tactlessly.

'No, no, my parents came here from Sicily. At first they were very poor, and worked as sharecroppers, picking cotton. Then they opened a grocer's shop here in Natchez, and ran it till they retired. The shop is still there. Here's my place.'

We alighted at a single-storey Spanish-style villa, and entered a front room decorated with beautiful antiques. I was shown to a room with a four-poster bed, and then joined Jimmy in his airy kitchen for a glass of orange juice. Jimmy lived alone in the house, but an elderly coloured maid came in once a day.

The kitchen door opened on to a back lawn fringed by banana trees. I was surprised at the short, chunky blades of grass. Jimmy said it was called 'St Augustine grass'.

After I had unpacked and rested, my new friend took me out to show me the town. It was already dusk, and the streets were lamp-lit. At one corner, we met Jimmy's friends, Paul and Mary Wincherterter, and they invited us to dinner the next day. Jimmy seemed to be very popular in his home town. He was kept busy saying 'Hi' to people, for unlike the people of Goodall Boyville, the citizens of Natchez walked about in the streets. Jimmy greeted a coloured youth, then showed me St Mary's Catholic Church (1841), a magnificent spired building which had once enjoyed cathedral status. It was the place where Jimmy worshipped. Next he led me on, through streets of gigantic solidly-built shops, to a 'Covent-Gardenised' brick railway depot, now converted to an arty shopping precinct. Across the road I saw the Mississippi River, a dark mysterious mass that moved and twinkled in the night.

'Have you heard of Natchez-Under-the-Hill?' Jimmy asked me.

I had not, so Jimmy went on to say that it was the oldest part of Natchez, a place of wooden houses below the main town, by the banks of the river. All through the nineteenth century it had been notorious for its hell-raising saloon life. Here black men and white, rivermen and cowboys had indulged in shootin', drinkin', whorin', gamblin' and droppin' the final 'g's off their words so as to sound more raffish. Now, however, most of the houses had crumbled away from the bank and fallen into the Mississippi – perhaps as a judgment from God. Jimmy led me down a steep path cut slant-wise into the cliff-like banks of the river and we came to a former fishermen's wharf, where solitary drinkers were sitting dispiritedly at the bars of the few remaining saloons.

Just as Jimmy was showing me a gap in the cliff where a house had slid into the Mississippi, a grey animal, between a rat and a cat in size, ran across our path and into an empty garage.

'That's a possum,' Jimmy told me.

It was the first one I had seen alive, though I had seen plenty of them dead on the road. We dined in a log cabin seafood restaurant, and walked back through the gracious streets to our beds.

Leaving his assistant in charge of the antique shop, Jimmy took me next day to see the sacred mounds made by the long-vanished Natchez Indians, who had given the beautiful city its name. He drove on to a road that followed the 'Natchez Trace' through green woodlands. Apparently the Trace was a trail that led up hill and down dale, like Offa's Dyke in Wales. It led from Natchez to Nashville, and had been originally made by herds of bison migrating through the forests. Then it had become an Indian trail, and then (in 1796) the mail coach route. Parts of it still resembled a 'green lane', and I am sure that it must be used by gypsies. Picnickers sat by the roadside, and I saw a run-over armadillo and a dead king snake. Finally we reached the parking space for the Emerald Mound.

This, a sign proclaimed, was the second largest Indian temple-mound in the U.S.A. It had been made by the forerunners of the Natchez Indians in the fourteenth century, and had flourished for three hundred years. I looked, and saw nothing but a tall, bumpy hill. It was hard to imagine an altar at the summit, or the strange fire-worshipping rituals of a bygone age. Just like the Bronze Age forts of England, it had been smoothed down and planted with carefully-mown 'Department of the Environment' lawn grass. I stood on the top of Emerald Mound and looked straight along a flat ridgeway that led to a smaller mound. Running down the ridgeway, I stood on the smaller mound and stared back at the Emerald Mound.

But it was no use. The Red Indians of yesteryear seemed just as remote as the people of the Bronze Age. Children of the conquering race ran up and down the wooden steps, while their parents poured coffee from flasks or threw sticks for their dogs. No Indian ghosts remained, at least not in daylight. I felt vaguely as if I were looking for relics of King Arthur in Wiltshire or Somerset. Negroes still appeared to be the indigenous people of the South. I rejoined Jimmy and he drove me back to Natchez. We nearly added to the roadside death toll, as a red squirrel, russet with a tail of flame, leaped from our path and vanished into the trees.

In a suburb of Natchez stood the remains of an Indian village, fenced around like a park. A path led among tall pecan trees to a large clearing.

'These are wild pecans,' Jimmy said. 'Most of the pecan trees you see round here are domestic, with large nuts.'

Mounds, like buried and neatly grassed-over castle walls, stretched from one end of the clearing to another. Again, the Indian spell had been broken, and it was hard to realise or to care that a village of round huts had once flourished here. Here women had planted maize and men had returned from the forest with slain deer. A little stream that ran beside the village may have been the scene of dalliance and flirtation, as maidens filled their waterpots and braves hung casually around. Now, alas, the place looked more like a golf course. A replica of a wattle-and-daub thatched hut, also in Bronze Age style, stood at one side of the village. A coloured girl of nine or ten was slowly walking round it, feeling the clay with her palms. When she saw me, she stopped, so I tried to look avuncular, and told her that I came from England 'where the Queen lives'.

However, she had not heard of the Queen, and received my explanation with scepticism. 'You mean she's Queen over y'*all?*' she frowned.

Then she saw her brother and signalled to him with a whistle-like shriek, 'Ee-oo-eek!' a finger stretching each corner of her mouth. I had often heard this noise among West Indian children in London, but this was the first time I had seen how it was made. Until now, I had always thought it was a whistle. So I had learned something at the Indian village after all.

On the following evening, the ever-obliging Jimmy drove me to the Church of God of Prophecy in another outlying suburb of Natchez. It was a long, low, brick building nestling under the pines. It was a 'white church', almost a 'poor white' church, and the pastor had been puzzled when visiting Black British members from Wolverhampton had called. In England, 'Prophecy' almost seems a Jamaican church, though London Greeks and Scots also belong to this Pentecostal fellowship.

Sitting in a back pew, I studied the Irish-looking congregation. Simple, warm-hearted people, they greatly admired the antics of a visiting preacher who ran up and down the stage, acting out the adventures of Elijah. Songs were sung from the *Country and Western Gospel Hymnbook*.

An emaciated old lady left her seat among her children and blonde mop-haired grandchildren and announced that she was going to sing a 'psalm'. However, the strange 'white spiritual' that she wailed in a nasal voice had certainly not been written by David.

> 'Jesus met the woman at the well.
> He knew that her soul was bound for hell –
> [Spoken] Think about it!'

When the service was over, the pastor and his wife invited me back to their house. Their home resembled a modern version of the wooden cabins I had seen in Beauregard County. It too stood under trees. Inside, the walls looked as flimsy as those in Casey Jones's house, and the place was sparsely furnished. No matter, the pastor and his wife were in great good spirits. They clutched large brown paper bags.

'We got a good pounding!' the pastor exclaimed with a smile.

'Don't y'all have poundings in England?' his wife asked. 'Every week, the congregation brings us presents of food so we can eat, an' that's called a "pounding". My husband's in the Ministry full time, you see.'

The pounding was tipped out on the table, Grace announced, and we had a feast. I arrived back at Jimmy's with my pockets full of food pressed upon me by the over-pounded pastor.

Jimmy attended St Mary's Catholic Church, where I met him one day after choir practice. The choir were just finishing 'God Rest Ye Merry Gentlemen' as I arrived, for in two months' time it would be Christmas. It was an all-white church, but among Jimmy's friends I met a priest who taught in a 'black school' for Negro Catholics in the country outside Natchez.

'Such bright, intelligent children!' he enthused, his eyes glowing. 'Some of them show truly exceptional talent!'

Jimmy collected another friend, a middle-aged Jewish lady, and the three of us drove merrily over the Mississippi Bridge. It was just after sunset, and the river glowed in the half-light. We walked along a log bridge over a tangle of undergrowth, and entered a large restaurant, which was designed as a mock frontier saloon and trading post. After our meal, we stepped out on to the porch and sat with drinks at a wooden table. A basket of popcorn stood nearby, and the other customers' eyes turned to the forested riverbank below the overhanging porch.

Jimmy told me to watch, and to my entranced delight I saw seven young racoons emerge from the undergrowth. Customers tossed them pieces of popcorn, and they stood up and begged like little monkey-bears. As the pieces of popcorn rolled on the grass, the racoons scrambled about on all fours, not on paws but on four black hands that fitted on their white limbs like gloves. Their dark, fluffy bodies were brindled and grizzled with peppery shades and their ginger bushy tails were ringed with black. All seven racoons peered up at the balcony, standing on their hind legs and gazing intently at the generous humans from bright, nervous and inquisitive eyes. No animal like them exists in Britain, though the badger comes nearest, with its whiffly black-and-white features.

Masked bandits, the racoons now climbed up on to the porch itself with their long-fingered burglars hands, and tried to carry off the popcorn from the source. A waiter emerged from the restaurant, threw out some popcorn and removed the rest. 'Keep back from them, they've got rabies,' he warned us.

None of the racoons looked very mad to me, but I'm sure they could inflict a nasty bite. They jumped off the porch and began hunting for stray scraps of popcorn. Soon they were joined by a giant grey rat with a long dark tail – an opossum! The opossum seemed unable to stand on its hind legs like the racoons, but remained low on the ground. Its eye caught mine, and I winced. Its long-jawed white grinning face wore a wicked, reptilian, alligatorial expression, as befits a marsupial, a mammal allied to the reptiles. Fascinated, I watched this gathering of Uncle Remus creatures until Jimmy and his friend announced that it was time to go.

Jimmy had kindly invited me to stay for a whole week, rather than the day or two I had at first intended. I decided to see some more of Mississippi and spend a day at Jackson. Early in the morning, my Trailways coach pulled out of Natchez, passing a suburban garden where life-size coloured models of white-tailed deer stood in attentive poses as if ready for flight. I dozed as we passed through kudzu jungles with dried-up creeks. Finally we arrived at Vicksburg. Here I had an hour to wait for the Jackson coach, so I roamed around the grassy motorway verges outside the waiting room. Earthy fire ant volcano-trails, familiar to me from the Walt Disney film *Tea for Two Hundred*, spread from the tussocky grass on to the side of the road.

I poked the ant constructions idly with my foot, then looked down and saw the ants were marching vengefully up the outside of my trouser leg. As I leaped in the air and sent them flying with wild swipes, a man slowed down his car and observed, in a laconic drawl, 'I never seen a dance like that.'

In the Walt Disney film, thousands of ants had carried Donald Duck away bodily, and I didn't want that to happen to me! Their tiny acid bites, harmlessly wasted on my trouser leg, left rows of black pin-prick marks. Looking down, I saw the largest ant I had yet seen in America, a King Ant come to avenge the others. It was a big black ant of a kind I have seen in Cornwall. I thought it would be safer in the waiting room, where a hugely fat white man had taken his shoes and socks off and unbuttoned his shirt. In England he would have been assumed a freak or a Trade Unionist, he was so fat.

'Moose-erleeny made the trains run on time,' he observed crossly. 'We need another Moose-erleeny.'

However, the Trailways coach arrived, sparing us from Moose-erleeny, and we were off once more. Passing briefly through cotton country, we finally arrived at Jackson. I had only a few hours there, and I knew what I wanted to see.

'To the zoo, please!' I commanded a taxi driver.

'From England, hey?' he remarked lazily, as he lit a cigarette and steered with one hand. 'What language do y'all speak over there?'

With mounting excitement, I hurried through the turnstiles, and found myself among artificial caves and canyons, green banana trees growing among concrete replicas of the badlands of Colorado. Here, for the first time in my life, I saw a Western grizzly bear; huge, bull-necked and bored, a thick-set version of the European brown bear. For some reason, animals often shown in American nature books, such as grizzlies, pronghorn antelopes, caribou and Rocky Mountain goats, are never seen in English zoos.

Apart from the grizzly, they did not seem to be shown in American zoos, either. Bears, lions, tigers and apes lived on the rockwork terraces. Their living space was not very large, and although the towering rocks gave an illusion of wildness to visitors, to the animals they were merely concrete dens. Elsewhere in the zoo were concrete dens and bars of a more traditional kind. It was not a first-class zoo, but pleasant enough, and the palm-studded antelope and zebra paddocks, enclosed by stone walls and ditches, looked very picturesque.

Visitors seemed to enjoy the zoo enormously. Innocent-looking sweethearts, perhaps out for a day from the country, walked hand in hand. Black and white people strolled happily around, usually with children. Everyone seemed to be enjoying themselves.

A white man pointed out the Giant Anteater to his little daughter: 'Whoo-oo, that big-nosed rascal looks like my Uncle John!'

Outside the zoo I pulled on my white hat to protect me from the sun, and hurried along the edge of the busy main road outside. I had promised Moonie acquaintances in London that I would look up the Jackson Moonies.

Very soon I came to a large grey and white house on a corner. There was no sign outside, but a large coloured family on a nearby porch confirmed that it was the Moonie commune. An interesting church, the Moonies have a name for being anti-Communist, yet their structure has come to resemble that of the Moscow-line Communist Party.

Only one communard was at home, a young Glaswegian called Frank. He welcomed me in, and poured me an orange juice.

'We're persecuted a bit,' he told me. 'The Authorities here don't like us buying houses, and they move us on if we don't register as churches. This place is registered all right. What we've been doing in the South, basically, is buying houses and letting just one couple live there at first, to blend into the environment, like. But if the authorities find out the house is owned by the Family, they make us register or leave. It's no' a bad place, this, but we're hassled a wee bit by the Black Moslems across the road. They dress in white sheets an' all.'

I had met a Black Moslem in New Orleans, who had sold me a paper which claimed that the white man was the devil and one Elijah Mohammed was God. He had been pathetically grateful when I bought the paper, as just like Moonies and Communists he was doomed to stand outside all night until he had sold his quota, or 'fulfilled his norm'.

'My wife's Japanese,' Frank told me with a dreamy smile. 'She's at the Family house at Montgomery, Alabama. We got married at one of the big Family weddings at Korea – there were six thousand of us there.'

This is a part of Moonie-dom or Family life, which is *not* very Communist. Members must be celibate for two or three years after joining, and are then 'matched' with a partner from the other side of the world. Such is the allure of a marriage to an exotic stranger, the stuff of a thousand daydreams about South Sea Islands, that the Church of Moonification will never lack new recruits.

Frank had to leave then, and offered to give me a lift. I asked to be dropped off at the Malaco Recording Studios at West Northside Drive.

'Fit?' he asked, when he was ready. It had been a long time since I had heard anyone say that!

I had long wished to visit Malaco, the company who produced the record 'Down Home Blues'. Run by three white partners, it was one of the few big-time record companies to deal exclusively in Southern black music. Singers and musicians from all over the South hoped to be talent-spotted and signed by Malaco.

When Frank dropped me off at the Malaco forecourt, I stared around in surprise. The studio resembled a garage. It was a long, low, flat-roofed building among rows of others on an industrial strip of roadside. I went inside and spoke to the secretary. Apparently Tommy Couch, who had virtually founded the company so he could record an old blues singer, Mississippi Fred McDowell, was no longer in command. His son had cancer, and this tragedy seemed to have cast a cloud over Malaco. Wolf Stephenson appeared and asked what he could do for me.

He was a tough-looking blond-haired man with his red shirt unbuttoned to allow the enormously long bleached hairs on his chest to grow upwards towards his chin like a reverse beard. As he spoke of Malaco's success, my eyes roved around the waiting room wall. A large poster showed Z. Z. Hill, singer of 'Down Home Blues'. 'Bluesmaster!' a large slogan proclaimed. The latest LP sleeves of blues, soul and gospel singers were plastered over the wall.

One showed a photo of a typical Negro café with a red neon sign in the window, 'Annie Mae's Café'. Annie Mae herself, visible through the window of her café, looked a formidable woman. She was the subject of a song by Little Milton, the only blues singer to be named after a village in Oxfordshire.

Wolf Stephenson mourned the loss of Z. Z. Hill, a fine blues singer who had died a few years ago, when a fractured leg sent a blood clot to his brain.

'We've got no blues singers here today, as we're doing a gospel session,' Wolf told me. 'Johnny Taylor may be looking in, but it's not certain. You're very welcome to sit in the control room and watch a gospel record being cut. It's the Williams Brothers helping out on a track by the Jackson Southernaires. Follow me.'

I entered the rabbit warren of corridors and untidy offices that was Malaco, constantly stopping to shake hands with some of the most sophisticated black people I had met in my life. P.R. Women, Production Managers, Sound Control Engineers – this was a strange and bewildering world. Apart from Wolf and his two partners, it was an all-Negro enterprise.

'We've got a big blues show in Jackson on Saturday night,' Wolf told me. Unfortunately, I would have to be back in Natchez by then. Having reached his office, Wolf introduced me to Engineer Tom Easley, and excused himself: 'I've got a lot on my mind – I'm getting married tomorrow!'

'You from Ingle-land?' Tom asked, impressed. He led me into a small room with a Coke machine and tables and chairs. Here the singers and musicians relaxed between sessions. Steps led up to a control room, where I was allowed to sit and watch a gospel record being made.

Tom and a friend sat at an immense control panel-cum-switchboard-cum-Cape Kennedy rocket firing headquarters. This was a mixing desk where sounds were captured and thrown together in a technological atmosphere as far removed from the origins of blues and gospel music as it would be possible to go. Behind a glass screen, three singers sat perched on stools. Everyone had earphones on. The music had been pre-recorded, and now the words were being stuck on. A guitar and a drum kit reposed in a corner, unused.

As machinery sets my mind in a whirl, I cannot recall with any clarity who was a Williams Brother and who was a Jackson Southernaire. The singers who wandered in and out seemed very sophisticated for gospel singers – tall, worldly, moustachioed men who gave each other odd-looking handshakes and boomed out, 'Hello, my man!' Various technologists shook my hand and asked me questions about England.

Now recording was to continue, and I was asked to keep quiet. My favourite looking singer, a big jolly man called James Burks, sat in the centre of the glass recording tank. A laconic moustache sat on his right and a cloth cap on his left (both with singers attached) and a soft orange glow lit up the proceedings. Their song was called 'You Got a Chance', about God's power to heal the victims of serious illnesses. As they began, moaning soulfully above a guitar from nowhere that kept repeating 'ta ta *ta* ta!', I could see that this was going to be difficult. Just as a film scene has to be shot again and again, so a Malaco song had to be repeated line after line, each phrase captured five times over and only the best one used. This procedure, I was told, was called 'punching in'.

'In Him you must put your trust! He's a strong tower over us!' the three men sang in high soprano voices.

Instructions were flung at them from the control tower (or whatever): 'That's gonna level out! Keep it level. Sounds like a lot of echo.'

For a joke, James Burks switched to a deep Paul Robeson voice. It was a great improvement, but not 'modern' enough to be recorded.

> SINGERS: Even in these times of tribulation . . .
> ENGINEERS: That's good! Let's dub it!
> SINGERS: Just thank the Lord for your salvation.
> ENGINEERS: Cut the Lord off and catch your breath. Salvation still sounds funny. We still not quite together.
> SINGERS: Make up your mind, you're gonna make it.
> ENGINEERS: Hold that same balance just the way you did it. Bring the drums up just a little bit more. All right! [Aside] He'd like to think he's the new Ray Charles.

SINGERS: With the help of God, you know you can take it.
ENGINEERS: That's good, let's dub it!

No wonder gospel music is so tortuous and soul-searing! Lights on the infernal dial shot up or down along with the singers' voices, and tapes spun round and round. I fled from the madhouse into the Coca-Cola room.

A white youth, son of one of the partners, was helping out by stacking boxes. 'I only hear blues and gospel when I come here to Malaco,' he said. 'The radio stations play nothing but rock music.'

I poured myself a drink and sat down at a table near two coloured youths, who introduced themselves politely. They were on stand-by in case their help was needed on a gospel record.

'I'm Granard McClendon, and I live here in Jackson and play the guitar. And this here is my buddy William Hardy from Detroit.'

I told them about the Black British in English cities who imported every American gospel record they could lay their hands on, and practised singing just like their heroes, the Williams Brothers and the Jackson Southernaires.

'I wish the girls from my church in London could be here,' I said. 'They'd faint at the sight of so many gospel records and gospel singers! If you ever come to London you must hear our choir. The Sisters dance round the church in a line singing "This Train".'

'Oh, I know that one!' said Granard. 'A man introduced that song to our church last year.'

I told them about the West Indians who had come to England, and their various forms of music, including 'Toasting'. At this name the boys looked shocked. To a Jamaican, 'toasting' means the quick-witted invention of a string of comic rhymes. But in America, the same term means the lengthy recitation, with appalling obscenities, of the sexual adventures of Shine or of the mythical pimp Stagger Lee. I corrected the misunderstanding.

'West Indian "toasting" doesn't have to be rude – it's allied to reggae music,' I said. 'You can be a reggae person or a gospel person, but not both – there's a gulf between them.'

'That's like our music!' Granard exclaimed.

Suddenly I saw the time, and quickly phoned a taxi to get me to the bus station. Tom Easley and his friends shook my hand, asked if I'd seen the Queen and showered me with priceless blues records from their store room. As I left, staggering under the weight of the records, I looked up at the wall. Hanging there was the large neon sign used for the picture of Annie Mae's Café. I had seen history in the making.

* * *

Back at Natchez, everyone in Jimmy's circle was eagerly looking forward to Halloween. On the great day itself, Jimmy and I spent the morning at a nearby stately home, 'Dunleith'. This was the house I had glimpsed from Jimmy's car on my first day in Natchez. Then it had seemed impressive, but now it appeared as one of a kind, so crammed was Natchez with white columns dreaming away their days behind ilex oaks, and giant magnolia trees.

A pleasant young lady named Margaret Brown showed us around. She explained that the panels that divided the great rooms were there to separate men and ladies after dinner. The present Dunleith had been built in 1856, the year after an earlier house had been burned. White guinea fowl pecked around the steps as we said goodbye to Margaret.

That evening, as party time drew near, Jimmy rushed into the room wearing a hideous bald-browed clown mask, made of rubber. It covered his entire head, a cascade of curly red hair hanging down from the back, white clown marks around the eye slits and a tomato nose. It looked terrible! I hate clowns, and shrank from the sight of my playful host. To my horror, he held up a similar mask for *me* to put on. I refused.

'Aw, c'mon, Roy, you're no fun!' he screamed, jumping up and down in great excitement. 'You *got* to wear a mask at Halloween!'

In the end, I compromised by wearing a paper bat mask. The eye slits did not synchronise with my glasses, and after a time I surreptitiously disposed of the mask.

His mask on his lap, Jimmy drove me to 'Longwood', yet another stately home, where a children's Halloween party was being held. I was a bit annoyed with my host, as he had caught a fine, dark specimen of the American toad in the street near his house and insisted on taking it to the party. Like myself, the toad was not an inveterate party-goer and sat in a bag and glowered.

There was a long drive beneath live oaks and other trees hung with Spanish moss before Longwood appeared, a gleam of white in the darkness. Ghosts made of sheets and pillowcases tied to the trees enlivened our journey. Parents with children strolled happily around the circular driveway in front of the house, which was locked. In a grove of trees on the roundabout-type lawn, dummy witches gathered around a cauldron, hollowed-out orange pumpkins with lit candles inside glared angrily, strange green lights illuminated patches of foliage and tape-recorded monster roars rent the air. Stalls selling food or toys had been set up beside the stables, as well as hoop-la and lucky dips. There were no Guy Fawkes-style bonfires, but the trace of a Harvest Festival could be seen in the bundles of Indian corn which lay beneath the trees.

Few of the adults wore masks, I was pleased to see, but many of the children were dressed as funny little witches, ghosts or goblins. Wildly

elated, Jimmy ran around waving the toad in the bag and asking children
if they wanted to put their hand in and take a sweet. White people from all
walks of life parked their cars and walked around. I wondered if black people
celebrated Halloween. Mocking the forces of evil, even on the one day of
the year when this licence is given, may seem a trifle foolhardy if you
believe in those forces. On the other hand, West African masqueraders,
who expect simple people to think that they are *real* spirits from the
Otherworld, are only a broomstick jump away from Halloween revellers.

Children queued for rides around the estate woods in an open trailer,
pulled by a small motor truck. I queued also, and sat uncomfortably on
the floor of the cart, which had no seats. In a second, we were off, hurtling
along a twisty path beneath the trees at breakneck speed. Various party-
organisers had dressed up as spooks and sat concealed in the shadows
until our cart approached.

'Look at that! Oh no!' the driver boomed out in a mock-scared voice
whenever this occurred.

First of all a mummy, with bandages flapping, rushed roaring towards
us through the pine trees. It reached the trailer and groped blindly over
us, before being overtaken by a sudden turn around the pines. Around
this corner, a girl in white lay 'dead' on the grass, her apron bespattered
with hideous bloodstains. Then we charged in and out of a shed hung
with boughs, where lights flashed on and off mysteriously. Our strangely
jovial driver slowed down at a spot where the sign 'Graveyard' pointed to
three newly-dug graves with lights shining from them. Here the driver
stopped. 'Can some of you get out and check the tyres?' he asked.

There were no volunteers, though all the children looked delighted at
the wonderful treat they were enjoying. We drove on, and a coffin lid
opened to reveal a girl of sixteen or so, dressed as a witch with her throat
cut. She kept lifting the lid up and down and grimacing.

'Oh no, the Chainsaw Massacrer has been here!' the driver exclaimed,
as a bend in the road revealed realistic severed limbs and a blood-
bespattered human trunk lying beneath a cypress tree.

'He's not here today, that's lucky!' the man continued. 'Oh no! Here he
is! But I think we can make it!'

A man rushed out of the blackness brandishing a chainsaw which
roared into life at the touch of a switch. It was a real chainsaw, so I hoped
he knew what he was doing. We overtook him and then encountered
Ninja Man, dressed in a black cat suit with I.R.A. eye slits. He leaped
towards us in a karate attitude, but was felled to the ground by a hero-type
curly-haired stranger, dressed in a Kung Fu outfit. We left them
grappling. A bogey man (pronounced 'booger man' in Natchez) chased us
for the last few yards, and then we were in safety. Both the happy children

and the so-called responsible adults appeared to have been reared on a diet of horror films and videos, their sensibilities dulled.

At the entrance of the great house, a ceremony was about to take place: Crowning the Wicked Witch. A line of little girls dressed as witches were being shepherded along by an adult witch and her consort, Dracula. But Jimmy was impatient to leave for the grown-up party, so I climbed back into his car. Cottontail rabbits scuttled out of the way as we drove down the long woodland path to the main road.

I watched as Jimmy released the toad in the same place where he had found it. It seemed none the worse, but it may have been psychologically scarred. Then he put on his clown mask, and we waited outside the Wincherterters' house. Just as they emerged, with giant mouse ears and whiskers on their faces, a very timid, hesitant coloured woman in her fifties appeared on the driveway, holding a cloth bag.

She stood transfixed for a moment, then whispered in a tiny voice, 'Trick or Treat?'

The idea of her attempting to trick us seemed absurd. Treats, I had been told, were supposed to be sweets, and she seemed a little too old for that. Seeing my hesitancy, she changed her tune.

'My cousin is a cripple, sir. Please give something,' she whispered.

'What kind of cripple?' I asked in surprise.

'Ever so crippled, sir. Three of my brothers are in Heaven and one is in hospital.'

Still looking terrified, the woman crept away with the meagre handful of silver I had given her. Mary Wincherterter scoffed loudly, saying that only children were supposed to go in for Trick or Treat. On our way in the car to the second party, we saw an eager, mischievous-looking troop of black children peeping round grand gateways, each clutching a bag.

We drove up to an elegant house, where a friend of Jimmy's greeted us on the porch. She was dressed as a black slinky vampire lady, with metal snakes hung around her neck. I wished it were not Halloween, so that I could meet people properly and talk to them sensibly. Fortunately, few of the guests were in fancy dress. Some sat outside at tables on the porch, others hovered around a buffet where jambalaya and other Southern delicacies were constantly replenished by a gentle Negro cook. Pumpkins with triangular eyes watched us with suppressed malice. I wandered around the huge house and found that a dummy witch or ghost sat on every chair. A prayer book lay open on a table with a wooden snake curled across the pages.

I ate some jambalaya from a bowl, and made small-talk with a silver-haired woman who looked like an English marchioness. Everyone perked up as two hairy gorillas rushed on to the lawn, performed wild antics for a moment or two, then rushed away Untreated. Presumably they were young bloods of Natchez in disguise. Feeling very awkward, as I'm no use at parties, I sat and talked to a young accountant who seemed to feel the same way.

Just then, a coloured family appeared in the gateway. Five children, aged from five to ten, trotted up to the porch in single file, led by their father, who seemed nervous but with his courage mustered up to do-or-die point. None of the children had any costumes, nor any tricks up their sleeves. All smiled in wonderment, eyes and teeth glinting in the pumpkin candlelight. They were very thin, and so was their young father, who looked shy but proud.

'Trick or Treat?' somebody whispered.

'Ah, bless them!' breathed the Vampire Lady, and every child went away with a reward.

CHAPTER ELEVEN

Black Natchez

O NE SUNNY MORNING, Jimmy handed me a newspaper along with my breakfast omelette, toast and orange juice. He believed in spoiling me. 'I know you're interested in blacks, so I thought you might like to see this,' he said.

Called *The Afro-American*, the paper seemed as dull as its white counterparts, until I reached the Lonely Hearts column. Here I was surprised to see that most of the lonely-hearted girls specified 'No Inmates'. Soon I realised that this was a euphemism for 'prisoners' or 'convicts'. The 'pen pal' section took the opposite line. Among the men who hoped for letters were an 'Incarcerated Male', a 'Lonely Confined Male', a 'Mature and Sensitive Thirty-Year-Old Incarcerated Male' and a simple 'Male Inmate'.

It appeared as if most of the male Negroes in America had been put into prison. However, the paper covered the whole United States, and chiefly dealt with the North. Perhaps matters were different in the South, where (so I had read) over-zealous sheriffs had once sought to restore the Golden Age by herding black vagrants on to glorified slave plantations called 'prison farms'.

Jimmy had tried his best to get me an invitation to one of the last of the 'plantation' State Prisons, the notorious Angola, in Louisiana. Failing in this, he had managed to charm the local Deputy Sheriff into letting me see the Natchez jail. I drank up my black coffee, for I had to report to the Deputy Sheriff's office in two hours time. I needed to roam around the town for a while first to steel my nerves. My eyes followed the advertisement columns down the page, and soon fell on the following: 'National Association for the Advancement of Coloured People (founded 1909). Tenth Annual Freedom Awards Banquet, Saturday, November the First, Natchez Convention Centre, Liberty Road.'

'Why, that's tomorrow!' I cried, showing the advert to Jimmy. 'And it's here in Natchez! Do you think I could go?'

'That'll be no problem,' said my affable host. 'The man who keeps the store next door to mine is black, and he can probably spare me a ticket.'

Leaving Jimmy at his shop, a cool, shady cathedral of art treasures and Audubon paintings, I loped rather aimlessly around the town.

Crowds of young people gathered on the steps of the Natchez Institute, or polytechnic. Most of them were coloured, merry-faced young men in T-shirts and prim girls, all in high good humour. An inscription on the wall read: 'In Commemoration of the Generosity and Far-Seeking Wisdom of Alvaresk Fisk, who Founded this College for the Education Forever of the White Children of Natchez.'

Alas for the Gothamite 'wisdom' of Alvaresk Fisk! Now many of the white children had to seek elsewhere for their segregated Education Forever. In Zimbabwe, the so-called 'integration' of a 'white college' turns it into a 'black college'. A private 'white college' is then opened elsewhere. So thanks to colour prejudice, black people become state-aided, supported to some extent by 'white taxes', which in turn breeds more colour prejudice. I was pleased to see that the Natchez Institute had a few white scholars who mingled happily with the rest.

With a feeling of foreboding, I walked down State Street to the Mississippi 'bluff' or cliff-edge, passing both the present Adams County Jail and the old prison, a macabre antebellum haunted house with boarded-up windows. The two prisons faced the pavement with no outer wall. A white office block, the modern prison shimmered in the sun.

Down on the grassy bluff, beside the blue Mississippi, I discovered a grey stone tablet, 'Erected in Memory of Those who Lost their Lives in the Rhythm Club Fire, April 23rd, 1940.'

Rows of names were inscribed beneath, in several columns. A glimpse at one or two of them – Pearl E. Jackson and Willie Mae Jackson – made me realise that the victims had been black people. I looked up and my eyes met those of a middle-aged coloured woman, who stood respectfully a few yards away from me. She was heavily built, her thick legs clothed in enormous stockings. The eyes that met mine were large and doleful. Sadness personified, the lady may have had nowhere to live.

'What a terrible tragedy!' I said, pointing at the memorial.

'Yes sir, about three hundred people were killed.'

'Oh dear. I hope you didn't lose anyone yourself?'

'No sir.'

I read on, and she silently passed behind me. When I had noted down the inscription, I found that the sad lady was now sitting on the roots of a pecan tree. Below her, in a hollow, an elderly man sat on the ground. He had a white grizzled moustache, and looked almost exactly like Mr Casey Jones back at Beauregard Plantation.

I sat down on a tree stump next to them, and introduced myself, adding that I came from England.

'Sir?' enquired the lady, a female Jeeves.

I introduced myself again, and this time extended a hand for one of the orgies of hand-shaking so beloved of white Americans. This broke the ice at once, and with smiles and much hand-shaking I was introduced to Annie and Billy the Kid, and also to Errol Johnson, a personable young man who happened to stroll along at that moment.

'Yes, that's my full name, Billy the Kid,' the elderly man told me. 'So you're from England! My, my, you're a *long* way from home! We protect your country, you know. Those Russians want to conquer the world, but we won't let them! You don't need to worry none, 'cos those Russians don't dare do a thing for fear o' what *we'd* do. We got bases ringed right round your country. You see, we'll protect you.'

'I know, and I'm grateful,' I said. 'Those Russians – at least the ones in the government – seem to be terrible people.'

It is not often that I meet people whose views accord so closely to my own. The Black South had never seceded, and the Confederate flag held no joys for them. They were Americans and pleased to be recognised as such.

'It's certainly a pleasure to meet Americans and to be in America,' I added, rising to leave, for my appointment with the Deputy Sheriff drew near. My new friends all beamed. They seemed scarcely able to contain their pleasure at being American. In a glow of patriotic fervour, we parted with many waves. Even the doleful Annie looked almost cheerful.

'Land of the Free! We'll protect you!' the Kid called after me.

'Robert Stutzman, Junior, Criminal Deputy of Adams County!' a big man introduced himself to me in the smart Reception office of the prison and sheriff's headquarters. He led me down a long corridor, the walls decorated with colour photographs of dynamite booby traps surrounding marijuana patches in the woods. A breathalyser machine, labelled 'Intoxyliser', stood in one corner.

Finally, we reached his private office, where he gave me a talk on the prison system in Mississippi. A tall frank blue-eyed man, wearing a star and a gun, he closely resembled the sheriff I had met in Georgia. I was impressed by his air of sincerity.

'Now, this is a County Jail,' he told me, 'and each county in this state has to have a jail. The State prison for Mississippi is Parchman Farm, that's for men who've done serious crimes. But seeing that Parchman's overcrowded right now, many of the inmates have been shared around the

County Jails. For instance, we got twenty-two to twenty-five men who should be in the state prison. This has brought problems, 'cos it's brought the County Jails under Federal court rules an' there's been a lot of changes. Nowadays, all the prisoners have got rights, same as folks on the outside.'

He paused a moment for this to sink in, and then he went on. 'Most important o' these rights is that we can't make the men work if they don't want to. Matter o' fact, we got no workshops here if they *do* want to! Up at Parchman, in Sunflower County, where the inmates used to work outdoors all day, now they only work if they want to! The whole prison farm is overgrown and going to waste.'

This was bad news for all the Lomax-inspired worksong-collectors with their portable tape recorders.

'At Angola, in Louisiana, they still make 'em work, picking cotton an' cuttin' sugar cane. But not in Mississippi. They have freedom of religion here now, and some o' these men seem to pull religions out of the air! Black Moslems with special diets, and I don't know what! Church ministers are allowed into the prison to talk to the men. This is a four-storey building, with seventy-two cells. I can't take you into the women's sections, the state section or the male juvenile block. We call 'em male juveniles – that's boys aged twelve to eighteen years. Women and juveniles have their own special officers, of course. We got a Detox Tank for drunks, that's where they sober up, an' what more can I tell you? You'd better come see for yourself.'

I followed him outside, and he first of all showed me a Holding Cell, the equivalent of a police cell in Britain. A bare room, the only decoration was an inscription carved on one wall: 'I Had a Dream That I'll be Free One Day.'

With great lockings and unlockings of doors, he led me into a room so jam-packed with gleaming technology as to put Malaco recording studios to shame. This was the control room for the whole prison. I was shown banks of buttons, flashing lights galore, a battery of closed-circuit televisions and impressive radio devices. Stutzman's right-hand man here was a very alert, smartly-dressed Negro, an eager young man who clearly took pride in his job. As Stutzman showed me around, I realised that no wardens patrolled the prison regularly. Everything was done at the press of a control-room button. Doors opened or shut, messages were delivered, all without the officers leaving their desks. With a shock, I learned that the prisoners were kept in their cells for *nineteen hours a day*. There was no exercise yard.

'Now, I'll just put this in here,' said Deputy Stutzman, removing his gun and shutting it in a locker, 'and we can be on our way.'

Throughout my trip around the prison, every door was opened and shut, self-unlocking and locking, at the touch of a button from the control room. At every doorway, Stutzman would speak into a radio and inform his cohort downstairs where he was, and the door would open and close. Sometimes his helper would be occupied at another task, and we would have to wait until he returned and took his order. By this means, Stutzman explained, no guard with keys could be seized by the men, his gun wrested from him and a 1930s 'prison break' film re-enacted in real life. Warder Technology grimly kept the men in their places, ridiculous 'rights' and all. Lifts took us from one floor to another. From top to bottom, the prison gleamed with modernity, the Victorian grimness of an English jail replaced by a more up-to-date inhumanity.

First of all, I was allowed a glimpse into a room for men who had committed 'misdemeanours', or fairly trivial offences. An open dormitory, with tables, but no decorations of any kind, it seemed an easy-going place.

'Hullo there!' the Deputy greeted the men, who gave him cordial glances. 'Most of these men are trusties,' he added in an undertone. A sag-bellied black man and a sprightly white youth with long hair recommenced their animated conversation as we left. Normal prison uniform seemed to be trousers and a white vest.

'This is the Recreation Area,' announced Deputy Stutzman, as his assistant downstairs opened the door. It was a small room with two tables, evidently used at mealtimes by the men I had just seen.

Another door opened, and I was shown a Cell Block for more serious offenders. I could only peep through a barred door into a lion house corridor (without the smells) of rows of cages, the thick bars all painted an institutional brown. Barred from floor to ceiling at the front only, the cells lined the walls, each containing one man, one bed and a gleaming stainless steel toilet. There was little room for anything else. No personal comforts or touches seemed to be allowed, no books, radios or pictures on the walls. Their 'rights' had deprived the men of their freedom to go out and work, thereby making friends and establishing a camaraderie of sorts. All they could do was lie on their beds and stare out through the bars. At least one of the prisoners, in the lengthy cell block, was a white man. None took any notice of us.

'These men don't even need to be moved out to get their meals,' Stutzman told me proudly. 'See these bolted metal hatches along the passage here? They open on to the cells, so you just place a meal inside, and slam the hatch shut again. That door leads into the women's prison. Even I can't go in there unless I'm with a female officer.'

Our lift glided to the second floor. Open Sesame, and I was shown a glimpse into a Cell Block exactly like the one I had just seen. The prisoners here were 'felons', a serious category, and they were serving several years apiece. I could see no white man here, though not all the cage doors were visible from where I stood. The saddest black people I have ever seen in my life turned yearning expressions towards me, and I felt deeply moved. Not one man seemed to have an evil or criminal face, although they may have been convicted on sound evidence. Still, it was hard for me to think of their possible victims when those soulful eyes were looking into mine. In the cell nearest to me, a man in a white vest lay face downwards on his bed, and as we left, he raised his head. I managed to give him a slight shrug.

'It's a funny thing!' said Deputy Stutzman, 'but these men usually curse and spit at you when you come up here. You have to take it! If you hit a man, he can sue you. I wonder why they didn't do it today.'

One last lift ride, and we were on the roof. It was a flat roof, with unsightly air conditioning machinery covering most of it. I wondered why we were there, but Robert Stutzman soon enlightened me.

'Look at this roof! Now many people are suggesting that this be made into an exercise yard!'

'Why, the prisoners would throw each other over the edge!' I exclaimed.

'Exactly, that's what I tell 'em! We'd have to make a whole cage with a roof here, and even then, the air conditioning plant takes up most of the space!' he said indignantly. We got back in the lift, and sailed down to the ground floor.

Here, in the control room, he greeted his colleagues heartily, and retrieved his gun. I was shown a glimpse of the prisoners' files, not the ones that come out of cakes, but the documentary kind. Each prisoner was categorised by race. Most of them were B.M.s or Black Males. Typical crimes were burglary, shoplifting and sexual battering. I presume that this was wife-beating.

Last of all, before Deputy Stutzman returned me to his office, I was shown the Visitors' room. Prisoners could face their loved ones through a transparent grille.

'That there is a Sallyport,' Robert Stutzman announced, pointing at a small door. 'If any visitor, like a mother or girlfriend, brings a present in, it has to go through that door, where it's electronically scanned. Anything in there that shouldn't be, the doors lock automatically and she's already *in* jail.'

I left Adams County Jail by the art gallery corridor, whose pictures showed heaps of seized syringes and other drug equipment, together with spiked boards used by marijuana cultivators to trip up their foes.

Before Robert Stutzman and I finally parted, I asked him why almost all the prisoners were black people.

'They think differently from the way we do,' he smiled. 'Also, their sexual mores are not those of white people. All the same, we use some discretion. We never put a white man on an all-black Block, or vice-versa.'

I was halfway towards Jimmy's shop before I began to wonder where he could find an all-*white* block in the Adams County Jail.

To my delight, Jimmy succeeded in getting me a ticket for the N.A.A.C.P. banquet. That night there was to be a mouth-watering blues show at the Ambassador Lounge in Pine Street.

'Little Johnny Taylor ("Part Time Love")', the poster read, 'Gary B. B. Coleman and Mean Jean.' Mean Jean, to judge by her picture, looked very like Joan Magee, the blues and soul singer of Bourbon Street; I knew now that Coleman's initials 'B. B.' stood for Blues Boy, and indicated that he sang in the style of the popular blues singer, B. B. King. I couldn't go to the show, as it coincided with the N.A.A.C.P. meeting, but I went along to look at Pine Street itself. Directly across the road from Jimmy's shop at 701 Franklin Street, the Ambassador Lounge marked the raffish frontier of the 'black quarter' where white men sometimes ventured a few yards in search of prostitutes. Respectable 'black streets' lay beyond.

A shabby little street, Pine Street that day was brimful of life. Every second doorway seemed to be a bar, with loud soul music blaring from the juke boxes. Big tubby men lounged outside in the street, talking and laughing. Many of them looked like rascals. Some sat on the kerbs, grinning wickedly, like bearded Fats Wallers in hand-me-down clothes. All ignored me. I crossed the road and went into a pub called the Harlem Hotel.

It was a dark place, lit by red lights, with a pool table, Space Invader machines, and a wall-long row of tables and chairs. Men and boys of all ages, from fourteen to seventy, crowded the lengthy interior. All looked at me stony-faced. There were few women there, but one of the few sat on the bar stool next to mine. A stocky, red-lipsticked young woman, her eyes said, 'Touch me if you dare.' Clearly, she could give Mean Jean lessons in meanness. I ordered a Budweiser and the big bald barman produced the tin in silence.

It occurred to me that if the place were an hotel, presumably for 'coloureds only', then perhaps my sister Amina could stay there when she joined me from London. 'Do you do accommodation here?' I enquired of the barman. 'It's not for me, it's for a friend of mine. This is her photograph.'

'No, we don't do rooms,' the man said woodenly.

'Is y'all from England?' the girl beside me asked.

'Yes, madam,' I replied. 'Do you want to see some pictures of England?'

I selected a few photographs from my pack, not wishing to go into the whole story of my African stepfather, my brothers and sisters, Jamaican in-laws and so on. However, the girl took the rest of the photographs uninvited, so I *did* tell her the whole story. She never cracked a smile, but looked at me musingly. I bought her a drink, and as I did so, a thin man in a peaked cap and raggy moustache came over and stared at the pictures over my shoulder.

'And this is my little nephew,' I was saying, in the same debonair tone with which I had introduced myself. At the same time, out of the corner of my eye, I could see the thin man return to his friends gathered round the pool table and whisper something to them behind his hand. Then he returned to the pictures, stared a while, then slipped back to his friends and sniggered behind his hand. Finally he addressed me directly.

'You may not know it, but you are in great danger here,' he said.

'Why is that?' I enquired.

'That's on account of the colour of your skin,' he explained, prodding his own cheek with a forefinger to make his meaning absolutely clear. 'You see, this is a rough neighbourhood. I don't have any prejudice myself. Nor does my brother over there' – pointing – 'but a lot of people here have prejudice, and they might decide to harm you. There's a lot of hate here, black against white and white against black.'

'Oh, I didn't know that. Perhaps you'd better see me to the corner of Franklin Street, as it's dark outside now. Have a drink first. My name's Roy, what's yours?'

'Charles. That's my wife there you just bought a drink.'

'Really? Any children?'

'Yeah, a boy and a girl, Anthony and Crystal.'

'Oh. I wonder if they like unicorns?'

So saying, I pulled my trump card, the drawing pad, out of my plastic bag and on to the bar. Within a minute, I was drawing unicorns to beat the band, augmenting them with google-eyed rabbits. When in doubt, draw unicorns, that's my motto. They were an instant success and soon I was tearing sheet after sheet of take-home unicorns from my book to satisfy the popular demand. ('Well, looky *here*! All *right*!')

Toast of the Harlem Hotel and very much in my element, I was kept busy turning down drinks, as I prefer to keep a clear head when drawing unicorns. A big fat young man with a bushy moustache held back the pressing crowds in return for a unicorn or two. Most of my pictures went to Charles, though I felt rather moved by the sight of an old man with grey hair who gazed at my sub-standard Disney drawings in passionate amazement. Finally, I waved them all goodbye, and Charles and I set off.

Outside, a few jovial men slapped their thighs and told each other jokes, and it became obvious that a bodyguard was unnecessary. Nevertheless, it was interesting talking to Charles.

'No one dares mess with my wife back at the bar. She can take care of herself,' he said, and I could believe it.

Together we walked down deserted Franklin Street in the lamplight, past Jimmy's shop and all the other shops. I told Charles my life story and he told me of his frustrations in Natchez, a town where he had to shun white people and found it impossible to better himself.

'You see these long fingers?' he asked, showing me his hands. 'These are piano-playing fingers. I love piano and guitar, but nobody wouldn't teach me.'

I asked him if he knew Sammy Price, a legendary piano player my sister had met in a club in Harlem, and he said he owned some of Sammy's records. He accompanied me as far as St Mary's Catholic church, near Jimmy Guercio's house, carefully steering me past a wooded square where he claimed 'a guy who robs people' might be lurking. At the beautiful porch of St Mary's he stopped.

'I ain't going no further here. Now I'm gonna slip through the back alleys to the black side of town. I could be shot here, just for talkin' to you! See, if the sheriff saw me here, he'd straightaway think I was robbing you. Supposing there was a robbery here, an' someone had seen me in a white district an' described me, brown trousers an' so on, I'd get arrested.'

'Do you want me to see you back to Pine Street?' I asked.

'No, I'm nervous here, but not scared. I can be back in less than five minutes. I won't never forget how you drew those pictures for Anthony and Crystal. So you're staying down that fine street? Are you staying with black people?'

He seemed disappointed when I said no, as if hoping that some black people in Natchez might be able to live in 'the white district'.

'Well Roy, I don't suppose I'll ever see you again!' he said, with great emphasis, looking me straight in the eye and shaking hands firmly.

'If I live right, and get to Heaven, I'll certainly see you there,' I said.

He gave a half-smile and was gone. I walked down to Jimmy's house thinking of George Orwell's poem about the Italian soldier.

> Good luck go with you, Italian soldier!
> But luck is not for the brave . . .

Jimmy dropped me off at the Convention Centre, a vast white building in the middle of nowhere. A smartly dressed young girl took my ticket with a smile, and ushered me to a table. A vast hall, the Centre was filling up rapidly, as guests took their seats at the rows of tables provided. I sat between a bookie-like man in a check suit and a churchy woman with glossy hair. To the left of the rows of tables was a stage and rostrum, to the right a lengthy buffet table. More women than men were present and, except for their lipstick, they looked almost exactly like Pentecostal West

Indians in England. In fact, the whole atmosphere of the Freedom
Awards Banquet was that of a Pentecostal Wedding Reception. Fresh
white tablecloths and sparkling cutlery were the order of the day. Instead
of the roar of conversation, loud callings-out across the hall and shrieks of
laughter that distinguish a West Indian and Black British occasion,
manners were restrained and voices quiet. Soon every seat was filled, and
the evening's programme began.

Dr Benny Wright, the toastmaster, opened with a brisk speech, and
introduced a girl who sang a gospel song, 'I'm On My Way', in
impassioned style. Dr Ben, I saw from my programme, had a dentist's
surgery in North Pine Street. Nearly all the businessmen who advertised
on the back of the programme were in the same street, evidently the
respectable end of the rowdy street I had visited. If politics had entered
the coloured churches, I realised, so had Christianity entered politics.
The two were mixed together, as I could see by looking at the four or five
white visitors. Blue-eyed men in short hair and neat suits, they were
obviously pastors. The N.A.A.C.P. had supported Martin Luther King in
his Freedom Marches campaign.

My neighbours smiled at me and made small talk. To great applause,
the white Mayor of Natchez, Mayor Byrne, took the pulpit. According to
Jimmy, he lived in an antebellum house and mixed with the Pilgrimage
Garden set, the Natchez upper class. Now he spoke of his involvement
with the Civil Rights marches of the sixties, when 'here in Natchez we
had shootings and bombings'. We then had to sing a hymn from our
programme, asking that we may 'Forever stand – True to our God and
true to our native land.' Lengthy prayers followed, and more gospel
singing from a green-jacketed male quartet: 'Is your name in the Lord's
little book?' Then we all filed off for dinner.

'There's nothing like this in England,' I said to the woman in front of
me, as we queued.

'Perhaps there doesn't have to be,' she observed.

Soon we were back in our places, the menfolk in their Moss Bros. suits
gravely cutting the chicken legs with the tips of their dainty knives and
forks.

For pudding, we were all served personally with a tub of delicious
Taking Care of Business Yoghurt, made by an N.A.A.C.P. businessman
from his own recipe. Members mounted the stage one by one to receive
awards for fund-raising and other activities. Most of the paper awards
went to women.

'I felt so proud as a girl to see Joe Louis fight and to hear Mahalia
Jackson sing!' one woman announced. 'Now I'm proud to be American,
and proud of you all in the N.A.A.C.P.'

The evening's main speaker, the Mayor of Ferriday, Louisiana, took

the rostrum. A big black man with glasses, he was named Sammy Davis
Junior, but was no relation to the show business personality.

'Marching for Civil Rights might be over!' he boomed, 'but that doesn't
mean to say that all Civil Rights are won! We want a black empowerment.
Not Black Power, none of that clenched fist stuff, but a hold on business,
an enablement to buy land and own property. How many of us know how
to do this? How many black-owned hot dog stands in this city? None at
all, I believe. We got to do it ourselves.

'You all know about the shoe-shine boy in Chicago? He was shining a
white man's shoes one day and he asked, "What's your job, sir?"

' "I'm a chemist," the man replied.

' "What's that?"

' "Well, I mix up potions and stuff."

'So the shoe-shine boy asked, "Could you mix something that could
make my hair straight?"

' "Sure could."

'So he mixed him up something, and sure enough, it made that shoe-
shine boy's hair straight! So he sold some to his brothers, and 'fore you
know where you are, that shoe-shine boy had a whole flourishing business
on his hands!'

Mayor Davis went on, in his bluff way, to pay tribute to Jimmy Carter
and Rev. Jesse Jackson, a pretty pair who surely deserve each other.
Statistics revealed, he claimed, that the worst town for segregation in
America was Boston, and the best was New Orleans. (Before the Civil
War, New Orleans had a large population of free Negroes, augmented by
French-speaking mulattos who had fled from the 'black rule' of Haiti.
Hence the unique atmosphere of the city.)

'Black people now work in white offices,' Mayor Davis continued. 'But
have you ever met anyone like *this*, a character who boasts, "All I do in
this job is drink coffee. Then later I clear up the coffee cups." He's so
pleased at his easy job, he hasn't noticed that he's been reduced to *janitor*!
Y'all know someone like that!

'I'd like to finish with a story of a wise man addressin' a meeting. This
wise man is suddenly challenged by a youth holding a dove. The youth
says, "Mr Wise Man, is this dove dead or alive?"

' "Oh oh!" The wise man thinks, "If I say it's dead, he'll release it and
it'll fly away. but if I say it's alive, he'll crush it in his hand and it'll fall
dead."

'So he says, "It's in your hands!"

'Yes, people, when you ask how we black people gonna succeed in life,
I say – it's in *your hands*!'

With that, the Mayor sat down to an avalanche of applause.

'The Mayor always *did* talk too long,' somebody said ungratefully.

Reverend Sherman Berry, who had led the prayers earlier, now led the singing, as the whole Convention sang 'We Shall Overcome' with crossed arms, as if it were 'Auld Lang Syne'. I joined in as best I could, which seemed to please the people at my table. Seeing my chance, I begged a lift back to Jimmy's. After the singing, which was embellished by all kinds of private frills, moans and 'amens', the Rev. pronounced the Benediction. Everybody streamed outside.

My lift had been begged from the lady who had been sitting on my left, and her friend. Both were a bit uneasy of me, and called me 'sir'. I began to talk about politics, telling them of the newspaper my mother and stepfather used to publish in London, *The African Voice*. Their unease continued, and finally one of the women blurted out, 'Do they have Christianity in England? Do they know the blessed Holy Bible?'

'Of course they do!' I answered. 'The Queen is the head of the Church, Defender of the Faith.'

This reply delighted them, and we talked merrily of church doings all the way back to Jimmy's.

There had seemed to have been a confusion of aims at the Natchez branch of the N.A.A.C.P. The main interest of the members was the Christian religion, yet the leaders had firmly espoused the American idea of salvation through business. Did they wish to make black people self-supporting? If, as I believe, they wished to be accepted as friends and neighbours of white people, then salvation was *not* in their hands.

Light streamed through the window shutters of Jimmy's palatial villa, sending bars across my four-poster bed. I had to leave Natchez that morning. As I was packing, I could hear Jimmy talking to a friend outside.

'I went to an N.A.A.C.P. meeting once,' the friend was saying. 'I had to be careful no one saw me coming out.'

Finally I had to take my leave of the lovely garden town. Jimmy drove me to the Greyhound coach station, passing a terrible-looking school with a rusty wire-netting fence, broken swings and a dirty building on point of collapse.

'That's the black elementary school,' said Jimmy. Good teachers and bright children can thrive in the ugliest and poorest of schools, and for all I know this may apply to Natchez.

There was also an all-black high school in Natchez. These schools were segregated by neighbourhood, not by law.

I bought a Greyhound ticket to Shreveport, Louisiana, 'change at Vicksburg'. The clerk served me, and then went on telling a friend about the day he had been held up at gunpoint. Jimmy was chatting away, as I looked around, waiting for the Greyhound. Suddenly, I noticed a building with a large hoarding outside, 'Taking Care of Business Yoghurt.'

'Look Jimmy! That firm's run by a coloured bloke who was at the meeting last night!' I exclaimed. 'He gave us each a tub of yoghurt.'

'Well I'll be damned!' Jimmy whistled in surprise.

Here came the Greyhound, silver, red and blue, and I said farewell to the effervescent Jimmy and rode off in search of more adventures.

CHAPTER TWELVE

Key to the Highway

'CLOUDS OF JOY', a sign by the road announced, advertising a gospel music concert. But as my Greyhound nosed into Vicksburg, the sky was overcast with gloomy clouds of rain. In the tiny waiting room and office, a fat white man in vest and baggy trousers slopped around on bare corn-encrusted feet enquiring about the bus to Shreveport. I knew nothing of Shreveport, but it seemed a good place to stop for the night before going on to Arkansas. Pictures on the waiting-room wall advertised lost or runaway children. Most of them were ten years old. Each smiling, innocent face was labelled either 'Black' or 'Caucasian'.

The Shreveport Greyhound arrived and we were off, over the Mississippi bridge and into Louisiana. After a while, we came to a university town called Grambling. It was an all-black university, and the smartly dressed scholars hurrying to and fro seemed to be bubbling over with inner merriment and delight. Part of the university was called the 'Booker T. Washington Complex'.

By now I had finished reading Booker T. Washington's remarkable autobiography, *Up from Slavery*. The Civil War delivered Booker from slavery early in life. All his considerable energy was spent in forming a Negro college that would do more than produce third-rate preachers or perpetual students, but would give the students practical skills. A tremendously earnest, Christian and hard-working man, he believed that if coloured people would prove their usefulness to white people, then the two races would each find the other indispensable. His favourite story, similar but better than the tale of the Wise Man and the Dove, was of a ship lost at sea in a fog, with no water. Finally the fog lifted and the captain spied another ship. Frantically he signalled for water. Back came the message: 'Let down your bucket where you are.' The captain of the first ship couldn't understand this, for sea water is no use for drinking. Always the message was the same, so in the end he obeyed. Behold the water was sweet, for they had entered the estuary of the mighty River Amazon!

To white employers looking round for skilled men, Booker gestured towards the Negro quarter and said, 'Don't look outside the South. Let down your bucket where you are.' To black people seeking better opportunities, he would say the same thing, pointing towards the white Southerners.

To applause from white Southerners, many of whom subscribed money to his foundation, he would explain that he wished to bring the races together *commercially* but not *socially*. For this viewpoint he has been heavily criticised by 'black militants' in our own day. The white men who cheered and stamped when Booker T. said that a man's social life was his own business seem to me to have overlooked a note of cautious irony and pregnant meaning in the savant's words.

'Your social life is your own affair. If you won't be friendly, and if you must be standoffish, then so be it. The reproach is on your own head,' Booker T. Washington seemed to be saying.

We were now travelling through wooded scenery, green birch trees tinged with autumn's gold amongst dark masses of firs and pines. There were few white people in the Greyhound. A thin coloured girl with a fat baby offered me a half-full cup of orange juice, and then kept on asking me the time. In the seat behind her, a young couple, he coloured and she white, sat joking and laughing, very much in love. Outside, muddy creeks burrowed their way into the undergrowth. In front of me a big spirited woman was talking to the driver.

'I had an aunt who was always dreamin' on me, saying, "Are you sure your house ain't gonna burn down? I dreamt it did. Are you certain there ain't gonna be a flood? I dreamt I saw you washed away."

'In the end, it got so I finally told her, "Look, leave me *out* of your dreams, honey! I don't wanna *be* in them no mo'." Now I got this cousin who's got a *dream* book. Every kind o' dream youse liable to have is in that book, an' she tells me, "Someone you know is gonna get married, 'cos I had a dream an' it says so in my *dream* book." She used to bet on the numbers, an' dream numbers an' dream things that the book said *meant* numbers, but she never won nothin'.'

Shreveport in the rain seemed an ominously ugly town. We crossed the Red River, famous in cowboy song, and crawled through decrepit industrial scenery to the coach station. It was still morning, and the waiting room was packed, with standing room only. The thin girl popped her fat baby on to the lap of a delighted white woman, a total stranger, and wandered off somewhere. The baby laughed as the woman tickled it under the chins. A vivacious Afro-headed girl at the ticket desk phoned a taxi for me and asked if I had met the Queen. I'm fond of Royalty, and felt flattered at this perpetual question.

However, the taxi driver looked me up and down and seemed to form quite a different opinion of my rank in life. 'Can you afford a five-dollar fare?' he asked. 'You *can*? Right then, we're in business. I know a ho-tel that won't be too expensive for you.'

So saying, he drove along a straight road leading out of town through a sprawl of small, seedy-looking businesses, garages and workmen's cafés, red neon lights shining. Finally, we reached an hotel that looked like the entrance to a small Hollywood studio, deserted since the 1930s. 'Plaza Toro', the neon sign announced. The hotel appeared to be a gigantic horseshoe-shaped row of connected sheds, with a huge driveway in the middle overgrown by grass and weeds. In the foyer, which resembled the waiting room I had just left, except for being empty, a large sign read 'No Refunds'.

A sullen, sallow girl with a baby appeared at a pay-kiosk window and gave me a key. So I paid off my taxi driver and tried to understand the girl's instructions. She was an 'Asian' refugee from Zambia, I learned, and her husband was South American.

I realised that this was one of the 'drive-in' hotels for which America is famous. I dragged my bag along rows of barrack-like dwellings made of brick and wood, with tiny dirt-encrusted windows. These strips of accommodation, which would have been called 'chalets' in an English Butlin's, had been divided into segments, each with a door and a window. Lorries stood here and there, which explained the large entrance and driveway. A rough-looking crowd of joking drivers showed me the right block of rooms.

My brown, dark, musty room, with jammed drawers and cracked, curling lino, made my heart sink. It was larger than my room at the New Orleans Y.M.C.A., but more forlorn. I put my bag down, killed a ferocious creature the Americans called a 'wasp', but I called a 'stinging daddy longlegs', and went out for a look around Shreveport. To do this, I had to call another taxi.

Peaks of grey skyscrapers appeared, their summits covered in grey mist, as Shreveport 'downtown' loomed ever closer.

'This city's founded on oil, and oil isn't what it was,' explained the taxi driver, a white man. '*Nothin's* what it was, if you ask my opinion. I remember as a young man going to Yellowstone Park, an' I saw *crowds* of huge bears snarlin' an' pawin' round the big rubbish dump. Huge grizzlies! One she-grizzly had a cub that was as big as a full grown Louisiana bear. We used to have small brown bears round here when I was a boy, but you never see them now. Last year I went to Yellowstone, an' the rubbish dump is gone an' so are the bears! This here's a good enough place to stop, near the courthouse.'

Big raindrops began to fall, as I hurried past a ranting open-air preacher towards the great doors of the Caddo Parish Courthouse, a gigantic nineteenth-century building amidst the grey modernity of Shreveport. At a statue of a Confederate hero, I paused for a moment to read an inscription beside an empty flagpole. 'The last Confederate Flag', it read. When the flag of the South had been lowered at courthouses everywhere, following the final defeat of 1865, Shreveport had stubbornly flown hers until the last minute. Rain behind me, I galloped up the steps, and reached shelter just as the main downpour began.

Another sign, this time on a wall, told of the 1835 Treaty between the U.S. government and the Caddo Indians, signed in that very courthouse. The Indians, 'represented by twenty-five chiefs and warriors', had sold their land for 180,000 dollars. Later, oil was discovered.

In a corner of the vast, highly polished and dimly lit hall, a cheap looking coffee stall was doing good business. Black janitors leaned across the counter and joked with the staff. A poster advertised 'Pickle Pig Feet, Seventy-Five Cents'. At a table, some kind of small-scale election was going on, perhaps for sheriff. Citizens drifted over, took ballot slips and wandered off. Coloured office girls in brown uniforms ran in and out of a door marked 'Sheriff's Office', holding various papers. Sheriff types with pistols and a man dressed as a cowboy hovered around.

Too absorbed in my book, the autobiography of Zora Neale Hurston, to worry about sheriffs, I sat down on a step and began to read. There were no seats. Every now and then, a violent explosion outside was followed by a blinding blue flash of lightning. A coloured youth in a yellow peaked cap sat on a stair near me and asked what I was studying. Forgetting that I was in a country where many people cannot read, I simply handed him the book. He gave it back as if it were red hot!

'No, man, only if it's got pictures!' he yelped, and ran outside into the rain, humiliated.

After two hours on the step, refreshed by coffee from the stall, I decided that the rain was slackening. So out I went, hoping to find a bookshop in which to browse. Instead, on a corner, I found an enormous record shop, Paula's.

Inside, I found myself in a blues- and gospel-lovers Paradise. The shop was apparently the outlet for a recording studio, Jewel Records, affiliated to Ronn Records, affiliated to Suzy-Q Records, who specialised in black music. Men flipped through LPs by singers with colourful names, such as Lightning Hopkins, who would feel at home in Shreveport that day. Women concentrated on the other end of the shop, in the large Gospel department. Not only were LPs of choirs and groups on sale here, but also recordings of fire-eating sermons. Sermon LPs had archaic pictures on the covers, resembling Negro newspaper advertisements of the 1930s.

'Put Down Your Whiskey Bottle' and 'Down in the Dumps with the Blues' were preached by the Rev. Leo Daniels, while another Rev., C. C. Franklin, told stories such as 'Satan Goes to Prayer Meeting' and 'A Bigot meets Jesus'.

Back in the blues half of the shop, beneath posters advertising Z. Z. Hill's 'Down Home Blues', I spoke to the young man in charge, explaining that I was writing a book about the South. He seemed delighted that his shop would receive a mention.

'I'm Lenny Lewis,' he said, shaking hands, 'and my father is Stan Lewis, the founder of the business. Our family came to America from Sicily, originally. I'm named after Leonard Chess, who once ran a famous blues company in Chicago. He was a friend of Dad. Suzy-Q records were named after Chess's daughter Sue, and so is my sister Sue. Suzy-Q are linked to Cobra Records, who are linked to U.S.A. records, who . . . well, they more or less come under one heading. But things are very hard in the blues business now – we can't get airplay and we can't get good distributors, so we may have to sell up.'

I remembered how, at Malaco Records, I had been told that only rock music could be heard on the radio, despite the obvious Negro interest in rhythm and blues. It seemed as if show business was intent on standardising itself. Stan Lewis, the founder, returned at that moment and gave me a curt two-minute interview in his office. He seemed more of a businessman than his son, who obviously loved blues for their own sake and constantly scouted the Lounges for new talent.

'We may not sell, but if we do, it'll be due to the lack of good independent distributors,' he snapped. 'If so all our master tapes of unissued songs by Elmore James and Jimmy Reed, well-known singers of the fifties, will be up for sale. Thank you.'

Back with jolly, boisterous Leonard, I waited to bid him goodbye, as he sold a customer a record by Little Johnny Taylor. I found him in an excitable mood. Just like the man at Malaco Records, he dashed to and fro picking me out the finest records as gifts.

'You'll like this one: "Spider In My Stew". And here's a new record by a discovery of mine! This man's just about the best blues singer alive!'

The picture showed a grinning curly-permed man named Blues Boy Artie White. So once more staggering under the weight of priceless blues records I tottered out into the rain. Luckily, there was an excellent public library nearby, where I enjoyed a rest, before asking the librarian where I could find a bookshop. He seemed amazed.

'A bookshop! You'll have to go out of town to one of the shopping malls for that!'

To my surprise, the rain ended, and a watery sun appeared, soon to go down. I crossed various roads, zigzagging between lumps of concrete modernity, theatres and so on, and soon found myself on a promenade beside the rushing, swollen waters of the Red River. Mockingbirds uttered liquid notes as they flaunted their long tails and swooped from bough to bough. Thick with pasty red mud, the river swept on its way. A dull Devonian red, the Red River lives up to its name. A river of romance, associated with cattle drives and Indian buffalo hunts, the subject of blues songs and a cowboy ballad, the Red River compensated for the grey town through which it flowed. Once a timber-carrying river, the rafts of logs had jammed near Shreveport, and in a sense these logs had founded the city. Yet another sign beside the river told the tale.

> *The Great Raft.* Captain Henry Miller Shreve came to Red River in 1833 to remove the log jam 165 miles long, extending from Loggy Bayou to Hurricane Bluffs; the removal of the raft by 1837 opened Red River to navigation and made Shreveport an important center of trade and gateway to the West.

Walking towards the West myself, I followed a pink sunset along the straight, dreary industrial road back to the Plaza Toro hotel. Factory chimneys stood black against the horizon. A passer-by told me that my hotel was five miles away, but that was all nonsense. Americans drive everywhere and so see no difference between one mile and four. I calculated that it was a three-quarters-of-a-mile walk. However, the records were heavy and the traffic was fierce, for of course there was no pavement.

At Kay's Pet Shop, I stopped to look at the animals. It was a tiny roadside shop, and the friendly young owner proudly showed me his fish and some tame rats who reminded me of my dear pet rats at home in England. Promising a great treat, he took me out to the back, where I was shown two lively ferrets in a hutch. One was almost a pure polecat, the ancestor of the working ferret. However, the pet shop man had never heard of rabbit-hunting with a ferret. In America, it seemed, ferrets were novel pets.

'My contact in South America supplies me with tropical fish,' the man told me. Shreveport, with all its faults, certainly had very friendly shopkeepers. 'The Plaza Toro Hotel? It's about a mile and a half straight on.'

Actually, it was five hundred yards away, to my relief. Before returning to my musty room, I crossed the road and enjoyed a meal at a wayside Bar BQ, served by two motherly women. Louisiana accordion-music, played by white and coloured musicians, swirled from the friendly juke box.

Back at the tawdry Reception kiosk, I had begun to ask the girl for an early-morning taxi, when a smartly dressed coloured man with spectacles dashed in and asked if he could see her first. Surprised, I agreed.

'I'm a police officer!' he barked, showing a badge. Glumly the woman admitted him to the office, where they spent some time discussing the movements of certain guests. Finally he left. I could hardly wait to do the same. Early in the morning, when I arose, I could hear a woman screaming and a man roaring at her. Soon, feeling much happier, I was on a Greyhound leaving Shreveport and heading for Texarkana, a town on the Texas-Arkansas border.

There was only one other passenger aboard, a young white man in Air Force uniform.

'You ain't a pilot, are you?' asked the stout young woman driver, also white.

'No ma'am, I'm a computer operator,' he replied, with pride in his voice.

'Well, that's good, 'cos I never met a pilot who was worth a damn. I've had it up to here with Service people! I drive for the bases sometimes, and last week I had two generals having a fist fight right in my bus. And one night I had to wait at the camp while a general got in a terrible fight with a policeman and just about beat him up. The M.P.s came along, but the whole affair was smoothed over. That surprised me some, as I always thought there was the same law for high as for low. It frightens me, that these generals are just like small boys, yet they have the power to start another *war*.

'Now, Marines, these young Marines from college, are so gung-ho, they're looking *forward* to a war. One young man still wet be'ind the ears talked big on my bus; claimed he was ready to lead his men anywhere. Man, I just tore into him! "You been brainwashed," I told him, "all that stuff about your gun being your best friend. Why there's no sense in just going out an' getting killed. *You* can die like anyone else, you know." Finally he gave in and had to admit he'd been brainwashed.'

The young man didn't quite like all this, but he was very polite. We passed through coppery woodlands, past occasional shanties and small farms, and at last stopped at a Greyhound waiting room miles from nowhere. A bright young man at the desk, who seemed very interested in England, phoned for a taxi. A pleasant old man drove me into the hybrid town of Texarkana, half-Texas, half-Arkansas.

'I'll take you to a hotel downtown,' he said. 'It used to be a fine place, but now it's none too sporty.'

A hotel *downtown*! Could this be possible! Just as if I were in England, I would be able to stroll from my hotel, along a pavement, into a real street with shops in it! Was it too good to be true?

But my driver was telling me no more than the truth. He drove into the centre of a clean, bright little town with a 1950s atmosphere, and along a wide street called State Line. One side of the road was Texas, the other Arkansas. Soon a very strange hotel came into view. It was a tall, brick building with rows of windows and a semi-derelict appearance, like a haunted house. One side of the hotel narrowed to a sharp point, like a neatly cut slice of chocolate cake. A big sign along the wall read: 'Hotel Grim'.

It seemed too apt to be true, but the driver assured me the hotel was named after a once-powerful local family, the Grims. The 'Grim Barber Shop' adjoined the hotel.

I crossed a vast parquet hall to a wooden Reception desk of fort-like proportions. Behind the ramparts, a young man in a cowboy hat was reclining in an office chair, his boots on the table, as he negligently dealt cards to a curly-headed youth. Two or three other young men were wandering in and out of the desk-enclosed compound, which they evidently used as a social club. Tipping back his hat, the cowboy flipped the last card down, gave me an enquiring squint and assured me that I could have a room. I returned to the taxi and fetched my red, white and blue bag.

Although the hallway was huge and highly polished, with newly-painted classical columns, a balcony, tall windows looking out to the street and other Riviera-like touches, it was unfurnished and faintly-derelict looking. A television stood in the middle of a parquet desert, with ill-assorted rows of shabby chairs and divans arranged in front of it. Two black construction workers were watching a programme, shouting angrily at the announcer on occasion. Both wore dirty overalls and one was still wearing his yellow safety helmet.

At the desk once more, I paid the remarkably cheap fee (fifteen dollars a night) and the curly headed young man took my bag, excusing himself from the staff poker game.

'No, the dining room's not in use right now, but there's a vending machine for Coke and coffee,' he said. 'The elevator's out of order, but I can take you up on the service elevator.'

So saying, he took my bag and led me into a dingy corner behind the scenes, where a wooden broken-looking lift jerked us up into the higher quarters of the Hotel Grim. Part of the side of the lift was missing. Instead of making one journey, we zoomed up and down picking people up and letting them out. Sometimes, we were out of doors, with views of brick buildings across the way, for several floors were disused, and some had their walls knocked away. The amateur liftman was friendly, but with rather a wild look in his eyes. At last I was released on a dusty floor of dark corridors, above two or three disused or ruinous floors.

'This is an historic hotel, built in the 1920s,' I was told. 'Bonnie and

Clyde the bank robbers once stayed here, and all kinds of famous people. We've got a grant to repair it, so in the end it'll be just as grand as when it first opened.'

He gave me a key, and left me in my room. I was entranced. This was a proper hotel room at last, with an old wooden dresser and a mirror, a big old-fashioned bed and a creaky wardrobe. At the refreshingly normal window, I could look down on a real street with shops and pavements. People walked about! At last I had discovered the perfect hotel – not a modern monstrosity with televisions in every room, and not a doss-house, for my room was clean and airy. I could have been in England, in the Station Hotel at Ipswich in the great days. How I had missed chests of drawers with knobbly handles! Time in the Hotel Grim had stood still, and I was in an American hotel bedroom of the 1930s. Everything I saw suggested a black-and-white film. Why did America ever have to change?

I settled on the large bed and turned in for a nap. At first I had switched on the great propeller-bladed electric fan that hung above my bed, but it roared into life with such energy that I was afraid it would take off with a chunk of cracked ceiling attached, and smash me to pieces. So I did without it.

Awaking much refreshed an hour later, I found the stairs after some searching, and made my way down past the disused floors in semi-darkness, kicking away pieces of broken glass. Soon I stepped out on to a newly restored balcony in some relief, whence a curve of safer steps took me down to the foyer. At the Reception desk, poker had given way to jigsaw puzzles, girls had arrived and the atmosphere was more domestic. All the staff at the Hotel Grim seemed to be young white people who had run away to see the wicked city (Texarkana); the boys raffish, the girls tragic-eyed with a touch of defiance. Once I was used to them, I could not have wished for a nicer crowd.

Helping myself to a coffee, I sat down in front of the television. As usual with American television, no pause intervened between a programme and the advertisements, so that a stunt-filled car chase careered straight into an advert for Shick's Nursing Home for Cocaine Dependency. Two young men sat on chairs with their legs curled under them. A girl with a baby arrived, and sat silently on the floor, resting her head against her boyfriend's knees. Now and again the helmeted man, who had a curly beard, got up and changed programmes. Nobody objected. Behind me, two young men sparred playfully. Out in the street, I could see the passers-by through the large windows. A peppery old man was walking stiffly along, an embodiment of the Old West in cowboy hat, white curly moustache and luxuriant sidewhiskers. Finishing my coffee, I too hurried out into the streets of Texarkana.

A clean, old-fashioned town, with wide streets, Texarkana varied in mood from the twenties and thirties to the 1950s. In the latter decade, apparently, a deranged murderer haunted the town, making Texarkana notorious. Apparently, the sheriff chased the killer on to the railway line. Just then, a train swept by, and when the dust had settled, there was no sign of a body. However, the murders ended after that. A film had been made of the story, entitled *The Town that Hated Sundown*. Or so I was told at the Hotel Grim. Perhaps the shock of these terrible events had stunted Texarkana's growth and kept the town in the 1950s. It's an ill wind . . .

Across the road to the hotel, in the museum, I admired a collection of pitiful relics of the Caddo Indians who once had lived on the site of the town. Later, the remnants of the Caddo had been sent to the ill-fated Indian Nation of Oklahoma.

'Some of the Caddo still live in Oklahoma,' the lady curator told me. 'Last year they came back and showed off their tribal dancing. We're hoping it'll get to be an annual event.'

A huge square post office loomed over Texarkana, and at the bottom of the steps, by the kerb, a sign pointed to the invisible county line. After playing at having one leg in Texas and one in Arkansas for a while, I wandered into the nearby Trailways coach station, had a coffee and watched a frenetic fiddle player on the video juke box. In America, each town seemed to have *one* post office, which had a status somewhere between the town hall (or courthouse) and the local newspaper office.

Pictures of scarlet wild boars with spiky humped backs dominated Texarkana, as these were the symbol of the Arkansas Razorbacks, a football team. An extraordinary tall thin deacon, with piercing eyes and a walnut-cracking jaw, allowed me to look around the small red-brick Episcopalian Church. Soothing, pastel-shaded stained glass windows were pleasing to the eye. A plaque caught my attention. 'To the Glory of God and in loving memory of Sarah Hauberger Grim', it read. Do any Grims survive today, I wondered?

A long street of solidly-built well-stocked shops dominated Texarkana. I bought a pair of patent leather shoes, and then discovered a wonderful Hunting Shop, full of mounted deer heads and snarling stuffed lynxes. Robin Hood would have gasped to see the 'Critter Getter', only one of a row of high-powered finely-etched wooden bows, made for deer-hunting, not archery. The bowstrings could be tightened by a wheel mechanism, similar to that of a fishing rod. Racks of finely-feathered arrows stood beside muzzle-loading guns, rifles of every description, bird and animal-calls and paintings and models of deer and other wild game. Blue-jeaned girls, who looked like film stars, served customers with expertise. It was the next best thing to a natural history museum.

A sidestreet led down to the railway station, a macabre and forgotten part of Texarkana. Passenger trains still stopped here four days a week, but for all that, the station had fallen into a ruin. Decorated by broken glass and rubbish, a long desolate platform stretched into infinity, the roof held up by rusty girders. 'Ohio Hobo Number One' had been chalked on one of these. Goods trains still ran frequently, and chains of trucks (or boxcars) stood on branch lines almost encompassed by secondary woodland. Some side platforms had crumbled away, leaving black doorways suspended, where once goods had been heaved to and fro. A ghost hotel, the Ross, vainly promised air conditioning in every room. Ruined storehouses stared with sightless windows.

Similar dereliction can be seen in the North of England, where diesel 'paytrains' flourish and stations all decay. But in Texarkana, the ruins were on a larger scale, and so rendered all the more mournful.

All of a sudden, I looked up and saw a smartly kept-up building that I took to be the ticket office. Bright lights shone from the windows. Steps, rather like those on a signal box, led up to the door. A laconic man behind a grille worked on, ignoring me. Two big men were talking loudly to one another. One was dressed as a cowboy, in jeans, boots and stetson. At first they shot me a suspicious glance and then went on talking. When they saw that I was hanging around and trying to get a word in edgeways, they seemed incredulous and inclined to laugh. With my pitiful enquiries about trains to Arkansas, I felt like a comic greenhorn among whiskey-drinking giants in the Last Chance Saloon.

'Train times on a board outside,' the cowboy snapped, and they went on discussing 'freight'.

Pondering the affair, for it was no use pondering a railway timetable, I came to the conclusion that I had been among 'railroad men'. Part of the legend of the West, railroad men no doubt saw themselves as mythological heroes or 'bad men', much as did lorry drivers. A rhyme from my Alan Lomax days floated back into my memory.

> Oh, I don't like a railroad man!
> No, I don't like a railroad man!
> A railroad man will kill you if he can,
> And drink up your blood like wine.

Darkness approached, and I made my way to Bryce's cafeteria, Texarkana's main restaurant, for my supper. Everybody in town, from the bank manager downward, ate at Bryce's. I piled my plate higher and higher with mouth-watering delicacies: black-eyed peas and candied yams. As I demolished my food-mountain, I admired the panorama of Texarkana society queuing to be fed, ponderous Teutonic captains of industry and loose-limbed coloured janitors. I didn't blame any of them, for the food was delicious.

Back at the Hotel Grim Reception desk, I found that a poker game had ended and a jigsaw not yet begun. So I took the opportunity to get to know the staff. This I did, in my usual way, by casually drawing a unicorn. The effect was almost explosive!

'We're all crazy about unicorns here!' one of the youths shouted, tearing off his shirt to show me his unicorn tattoo. 'You ought to be a tattooist! Unicorns are special to us! They show individuality.'

Three eager young men and two girls in 'cowgirl' checked shirts and jeans gathered round as I drew more unicorns. One of the girls, who was in love with a wild-looking boy, had the most soulful brown eyes I had ever seen outside Crufts. Shouting and snatching at unicorns, the youths (who were all white) used Negro slang with great emphasis.

'That's ba-a-ad. Now is that bad or ain't that bad? Whoo-ee!'

In England, my better unicorns would have been labelled 'wicked'.

One of the young men showed me a photo of a huge grinning bull terrier. 'That's a pit-bull! I breed these,' he said. 'Folk put 'em in a pit, fight 'em. Bingo is a great fad here, too! Look, this here's my Bingo card.'

'Put my name on my picture – my name's Phil,' a tall curly-headed youth, also with vivid brown eyes, requested. He worked for a garage, and had black oil slicks all over his overalls and on his face and hands. 'I'm a country boy – my folks farm out near Shreveport. It's a real old-fashioned farm. My daddy has even built a wooden house specially so that neighbours can set in it while the whole family plays 'em music on banjos and fiddles. They play some French tunes, but mostly bluegrass. Bluegrass is really fast music, kind of like a square dance. I like rock music, myself. It's funny I stay here, 'cos I'm a second cousin of Bonnie, an' Bonnie and Clyde made this hotel famous.'

'Ask me tomorrow, when it's light, and I'll take you on a tour of the haunted floor,' the cowboy-hatted youth said, as he rattled me up to bed in the service lift.

Texarkana public library, which I found next day after some trial and error, gave me a contented hour's browsing. On my way down to it, beside a car park, I had been struck by a gigantic mural showing 'Scott Joplin, American Composer' on a car-park wall. Apparently the Father of Ragtime Piano had been born in Texarkana. On my way back to the town centre, near the mural, I stopped to look at some poky little shops. 'Black Chamber of Commerce' was painted in black sprawly writing over one dusty window, but there was no sign of life within. Next door's window, equally gloomy, bore a faded card with the legend 'Jimmy Ellis's hit on Kris Records – "Move to the Outskirts of Town".' No other sign showed what the shop might be used for. I pushed the door and went in.

Inside, I found myself in a tiny and very closed-looking nightclub. A big coloured man was wrestling with the cable of an electric guitar that stood beside an amplifier and drum-machine. He gave me a harassed glance from a bespectacled face beneath a curly-perm hairstyle.

I introduced myself politely, and asked him if he were Jimmy Ellis. He nodded, and I asked if he would like to be put in a book.

'Hmm, I guess so,' he ruminated. 'Y'all come back about ten o'clock tonight when I start to play. I keep playing from then on till early morning. Guitar is my favourite instrument – wisht you could o' heard me when I had a band behind me. Then I could *really* play. This place? Well, it's just called The Lounge; got no other name. I run this place from Thursday to Sunday and the rest o' the time I live at Dallas, Texas, where my house is.'

Bidding Mr Ellis a temporary farewell, I returned to the Hotel Grim to see the haunted floor. In great good spirits, the cowboy-hatted youth took me straight up to the roof in a series of vivid flashes of Hotel Grim scenery, floor by floor, like a life passing before someone's eyes. We climbed out on to a flat roof dotted with rotting divans. There was an excellent view of the defunct McCartney Hotel, once one of the Grim's rivals. Hotel Grim now stood in a class by itself.

We then climbed back into the lift and plunged to a lower floor. Every room here had been gutted, and pipes emerged crazily from holes in cracked plaster beside heaps of bricks. Following my guide, I carefully stepped over holes in the floor. Windows had been knocked out, leaving holes that faced on to mid-air.

'This is the haunted floor – someone said they saw somethin' here once. We're trying to restore it, but the plaster just won't stay on the bricks no matter *what* we do.'

To my mind, the floor below seemed far more haunted. Each floor of door-studded corridors now housed only two or three guests, mostly migrant workers. On this particular floor, doors stood open and stores were piled in dusty ghost-rooms left over from the 1920s.

'Bonnie and Clyde stayed on this floor,' I was told.

Thanking Cowboy Hat for his kindness, I had a meal, a sleep and a coffee, and then set out for The Lounge and Jimmy Ellis's club. As I approached, I could hear the familiar notes of a blues guitar being picked in a steady rhythm. With bright fairy lights winking all around the curtained window, The Lounge looked an enticing place indeed.

Inside, I found the place transformed. Dim red lights illuminated an attractive coffee-bar-like club, with chairs and tables set before a small stage with a special chair for the singer beside the ubiquitous drum-machine.

Jimmy Ellis put down his guitar and cheerfully called me over to the bar, where he introduced me to his wife Dolores. (He spelled her name 'Deloris', so in future I shall do the same.) There was only one customer, a tall coloured man in a lumber shirt, who drank his whiskey quietly and listened to us with interest. He looked like a farm worker. A doorway led into a dimly-lit cave-like dance hall, with a barred window looking on to the music room. The juke box gently glowed with dormant records, such as 'The Welfare Done Turned Its Back On Me'.

'I was born on a cotton patch in Arkansas,' Jimmy told me. Deloris, a tough-looking girl with her hair in long plaits, nodded approvingly. They seemed to be very fond of each other. 'I'm named after my grandfather, Jimmy Ellis, who used to run a car ferry on the Red River. I began singing gospel; fact is, I used to preach some. That's why folks call me Jimmy "the Preacher" Ellis. When I was only fourteen, I went to Seattle with the Kansas City Gospel Singers. They used to call me Little Jimmy. It wasn't till I was in the military that I went over to rhythm and blues. I've played in supper clubs all over, done rhythm guitar for a blues singer called Lowell Fulson and for another named Joe Blue. I also was a fighter once, a boxer. I been a lot of things. Me 'n Deloris run a liquor store back in Dallas. Too bad you here on a rainy Thursday, when custom is slow. You should be here on a Friday or a weekend when the place be really jumping! I play best when the dance floor is full, in the early morning, with folks just swaying to the music.'

'You gonna play?' asked the customer, not unreasonably, and Jim galloped back to his music seat. He adjusted the drum-machine, which emitted a steady beat from its electronic interior. Where had all the real drummers gone?

'I'm gonna move, baby, way out on the outskirts of town,' Jimmy sang mournfully, plucking notes from his guitar and leaving them hanging in the air. He sang well, but I hoped his song would not have too much influence. Far too many people seemed to be deserting town centres in the South.

'Now, here's Z. Z. Hill's great song, "Down Home Blues". I knew Zee Zee well – I was at his funeral.'

For the next half-hour, Jimmy sang both blues and sentimental ballads with great feeling. He was an admirer of the Welsh singer, Tom Jones, and of Blues Boy King. After each song, the customer and I clapped heartily. Taking out a harmonica, to my great surprise, Jimmy began to play vigorously, jigging about and fanning at the instrument. After so many sombre songs, the light-hearted dance music galvanised the customer into action. Quickly masking a fleeting smile of delight, the tall man put on a dead-pan face as he danced round and round the bar-room first on one leg, then on another, gyrating and slapping himself on the rump of his jeans. I was most impressed. As the dancer cavorted, and

Deloris nodded appreciatively, Jimmy sang a few lines, then played, then sang.

> 'Racoon in the tree and possum on the ground,
> Hound dog come along and he chase 'em all around.
> Chicken in the bread pan, peckin' up dough,
> Mama, kin I have some? No, child, no!
> Ida Red, oh Ida Red!
> You can't beat old Ida Red!'

Scarcely pausing, Jimmy sang us the song of the bad man Stagger Lee. When he finally stopped playing, the dancing customer tipped back his drink and left. We gathered at the bar once more. My drinks were on the house.

. 'I sure wish you could see this place when there was more people here,' Jimmy lamented once more.

To cheer him up, I told him all I knew about Tom Jones, which wasn't very much. 'Wales is a land of male voice choirs,' I explained. 'They sing without musical instruments, as music might be sinful. Sometimes a singer will develop his voice in a choir, then leave to sing popular music.'

'That's like our people,' Jimmy said. Deloris didn't speak much, but listened very attentively. I showed them my photographs of the Mount Zion Spiritual Baptist Church of Kensal Green in full song.

'What fine-looking black people!' Jimmy Ellis marvelled.

'They sing Jubilee songs,' I told him. 'Stuff like "Go Down, Moses", "No Hiding Place", "The Great Trumpet Sounds".'

'Jubilee Songs!' Jimmy exclaimed, pleased that I had not said 'spirituals', as that has now become a 'condescending' word. 'I know all those songs! Too many of our people here are forgetting the church. Have another drink and I'll sing y'all some more songs. There's a singer called Howling Wolf – I do some of his songs. But you know the blues is a *feeling*. If you don't have the feeling, you can't do 'em. That's why I don't like auditions. Now, this here's a record I made on my own label, Kris Records. It's called "Party Time", an' I'd like you to have it. It got played a good deal out in California. I even got a trumpet player and a brass section. I'll do it for you now, in person.'

'We're gonna party all night long,' he sang, leaning back and whomping on his guitar. The words and tune reminded me of Desita's singing in Jackson Square. He even put me in the song, as Desita had done. I go to more parties in songs than I do in real life.

'Roy gonna pa-a-arty all night long!'

From then on, Jimmy sang nothing but blues. Deloris sat on a stool at first, rocking along with the rhythm and breathing out a heartfelt 'yeah' at each song's conclusion. She seemed justly proud of her husband. Finally she could contain herself no longer, and moved out to the dance floor. There I could see her, reflected in the mirror above Jimmy's head, loosely swaying her arms and body, her plaits swinging in rhythm and an expression of religious concentration on her face.

'The blues is a *feeling* . . .' and without doubt the blues are religious, a vestige of all the non-Christian religions brought from Africa to be dissolved in the agony of slavery. When country music received such a large injection of blues that it became rock and roll, it was felt by its white devotees not to be entertainment but a religion, something you got converted to. In true African fashion, the blues has two meanings, a mood of deep melancholy and the music that, by expressing that melancholy, exorcises it. A witch doctor is not a witch, he *finds* the witch and by his own magic, lifts the spell. Many blues singers compare themselves in verse to doctors, and address the Blues as if it were a mysterious person or a spirit of possession.

'When you get the Key to the Highway, that means you got to hit the road,' Jimmy looked up and told me, then bent to his guitar once more. At the first note, Deloris closed her eyes and swayed in a trance.

> 'I got the Key to the Highway,
> I am out and bound to go,
> I'm gonna leave here running,
> 'Cos walking is far too slow . . .'

I felt awestruck at Jimmy's talent. Nothing daunted, I stood up during a pause and sang 'My Old Man's a Dustman'. When Jimmy and Deloris had finished laughing, it was back to the blues once more. Jimmy seemed to be directing his words at Deloris, and there was a strong feeling between the two of them.

> 'I'm gonna write you a letter, baby, sign it with a seal,
> Yes, write you a letter, sign it with a seal.
> Saying I still love you, I'll be your driving wheel.'

At last Jimmy laid his guitar down, looking overwrought, and switched off the drum-machine.

'You must be proud of him,' I said to Deloris.

'I *am*,' she answered. 'What kind of funny song was that you was singing?'

I told her about Cockneys and East Enders. Jimmy came over and listened keenly. When I told them about rhyming slang, and how it had probably begun as a way of mystifying the police, he gave a loud laugh.

'That's just like with us and jive talk!' he cried. 'It just shows, people are the same every place, the wide world over! At one time, the police had to get a jive-talk dictionary. We'd say, "Man, give me some skin!" [With that, he shook my hand.] Or some guy would say, "Hand me my lead, 'cos my kickers want out of here." That means, "Hand me my hat, 'cos my feet are leaving." '

It was now rather late, and I felt that my own feet ought to be leaving. With a great deal of shaking hands and slapping backs, I said farewell to Jimmy and Deloris. 'Do you think it's safe on the street?' I asked.

'I think so. Anyhow, I'll stand out here and look over you.'

And so he did, for as I walked down the long moonlit street, the rain-washed pavement gleaming, I was conscious of Jimmy's huge form standing there in the road and watching me out of sight.

Next morning, I handed in my room key at the Hotel Grim, and took the Key to the Highway. In other words, I rode out of Texarkana, most delightful of towns, on a Greyhound in the pouring rain.

Nearly all the other passengers were going on to New York. A coloured girl slept across one seat, covered by a patchwork quilt. As usual, there were few white passengers. A large chubby-faced woman, whom even I thought slightly dotty, handed out religious tracts to everyone within reach.

'I'm going to Memphis,' she told me. 'So you're from England? That's a fine country! God created England.'

'Ye-e-es. Still, as He created everything, it sort of evens out.'

'Praise the Lord! Is England different from here?'

'Yes, in some ways. There's no cornbread in England, for instance.'

'No cornbread!' Shocked, she began to make magic signs to God with her hands.

'This is the nearest I go to Arkadelphia,' the driver announced.

I staggered out into the rain with my bag. As the driver had promised earlier, there was an hotel nearby. Taking a key, I staggered round the side of the plate glass building, looking for my room. Juggernauts stood outside a mock Tudor social club for lorry drivers. At last, drenched and weary, I found my room, and lay on the bed watching blue explosions of lightning and thunder that made the glass wall vibrate.

'What next?' I wondered.

CHAPTER THIRTEEN

The Arkansaw Traveller

TOMMY HANCOCK, A genial moustachioed young man who had been to Vietnam and had returned safely, drove me to the town of Arkadelphia in his taxi. The absurdity of having hotels miles outside towns and nowhere else made me despair of the United States. America, America! When will you forget your infatuation with the motor car?

A damp stillness hung over Arkadelphia, as if the weather were a trifle bleary-eyed after its exercises of thunder and lightning the day before. I found myself in a small peaceful town with a brick Wild West Main Street of dingy shops. Leafy suburbs stretched away to the busy main roads which sealed all access to the Arkansas woods. Everyone in Arkadelphia seemed mild. People on the streets greeted me with a gentle 'hello', as they might in a small country town in England.

Two old men walked along talking, and I walked along behind them.

'Now some white men marry coloured women,' one gnarled man muttered in a disgusted tone. 'But no coloured man has ever married a white woman!' he concluded, with pride in his voice.

Coloured youths walked by brightly, as if on a livelier plane than the rest of the sleepy town. They talked so quickly that I could not understand them.

I noticed a large crowd standing on the road and pavement outside a shop window. They seemed excited, so I hurried along to see what was the matter. The shop had been made into a small gymnasium, and the window looked on to a scene of young white-clad people surrounded by vaulting horses and parallel bars. A karate class was evidently holding its final examination. Formal displays of martial arts were taking place before a grim panel of judges. Each young candidate, dressed in white robes with a belt, bowed stiffly, then whirled into the attack. No sound from within could be heard through the shop window, but the crowd outside buzzed with conversation.

A girl bowed deeply and then leaped at a piece of wood held high in front of her by two impassive youths. She split the wood with the side of one hand, then spun around without pausing and kicked a second piece of wood held behind her. Unfortunately, she only dented the second target. Next came a boy of ten who split both pieces.

I looked beyond the contestants to a group of onlookers, who sat on a row of chairs at the rear of the gym. Some without chairs kneeled on the floor or sat with their legs stuck straight out in front of them. Their narrow-eyed 'mean' expressions and shabby clothes made them seem like a group portrait photographed in the rural Arkansas of the twenties. A round-faced Indian squaw, sitting cross-legged, looked as if she ought to have been preserved in an album. Her immobile features had a hint of Eskimo about them.

Meanwhile, the show must go on, and a fat coloured boy came forward and bowed with great bombast. With the air of someone about to perform an heroic and self-sacrificing deed, a *thin* coloured youth jumped up and volunteered to bend while the first youth leapfrogged to and fro over his back on lightning wood-splitting excursions. Unfortunately, he was a little *too* thin, and staggered under the other's weight. So the fat boy's first two attempts at karate leapfrog failed. I walked off down the road, and a moment later loud applause from the street audience showed that it had been a case of third time lucky.

Wandering around, I came across an old-fashioned English-style red-brick public library with near-Greek columns by the door. A bright coloured girl was the sole assistant in the delightfully musty old building. Old men sat at a table and chuckled in rich farmer-like tones. Hitherto I had only heard chuckles like that uttered by old white-bearded Bootle Beetle, a lesser known Walt Disney character, who smokes a clay pipe and sits on a mushroom.

Many curious old books could be found in this library, and one curious new one. This was *Essays on Segregation by Southern Episcopal Churchmen*, edited by T. Robert Ingram and dated 1960, the time when Martin Luther King was marching. All the Southern Episcopal Churchmen opposed racial integration. None more so than Henry T. Egger, who began his essay in ringing tones: 'Let God be my judge! . . . Egypt, the most cultured and refined nation in antiquity, became degenerate through the interbreeding of whites with Negroes. [A reader had ticked this passage.] Mixing Negro blood with white blood, on an even larger scale, will destroy America!'

Reverend Egger made a seemingly valid point when he stated that he could not accept 'that Christ requires us to destroy the Negro

Community'. However, a careful reading showed that by 'destroying Negroes', he meant diluting their African blood through marriage to other races. He praised Booker T. Washington (whose deeper meanings escaped him) and equated Negroes with Communism throughout.

Just as many English libraries have a 'Local History' room, so the Arkadelphia library had an Arkansas Room. This was where the old men sat and chuckled over books about the Arkansas of their golden days.

According to a book about Arkansas animals, dated 1940, Arkansas was known as 'the Bear State' because it teemed with wolves and bears. A long section of the book was devoted to bear- and wolf-hunting, activities which have, I fear, greatly diminished, if not exterminated, these creatures. However, scrubby woods arising from former cotton plantations will probably lure them back again. Many Irish have settled in Arkansas, and according to the spelling in this quaint book, even the Opossum is an O'Possum.

My favourite book in the library was *The Arkansaw Bear* (1898) and its brilliant follow-up, *Elsie and the Arkansaw Bear* (1909), both by Albert Bigelow. Possibly meant for children, these charming stories with their spidery illustrations told of a marvellous fiddle-playing bear who befriended runaway children in the Arkansas woods. Wherever the bear went, he fiddled his favourite tune, 'The Arkansaw Traveller'. Will no one rescue and reissue these tales?

The girl at the desk turned up her radio, which began to broadcast warnings of a tornado.

'Big storm coming!' said one of the old men. Both rose to leave. Nervously, I asked the girl what a tornado looked like.

'I never rightly seen one,' she replied politely. 'We're so low, they usually sail right over. It's kind of like a whirlwind, and when it's coming the sky goes a weird colour, like green. If you see it coming, get into a ditch. Me, if it comes, I'm going down in the basement. It starts as a thunderstorm, that's why they reckon we might have one, through that storm we had last night. But I don't think that radio said "tornado warning", I think it said "tornado watch". It's only when the "watch" goes to a "warning" that you have to take cover.'

All the same, I felt very uneasy outside, as I searched for the taxi hut. I kept an eye on the sky, but it remained a dull white, with a shiver of breeze. A sign outside a pawnshop read 'We Buy Guns, Jewelry, T.V.s.' On a corner, not far from the karate gym, I found a most unusual shop. Black cellophane hung across the windows like curtains. Over the glass, in giant whitewashed lettering, I read 'Southern Swing Jamboree.'

A girl in a nearby fashion shop explained that a country music show was held there every Saturday night. I vowed that I would attend and see how Arkadelphians enjoyed themselves.

Tommy Hancock the taxi driver, when I found him, booked me a seat on the train to Texas by telephone. Apparently, American passenger trains had been all-but abolished for a long time. Then they had re-emerged as 'Amtrack', a nationalised body, and were now conceived of as groundborne aeroplanes. Seats had to be secured by advance booking. No one ran for trains any more, or leaped aboard one on impulse. Musing on the Romance of Rail, I returned to my hotel.

No tornado occurred, and next morning I sailed off in Tommy Hancock's taxi to see the resort town of Hot Springs. Tommy was in fine form, the sun shone and the blue waters of Lake Degray, just outside town, sparkled. It was an artificial lake beside a forest tinted with autumn's gold.

'I go swimming here!' Tommy told me. 'The water's pretty low today, considering all that rain we had. Go fishing here, too, an' catch catfish, crappie 'n perch. We call bluegill fish "perch" over here. What's a crappie? Well, maybe it's a kind of trout.'

Soon, we were driving through vast secondary forests, the sun shining through the light foliage. Forested hills formed a patchwork quilt of pastel shades; red, gold, orange and green. No two trees were the same colours. Tommy looked at them appreciatively. He was happily looking forward to his next day off, when he was going deer-hunting.

'I've got an old .303 Winchester!' he said, swelling with pride, his eyes sparkling. 'I'll get to the deer stand real early in the morning, before light. A deer stand's a platform up in a tree where you can shoot from. Right near my deer stand, the earth is all turned up round the base of the trees by razorbacks. That's wild boars! It's my ambition to get a razorback – I never shot one yet. I'm either gonna get me a razorback or a buck. If I get a buck, I'll get its head mounted. Lots o' taxidermists round here. I wish you could o' come hunting with me. You'd have to get bright orange armbands, or you'd get mistook for game an' shot by someone. After the buck season, it'll be the doe season. We have bears, wolves and mountain lions in this state, but you have to go deep in the backwoods to see them.'

'There used to be wild boars in England,' I told him. 'Until turkeys were brought to England from America, a boar's head was the traditional Christmas dish. Boar-hunting used to be a noble sport, but our boars are all extinct now.'

'I'm sorry to hear that! I reckon a boar's head at Christmas is better than a turkey. Is there much hunting in England?'

His eyes opened wide in astonishment as I regaled him with horror stories about our Hunt Saboteurs. 'Sabs' are unknown in America, where hunting is a working man's sport. Tales of random violence led to talk of the Ku Klux Klan.

'The Klan used to be real strong when I was a boy,' he said. 'Now it's secret an' small time an' you hardly ever hear of burning crosses. People here had to accept integration, seeing it's law. The old people don't like it, but the young people don't mind. There used to be a black side of town, but now they live anywhere and do anything. Why, our Mayor of Arkadelphia is a black man!'

I glimpsed an old log cabin amid the trees, with a washing line attached. Clay had been tightly packed between the logs of the matchstick house. Cattle trucks rattled by, filled with mooing occupants. We left the 'dry' alcohol-free neighbourhood of Arkadelphia behind, and entered the boom town of Hot Springs, an American spa.

Hot Springs was approached by two bridges across wide Lake Hamilton, a virtual inland sea caused by a modern dam. Hotels reared their Spanish façades from the shore, and large amphibious 'ducks', white vehicle boats with wheels, cruised around with holidaymakers on board. We passed Oaklawn Racetrack, with its bronze equestrian statue, and, on the far side of a neon jungle of cheap hotels and eating houses, reached the opulent centre of the town of Hot Springs.

Even now, years after its turn-of-the-century heyday, the beautiful resort of Hot Springs must be one of the wonders of America. Built at a time when the brash 'nouveaux riches' looked to the Old World and not to the science-fiction future, its sequence of Grand Hotels came as a relief after the horrors of Interstate America. Tommy and I ascended Hot Springs Tower. There was no Vulcan statue on top, but the lift of the modern tower took us to an observation balcony with views over all Arkansas. Vista upon vista of mountains met our gaze, each one densely clothed with trees. Scrubby forest stretched from horizon to horizon, pioneer days recreated. Sugarloaf Mountain stood nearby, and Lake Catherine gleamed in the distance, beyond boat-covered Lake Hamilton. We were upon Hot Springs Mountain itself. Below us, forty-four hot springs were gushing from the heart of the mountain into pipes that led to the spa hotels of Million Dollar Bath House Row.

According to a notice fixed to a rock at the foot of the hill, the Indians had called Hot Springs Tah Ne Go, or Place of the Hot Waters. It was holy ground for the first Americans, a neutral territory of safety for the warring tribes. Indians made pilgrimages to the Springs, along high ridges, from as far away as Canada. Hernando de Soto was the first white visitor to Hot Springs. He arrived in 1541, had a bath and stayed for a month. As at Bath, in England, the waters contain minerals with healing powers.

Tommy drove off to park his taxi, and left me beside the forty-fifth hot spring. This spring had been uncapped and restored to its original appearance. Boiling water, surrounded by steam, gushed out of a cavity in the rugged hillside. Steaming leaf mould, like cabbage in a saucepan, hindered the waterfall's descent to an artificial pool. Tourists, clean-cut young men and women, dipped their fingers in and pulled them out again quickly. Nearby, a giant boulder had tumbled down from the mountain top and stood beside the pool, a lesser version of one of the great rocks of Tunbridge Wells.

A landscaped path took me above the hotel roofs and along the side of the hill. Birds sang in the young trees, and a second steamy spring could be seen through a barred window in the hill. It was as if I were walking along the edge of a huge tree-covered kettle. Thanks to the birds, it was a whistling kettle. My path led to a tall brown hotel now used as a Rehabilitation Centre, and another which was headquarters of the National Park. The whole town belonged to Hot Springs National Park, and the Million Dollar Bath Houses were well-preserved, even though most of them had been closed.

A public fountain spouted steamy water, and small drinking fountains released the brew in spurts. Now down at street level, I walked along Bath House Row beneath the shade of the magnolias.

Each grandiose Bath House had its own Hollywood-flavoured style. One had an Oriental dome, another looked Spanish, while a third was a rococo dream of elegance. The Oriental hotel, named The Quapaw, boasted an incongruous Red Indian chief's head over the door. A plain white bath-hotel, the Lamar, was managed by W. R. 'Bob' Grim. So the Grims had moved from Texarkana to Hot Springs! Were these bath houses ever open, and if so, who were their customers? I never found out.

Across a wide road, a line of seasidey-souvenir shops included an 'I.Q. Zoo', a performing animal exhibition. Arriving back at the Tunbridge Wells boulder, I met Tommy again and we went on a two-mule-drawn train ride. The muleteer proved to be an Arkadelphia lad, like Tommy, and the two of them compared notes. Apparently the mules, named Buck and Sadie, had spent most of their working lives hauling logs down the mountains. They were now in semi-retirement. The driver pointed out places of interest, such as the spot where a landslide had recently buried six parked cars with no one in them.

'See that amusement park? They once had an ostrich farm there, and the owner used to organise ostrich races. Once an ostrich and trap raced a pony and trap, and the ostrich and its driver won. Whoa, Buck!'

Buck stopped and so did Sadie. We were told that there was a halt of twenty minutes outside yet another I.Q. Zoo and an indoor model village. The crafty mule-driver must have made a deal with the two proprietors. We decided to visit Tiny Town, where Mr and Mrs Moshinskie greeted us. Mr Mosh had made an enormous model village, with a mountain range and railway line, all out of tins and other cast-out rubbish. Toy aeroplanes wheeled above the famous sights of toyland America. Niagara

Falls gushed real water, and the gold-fingered spire of Port Gibson pointed to Heaven. Little Noah's Ark figures, purported to be 'T.V. personalities', promenaded round and round over grass made of painted sawdust. Trees were made of 'dried weeds'. Frank Moshinskie's first model, a lady forever hanging up washing, took her place in a miniature world where cowboys and Indians fought anew. An arrow-stuck cowboy shook with mechanical death twitches, as the Indians in their village performed a war dance. Lights blazed in the windows of tiny houses, and toy boats floated from pool to pool. Glimpsing below the model-covered table, I could see various wheels and pulleys spinning round. Most of the miniature puppets were connected through slits to the machine beneath their world.

'My husband began making toys for the Christmas tree, and then found he couldn't stop,' Mrs Moshinskie explained. She seemed to be very proud of him, and no wonder.

In Yellowstone Corner, a troop of black bears had taken over a picnic. While some of the tiny mechanical bears ate the food or drank from minute bottles marked 'Seven-Up', the ranger was busily trying to beat them off with clubs. A cowardly toy man had climbed a toy tree, leaving his wife (a mere toy) on the ground.

Our mules took us back to the real town, and soon Tommy and I were heading back to Arkadelphia.

'I used to drive four racehorses from Florida to California and back, for race meetings,' Tommy told me. 'I'd carry water in the truck, and every now and then I'd let the horses out for a run around. Now that was a job I really enjoyed. I certainly saw America! In the Arizona desert, I saw boulders balanced one on top of the other. How did they get like that? And what's more how do they *stay* like that?'

Leaving these questions unanswered, Tommy dropped me off outside the Southern Swing Jamboree, in Arkadelphia. I went in, and found myself in a long hall which had been made by tearing out the wall between two shops. At the far end of the room, musicians were tuning up on a stage before a backcloth of black cellophane that hung in crinkly folds that resembled gnarled tree trunks. All the musicians wore their everyday clothes. An elderly white-haired man plucked meditatively on his fiddle, four young guitarists tightened or loosened their instruments' strings and a drummer rapped out a tentative note. Below the stage was a shiny dance floor, and on a carpeted section nearer the door, row upon row of cheap canvas chairs.

Nearly all the seats were full. Most of the music lovers were in their sixties, the men fat in shirtsleeves, the women thin and wearing spectacles. All seemed relaxed and friendly. Young people and children made up the rest of the audience. Pink or blue patches of hardboard had been nailed to the walls as a decoration, together with hand-coloured and clumsily cut-out paper stars and pumpkins.

I paid a small fee at the counter near the door, and was given a soft drink. Everyone looked Irish, if you can imagine Irishmen content to sip Coca-Cola or orangeade.

'There's another country music show in town, held in the old theatre, and that goes on till late, with a bar,' I was told. Perhaps that was where the thirty- and forty-year-old Arkadelphians had gone.

'You can ask any of these women to dance!' a grinning gap-toothed woman at the door told me, gesturing expansively across an audience who looked poorer and less sharp than most modern Irish people.

Kindly faces turned towards me, and I felt at home, even though I could not dance.

'I'm a full-blooded Irishwoman,' the gap-toothed lady told me proudly.

Several men turned round in their seats and shook my hand.

'So you're from England, hey? I'm a full-blooded Irishman!'

'So am I!' another chimed in. 'The band's all Irish, with one Swede.'

They were referring to the nationalities of their settler forefathers. Until then, I had never known that an Irishman could be 'full-blooded'. I had always thought that the term was reserved for Red Indians and Romany Gypsies. Theron Freeman, the tall, burly owner of the club, claimed to be part French. A granite-jawed man, his tough face full of character, he could have been taken for a Geordie dustman, or an East End Cockney. His peaked cap was jammed on back to front in a very English fashion.

At last the fiddler struck up a slow waltz, and the rest of the band followed. All the lively children scampered across the floor back to their seats. A few couples rose and made for the floor, where they swayed slowly. More and more people left their seats. Three pear-shaped single girls were asked for dance after dance. A slinky woman in black leather trousers accepted a dance. When she turned, I saw that she was middle-aged and wore dark glasses.

A big man in a suit and tie pointed her out to me with an air of great dignity. 'That lady is blind,' he said impressively. 'She used to be a country and western singer, but gave it up when she lost her sight.'

Before heading for the dance floor, couples approached me and shook my hand. All the women beseeched me to learn to dance. News of my unusual nationality swept the Southern Swing Jamboree. Soon the musicians stepped up the pace, and the fiddler swung into a Chicken Reel. Everyone, in happy excitement, began to hop on one leg, flap their arms and career in chicken-fashion around the floor. The musicians clucked and cackled loudly as they played. Waltz-time returned, and two of the guitarists crooned soft ballads: 'You Win Again', 'I Wouldn't

Change You If I Could' and 'Does Fort Worth Ever Cross Your Mind?'

Suddenly, the lead guitar rang out with a rocking blues I had heard everywhere in the South, from black or white musicians – 'Going to Kansas City'. Theron, the Geordie dustman, took the stage and sang Gene Vincent songs with great feeling, waggling his cap and his eyebrows saucily. Gene Vincent, like Elvis Presley and most other fifties rock and rollers, was a white country boy who knew the blues and transformed them to a white Southern style. This early rock and roll had been deemed 'too black' by the established country singers of its day. Now as archaic as Elizabethan ballads, it had been absorbed into country music and formed a part of every singer's repertoire. The cheerfully jiving couples looked as if they were performing a country dance. I had seldom seen people with such a delight in dancing. Haunting, liquid notes from the fiddle heralded a return to waltz time, and the big, stout men swayed with their eyes shut. I could have been in Kilburn.

'Anyone here from another state?' the band leader shouted.

'Ohio!' shouted one person, 'Mississippi!' another.

'There's an Englishman here!' somebody roared.

'An Englishman!' the band leader echoed in amazement.

Feeling like an ambassador, I stood up, shouted out my name as requested, bowed deeply and sat down.

'And now, for Roy there, we'll play our national anthem,' the bow-legged fiddle player announced. 'The Arkansaw Traveller!'

Stamping one foot, he sawed away at a tune that sounded very like 'Turkey in the Straw'. With many loud whoops and cries of 'Now git it!' the other musicians joined in. Just before the dancers grew out of breath, a Paul Jones was announced. Dancers joined hands in a circle, then formed pairs who spun around the floor to the fastest fiddle I had ever heard in my life. A whistle screeched and everyone changed partners, to whirl around anew. Falsetto howls, whoops and yips spurred the dancers on. When everyone was exhausted, an interval was announced. At once the floor became a playground for the children.

I hurried up to the stage to meet the band.

'That tune you might know as "Sleepy Eyed John", but a lot of us Arkansas fiddlers call it "Leather Breeches",' the fiddler informed me gravely. His remarks suggested a troubadour fraternity of fiddlers roaming around Arkansas. 'My name is Erbie Meeks, an' I used to go on tour playing fiddle for well-known country singers like Carl Smith and George Jones. Talking of George, my great-great-great-great-uncle Nathanael fought along with George Washington. I got his discharge papers at home. After that, some o' my folk married Cherokees. I got a grandfather from Ireland and a grandma who's a Cherokee Indian. And that's a fact!'

Lincoln Wilson, the band leader, affably introduced me to the guitarists Jimmy, Jack and Scooter, and to Larry Wharton the drummer. Scooter, in his check lumber shirt, was the heart throb of the band. Just then I felt a tap on my shoulder. It was the dignified man in the suit again. 'She's just found out, they can do an operation to bring her sight back,' he told me.

A gnarled man told me of a stay in a London Hotel near King's Cross, and an even gnarleder man said, 'I'm an old has-been now, but I used to play guitar and yodel like my idol, Jimmy Rodgers.'

I showed him some of my photographs of England. The sight of so many coloured people made him feel gloomy, even though Jimmy Rodgers had achieved fame and fortune by borrowing verses and rhythm from the blues.

'So you've got 'em!' was all the man said. 'We have to have them in our schools now.'

Just then, the band struck up once more with a boogie rhythm that was pure Negro, even down to the cries of 'Mercy, Mercy, Mercy!' So the old man cheered up.

Couples linked arms and spun around to the fast blues of 'That's All Right, Mama' and 'Mean Woman Blues'. A song about a hot Louisiana dish I had sampled in New Orleans followed – 'Jambalaya and a crawfish pie'.

'Fräulein!' shouted a woman from the audience.

Obligingly, a song about a German girl was warbled, then a ballad called 'Crazy Arms'. A piston-rhythm train song, with realistic whistle hoots, brought the merry evening to a close.

'I hear that train a-coming . . .'

A guitar player drove me back to my traffic-island, where, in the Waffle House at midnight, I met all the music-loving Arkadelphians all over again, eager and ready to hear about life in England.

Early next morning, I stood with my bag on the forlorn, semi-derelict railway platform of Arkadelphia, wishing that I *could* hear the train a-coming. The ticket hall had long been boarded up. Workmen locked their tools away before driving home. One of them assured me that the train would be coming by and by. For three-quarters of an hour I stood there in mounting despair; by now the train was an hour late.

'How wonderful if an old Western train were suddenly to appear puffing round the bend, steam pouring from its funnel and the whistle hooting,' I thought to myself.

Just then, I heard a loud hoot, and an enormous train appeared, black smoke pouring from the chimney. Amazed, I watched it draw near and then stop. Close up, it didn't seem like a train at all, but a huge sealed-up silver-caterpillar space rocket, each section taller than the station roof.

The smoking chimney appeared to be an upturned exhaust pipe leading from the gigantic engine. *The Eagle*, a name-plate proclaimed.

A small spacecraft door slid open, and steps were placed outside. The uniformed guard and an old grey-haired Negro steward looked out, smiling and beckoning. They seemed relieved and half-surprised to see a passenger, but not as relieved and surprised as I was to see *them*.

'Mr Roy Kerridge, bound for Fort Worth, Texas?' the guard enquired, consulting a document.

That was me, so I climbed thankfully on board and was shown to a seat upstairs. The train was a double-decker. Narrow steps led up to the top floor, where rows of narrow aircraft seats were filled with passengers. From outside the windows had been invisible, but from inside they were real enough. I sat next to one, and soon we were off. I had often wondered how Lenin had felt, riding on a sealed train, and now I knew.

In a moment Arkadelphia was left behind and we were riding through tangled, swampy Arkansas woods. Cypress trees grew from pools of water amid the lesser forest trees. Once the blue tent of a deer-hunters' camp appeared for a moment between the leaves. Drizzle sprayed against the window, and the broad-leafed forest went on and on.

Southerners seem to have forgotten that trains exist and we sped through Texarkana and other stations without stopping. Most of the passengers, I gathered from their conversation, were from Chicago heading for San Antonio and the dry South West. Not precisely Yankees, but non-Southern Americans, the sort who come to England on holiday.

A fat, elderly man in a grey suit and spectacles got shut in a self-closing door as he entered the carriage. He gave the door a spiteful, childish glance and began to swear at it. Still spluttering 'goddams', he sat down in the seat behind me.

Out in the wet world beyond my window, logging camps began to appear within the woods. Soon after that, the woods ended. A brickworks, complete with old kilns, flashed by and then we were among open fields, speeding through Texas. Huge Hereford bulls, with unpolled horns, lorded it over their wives. So it was true that everything is bigger in Texas! Donkey engines (or 'Pump Jacks'), pumping out oil, nodded their heads in the middle of arable fields. Oil drilling and farming can apparently take place side by side. Real donkeys, or *burros* as they say in Texas, cropped the grass around oil storage tanks. Large oil refineries appeared as industrial patches in the wide-open landscape. Still the rain pattered down.

Drowsily I hummed a tune I had heard at the Southern Swing Jamboree: 'Does Fort Worth ever cross your mind?'

'Do you intend to hum all day?' the fat man leaned forward and asked me irritably.

'Sir, if you request me to stop humming I will do so,' I replied austerely. 'I am an Englishman and I was unaware that humming was forbidden.'

A deathly silence was all the answer I received, and as I *did* stop humming, this silence continued for a while. Then the hum hater recognised a friend and shouted out a greeting.

'I'm eighty-two years old, and I feel fine,' the friend replied, sitting down heavily. 'All my life I've done what I wanted to do, and drank as much as I pleased. My sister's in a nursing home, and she's younger than me. I called to see her and she said "Jimmy, after the life you led, you look fine. I've lived clean, an' here I am broken down and sick." It makes you think.'

> HUM HATER: That's right! There's no harm in doing whatever you please! That's what made America great! If I want to spend my money on a whore, I do so.
> JIMMY: That's right! There's nothing wrong with prostitutes. They're just making a living. There'd be a lot more rapes if it weren't for prostitutes.

Their loud conversation continued to deteriorate morally, and I fell asleep. A moment later, I awoke to find a tall, white-haired, red-faced man bending over me. 'Are you going to Fort Worth?' he asked.

'Why, are we there?'

'No, we don't get in for hours yet,' he replied, and walked off.

I decided that he had awoken me because someone had told him that I was English, and he wanted to hear my accent. Drowsily, I made my way to the buffet car, a splendid carriage with outsize windows and room to stretch your legs under the tables. Drinks were served from a tiny hatch at the carriage end. Two middle-aged men, drunk and shouting, were analysing America's political situation. At a nearby table, two spotty young men conversed entirely in swear words. By contrast to these Chicagoans, *every* Southern man was a gentleman.

Hum Hater waddled up to the hatch and ordered a drink. 'See that man? He's English!' he loudly informed the barman, pointing at me.

At that moment a beaming, well-dressed man, the railway entertainments officer, walked to the head of the carriage and greeted us. A badge on his impeccable suit read 'John W. Mohammed', so I presume that he had been a Black Moslem in his younger days. He handed out pencils and paper to those who wanted them, and announced a game of Trivial Pursuit.

This turned out to be a quiz with prizes.

'Do we get Chevrolets or trips to Florida?' a woman called out.

'No madam, our prizes are much smaller than that.'

Now the good train *Eagle* seemed less like a plane and more like an ocean liner. The tall man who had woken me sat by my side, and I whispered wrong answers to him. He seemed very drunk, and his face was redder than ever. Most of the questions were about pop music.

'What caused poverty among the farmers in the South East in 1985?' Mr Mohammed read out.

'Reagan!' shouted the woman who liked Chevrolets. Everyone cheered.

'That's naughty! I meant *natural* cause,' said Mr Mohammed.

'Reagan *is* natural.'

'Funny!' mused our compère. 'Only a year ago, everyone loved him, and now everyone's against him.'

Slowly we drew into Dallas, a horrendous town of grey concrete skyscrapers.

'Look, that's the very spot where Kennedy was shot!' a woman called out dramatically. 'And that building there is where the bullet came from!'

At Dallas Station, the loudspeaker paged a woman passenger, but she could not be found. So after a long wait, the train moved on. All at once the loudspeaker roared out, 'Stop the train!'

We stopped and reversed back into Dallas. The old lady had been found, and was helped solicitously down on to the platform by the guard and steward. Then we moved off once more. British Rail could learn some lessons here.

Not long afterwards, I left Mr Mohammed and the others in mid-quiz and descended to the lower deck as Fort Worth, Texas, drew near. A mother screamed abuse at her child, as she dragged him towards the doorway. The two hulking, spotty boys, conversing loudly about drugs, took their suitcases down from a rack. A small crowd formed, ready to disembark.

'I used to have long hair, but I cut it off when I went to see my grandfather, and then I sold it!' one of the boys remarked.

'That man's an Englishman!' somebody interrupted. All eyes turned towards me.

'Do they have many punks in England?' the hair-seller asked me keenly.

'Well, they have a few Mohawks, with spiky red crests on their shaved heads,' I answered.

'I used to have a Mohawk hair-do!' the boy cried. 'That was when I was at school.'

'Schools in England don't allow them,' I mentioned.

'Most don't here, but I went to private school,' he replied, blushing around his spots. 'What politics have you got?'

Flustered at such an abrupt and personal question, I began to explain that Conservatism in England was different from American conservatism.

Luckily a shabbily dressed young man interrupted to ask me if I had heard of a place in England called Essex.

'I met someone from Essex when I was in South Africa,' he continued. 'He was on the run from the police. I thought you were a South African, with that accent. My buddy went back to England, and got murdered by his stepfather, who shot him. He was my best friend!'

I didn't know what to say.

Just then, the *Eagle* glided to a halt, the door opened, and the guard produced the steps. I was in Fort Worth, Texas!

With a last look at the immense silver train, which dwarfed the station, I dragged my bag into the spacious ticket hall and out on to the station forecourt. Here the railway buildings were in good repair, and passengers queued for tickets or sat on benches. There was a taxi rank, hotels on the horizon and familiar red-brick Victoriana everywhere. Only the huge goods trucks and the names of the depot outbuildings showed that this was not an outsize Worthing or Stoke-on-Trent.

'Union Pacific and Sante Fe', the signs read, an echo of the railway ballad of Casey Jones.

Within minutes I was unpacking my red, white and blue bag in a bedroom of the Park Central Hotel.

CHAPTER FOURTEEN

Fort Worth, Texas

MY HOTEL IN Fort Worth had its own elegant dining room, a luxury almost unheard of in America. I toyed over my delicious breakfast, admired the picture of the *Flying Cloud* clipper ship on my sugar packet, and watched the crowds outside from my seat near the window.

I emerged to find myself in the midst of a highly sophisticated city. A type of Superdome (Tarrant County Convention Centre) and other chunks of white concrete modernity surrounded the hotel, but I soon circumvented these. Passing a large post office and a chain of recruiting offices side by side (Army, Navy and Air Force), I found myself in Main Street. A high-class shopping street, with old shabby buildings among the glitter, Main Street led to Sundance Square and on to the magnificent old courthouse that dominated the city.

Sundance Square did not resemble a London square, but was merely an open space, full of parked cars, among shops and offices. A large bright mural showed longhorn cattle thundering through the main street of a long-lost Fort Worth that seemed scarcely imaginable. Soaring white skyscrapers behind the square alternated oddly with nineteenth-century shops that were being restored. To my surprise, I found a street of fake shop-fronts with paintings of their supposed interiors on the bricked-up windows.

Smart Fort Worth ended at the front steps of the great domed courthouse. Below the *back* steps of the Tarrant County Courthouse, Main Street continued in a straight line to the horizon, crossing the Trinity River and continuing through rows of small factories and businesses. In the palatial courthouse, I admired the gracious stairway that spiralled past floors of courtrooms with wooden pews and American flags. Photographs of bygone Fort Worth lined the walls.

Beyond the courthouse, tucked to one side of Main Street, I found a run-down but friendly district of wooden houses with porches and front lawns, the home of Mexicans and of a few coloured people. In a poor people's shopping street here, I observed Mexicans and Negroes mixing together without seeing each other, just as do West Indians and Pakistanis in England. I had never seen Mexicans before in my life, and looked with awe on these tall, handsome Red Indian-like brown people. Some of them appeared to have hardly any Spanish blood.

Scruffy old men with moustaches pottered in and out of the dark narrow open doorway of the Workman's Hotel. The ground floor was a pool hall where down-at-heel men of three races watched the players through narrowed eyes. Poverty and wealth in Fort Worth could be seen side by side. White people spoke in gentle, slow, soft accents, black people rattled their words out in a hurry and Mexicans spoke Spanish.

Spanish 'teach yourself English' books were on sale in the crowded Courthouse Market, a boisterous supermarket, whose customers were Mexicans and black people. Hot peppers of every kind were on sale, some bearing Spanish names such as *Burrito*. Young mothers with children queued at a pay-desk for customers with 'food stamps', a Welfare scheme to prevent 'relief' money being wasted on luxuries. The whole shop sizzled with life. I bought a pencil.

Back on Main Street, near Sundance Square, I chanced upon the Sid Richardson Gallery of Western Art. This wonderful art gallery is one of the chief ornaments of Fort Worth. All the paintings are of Wild West themes, and all are the work of two men (both with unfortunate middle names). Frederic Sackrider Remington (1861–1909) and Charles Marion Russell (1864–1926) both went West in search of adventure and both worked for a time as sheepherders, the Western form of shepherd. Now their vivid oil paintings, collected by a rancher and oilman named Sid Richardson, are hung side by side in a long white room decorated with a silver-trimmed cowboy outfit and guarded by a young man with a pistol at his hip.

Frederic Sackrider only spent a year among the sheep, and thereafter merely visited the West. His relative inexperience only showed itself in one picture, 'His Last Stand', where a hunted grizzly has obviously been drawn from a stuffed specimen. Russell's grizzlies are living creatures of flesh, bone and silver-tipped hair. Frederic excels at night paintings, perfectly capturing moonlight, that elusive substance, on canvas. His daytime scenes depict a pitiless sun. For him there is no dusk. Twilight, my favourite time of day, is Russell's forte, and that is one reason why I think he is the better man.

Frederic feared and hated Indians, and conveyed his horror brilliantly in uncanny paintings such as 'Apache Medicine Song'. A night picture, painted from life, this shows fierce, chanting warriors sitting round a campfire and ritually praising a demonic god. Charles Russell remained in the West all his life, and developed a strong admiration for Indians, 'the real Americans'. He made friends with Montana tribesmen and took the name 'Ah-Wah-Cows', the Antelope. His pictures are signed with a buffalo skull. I remembered reading Russell's accounts of Western life, which I discovered years ago in the Central Library at Liverpool. I had been particularly impressed by his interview with a 'squaw man', a white man who had taken an Indian wife and 'gone native'. 'Women make us what we are,' Lindsay, the long-haired white Indian, had told Russell.

Russell's painting of Lindsay, 'When White Men Turn Red', showed an idyllic twilit scene of the squaw man with his two wives and his two wolf-dogs riding back to his tepee village after a successful trapping expedition.

Among the Russell paintings I admired was one which showed two white hunters returning to their mountain camp with a slaughtered mule deer, only to find a couple of skunks playing havoc with their pork and beans. They have to wait until the playful pests have finished, for 'Man's Weapons Are Useless When Nature Goes Armed'.

'The Defiant Culprit' shows an Indian lawbreaker, in a dramatic night scene, boldly facing his tribal executioners. 'A Quiet Day in Utica' gives an excellent idea of what a sleepy, dusty cow town might have been like. Originally, this had been painted as an advertisement for the Utica Mercantile Store, which now appears in the background as guffawing cowboys watch a terrified dog with a tin tied to its tail trip up a horse and rider. One stretch of wall was given over to Russell's paintings of buffaloes (bison) and Indian buffalo-hunters. The frantic gleam in the eye of the hunted beast is captured perfectly. 'Guardian of the Herd' shows a wise old buffalo bull defending his wives from a prowling wolf.

Charles Russell was not always very apt with titles, but at least 'Captain William Clark of the Lewis and Clark Expedition Meeting with the Indians of the North West' is self-explanatory. Clark is shown as arrogant, and the Indians of the North West, by contrast, look very polite. One old crone, however, is clearly prophesying Trouble. Russell seemed to enjoy painting Indian hags with wild, glowing eyes, pointing with claw-like fingers and uttering toothless curses. A proud buccaneer-like black man stands at Clark's side, and an Indian coyote dog instinctively cowers with its tail between its legs.

Apparently, Russell toyed with the idea of taking an Indian bride. In the event, he married a white girl whose sound business head helped to make him successful. When I was a teenager, I longed for a South American Indian bride, as my boyish heart had been swept away by the romanticising pen of Lewis V. Cummings, author of *I was a Head Hunter*.

An American, Cummings claimed to have taken three jungle brides following his initiation into a tribe of Colombian Indians. Too timid to leave grammar school and run away to South America to hunt heads, I devised a board game where the winner could live happily ever after in a thatched Amazonian hut with an Indian girl. My grandparents with whom I played always allowed me to win.

After admiring the wonderful paintings in the gallery, I approached the young man who stood beside the ornamented leather chaps and saddle. Himself a living relic of the Old West, he wore a silver star.

'No, I'm not a sheriff. This star is my security guard badge,' he told me.

'In England, art gallery attendants don't carry guns,' I informed him.

'Don't they?' he asked in surprise.

'No. It must be frustrating for you, having that gun. I daresay whole *days* go by without you shooting anyone.'

'I'm glad – I don't want to shoot people,' the guard confessed.

Across the square to the Western art gallery, I found more exquisite artwork in a luxurious modern theatre, the Caravan of Dreams. Not only a theatre, a dance studio and a nightclub, the Caravan boasted a gigantic dome of crystal-like glass high up on the roof garden. Greg Dugan, the General Manager (who hailed from Boulder, Colorado) proudly showed me around. Originally the building had been a warehouse. Now every room boasted brilliant and expressive murals from floor to ceiling. In the nightclub, the finest mural of all showed the history of jazz musicians from slavery times on to a racy New Orleans in the twenties, then up a Spanish-moss-hung Mississippi River to Chicago. Jazz finally ended among pretentious hipsters and white bohemians in the far right-hand corner of the room. Live jazz played nightly on a stage before the mural, and Greg reeled off a list of famous Caravan names that I ought to have heard of. I recognised one – Albert King, a bluesman whose records I had seen on Jimmy 'the Preacher' Ellis's juke box in Texarkana.

The Caravan's finest pictures, those showing sharply-dressed loose-living coloured folk with beaming smiles, had been painted by the talented team of Flash Allen, Corinna MacNeice and Felipe Cebeza de Vaca. Up on the roof, under the great diamond dome, or solarium, rare cacti grew among weird artificial rock formations. Different parts of the crazy kopje represented South West Africa, Mexico and Madagascar. The Malagasy cacti resembled giant prickly cabbages.

'Come back tonight, we've got a reggae band called the Killer Bees,' Greg promised.

Rather at a loss, and a little overawed by Fort Worth, I wandered between towering glass skyscrapers as I killed time before the Killer Bee concert. On Main Street, both the road *and* the pavement were made of polished red bricks such as I had seen on the pavements of New Orleans. In a hidden, leafy little square near the Park Central Hotel, I saw my first grackle. It was a Great-Tailed Grackle, a typical Texan bird, that resembled a cross between a glossy starling and a magpie. A yellow-eyed, blue-velvety-purple long-tailed blackbird, once seen it could not be forgotten. Nearby I found the Greyhound Bus station and bought a ticket to Bryan in Southern Texas. Here at Fort Worth the weather was dull, and after sunset it grew freezing cold. November had rolled around, though with no Guy Fawkes' day to distinguish it.

Few people were about, but a troop of ten Mexicans suddenly emerged from the coach station, all with bundles and sleeping bags on their shoulders. Tall and dark, with Mongolian cheekbones, they looked just like Charles Russell's pictures of Red Indians. However, they spoke Spanish, in loud guttural tones. Noticing my admiration, one of the men asked me for a quarter. You're welcome.

I returned to my hotel room and had a little sleep. It was nearly dark when I awoke, and the rain was cascading down. I struggled out to Main Street, and found a cheap café near the Caravan of Dreams. Here most of the customers were uproarious young coloured people, the boys laughing, joking and pushing each other around, the girls sitting primly with armfuls of text books. A white man walked from table to table trying to sell a pair of gloves. Behind the counter, a fat coloured girl carried on a shouting conversation with a thin man.

'Is you hear 'bout Sam Johnson and that white man? Seems the white man says "Come here, boy," to ole Sam an' Sam don't like that . . .'

With my head down, I braved the rain and galloped into the Caravan of Dreams. My English accent aroused some stir at the box office. Just then a sophisticated-looking blonde girl, with a nervous Mexican on her arm, made her way towards me. 'Do the Celts still paint themselves blue?' she asked me in ringing tones.

'Only the women, and that's just their eyelids,' I riposted a moment after she had gone. Her vision of the modern Irish and Cornish as princely barbarian warriors and bards had taken my breath away.

In the darkened bar, I met Kelvin, Mal, Stan, Michael and Brady, the Killer Bees. All were as sophisticated as their decidedly un-Kerridgean setting. Couples kept arriving, mainly white people, and taking their tables near the stage. Kelvin wore his hair in Rasta dreadlocks but none of the group had been to Jamaica. They were college-educated lads from Louisiana.

'I like reggae, as it has its roots in jazz,' Kelvin told me. 'I began in modern jazz. No, I'm not a Rasta believer, but I don't go to the Episcopal Church any more. That's what I was brought up in. Organised religion can't be right. Okay, so Rastas say Haile Selassie is God, so what's wrong with that?'

When young people turn against 'organised religion', they usually become the slaves of a guru. The Killer Bees played a modern jazz-styled reggae. In America reggae was a cabaret art and attracted the well-to-do. In England and Jamaica it is a rough people's music. However, the Killer Bees play reggae no more, and are touring England as I write, playing sweet music for the Louisiana soul-singer Percy Sledge.

Outside the Caravan of Dreams, central Fort Worth gleamed in the aftermath of the rain. Every skyscraper was outlined with straight rows of yellow light bulbs. Lights hung from the branches of the trees, and the lampposts glowed green. At the hotel they told me that at one time the town was illuminated only at Thanksgiving, in late November, and stayed lit up till Christmas. Switching on the lights had been a great occasion, presided over by the Mayor. Now, in the hope of attracting tourists, the lights came on every night of the year, and the taxpayers footed the bill. The illuminated skyscrapers looked like gigantic neon cornflake packets in an advertisement.

To my delight, I found that Fort Worth had a zoo, set in an attractive park. In the morning the sun shone, and the grackles hopped from stepping stone to stepping stone across the little stream that ran through the flowery zoo. Near the entrance an elaborate sequence of elephant stockades, designed to facilitate breeding, evidently did not work, as no elephants could be seen. Careful landscaping and use of moats made it seem as if the fluffy-tailed herds of springbok, the lions and the Barbary sheep, all from Africa, shared the same rocky compound. Wild sheep on concrete crags leaped on to ledges that perilously overhung the lions' den.

Fort Worth Zoo Aquarium must be one of the finest in the world. Pools by the doorway teemed with ornamental carp, and a third tank was fixed over the door itself. Inside, steps led down to a green window on the outdoor sea lion pool. A gigantic male sea lion, black with a white bear's face and a bull neck and bloated body, moved lightly through the water. His wives were thin and streamlined. One of them tried to snap at me underwater, through the glass.

In an upright tank, in the middle of the floor, Missisippi paddlefish, like grey pygmy sawfish, darted up and down. Bengal finches, bright tropical birds, flitted among the ferns and the rockery above one exotic tank. A deep, clear pool filled a large hall, with a slope leading down to submarine windows below. Large terrapins clung to the branches of a fallen tree, and still larger cichlids, smooth gulping fish with baleful African expressions, could be admired from above or below. The Reptile House had been built on a similar plan, with a false Congo River and an imitation Amazon.

Dwarf crocodiles sat like stones by the riverbank, never moving and tricking the visitors into thinking that they were stuffed.

Malayan sun bears and Siberian tigers, however, were forced to live in minute concrete and iron prisons. Fort Worth Zoo has room for improvement. However, I could forgive anything for the sight of a steep mock mountain alive with a tide of mouflons, or mountain sheep, who surged up and down in a nimble light-footed flock, pouring over stones like quicksilver.

Outside the zoo, I waited at a bus stop, where I was soon joined by a disgruntled-looking coloured man. 'All these chalets belong to one hotel,' he said, pointing. 'I work there. Just now the dining-room table is laid and ready. Why don't you go in and eat? I'll show you where to go. Everyone will think you're a guest.'

'I don't dare to,' I admitted. 'Supposing I was caught, I don't understand the laws and the jails in this country.'

'I hear you!' the man acknowledged. Revenge on his boss would have to wait.

I was not the only English person at the Park Central Hotel. To my surprise, the middle-aged receptionist asked me wistfully how England was getting along. She had been a G.I. bride from King's Lynn in Norfolk. Now she was divorced.

'Texas doesn't have alimony,' she said, 'and my husband never paid his child support money in full, so I came to work here. A few years ago, I went back to have a look at England again. It looked horrible! All the young people were experimenting with new lifestyles! So I decided to bring my children up here in Texas. People still go to church here. Still, I often wonder what happened to the carefree Irishman I jilted when I met my future husband.'

Did any trace remain of the Old West, when Fort Worth really *was* a fort, standing alone in a prairie full of Indians? The paintings of Russell and Remington seemed to depict an America that is further removed from the present day than is the England of Chaucer. The Old Chisholm Trail, famous in cowboy mythology, had led to Fort Worth Stockyards. These Stockyards still existed, in the district known as Cow Town. I hailed a taxi and asked the driver to take me to Cow Town.

A genial old coloured man, he responded with an enthusiastic, 'I hear you!' to almost everything I said.

'I'd never seen a Mexican till I came to Texas,' I told him.

'Is that so?' he shouted in astonishment. 'Never seen a Mexican! I declare!'

'What kind of people are they?' I enquired.

'They're craftsmen! They can paint and work metal and do engineering work. Anything craftsmanlike. They're in great demand here. Some Mexicans do menial work that Americans won't do, for less money. See, they can live on tortillas made with just a little bit of flour. All the same, they get more money here than they could ever get in Mexico. So they save, and then they send for their families. A hard-working people, the Mexicans. In a moment you'll see Spanish Town, our Mexico City.'

Soon we were driving in a straight line along Main Street, past the courthouse, the river and the dismal factories and through a run-down 'Spanish Town', full of Mexican shops. All at once, still in Main Street, Fort Worth, we entered a strange cowboy realm of saloons and shops, enormous signs hanging from posts or standing above doorways. Effigies of saddles, horses, whiskey bottles, cowboys and Indians advertised various wares, sold from dark interiors framed in grey, weathered wood. Porches with hitching rails took the place of pavements. A large figure of a white elephant advertised one saloon, mounted steer horns another.

Beyond Cow Town, in a large, newly-cleared open space, the driver set me down beside a statue of a group of Texas longhorn cattle. This hardy breed, ideal for droving but no longer needed in a railway age, once epitomised the West, just as Highland Cattle represented Northern Scotland. Now both these sturdy long-horned breeds are only kept as a novelty to attract tourists. Another statue, of a horse and cowboy, stood nearby.

'That's the entrance to the Stockyards,' the driver pointed. 'That's Billy Bob's, the biggest honky tonk in the world. A honky tonk is kind of like a bar for music and dancing, but right now they're playing bingo in there.'

Cowboys playing bingo! Would wonders never cease? Did they pull out guns and challenge the caller? A long, concrete barn, Billy Bob's did not look inviting, so I walked on, through pantiled arches and spacious patios that reminded me of the entrance to Alton Towers in England. Trees in tubs and broken-down pioneer covered wagons stood as ornaments in the vast paved Stockyards. Cowboy hats and stuffed rattlesnake-head key-ring holders filled the windows of souvenir shops. Not many people were about, and the smell of straw and cowpat was noticeably absent.

Yet, as in the French Quarter at New Orleans, there was a kernel of reality within the tourist flim-flam shell. Real cattle offices where herds were bought and sold appeared between souvenir and craft markets. Rows of wooden stock pens, empty now, testified to the existence of cattle and cattlemen somewhere. Much of nearby Cow Town was fake Wild Westery, yet many of the buildings actually did date from the days of whooping men with lariats and the big cattle drives. Cow Town had been de-modernised, decorated as if for a film set. From the wide avenues of the Stockyards I could catch enticing glimpses of the narrow Cow Town streets through gaps between storehouses.

Most imposing building in the Stockyards was the 'Live Stock X-change'. Steps led up to a pantiled Roman villa with a bust of a longhorn steer above the wide entrance. Inside, I found myself in a cool arcade of cattle offices and craft shops. Glass shop-fronts of offices showed desks, files and stuffed longhorn heads on the walls. One of the most interesting of the old-fashioned offices had a bison head on the wall. The bison was wearing a hat. Directly below this unfortunate bison, a fat, tough cigar-chewing man appeared to be paying off a couple of over-awed cowboys. Both men wore enormous stetson hats, blue shirts, jeans and leather boots. Their irascible bald-headed boss shot an irritable look in my direction.

A sign on the window welcomed sightseers with these words: 'Answers to Questions – Seventy-Five Cents. Answers Requiring Thought – One Dollar Fifty. Dumb Looks are Still Free.'

I took a long dumb look, and observed another sign on the wall below the bison. 'Steer Beef, Heifer Beef, Cattle Kill, Hog Kill', I read. The office looked very different from that of an English cattle auctioneer. Mythology had been at work upon the American cattle industry. One of the cowboys, his business concluded, stepped into the office doorway. Here, he swelled out his chest, tucked his thumbs into his jeans and gave a lazily amused he-man's glance up and down the office corridors, from the window to the water-cooling machine. In his mind's eye, he was no doubt glancing up and down the dusty main street of Dodge City to see if Wild Bill Hickok and Yosemite Sam were shooting it out as usual. For a living, this man probably drove lorry-loads of Hereford cows up and down the interstate highways.

Outside, I stood at the Main Street crossroads of Cow Town and watched an ancient cowboy, a tall man in a stetson, with a white beard and longhorn moustache, walk slowly towards the saloon of his choice. Cars, not runaway horses, missed him by inches. Amidst the saloons and honky tonks, the souvenir shops and musty old stores marked 'Saddles Repaired', there was a first-class hotel. That was a *very* French Quarter touch. Opposite this hotel stood the Cattlemen's Restaurant. Here buyers and sellers of roped and branded cattle herds had been dining in an aura of cigar perfume ever since the days of Charles Russell and Frederic Remington.

Their heirs, sleek businessmen, still sat at the long tables while waitresses scurried around. Photographs of prize-winning Hereford bulls, too fat to last a mile on the Old Chisholm Trail, looked down from the walls in bovine stupidity. I selected a dish called an 'Arkansaw

Traveller'. Hot beef with gravy on cornbread, it was so tender and delicious that I can taste it yet.

'Can you no' tell my accent?' my waitress enquired. 'I'm from Glasgow, but I went and married a Texan. We're divorced now, that's why I'm working here. You know Lulu, the wee Glaswegian pop singer? Her mother used to be a friend and neighbour o' mine at one time.'

Bidding Lulu's mother's friend goodbye, I set out to walk to Spanish Town to see the Mexicans. Before I had gone very far, I came across the Bob Wills Museum.

Bob Wills, the famous country and western fiddle player, died in Fort Worth in 1975. His band, the Light Crust Doughboys, were to give their farewell performance within a few days of my visit to the city. When Bob Wills had mastered the cowboy fiddle styles that derived from Irish, Scottish and (probably) Swedish music, he went on to learn the Negro or 'alley' fiddle and to play blues and hot swing. He and his Light Crust Doughboys helped to create the style of cowboy jazz known as Western Swing.

Once more, a touch of the jazzy blues had livened up a white man's music. Inside the little museum, a video showed excerpts from films starring Bob Wills and his band, and the rooms rang with joyous fiddling and shouts of 'Mama Don' Allow No Fiddle Playing Here!'

There, behind glass, reposed the best-loved fiddle in Texas, together with the curious flat metal guitar played by sidekick Leon McAuliffe ('Take it away, Leon!'). A yellowing book, *The Life of Bob Wills*, lay open in a showcase.

'Chapter One,' I read . . .

> *A Fiddler is Born.* A flash of lightning momentarily lit up with blue white fire the lonely, rolling landscape. The sign of a small house ahead danced in the doctor's blinded eyes as a blacker night followed the crash of thunder. A tall young man with worried eyes threw open the door and helped the doctor strip off his sodden greatcoat. 'Doc, Emma's pretty bad,' he said in a choked voice. 'I was scared you wouldn't get here in time. . .'

Ah, they don't write books like that any more!

On my way out I glanced at the woman at the pay-desk. She was a sad-faced, courageous-looking, bird-like little woman, a streak of white in her black beehive hair. Could it be? Surely not . . .

'Yes, I am Mrs Bob Wills,' the lady told me. 'No, I didn't sing mahself, I raised young 'uns. So you're from England! I been all over Europe with my husband and the Light Crust Doughboys. We were out in Switzerland once –'

'Where the yodel comes from,' I interrupted.

'Yeah, and those Swiss didn't know what to make of us. So Bob sung fifties songs and they liked that. Then we was in Germany. Someone there said to me "Look at all those Friesian cattle." "I don't see nothing but them ol' Holsteins," I said. Seems they calls Holsteins Friesians over there.'

So in America, Friesian cattle are called Holsteins! Now I knew why everyone looked blank when I talked cattle and mentioned Friesians. You learn something new every day. Bidding farewell to Mrs Wills, I walked on out of Cow Town.

A young Mexican was walking in front of me. Suddenly he crossed the road and entered a tiny ramshackle shed with 'Mexican Café' painted on a board over the door. Sheds and shanties leaned against one another, business names such as 'Rodriguez, Mechanic' painted roughly on the planks. I ducked my head and entered the Mexican Café.

Stout motherly women, lean moustachioed men and brown flashing-eyed youngsters froze in surprise as I stepped down into the dingy room. Instantly I gained an impression of domesticity and warmth, and in that moment I realised that I was not comfortable with the white people of Fort Worth. Waves of relaxation flooded over me as I greeted the Mexicans and explained that I was English. I even produced a map of England for them to pore over, unfolded on a red formica-top table.

'Where are London and Liverpool?' a young man asked. I showed him, and after staring at them hard, he folded up the map and handed it politely back to me.

Next I produced an English pound coin and showed it around. One of the men took a great interest in it and offered to buy it off me. He showed me a coin and asked me where it was from.

'*Belgique*,' I read. At once, the man dashed out of the door and returned panting a minute later to show me an Italian lira.

A jolly curly-haired woman owned the café, and most of the customers were relatives. At a table in the furthest corner, an English lesson was taking place. These Mexicans were not tall and Mongolian, but short and Spanish. The young man I had followed, the same man who had admired the map, was named Mark Berzoza. To my surprise, for he looked a grown man, he told me that he was seventeen years old and still at school.

'This is my girlfriend, Marie,' he said, showing me a photo. 'I like rock music, *not* country. That's for cowboys! I do bench-pressing, weightlifting an' I like football. I got prizes at school for athletics and drawing . . .'

'Drawing!' I exclaimed. 'Here, draw some pictures in my notebook.'

With great care, his family looking on, Mark drew two stylised rabbits dressed as Mexican gentlemen drinking tequila. Beside his signature, he drew a thundercloud spitting lightning and a hand with two horn-like fingers reaching up to it.

'That's the sign of Hades,' he explained. Such horrid imagery came not from Mexico but from the world of rock music. I praised the rabbits. All the while, a dark-eyed girl sat looking towards us fervently.

'She's my sister, Sara Maria,' Mark told me. 'I think she wants to draw, too.'

Shyly, Sara Maria took my pen and paper and drew a beautiful doll-like girl with limpid eyes, short arms and a strange flowing dress decorated with geometrical patterns. Everyone approved.

'We came from Mexico,' Mark murmured, as if to himself.

'You want to hear Mexican music?' the jolly woman asked brightly, and pressed a button on the juke box.

Enchanting music, such as I had never heard before, filled the room. It sounded like a mixture of Western Swing trumpets and the French accordion music I had heard in Louisiana, held together by a drum rhythm that resembled Spanish castanets. I sipped coffee and listened to the music for a while, before heading back to the Stockyards for a look at Billy Bob's. Mark, Sara, the coin collector and the jolly woman all waved me goodbye, then fell to talking rapidly in Spanish.

In the Stockyards, I saw a poster advertising the Cowboys' Church, 'Pastor Copenhagen, champion calf-roper, will conduct the Stockyard Service.'

Restive, rowdy characters hung around the doorway of Billy Bob's, for the pub-crawling night was now underway. The admission was expensive, and as I wished no more than to peep inside, I showed the doorman a letter from my publisher. 'Please help this man, he knows not what he does,' it read (more or less).

'Y'all can go in, but you'd better see the manager,' the doorman said gravely.

Inside, I found myself in a vast alcoholic amusement arcade. Bars, cafés and fruit machine stalls formed separate pools of light within the black hangar-like interior. Crowds of excited young people dressed as cowboys and cowgirls swirled from one pleasure pin-point to another. Stetsons were not compulsory, but checked lumber shirts and blue jeans were worn both by the tall young men and the red-faced, bubble-haired, over-excited girls. A door opened on to an empty rodeo stadium, but few of the drinkers, I would guess, had any connections with cattle or the open range. Most seemed to be the Texas equivalent of Hooray Henries, well-to-do youngsters on pleasure bent. Armed policemen, both black and white, stalked menacingly up and down through the crowds. Each bar, stall, or café seemed to be an independent business. Whoever Billy Bob might be, he was clearly making a fortune.

A Great Rift Valley bisected Billy Bob's, and drinkers could lean over the railings and look down on a countrified rock and roll group, with a black saxophonist, launching into the well-worn blues 'Going to Kansas City'. Rows of chairs surrounded a vast dance floor swathed in rippling disco lights. On the far side of the floor, the inhabitants of a distant illuminated island tuned their guitars and waited for the first group to finish. Couples weaved and bobbed, but most of the patrons preferred drinking to dancing. I descended to the lower floor and walked for a while beside a bar that must be the longest in the world. It stretched away into the blackness like a perspective drawing of Infinity.

Having seen all I wished to see, I sought out the manager to thank him or her. I knocked at a door marked 'Employees Only', and was about to enter when two black-clad security men rushed at me with terror-stricken faces. One seemed to be tugging at a gun, while the other waved his arms about wildly. Obligingly, I backed away.

'The man at the door said I ought to see the manager,' I explained.

'You can't just go in there!' one of the men gasped, glancing at his friend in relief as if to say 'That was a close call!'

So I left Billy Bob's without paying my respects. I still don't know what Billy Bob looks like.

Outside, in Cow Town by night, the porched streets were full of uproarious revellers, nearly all young people of the Billy Bob variety. Rocked-up country music blared from every saloon, and I found myself in a country and western Bourbon Street, with steel guitars instead of jazz trumpets. Music blared from open doors all over crowded Cow Town. Raucous, amplified country music, with thumping rinky-dink pianos, lacked the Irish charm of the Southern Swing Jamboree of Arkadelphia. One honky tonk had a device where a lever released a bat which hurled a ball towards a basketball net. Big men clumped on a tiny dance floor.

Further up the road, at the coyly named Filthy McNasties, the large dance floor was packed with sweating couples. I searched in vain for a honky tonk where someone played a fiddle. Fiddle music is my delight, and the Bob Wills video had whetted my appetite.

'Come on in, it's *fun*!' a red-faced girl screamed at me, as I paused in the doorway of the Pickin' Parlour.

'I won't go in anywhere unless the band has a fiddle,' I pronounced firmly.

'The band's gotta have a *fiddle*?' she shrieked incredulously, and ran inside once more. I had taken her for a tout, but later I met her again with a group of friends, rollicking from pub to pub. 'Found that fiddle yet?' she bawled.

I had not. Faced with a total absence of fiddles, I made the best of a bad job and settled for the Longhorn Saloon. A big man dressed as a gunslinger took my entrance money, popped the lid off a bottle of beer and handed it to me instead of a ticket. Nobody used glasses, so I sipped decorously from the bottle. My perch on a stool was near the small dance floor, where couples performed a spinning dance to a tune called 'Cotton-Eyed Joe'. As good as a fiddle-less band can be, the musicians next struck up a mournful tune while a vocalist sang about his uncalled phone number, 'Lonesome 77203'.

A goofy man with buck teeth, glasses and an enormous Adam's apple sat on his own at a nearby table. He looked the complete greenhorn, so I naturally supposed him to be English. However, when I asked him, he turned out to have come from Philadelphia.

My beer finished, I set out for the long walk back along Main Street to the centre of Fort Worth. I left the neon lights and crowds behind, and entered the quiet Mexican district. It felt very safe there, just as Indian areas in England feel safe. My café was shut, but a huge, brightly-lit record shop was open. It was filled from end to end with Mexican records, all with glossy romantic pictures on the sleeves and the writing in Spanish. No other records were on sale at all. I could have been in the Indian record shop at Southall. Even the silent, sarcastic, brown-skinned shopkeeper looked the same.

As I walked, I peeped into bars, lounges, clubs and 'liquor stores' where Mexicans took their pleasure quietly. One club, where Mexicans and black people drank amicably together, looked particularly cosy.

Card players in overalls were sitting around a table. Noticing my face at the door, they smiled and beckoned me to come in. But I pressed on, as I make it a rule never to go into a club straight after hovering. Learning the geography of the place, I stride in boldly next day and make straight for the bar, ignoring all quizzical glances on the way. That way, I can 'belong' somewhere from the first.

On I walked, beside the road, and I soon reached the industrial area. Huge oil and gas (petrol) installations poured out steam. Small car-hire firms were protected both by wire-netting fences and by ferocious dogs. By now I was a lone figure stumping doggedly down a lamp-lit road. Brainwashed by America into thinking that all walkers were ne'er-do-wells, the hounds of hell flung themselves at the wire netting with foaming fangs bared. First a Doberman, then an Alsatian would make a sudden sagging bulge in a creaking wire-netting fence. But the wire held firm, and the dogs bounced back.

Then I came to a firm where a man opened a wire-netting gate and drove his car inside. He left the gate open behind him, but luckily the guardian Great Dane, a night-black animal the size of a horse, was too busy trying to get at me through the wire to notice. Suddenly the animal stopped, halted by a sudden thought, and wheeled rapidly around. Pell-mell it ran towards the open gate. I too ran for a while, then slowed down, but there was no dog behind me. Perhaps the man in charge had slammed the door.

Bright yellow lines ruled on the night air, the outlines of the skyscrapers lured me onward. Before long I was crossing the bridge over the Trinity River. Trinity's great rocky gorge reminded me of Durham. Oil installations loomed on the far bank instead of a castle and cathedral. A proposed canal link with the river had been finally turned down in 1970 in case it brought not only industry but Yankee 'undesirables' to Fort Worth.

Footsore by the time I reached Sundance Square, I sank exhaustedly into a seat in the Bar BQ. A friendly, elderly waitress served me a coffee, and a very tall, black old man with white hair and moustache smiled and asked how I was doing. He wore a peaked ship captain's hat, but looked every inch a Texan. A high moon hung over Fort Worth like a suspended balloon, and the strange diamond dome of the Caravan of Dreams reflected the silver rays. Why did the Texas sky seem so tall?

In the morning, a dishevelled man walked into the hotel dining room and poured himself a free cup of coffee. He looked as if he had been out all night, his breath smelled of wine, but a hawk nose lent arrogance to his features. 'Hi, my name's Rudie,' he volunteered. 'Like Rudolph Valentino. A Spanish name!'

It turned out that he too was taking a Greyhound that day, and he kindly helped me to carry my bag down to the coach station. Then he took the Greyhound to Dallas, while I left for Bryan, Texas, down in the sunny South.

My Greyhound passed through flat, sandy countryside of scrub oak, sagebrush and the occasional cactus. A dead armadillo lay shattered beside the road. Grey and pastel yellow seemed the predominant colours. Tall wooden gateposts bore ranch names nailed high across them on rough bark-rimmed planks. Cattle grew larger and larger and a herd of black Aberdeen Angus seemed to be trying to evolve into longhorns. We crossed the Brazos River at Waco. As in other Texas towns, white *Misión* buildings remained from Spanish days. Brick Wild West false fronts to the shops and offices seemed to have a touch of the Aztec pyramid about them, and there was a glorious wedding-cake of a Catholic church.

My fellow passengers, all Mexicans and coloured people, slept peacefully as we rolled along. I fought back sleep. There were few fences, but the open scrubby country was criss-crossed with roads. Man-made lakes or ponds gleamed in the desert sun. Once I awoke to find myself in a town of white Spanish houses, neat in a row, leading to a great church. Here the past was easier to imagine than it had been in the Old South, east of the Mississippi.

Near my destination, the countryside looked more fertile. Horses, ploughed fields and green grass began to appear. Innocent-looking coloured families stared at the Greyhound from cabin doorways. Myriad children played around the front garden of one wooden house, while in another, the whole family were at work in their vegetable garden. I gave up and let sleep overcome me.

CHAPTER FIFTEEN

Auction in Aggieland

AT BRYAN, TEXAS, I stood forlornly outside the Greyhound shed with my bag, as the coach rolled on to pastures new. The clerk phoned for a taxi, and in due course of time one arrived. I asked the driver to take me to an hotel, any hotel.

'So you're from England? Pleased to meet you. My name is Christian,' the driver said, in an unmistakable West African accent. He proved to be an Ibo from Eastern Nigeria. Bryan, I learned, was a university town, and where there are universities there are West Africans.

'I'm only driving a cab in my spare time, so as to pay my way through university,' Christian told me. 'I'm studying Agriculture. The university here is called Agricultural and Mechanical, or A. and M., and the students are called Aggies. All round the campus, the area is known as Aggieland. It's not like an English university – they take care not to have English books in the library in case the students pick up English spelling, and put a "u" in "coloured" or something.'

A note of regret in his voice, plus the assumption that English spelling was 'correct', told me that Christian, like most Nigerians, wished to study in England, the mother country. By raising the fees for overseas students, Britain has banished Nigerian students and sent them scattering about the world. Since Nigerians are bound to be students wherever they are, I don't see why they cannot fill our British universities, their evident ambition, and leave English youngsters free to pursue more sensible aims.

'Here is a fine hotel, from where you can see the university in the distance!' Christian announced. In fact, a strip of modernistic hotels faced a wide stretch of flat parkland that bordered on the campus. Expansively, Christian carried my bag into Reception, flirted grandly with the Receptionist, and promised he would collect me in the morning for a drive around. So saying, he charged me a large fee, and made off, all smiles.

After unpacking, I strolled out in search of a restaurant, and found one in a nearby hotel, the grandiose palm court (well, banana tree court) Ramada Inn. On the wall was a picture of two cowboys, who had lassoed a red devil and tied a knot in his tail. One of the cowboys had a squint, a nice local touch, and the devil looked extremely angry. Beside the painting, a dialect verse told the story. Cowboys, devils and prairies seemed singularly inappropriate to my ultra-sophisticated surroundings.

In the morning, Christian greeted me bright and early, picked up his flirtation with the Receptionist where it had left off, and swept me out to his car. It was his private car, this time, not a yellow taxi. On the outskirts of town, suburban houses set among lawns and trees merged into small farms. In one field I saw a herd of slim-legged brown animals grazing. I took them for deer, and as we were miles ahead by the time I had told Christian, he said he would stop there on the way back.

Flat ranch country, dotted with thornscrub, gave way to verdant, jungly growth on the banks of the River Brazos, celebrated in cowboy lore. I asked Christian to stop beside a white concrete bridge, and he and I followed a narrow path down through the trees. It soon grew too steep for our comfort, so I looked through the foliage at the swift brown river and tried to imagine longhorn cattle swimming across, herded by whooping men on horseback. Near Christian's car, a tablet half hidden in the coarse grass told a story of a Lost City.

'Site of the Town of Nashville,' I read. Named after Nashville, Tennessee, it had been founded as a county capital. 'Surveyed 1835. Seat of Justice, 1836–1837.'

No ruins could be seen, only a concrete bridge, a road and a river. Where was Nashville? Perhaps a surveyed and pegged-out town had never been built. I pictured an irascible hanging judge passing sentence on horse thieves in a makeshift shanty with a flag outside on a stick.

Returning to sprawling Bryan, we passed another Brazos, a tributary called the Little Brazos. The legendary Brazos Valley was now a tame and sleepy country.

'Now I'll find out about those deer!' Christian announced, parking the car once more and sauntering up a bungalow path. We could not find the right spot, but he felt he was somewhere near.

No one answered his knock for a long time. Fretting, Christian considered going round to the back and looking round. However, an elderly man with glasses opened up and stood shaking with terror at the sight of a black intruder.

Holding both sides of the doorway for support, the man faintly replied that he thought the 'deer' were in reality wild sheep. He pointed the way, and quickly closed the door.

His confidence shaken, Christian seemed to brood for a few minutes. When we arrived at the sheep pasture, the animals had vanished.

'You go and ask the man this time,' Christian said, hanging back.

A man emerged from a farm-sale shop, a lengthy shed beside a market garden. However, he was very courteous to us both. 'Yes, I'm the farmer,' he said. 'I'll show you my sheep. They're wild sheep called Bardos, or Barbados, an' they tell me they come from the Persian Gulf. They was breeding 'em experimentally up at the university, an' they sold me some lambs. That's how I got started. So I bred 'em, did very well, an' now people round here eat 'em at barbecues.'

He led the way, opened a gate, and we entered a wild-looking pasture, with clumps of trees here and there. All at once, the sheep started up from the long grass and fled before us like startled antelopes. Below some trees, they stopped, and the big ram glared at us in defiance. He was a magnificent animal, with curly horns and a heavy mane around his throat. He and his wives were vividly marked in dark red and black, with fawn underparts.

'They look to me like mouflons, the European wild sheep,' I commented.

'No, I got a mouflon in the front paddock,' our host said. 'I'll show you the way.'

In appearance, our host was a tall, thin man in blue overalls, a cowboy hat and spectacles. His speech, movements and character were all very gentle. Tall, thin country people seemed to abound in this part of Texas, but they were elderly. There were giants in those days . . .

Jumping up in alarm, the mouflon ram leaped up from his grassy bed near a fence and ran across the field, followed by his many wives. He was not quite as large or impressive as the Bardo.

'I bought him off a rancher buddy of mine from World War Two,' the farmer observed mildly. 'Put him in with Barbado sheep, an' they seem to be doing all right.'

In reply, I began to curse and dance up and down, as a malicious gang of fire ants had invaded my right leg and were busily biting great chunks out of it. Tactfully, the farmer walked back to the sales shed with Christian.

When I caught up with them, ruefully rubbing at minute red spots, the farmer was telling Christian about his rancher friend who bred exotic deer, wild sheep and antelopes on his land. Today, some parts of the Texas prairies resemble Africa or India, teeming with rare game imported from the tropics and turned loose for private hunting. Wealthy ranchers vie with one another in providing sport for their guests. Ranches are often so large that the fenced-in animals no doubt feel that they are wild on their native savannahs.

'Yeah, my buddy owns all the ranch land and farms around here a good deal further than you can see. After World War Two, we both aimed to buy a farm together. The price was seven or eight hundred dollars, and we couldn't neither of us afford it. Now he's got five oil wells on his land, cattle and every kind of foreign game animal. Nope, you can't go see him, 'cos he's seventy-five years old and very sick, laid up in bed. Sees no one.'

The old farmer waved us goodbye and we were off once more. Despite being a student of Agriculture, Christian seemed amused at my interest in country topics. I gave a squeak of excitement as he sped past a field with a banner over the ranch gateway: 'Mule and Donkey Show'. I could see rows of parked cars and crowds in the distance, but Christian pretended not to hear when I suggested that we turn back.

Negro cabins stood in rows along the top of a high green bank rising from the edge of the road. The small wooden houses looked well-kept, happy barefoot children played on the slope, and smartly-dressed fashionable couples emerged from a Baptist church. In sunny weather, at least, this seemed a pleasant place in which to live.

'There's a donkey,' Christian observed indulgently, as two children appeared leading a black and white Shetland pony.

'I suppose when you get your degree, you'll apply for a post in the Nigerian Ministry of Agriculture?' I hazarded.

'Most certainly! What I would very much like to do is visit England. I shall give you my address here, and my wife's address in Nigeria. If you write to us both and invite us to London, then we can get a visa.'

I agreed to this in the interests of Commonwealth unity. Meanwhile, I admired the chickens and pigs belonging to the roadside dwellers. Red pigs with black blotches rolled in the red earth, and brightly-coloured roosters scratched around, pale freckles on their dark green tail feathers. Boys on bikes whizzed to and fro, scarcely disturbing the majestic pigs and chickens. High in the air, large hawks wheeled on the air currents. It seemed an ideal setting for a childhood novel.

Christian slowed down as we reached a man-made lake, and drove around it. Some of the coloured people fishing from wooden piers waved and smiled at him.

'It is lonely for me here,' Christian admitted, as he returned their salutations. 'Just because they are black does not make them the same as me. I cannot be fully accepted. England is the place I would like to see. If you are interested in the black people, I will show you where the poor blacks live.'

So saying, he drove me into a large concreted square amid the greenery of the roadside. Barrack-like strips of two-storey brick dwellings stood here and there at angles to one another, separated by yards of dusty concrete. I had seen similar 'council estates' from my various Greyhounds all over the South. Usually, they were named after Martin Luther King. Although they looked fairly new, many of the barrack-houses were boarded up and derelict. Despite their Spartan homes, everyone here seemed cheerful. Neighbours stood in groups gossiping and laughing outside unboarded doorways, and children played merrily. No one took much notice of us.

'Now I'll show you where *I* live,' Christian said, and drove back into Bryan.

Small plank houses, surrounded by trees and lawns, stood in suburban rows. Mexicans and Negroes amicably shared this leafy neighbourhood. Christian stopped to show me his house, a plank dwelling, or suburban shanty, similar to all the others. A moustachioed Mexican ran out of the doorway and began to shout excitedly to Christian in Spanish.

West Africans are the world's best pickers-up of languages, a skill they think nothing of. So I was not surprised to hear Christian answer the man and pacify him in his own lingo.

'He works for me,' my driver explained loftily.

I sensed wheels within wheels, and also concluded that Christian spent more time driving than studying.

'There are many nightclubs and lounges here in Bryan, where the Mexicans go,' Christian continued, pointing at Spanish buildings with garish signs. He drove rapidly through the town and then entered the university campus, a city of its own. Here he drove slowly and blissfully along tree-lined avenues between grand magisterial buildings. The fine architecture showed that most of the university had been built a long time ago.

'Aggieland' had developed, I learned, from a Confederate (Southern) stronghold in the Civil War to a military cadet college and finally (in 1875) to its present form, the Agricultural and Mechanical University or A. and M. There had been a disastrous fire in 1912, but a new Aggieland had arisen above the ashes of the old.

Happily reciting the names of all the distinguished-looking buildings, Christian paused to allow flocks of brightly-dressed girl students to cross the road.

'These are the dorms,' he said, pointing. 'The students share two in a room. Girls have separate dorms to boys. All the students hate the U.T. students from the University of Texas at Austin, and try to beat them at football. At Thanksgiving they burn the biggest bonfire in the world. It's in the *Guinness Book of Records*. If the centre pole of the bonfire is the last to fall, they say it is a sign that the Aggies are going to beat Texas at the football.'

He chuckled at such superstition, and asked me where I wanted to go next. I had seen a public library in the centre of Bryan, so I asked to be set down there and collected in two hours' time. Friendly though Christian was, I felt relieved to be on my own once more. After browsing around the well-stocked library, I set out to explore the town.

This was the mild West, for Bryan, dozing in the hot Texas sun, seemed a sleepy little place. Gentle sack-like women, white or coloured, pottered dreamily around shops selling plastic bowls and other household implements. Everything seemed old and faded, both the shops and the people. Old Bryan, a Western-cum-Spanish town of shops with nothing much in them, seemed to have been built as a contrast to the youthful hustle and bustle of the Aggieland campus. Steps led up to long porches of cracked concrete in front of the shop doorways. The road was very wide, but there was little traffic. Steps led down between the shops to the Mexican and black suburbs, where stooped men picked pecan nuts from the grass.

In a Mexican café, aged cowboys, tall rake-thin men in stetsons, sat dreaming of the Old West. Mexicans also sat in silence, dreaming of the days when Texas belonged to them. I too sat dreaming – dreaming that I knew what other people were dreaming about.

Outside a shop marked 'Mission', a crowd of coloured people, men and women, were busily buying cheap furniture and carrying it from the pavement to their cars or pick-up trucks. I went inside and asked a white lady behind a desk what was going on.

'We receive donations of goods from well-wishers,' she explained, 'and then we sells them and uses the money to help the needy. You're not in any trouble yourself, are you? You're a *long* way from home. Can we help at all?'

In her kindness, the Mission lady resembled the long-lost voluntary workers at Christian Missions in England, before charity got organised.

'I'm sixty-seven years old,' a tall man with humorous crinkles round his eyes told me as I left the Mission. He wore a stetson, of course, and also a white bristly moustache. 'I was posted at Grantham, England, during World War Two,' he continued.

'That's where our woman prime minister was born,' I interrupted.

'Wal, I had a little girlfriend there, an' her family were real nice to me. They drove me round everywhere – Nottingham, Retford, you name it. Now, what was her name?'

Surely it couldn't be . . .? No – 'Hazel Swinger! That's it. Hazel Swinger was her name. Sweetest little thing you ever saw. Y'all must have a drink with me sometime.'

Murmuring politely, I passed on to the next doorway, where a sign on a board read 'Auction'. I entered, and introduced myself to Auctioneer

Fletcher, a stout genial man in shirtsleeves. He pulled up two chairs and a litter bin and we sat down. As he spoke, he spat accurately into the bin at the rate of one spit for every two sentences.

'So you're from England, hey? I seen your English auctions on T.V. and they're kind of slower than ours. Also you only sell real valuable items, but here in Bryan, anything goes. We got an auction at seven-thirty tomorrow night, so you're welcome to come an' see for yourself.

'You ever been to Scotland? I sure would like to go. That's where my ancestors come from. I know that, 'cos I sent off for information an' they sent me the Coat of Arms of the Fletcher Clan. My ancestors used to make arrow shafts with feathers, out there in Scotland. That's what "Fletcher" means, you know. Well, do tell me about life in England.'

However, Mr Fletcher had to make do with a quick, garbled version of that topic, as it neared the time when I had to meet Christian back at the library. Soon I was enjoying a Ramada supper beneath the picture of a devil with a knot in his tail.

Towers of Aggieland loomed on the horizon, as, next day, I avoided Christian's expensive taxi and walked over to the campus. Soon I was strolling along magnolia avenues, among fountains and lawns, amazed by the opulence of all I saw. Cadet students, dressed as soldiers and wearing knapsacks, hurried into one of the vast buildings. Modern glass and concrete blended well with older stone buildings of imperial design, each well suited to be Town Hall of a prosperous English spa. All the students, who walked around in chattering groups, looked excessively clean-cut, fresh-faced and well-behaved, like good children on an outing. They dressed in brightly-coloured clothes, both boys and girls in jeans, with not a beard or a moustache in sight. I saw only a handful of coloured students, and one of those walked sedately arm in arm with his white girlfriend. One or two tattered feminist and gay posters could be seen pinned among the sports fixtures on open-air boards or kiosks, but these were the only concessions made to the dreary English idea of a university.

A marker stone showed the site of the cadets' parade ground when A. and M. had been a wholly military foundation. Another memorial gave the names of 'Fallen Aggies' in the wars. It was surrounded by a lawn with a sign reading 'Stay Off Of the Grass'. Outside the boys' dorm, banners with football slogans hung from windows. 'No Fat Girls', one unchivalrous motto read. Nearby, a peaceful soccer match was taking place, and in the distance a huge array of football stands, higher than the stalls at Wembley, showed the site of the epic struggles with the University of Texas.

Strips of pavement, steps and patios threaded their way among parkland and college buildings. I particularly admired a college with a St Paul's dome on top, the first building to be completed after the fire. A group of lecturers emerged, dowdy and leather-elbowed. One had a pipe poking from his jacket pocket, and all resembled kindly and conscientious prep school masters. Inside, I found the college to be divided into classrooms, exactly like an old-fashioned English school. Rows of desks faced a blackboard. Quickly, I darted into one room, chalked a funny face on the board and wrote 'Teecher' under it. Schools bring out the devil in me.

Hurrying from the scene of the crime, I reached the edge of the campus, and found a neon jungle of makeshift shops and cafés thrown together, boom-town-style, to be of service to the Aggies. So-called 'bookshops' sold T-shirts, badges and other Aggie souvenirs. Every Aggie seemed proud of his or her Ag-hood, and ready to proclaim it to the world.

'We have some text books out back,' a blonde girl assistant said helpfully. 'Otherwise the only books we have are those old ones in the corner. There's an official bookshop in the campus, but Aggies aren't great readers by no stretch. In fact, where I live at Bryan, we tell Aggie jokes, like, "How many Aggies does it take to change a light bulb?" stuff like that.'

However, I found a book called *Log of a Cowboy* (1903) which described the Brazos and Red River valleys in the great trail-herding days of the late nineteenth century. It was written in more sprightly prose than any modern American could manage, for Andy Adams, the cowboy author, had lived before the Age of Colleges had got into its stride. So I was more than satisfied. Later I realised how apt the name *Log* really was, for the cowboy's life had resembled that of a sailor on a sea of prairie, the wide-open rest towns, in the middle of the plains, resembling ports with red-light sailor towns. Near the bookshop I found a pub, made of logs in pioneer style, where Aggies no doubt refreshed themselves after thrashing the University of Texas at football.

Back at the campus, I found my way to the magnificent Memorial Hall, a place of barbaric splendour, where Red Indian art hung amid palm trees and divans with richly patterned leather cushions. Below this hall, a few students looked at comics in a corner of the empty bookshop. Others played at Space Invader machines. I left them to it, and crossed the quad to the library.

A huge glass skyscraperish building, the well-stocked library was full of students, all working hard and speaking in whispers. There were plenty of English books, so the students could spell 'coloured' whichever way they chose. Not caring for lifts, I climbed from floor to floor on narrow shiny brick staircases. On the higher floors, rows of books gave way to tables and chairs. 'Group Tuition', the signs proclaimed.

Worried young people sat around these tables, evidently trying to help one another with their homework. From their harassed faces, it appeared a case of the blind leading the blind. Where had the grown-up Tutors gone? Each table buzzed with half-whispered talk. I paused at one, where a fair-haired boy with more confidence than the rest had appointed himself Monitor. All eyes turned to him trustingly.

'One example of a Symbol is a wedding bouquet,' he said. This pleased the girls. 'It's not just a bunch of flowers, as it has a Symbolic meaning.'

In a nearby Lounge, small girl students sat chatting about boyfriends. I liked A. and M. University, as it reminded me of Linbury Court School, the setting of the 'Jennings' school stories by Anthony Buckeridge. If the students could be seen as boarding school children, madly loyal to their school on the playing field and trying hard to please grown-ups at all times, then their behaviour began to make sense. Schoolboys and girls read comics for pleasure, but take homework books very seriously. A. and M. was an idealised prep school, not a public school where teenage cynicism or coarseness might have its way. It was certainly nothing like an English university. Where was the arrogance, the uncouthness, the sneering rudeness to adults and the one-upmanship of pretending to be gay or working class? Even if most of the courses at A. and M. were nonsense, as I daresay they were, the atmosphere of innocence, earnestness and eagerness to be good did the students credit.

Mentally patting the A. and M. students on the head, and wishing that I could grant them a half-holiday, I trotted out into the quad and asked a young scholar the way to the Thanksgiving Bonfire. A youth of military appearance, the young man had a cropped head crowned with a flat top, a fashionable hairstyle. His self-absorbed expression changed at once into a look of great concern. As for his directions, they were almost lost in a sea of 'sirs'.

'Sir, my name is Sutton, sir,' he told me. 'I am studying History here, sir, and I would certainly like to visit your country, sir. It's so full of History, sir, that I just know I'd like it, sir.'

'Here is my address, Sutton. When you come to England, you may stay in my house.'

Leaving Sutton to his broken thanks, I made my way to the football stand. Beyond it I discovered the Largest Bonfire in the World, as yet unlit.

The centre pole of the bonfire was an upright pine trunk, at least three hundred feet tall. Neat circles of logs had been leant against this pole, layer upon layer, lesser logs balanced on the heads of greater ones. Outside the perimeter, large up-ended logs, embedded on the ground, acted as tent pegs. Ropes connected them to the main pile, and these tent-poles leaned outwards with the strain. At the top of each pole, a battery of floodlights and loudspeakers had been attached. Muscular

Aggies in construction hats wielded electric saws or drove small bulldozers. A fanned-out field of logs, laid on the ground in rows around the main pole, awaited the Paul Bunyan who could lift them into place and tie them down. Tough Bonfire-Aggies, a hardier breed than the Studying-Aggies, scowled as they worked. So far the bonfire resembled a strange, giant wooden wigwam.

Local farmers had donated the logs, and each night an Aggie guarded the pile in case an enemy from the University of Texas crept up under cover of darkness and set it on fire before the right time. Where had I heard of such a custom before? Of course, in Northern Ireland. There the Bonfire Boys of County Antrim celebrate the eve of 12th July, the Protestant Orange festival, by building enormous bonfires. At one Irish village I had seen a farmer stop his lorry beside a field, hurl armfuls of copper beech branches towards the Bonfire Boys and then drive on. Each bonfire gang attempts a larger fire than their schoolboy neighbours. In Belfast, where bonfires blaze at every third street corner in the Protestant area, twelve-year-old boys sit up all night to guard their bonfire from a surprise torching. For the fire to burn before the correct hour of midnight would be a calamity. In Ulster, branches, not whole logs, are used, but the principle seems to be the same.

Celtic fire worship is sometimes cited as being the true origin of the Northern Irish Bonfire. Could such folk memories of a pagan past have been carried to Texas, there to influence the football-mad Aggies? I thought it probable.

Flocks of long-tailed grackles, whydah-starlings of Texas, flew to their roosts as the sun set over Aggieland, purple clouds on a roseate sky. I returned to my hotel, from whence I later phoned for a taxi to take me to Mr Fletcher's Auction.

It was Christian's day off, and a young white taxi driver collected me. When I described our previous day's ride-around, the young man stared. 'Christian told us he wasn't working yesterday!' he said.

'Well, now I come to think of it, he was using his own car.'

'That makes it even worse! This here's the Auction Room now. You sure you want me to leave you here in the rough side o' town?'

I arranged to be met by yet another taxi, since short-distance buses have yet to make their mark on Texas.

'Hi there Roy, come on in!' Mr Fletcher welcomed me. He introduced me to his daughter, who sat in a kiosk by the door handing out cards with numbers on to all who entered. Citizens of Bryan, looking rather like the Arkadelphian Swing Club patrons, wandered round examining the items to be auctioned, which stood on display as if in a shop. Everything looked very second-hand, rather like the goods at a trestle-table sale inside a former Woolworth's in Kilburn High Road. Even the patrons seemed rather faded. A few black people and Mexicans were present, peering around shrewdly.

Auctioneer Fletcher and his daughter then mounted a high desk, like a pulpit, and the auction began. Bids were made by holding up the numbered cards. Two helpers walked around holding up the merchandise and leering horribly. One was a giant bearded young man who looked like a wrestler and wore a hunter's cap. The other was an older brown-skinned man in shirtsleeves.

'First lot tonight is a hunting knife!' Mr Fletcher announced.

The hairy man unsheathed the murderous blade dramatically, and declared, 'Ah've skinned three deer with this knife!'

'Liar!' somebody shouted.

I sat with the audience in a tiered row of wooden benches. The demonstrators paced up and down waving the merchandise above their heads and uttering loud cries of 'Here!' or 'Yip!' to stimulate the bidding. When Fletcher was in full swing, the auction sounded like a square dance. Number Twenty-Six, a lean, severe, chain-smoking coloured man, evidently saw himself as a serious bidder. He crouched in his seat, staring forwards.

'Now, to set this here auction rolling, I've got a surprise box with not only high quality goods but also money in it! Do I hear two dollars, two dollars – Sold! To Number Twenty-Six!'

A sealed cardboard box was handed to the serious bidder. Excitement swept the hall. Another coloured man helped Number Twenty-Six to tear off the sticky tape.

'Look out, there may be a rat in there!' someone sang out.

But there was not. Triumphantly, Number Twenty-Six held aloft a crisp brand new dollar bill. Then he pulled out not one, but seven plastic carrier bags! Elated by this successful start, he bid for almost every item on display and bought quite a lot of them.

Garage tools, kitchen implements, plastic ornaments and jumbled odds and ends, called 'box of contents' were the usual auction fare. If any item sold for more than three dollars it caused a sensation. As bids were made by card only, the audience felt free to stamp, wail, shout and cheer. Valiant Number Twenty-Six was the hero of the auction. Meanwhile, Mr Fletcher's voice rolled on.

'Two dollars, two dollars, will you make it two fifty, will you make it three, three, three . . .' ('Hyar!') 'Three, three, three!' ('Hyarp!') 'Willermaggerfour, four, four, four. Wilhelmina Five Dollars! Five, five, five! Sold to Number Twenty-Six!' (Sensation. Cries of 'Hyarp!')

Patrons rose from their seats occasionally and made their way to a soft drinks counter for refreshment. No children were present, except for a small girl of seven who belonged to the place. When the auction stopped briefly for a raffle, the girl drew out the winning number and handed a bag to a housewife. Jewellery was then produced and dangled tantalisingly in front of the women. A man inspired, Fletcher described each item in ringing tones.

'This here's fourteen carat gold! . . . A bracelet covered in diamond dust! . . . And now, a pearl necklace straight from the blue deep!'

Bidding opened at one dollar per item, and closed at two. Priceless gems disposed of, Mr Fletcher stepped down and opened several bags of heavy, old-fashioned-looking electrical equipment. Leaving the bearded man to shout 'Hyar!' or 'Hyarp!' the shirtsleeved man stepped up to the auctioneer's rostrum. He took over the sales patter, while Mr Fletcher tested each item at a socket connected to a cable draped over a desk. A tape recorder, electric razor, iron-winged fan and a slide projector were each plugged in, to a happy cry of 'It works!'

Now, with a new auctioneer in charge, the patter grew so rapid and ridiculous that the audience began to laugh. Many had come for the entertainment, not the bargains, and made no attempt to bid.

'Two dollars, make it three, three make it four, four, four, four, make it five!' ('Hyar! Yip!')

The words 'make it' added a new rhythm to the auction. Wilhelmina Five Dollars had been replaced by her cousin Wanamaker. It was now time for my taxi, and I left the auction in full melodious song. Any minute now, they would begin to dance. Number Twenty-Six sat surrounded by booty.

Outside, it was a warm muggy night. Mexican youths strolled by in twos and threes. Soon my taxi arrived, with a coloured driver.

'What I like about this town is that it's so safe you don't even have to lock your door when you go out,' he told me. 'I'm a blue-collar worker, so I cain't afford much, but I got a car here, a trailer and a boat. I could say I'm a happy man.'

Full of plans to come to England, a beaming Christian drove me to my southbound Greyhound in the morning. If I had got him into trouble with his boss, he didn't say so. I shook his hand and was off once more, heading for Louisiana.

I looked back at the campus, and noticed an Aggieland Hotel. So the name Aggieland was quite official. A strange land indeed. Further south, I saw an hotel called Sleep Shop, a good name for a place with no dining room. Tall skyscrapers appeared – the city of Houston. Shabby Negro lounges stood shakily beneath huge concrete flyovers, neon beer signs in their tiny windows. Most of the skyscrapers were of mirrored glass, but one looked like the Gothic castle of an evil space-age monarch. Larger than all its fellows, and made of brick, it ought to have been built upon a lonely crag-top. Pinnacles and spirelets grew from the jagged ramparts, with a centre tower in which to imprison a princess or a unicorn. Evidently Houston was a riverport town, for I noticed two rusty-looking steamers in a shabby dock.

South of Houston the West was left behind. Small fields took the place of sandy ranches, and thorny trees were replaced by Southern greenery. After a while, rice fields began to appear, half flooded, with white wading egrets. Dignified grey-white Zebus, the Eastern sacred cattle, walked slowly along, led by enormous hump-backed dewlapped bulls with sad eyes. In America these beasts are known as 'Brahma cattle'. Flooded forests of coppery trees and winding rivers hinted at the swamp country to come. Hours passed, as I dozed and woke in starts.

Beside an immense oil installation, part fallen into decay, a wide bridge pointed up at the sky. I expected cars to shoot off the top into space, as they might at Tower Bridge when it raises. Our Greyhound, however, plunged down the other side. Perhaps the engineer had designed the bridge by balancing two playing cards together. Cars poured over it like lemmings.

Near a calm blue lake, the driver shouted, 'Lake Charles, Louisiana!' and I dismounted. A friend of a friend of my Natchez host Jimmy Guercio had promised to meet me here.

'Hi, I'm Lana Brunet!' a nervously fashionable girl in trousers and bright lipstick greeted me. 'So you're the writer who's going to put Lake Charles on the map tourist-wise! I think that's wonderful! I help organise Contraband Days, a thirteen-day pageant here. It's all centred round Jean Lafitte and the legend of his buried treasure lost in the bayous some place. Folks dress up as pirates and seize the Mayor, an' there's all kinds of revelries. Only thing is, Contraband is unpopular with the blue-collar workers here, on what's left of our vanishing oil industry. They don't like tourist foolery, they only want work.'

'Oh I've heard of Jean Lafitte, the pirate, of course.'

'He wasn't really a pirate, only a slave trader and merchant who *dealt* with the pirates,' she corrected me. 'I've booked you into the Downtowner Hotel, with one night free of charge. In the morning we can discuss our plans.'

Bemused, I found myself leaning over the balcony of a luxury hotel, looking out over a vast twilit lake with boats on it. Banana trees grew beside the shores, and nearby an artificial palm beach with imported sand had been created.

CHAPTER SIXTEEN

Lake Charles, Louisiana

LANA BRUNET WAS at my breakfast table in the morning, leafing through a glossy wad of tourist literature. I tried to explain to her that travel writing (which is full of misadventures) is different from *tourist* writing (where nothing can go wrong). But she brushed all such distinctions aside, and said that she was sure I would do my best to promote Lake Charles as a resort. I looked out through the banana trees at the window towards the blue lake, and wondered if anything I wrote could lure holidaymakers to Lake Charles. Well, the Downtowner Hotel had a restaurant, for a start, although paying twice for bed and board still seemed to me peculiar. However, I had enjoyed a free night's repose, thanks to the kindness of the tourist people. Lana told me of her love for workouts in the Y.M.C.A. gym, and then went on to tell me about a book she had been reading.

'It's by this psychologist, and he's proved that the people who batter children have themselves been battered when young, and the people who divorce have had divorced parents. It's a never-ending cycle of deprivation unless the patient chooses counselling with the right kind of psychologist.'

'You mean the kind who wrote the book?'

'Right. If you're ready, Mr Kerridge, I'll take you to the Convention and Visitors' Centre.'

The Centre proved to be a one-storey glass tourist office facing the artificial palm beach of Lake Charles. It seemed absurdly overstaffed, and a gang of forceful women and men in grey suits fell on me, shaking hands like an over-enthusiastic octopus. A girl reporter appeared from somewhere, and tried to interview me, and a slice of cake was thrust into my hand. One of the women was having a birthday party, and my reception and her party somehow merged. Everyone talked so much that I was unable to get away to explore downtown Lake Charles. However, it turned out that there was method in their madness, for downtown Lake Charles had been pulled down in the 1960s and there would have been nothing to see.

'I went on a course of counselling recommended by a college professor I know,' one of the men was saying to a group of cake-eating friends. 'It consisted of mind-games and hypnotism. Then I saw the name "Moon" on the paper, so I left real quick! I'd been taken for a ride by Moonies, and they refused to refund my fee. "Stay till Saturday," my friend said. "That's the day I really took off on it." I said, "Yeah, that's the day you got brainwashed." Now I'm gonna see if I can try find a deprogrammer to help him get out of it.'

I was rescued from the bewildering babble of conversation (in which tourism, counselling and birthday greetings had been nicely mixed) by the Convention Services Manager, Sabrina Sonnier. She bundled me into a car and drove off with me.

Sabrina was a pale, plump round-faced girl who called me 'sir' all the time. 'I was brought up always to say "sir" and "ma'am", sir,' she explained. 'I had to show respect to all adults, beginning with my parents.'

As we drove further and further away from the tourist office, Sabrina seemed to grow less and less like a tourist official. She soon reminded me of the type of sweet unsophisticated English girl who stacks tins in the village supermarket and tells everyone how important it is to pass a C.S.E. exam.

'Sonnier is a French name, isn't it?' I asked.

'Yes, I'm a Cajun, sir,' she replied. 'But I don't speak French none. All I can say is *Laissez le bon temps rouler*, which means "Let the good times roll".'

Jimmy 'the Preacher' Ellis had sung me a song with that title, back in Texarkana, I remembered.

Lana Brunet, my breakfast hostess, had also told me that she was a Cajun, and had added with pride that her father 'could understand the French they speak in France'.

In 1713, a hundred years after a previous attempt at conquest, the British finally took the snowy Northern island of Nova Scotia from the French. Before being renamed in Latin as New Scotland by the oncomers, the Canadian isle had been known as Acadie. The French farmers, whose ancestors had driven out the Mic Mac Indians and settled the land in 1605, were called Acadians by the British. In 1755, these farmers were required to swear their allegiance to the British flag. This they refused to do, and so were ordered to leave. After many vicissitudes, most of the six thousand refugees arrived in Louisiana, then a French territory, and settled down anew. But thrifty peasant values had no place

in a land of semi-tropical swamps, where a plough might sink and a horse
be seized by alligators. Nova Scotian-type dwellings, small wooden
houses, were built, with steep roofs to shake off the non-existent snow.
But life was never to be the same for the Acadians. Even their name was
to be worn down into 'Cajun'. Through hurricane, hell and high water
they retained their pride in being French.

Gradually the former peasants became easy-going swamp hillbillies,
their lives spent scouring the waterways in flat-bottomed boats in search
of shrimp, crawfish, crabs, gar and other delicacies. Their French
language became a unique patois. Lana Brunet had told me that in fairly
recent times, French speaking had been banned at some Louisiana
schools. Those who spoke it were punished by being made to walk round
and round a tree. However, *all* the Cajun children walked round the
punishment tree, and so the rule had been forgotten. This story reminded
me of the brave action of the Danes during the German occupation.
Danish Jews had been ordered, by their new masters, to wear the yellow
star. So *all* the Danes wore the emblem, and this rule, too, was dropped.
Welsh, Scottish and Irish schoolchildren have been punished for
speaking their own languages within living memory. Good jobs had gone
to English-speakers, and so the older tongues grew weak and died. The
same rule applied in Louisiana. Cajun French is now a healthier language
than is Gaelic, and half holds its own.

However, as Sabrina and everyone else told me, the Cajun style of life
has proved so attractive that everyone in the flat swamp country tries to be
French. If France should ever repossess Louisiana, most of the
inhabitants would be delighted. A French surname, around Lake
Charles, is an absolute must.

Descendants of nineteenth-century German settlers and eighteenth-
century Spanish adventurers have nearly all Frenchified their names.
Poor people of German stock have become an important element of
Acadia, the Cajun nation. So have the swampland black people, who sing
the blues in French and call it Zydeco. Cajuns never had slaves, but there
are now thousands of 'black Cajuns' or French-speaking coloured people.
Poor brown-skinned Cajuns have been more friendly to black people than
poor whites ever were. But why are so many Cajuns brown-skinned? It is
a fact seldom spoken of in Louisiana, but the hunting, fishing, creek-
dwelling Cajuns have all-but absorbed, by marriage, the original owners of
the swamps, the Red Indians. One tribe, the Houmas, have lost their official
identity, since no one knows where a Cajun ends and a Houma begins.

Sabrina Sonnier, however, was very much a white Cajun. Most of the
Lake Charles white people seemed to be of British or non-Cajun French
ancestry. The latest arrivals had been a group of Syrian immigrants who
now seemed to be popular.

A huge modern Civic Centre dominated the shore of Lake Charles. Some way beyond it, we entered an opulent estate of tall white houses set in palm-fringed parkland. Many of the mansions were as old and as delightful as the stately homes of Natchez, but they were not open to the public. Smart bungalows with private beaches and moored boats lined this part of the mighty lake's shore. Lake Charles was only one of three huge lakes in the neighbourhood. Streams isolated each house from its neighbour.

'This here is the Goss Cemetery, sir,' Sabrina pointed out. All I could see were the trees growing around it. 'Captain Goss lived in a big house here at the time of the War Between the States. All the Gosses were buried here. Captain Goss had fourteen children, sir. He was a real good man, and when the soldiers came down with yellow fever, he had 'em nursed. When they were strong, he paid their fares home to their families, even if they were Yankees. Now I'll show you the port, sir, if they'll let us in. We'll have to show identification. You see, Lake Charles is linked to the sea by the Intercoastal Waterway, a big canal.'

A high wire fence surrounded the port of Lake Charles, which was far outside town, among overgrown scrubby woods. We had to follow the car of a friendly security man who drove ahead of us.

Just as in an English port, there was a forlorn atmosphere of gloom and rust. However, the port had its own railway platform linked to the Louisana railway system, and a few deserted boats stood at anchor. As in England, private pleasure boats have superceded commercial water traffic, and a trip through the Intercoastal Waterway amid the wild game-infested swamps would surely be the holiday of a lifetime. Day trips by pleasure boat, or the hire of a holiday barge, are concepts unknown and unheard of at Lake Charles.

'Now I'll take you to see the Sallier Oak!' Sabrina remarked, brightening up as she headed back into town. 'It's a wonderful old tree, with a legend around it. I know you'll like it, sir!'

The Sallier Oak, an old ilex tree with dark leaves and mighty spreading boughs, stood in the garden of a small museum where Audubon paintings and Atakapo Indian arrowheads were exhibited. Lightning had once struck Lake Charles's Guardian Oak, and the broken tree had been bound together with an iron chain. Now the chain had sunk into the ever-growing tree, its traces covered over by bark, but the two ends still dangled from the trunk.

'It looks a good tree for climbing on,' I commented.

'Oh, it is!' Sabrina cried. 'All my life I've loved that oak! When I got married, we posed for photos right here under the oak. Me and Mark were wed last February.'

'Oh, so you're a newly-wed! Congratulations!'

'Thank you, sir. Mark will be real interested when he hears I've met an Englishman. Now, as best I remember, the story of the oak goes like this. Back in Nova Scotia, there was a young French couple about to be married. The English invaded, and separated the lovers when they expelled the Cajuns. They put the young man into one boat and his sweetheart into another. When the poor girl got to Lake Charles, she didn't know what had become of her fiancé. So she sat under this oak and looked out across the lake for his boat coming in. Some people say that he found her here when they were both old and grey. He kissed her and they died in each other's arms. It's very sad, isn't it? Let's go back to the car.'

'I liked the Audubon pictures,' I told Sabrina, as we drove off once more. 'Are you fond of nature?'

'I was brung up in the country,' she said animatedly. 'I just love hunting and duck-shooting!'

'Do you know when they killed the last wolf around here?' I asked eagerly. Among the Celtic fringes of Britain, there is always a spot where the 'last wolf was killed', a place of eerie fascination.

'Ain't got 'im yet!' Sabrina said cheerfully. 'I remember hearing wolves howl outside our cabin when I was a girl. I was scared to go out! In the morning Daddy showed us the footprints and said they definitely wasn't coyotes. There's still a few packs of wolves left, out in the swamp. Once we had a wild pig that came an' made an awful mess outside. A fox came one night an' killed a little pup my Daddy was raising to be a hound. Poor Daddy took it real bad. Our other hound died from eating strychnine bait left out to kill the wolves and foxes. My Daddy's daddy, my grandfather, died when Daddy was only fifteen. He worked in a bakery, and one morning there was a gas explosion.'

We stopped at a small café that advertised 'Poor Boys'. Sabrina took great delight in showing me the different sorts of Louisiana snack. A Poor Boy proved to be a soft roll stuffed with meat and barbecue sauce. A long Poor Boy would make a good working lunch for a real poor boy at the tractor or plough.

'This pickle's very dill,' Sabrina said, meaning 'sour'.

'Links', I learned, meant sausage strings, or sausage in the skin. 'Sausage' in America meant loose sausage meat. Sabrina was a useful guide, yet I rather chafed at her patronage, afraid of being shown only tourist sights and of missing the real Lake Charles.

I hoped to leave Lake Charles by train, travelling across Louisiana to New Orleans once more. Had it not been for Sabrina I could never have done this, as buying a train ticket threw everyone at the Bob Winfree Travel Agency into a fearful spin. Such a thing had never been heard of, and some doubted if it could be done at all. Phone calls were made, timetables studied and tickets drawn up only to be scrapped as the procedure began anew. Adversity drew the staff of the travel agency into a web of comradeship, and by the time the ticket was at last procured, Sabrina and I were the centre of a happily chatting group. One of the men had been to England in winter, as cheap off-season holidays were a perk at Bob Winfree's. A friendly girl named Tinnie Cobb, who hoped to visit England, looked as if she might have been of Syrian ancestry. Sabrina and I left in triumph, waving goodbye, and the staff went back to relatively simple tasks such as booking flights to Outer Mongolia.

'Don't be angry!' Sabrina suddenly remarked, giving me a look of tragic earnestness.

'Why should I be angry?' I asked.

'You might think that I'll take you to places you don't want to go, when you'd sooner be on your own,' she said.

This was the first instance I had seen of the mind-reading gifts of the Louisiana French, gifts I later found to be remarkable. How could Sabrina know that I liked walking and solitude, forgotten ideas in America?

'There *isn't* a downtown no more, only these few shops waiting to be restored,' she continued. 'What's more, I'll take you *any* place you want to go, not just tourist places. The Convention Centre is arranging and paying for it all. I really want to drive you around every day, sir, but you can do anything you want.'

'Can you fix up *anything?*' I asked, and she nodded mutely. 'Well, can I visit a black school and a studio where blues and country records are made? You see, I'm not really writing a tourist guide, but a description of things that just interest *me*.'

'A black school and a record studio? I know I can do that! Just wait in the lobby of the hotel after breakfast tomorrow. I'll be there! Now, where can I drop you?'

I chose the public library, and so waved Sabrina Sonnier a friendly if guilt-stricken goodbye. A dingy building, the library was guarded by an elderly man in a brown uniform, a pistol at his hip. I'd hate to go there with an overdue book! Next I strolled down to the huge white Civic Centre, where the signs were both in English and in French. Lana Brunet's office, Contraband Days, Inc., was there, but Lana had gone home. A vast auditorium within the Centre was being prepared for a teachers' pay claim protest meeting, just like in England. Hunger called, and I returned to the Downtowner Hotel, which was within walking distance of the town.

Later, in the blue tranquil dusk, I walked back to the Civic Centre along the seaside promenade beside the lake. Just as at Hove, in Sussex, wide lawns swept from a main road down to the front. Instead of a pier, the strange crook-backed bridge dominated the shoreline. Beyond it, oil installations did duty for the factory chimneys of Portslade. Small boats, some with lights, bobbed in the waters.

A tall black man kept a fatherly eye on his small son as he fished from the shore. He was hauling in a small struggling silver fish.

'Excuse me, I'm a foreigner from England,' I intruded. 'What kind of fish is that?'

'That's a crappie. It's no good!' the man exclaimed, throwing it back. 'Look, here's a trout!'

He opened his basket and I saw a fresh, gleaming brown trout with black speckles.

'What do you call that in your country?' he asked, not realising that the languages were the same.

As I continued on my way, I reflected that if this were truly England, holidaymakers in Lake Charles would be confronted by pedalo boat rides on the lake, donkey rides by the shore, a children's railway, stalls selling Lake Charles rock and possibly a Punch and Judy show. Coaches would line the road, each with a board advertising a trip to a nearby town or beauty spot, not forgetting the Swampland Mystery Tour. Swingboats and roundabouts for children would be spinning merrily. All these attractions would be taken for granted by everybody, and not thought of as 'tourism' at all.

Further along the prom, I encountered a big bearded man who was throwing a white string net over the water. A girl angler in jeans, who looked like a country and western singer, struck up a conversation with him.

'Me and my brother used chicken as bait,' the man was saying, as I drew near. 'We figured that when the alligator took it on the line, we could shoot it an' haul it in. Sure 'nuff, we caught a 'gator, but he bit the line through. I shot him, but I couldn't tell if he was dead or not. Well, I waded in on after him. You should o' seen me jump an' run when that sucker started threshin' around! Finally got 'im, though. Pulled 'im ashore. Their tails taste real good, don't they?'

The fisherman looked surprised when I asked him what he was trying to catch, and showed me a dead brown shrimp about one and a half inches long.

'Use 'em for bait,' he explained.

I walked up to the Civic Centre which was the main landmark of the flat, sprawling Lake Charles town, although a few grandiose neo-classical civic buildings stood some way away. The auditorium was full of teachers, nearly all of them young women. They looked sophisticated but irritable. In the front row, below the stage, the teachers were dressed in ironical mourning clothes of black. On the stage itself, the municipal politicians (referred to not as councillors but 'Legislators') were greeted with laughter or sarcastic cheers.

As I entered, a smart coloured youth, the Lake Charles equivalent of a sixth former, was making a speech in praise of teachers. He was cheered by the audience, whereas a middle-aged coloured Legislator was met with groans.

'Y'all know the oil crisis has hit Lake Charles real bad, but we'll raise money for schools somehow,' he said. 'Public lotteries might not be a bad idea.' (Groans, jeers and boos.) 'You say lotteries are immoral, but they raise money, don't they?'

Taken one by one, the teachers of Lake Charles were probably pleasant enough, but a mass-meeting devoted to shouting for money necessarily brought on a harsh, selfish atmosphere.

Just as everyone was making for the exits, a young woman sprang up and called for a certain legislator by name. It was a panicky moment, for the unspoken question, 'Is she armed?' seemed to echo through the hall. Luckily she only wanted to heckle, and her angry shrieks were cheered by the other teachers.

'My voice is a bit hoarse from making political speeches,' the Legislator apologised ingratiatingly.

'Try teaching!' the girl yelled.

'I have, but then I took up politics,' he replied thankfully.

I hurried back to the hotel, where soon I was dining in splendour to the sound of country and western religious ballads sung by a young lady in the bar next door. In the lounge, a lively school football team, coloured youths visiting Lake Charles for an away game, took over the hotel and began to ride up and down on the lifts. Order was restored, and then someone turned on a radio. A shooting had just taken place at the Civic Centre, supposedly unconnected to the teachers' meeting, and a man had been taken to hospital with his face blown away.

In the morning, I was woken by the football youths running up and down, and I arose and stepped out on to the balcony. Lake Charles shone in the sun, the further shore as invisible as France appears to Brightonians. Sandpipers cried plaintively from the water's edge, near the Downtowner Hotel's private jetty. After breakfast, I sat reading in the lounge.

Someone called my name, and there was the soft-spoken Sabrina, a pleasant contrast to the harsh young ladies of the night before.

'Good morning, it's your busy day today,' she said. 'I've fixed for you to see a black school first of all, and then a record studio. This afternoon another lady, Mrs Anne Hurley, will give you a historical tour of Lake Charles. How about that?'

Sabrina looked pleased with herself, and no wonder. Amazed, I stepped into her car.

'I'm taking you first of all to Ray D. Molo Middle Magnet School,' she said. 'That's a black school for children aged ten to fourteen. The schools don't *have* to be black or white like they used to, but some have just stayed that way.'

On the way, near some shabby outbuildings, I noticed a bearded tramp, an off-white man, carrying a rolled-up festoon of tins on his back, all strung together.

'I've been seeing him round town for years,' Sabrina said. 'He hunts for them ol' tins all day and sells them someplace. Here we are! You haven't got too long here, as the whole school is closing for the football this afternoon. I'll meet you back here in an hour's time.'

I found myself outside a modern flat-roofed school set in a tarmac playground. I went in. A secretary met me and led me to the headmaster's room. Sabrina had managed things splendidly.

Edward J. McKinley, the stout, genial headmaster, shook my hand and showed me to a chair. Then he sat at his desk below an American flag and asked me what I wanted to know. Photographs of his family stood here and there, and he seemed a relaxed, contented man. In my quick glimpse around the school, as I entered, I had seen no white children or teachers.

'Could you explain the name of the school to me?' I asked.

'Certainly! We are named after Dr Ray D. Molo, our former headmaster. Before that we were known as Lincoln Elementary. Dr Molo was a brilliant man, a bachelor of science of Grambling University.'

This was the black university I had seen from the Greyhound near Shreveport.

'I see, but what does "Magnet" mean?'

'Ours is a school for bright children, and it is intended to draw pupils here from all over the Lake Charles area. To make this school particularly attractive to all comers, the Legislature allots us more money for books and for better facilities. We want *all* the bright children to come here to Ray D. Molo.'

His eyes strayed to a school photograph on a shelf beside some silver cups and a shield. I noticed that four or five white children had been placed in the front row and the others, all coloured, were posed behind them.

'So this is not a black school at all?'

'No, no. It *used* to be, in the early days, but now we intend, by our Magnet policy, to attract children from white homes also.'

'Really! And how do you tell if a prospective pupil is bright or not?'

'We give each child a six-week trial period. During this time, the pupil's intelligence is measured in Carnegie units. If two and a half units are earned, the child can stay. Intelligence is monitored in units throughout a pupil's time here, and it takes twenty-one Carnegie units to graduate.'

Could these units have been invented by the same Carnegie who blessed the world with so many free public libraries? If so, like the Lord, he giveth and taketh away, for I am sure that units can do no good to the brain cells. Mr McKinley gave me an Information Sheet where units and other subjects were described in Gradgrinding jargon.

I asked if I might be shown quickly around the school. Importantly, the headmaster spoke into an intercom device and told everyone that I was on my way. The football match that afternoon seemed of great importance to him, so I knew I would have to rush through Ray D. Molo for fear of harassing him out of his wits.

Smiling benignly, the headmaster rolled along the corridors, pausing now and again to ask a boy where he was going. From the ready answers, I could see that he was by no means an ogre putting on an act, but a fairly well-liked man. Glancing through classroom windows, I saw many white teachers of the sharp young woman type who had attended the meeting. Half Molo's teachers were white. I saw no men teachers. Two pupils only were white, so the Magnet had not exerted much pulling-power. Seeing rows of red metal lockers on the walls, I groaned inwardly. These meant that a child's desk, or classroom, was not his castle. Give me a desk with a liftable lid any day, in which to store books, rulers, comics and conkers. There are no conkers in America now, following the great nineteenth-century Chestnut Blight, but the principle remains. A secure cosy den of his very own, in which he can be concealed by a raised lid, does wonders for a boy's morale. Sure enough, the first classroom we entered revealed table-top lidless desks.

This was an English class. Rows of brown faces looked up at mine, but they seemed, I thought, a little careworn and repressed. Perhaps the teacher had put the fear of God into them after hearing the intercom message, or perhaps the Carnegie units had taken their toll.

'We have one computer and one typewriter per child in this school,' the headmaster rumbled reassuringly.

As I can neither type nor compute, this cut little ice with me, and I asked if I might look at their school books. Before I did so, I gave my standard speech on Britain, dragging in the poor Queen as usual, and then asking if there were any questions. To my surprise, there were none. Most of the faces that stared humourlessly towards me looked blank and stunned. The children were about eleven years old. I asked again, and girls screwed up their faces as if in an agony of thought, but no questions emerged. Some of the pupils looked bright, with open faces and sparkling eyes, but no one spoke.

I walked up and down, inspector-style, and looked at their books. Text books were very simple, and most of the exercises consisted of filling in a single missing word, ticking a word, or stating which was the 'odd word out'. In the exercise books, handwriting was joined up in most cases, but the attempts at essays had produced only confused and misspelled ramblings. I said goodbye to the English class, no doubt to their relief.

Next door, a History lesson was taking place. The headmaster kept glancing at his watch and murmuring about football, so I didn't look at the books, but merely rattled off my Great Queen Over the Sea speech and asked for questions. A girl in plaits at once put her hand up and asked if every child in England went to Oxford. I had to disillusion her, but cheered her and the class up by drawing a comic-gowned undergraduate on the blackboard.

'My, my!' marvelled the headmaster, and I left to popular acclaim.

I only came into my own at the Maths class, where rows of eager faces beamed brightly towards me. In England, aptitude at Maths seems linked to a working-class or mechanical frame of mind. English is a subject linked to Royalty, for do we not say 'the Age of Dickens' or the 'Victorian Age' interchangeably? Likewise, we can say 'Georgian times' or 'Jane Austen's day'. Perhaps I am biased. I hope that Maths in America is linked to the Presidency, for a brighter bunch of ten-year-old hopefuls I have yet to see.

'Do they have school uniforms in England?' a girl asked me.

'Some schools do and some schools don't,' I replied. 'At my school, Holloway Comprehensive, we had black caps with metal badges on in the shape of a bird. If we saw a teacher in the street, we had to raise our caps and greet him. There were no girls in our school, so we used to sit thinking about them. Sometimes a girls' school would go by outside, and the bad boys would rush to the window and howl like wolves, bang their desk lids up and down and shout, "Lemme at 'em! Lemme at 'em!" '

All the class seemed interested in this information.

'Sir, if a boy at a private school gets expelled, does he have to go to a public school?' a boy asked me.

I knew that in America a 'public school' means *not* a first-rate fee-paying school but the equivalent of a state school or Comp.

'It's up to the boy's parents what they do,' I said. 'If he had been expelled from a really good private school, they'd be very upset. What's your name?'

'Jason, sir.'

'Well, here's how the boy's father might carry on.'

I coughed, and advanced on Jason, trying hard to look like a choleric Lord or a gout-ridden general.

'Jason! Sir!' I shouted, jumping up and down in uncontrollable rage. 'What do you mean by letting down the good name of the Jasons? Ours is an ancient family, known and respected far and wide, and you have to let down our name, sir, by setting your school on fire! What do you mean by it, sir? Eh? What? What? What?'

Jason responded at once in character: 'Well, sir, I was just playing with some matches . . .'

We were both drowned out by deafening applause, under cover of which the headmaster whooshed me down the corridor to the Remedial Class. Here eight desks were drawn closely around the table of a serious-looking young white woman teacher. She did not seem to want to break off from her English lesson, so I asked if I might glance quickly at the exercise books. All the children, aged about ten, looked very quiet and worthy.

'Julie, you've won half of the battle if you've realised that you must be responsible for your own actions and take the consequences. Congratulations!' the teacher had written at the foot of one essay.

A very curious essay had been titled 'The Enchanted Turtle from the Magic Waters'. It showed great imagination, coupled with a rambling, disorganised mind. The story ended like this: 'While she was talking she died and after this he and his father were sad for a little while but after that they were enchantedly swell.'

'There's just time to show you the school kitchen!' Mr McKinley said breathlessly. I could tell he was proud of the kitchen, and so he should have been, as acres of stainless steel and smiling cooks presented themselves. The cooks were heating up frozen chips, a nostalgic taste of England.

'Thirty per cent of the children pay for their own lunches!' Mr McKinley announced grandly. Then he barked into the intercom. A moment later every door burst open and the children rushed out shouting like the Bash Street Kids. Many paused for a friendly word or a wave for their headmaster. Instead of mechanical bells, lessons apparently ended at the whim of the headmaster and his portable radio. No wonder the classes had seemed rather repressed, as I had obviously been 'keeping them in'. Now, as the children rushed off for football, their joy was unconfined.

'So Sabrina Sonnier has been showing you around?' beamed the headmaster, as eager to leave as any of his pupils. 'Her husband Mark was here to mend the school copying machine. Such a nice man! We all became great friends. Now you wait here in the secretary's room, and I'll give you a copy of a magazine the pupils wrote themselves. Then I must say goodbye. Maybe I'll come to England some day, but people who've been, say I wouldn't like it. It's full of old things, and I like everything to be gleaming and modern.'

And so I settled down with a well-produced copy of the *Astro Gazette*. Apparently written entirely by fourteen-year-old girls, it resembled *Jackie*, an innocent romantic magazine.

'Valentine Secrets, by Unknown Reporter', one column was headed.

Gossip columns abounded, signed by initials. The preoccupation of the school seemed to be Love: 'S.J. and S.R. are really getting involved.'

A list of 'Top Ten Books' ended with *Huckleberry Finn*, I was glad to see. I had not heard of the other nine.

'What Would You Like To Be?' another column was headed. Everyone wished to be a doctor, a teacher or a lawyer, except for good old Ronnie Bartie, who put 'An Undercover Cop'. Girls' names had a strange music about them: Nicole Celestine, Margaret Champagne and La Shonda Bilbo. There were lots of photographs and class news, such as, 'We in 8A are the liveliest class in the eighth grade, and this is not an opinion but a fact.' A 'Just Suppose' column by Mallory began: 'Just Suppose Mrs Vincent was a Russian spy . . .'

A girl named Zonya had submitted the following poem as her own work.

> January brings the snow, makes our feet and fingers glow . . .
> April brings the primrose sweet, scatters daisies at our feet.

Since snow is unknown at Lake Charles, and primroses don't grow in America, you would think that she might have been suspected of cheating. However, back in my secondary school days, a boy palmed off Housman's 'Cherry Tree' as his original composition. Despite the words referring to the poet's age, it appeared over the name 'Hibbard, 2B' in the school magazine. The standard of work at Molo seems to be about the same as that of a not-very-good Middle School in England now.

Almost two pages of the Gazette were devoted to an extract from a reading book called *The Black B C's*.

> C is for Cowboys,
> Kings of the West
> Some of the black men
> Were some of the best.
>
> G is for Ghetto
> A place where we
> Can be at home
> Loved and free.

I was so used to seeing books like that in English schools, imported for the children of West Indians, that it seemed odd to see one in the land of its birth. It made no more sense in Lake Charles than it did in Tottenham. Sabrina arrived, and I followed her to the car.

'How did you like it?' she asked.

'Well, the school work isn't up to much, but the place is beautifully kept up, with masses of new equipment.'

'That's because of politics!' Sabrina said bitterly, driving away. 'The black people are getting in power now! We got black legislators, an' they say the black schools are getting the worst of everything, so they give 'em the *best* of everything! And then the white schools suffer! Now the *white* schools are poor.'

'Oh dear. Are the white schools in Lake Charles really run down, then?' I asked.

'No, they're better than the black schools, but that's only 'cos they're in a rich area.'

Headmaster McKinley, and other headmasters like him, I reflected, try to improve their schools with more money and equipment in order to attract white pupils. They do not see their schools as black schools at all, but hope to run schools that are good enough to welcome hundreds of white pupils. However, to most of the Southern white people, these efforts are construed as 'the black schools getting the best of everything', and they grow more prejudiced than ever. Few would dream of sending their children to a black school. In their hearts, many seem to believe that black people are ineducable and that *any* money spent on their schooling must be a total waste.

Mr McKinley reminded me of the West Indian pastors in London who vehemently deny that they run black churches, but hope in vain to gain at least one white member. White people in England, however, do not even realise that they are *allowed* to go in a black church and have no wish to do so. To Headmaster McKinley, school segregation had ended, but to Sabrina it was an unquestioned fact of life.

Later, Sabrina showed me her own school work, beautifully written essays in faultless copperplate writing. She too had a vivid imagination. In her last year at school she had written a lengthy treatise on the Moonies.

'I've found a record studio for you!' Sabrina said, brightening up. 'All my life I've lived near Lake Charles and I never knew it was there. Now I'm takin' you to a black quarter of Lake Charles that I never knew existed at *all* until last week when Mark took me there.'

We drove past the railway station, which looked as derelict as the empty brick buildings around it. Wooden shacks, some painted and well kept up, but most shabby, lined the wide weed-grown streets. Hopeless, apathetic-looking black men lounged against the plank walls, sipping from bottles wrapped in brown paper. One scraggy-bearded man in a dirty vest resembled a human skeleton. He had a dreamy faraway look in his eye, an empty bottle at his feet. All at once he saw a friend across the overgrown street, brightened up and waved happily. Few if any coloured people seemed to be employed in the prosperous parts of Lake Charles, and everyone here looked as if they had been out of work for a long time.

Only one place of luxury could be seen, the Sapphire Blue Club, whose neon light beckoned above an open door revealing a gleaming bar inside, sumptuous furniture and posters advertising singers.

'Prostitutes come here at night,' Sabrina whispered, 'and white men come after them. All these old wooden buildings are bars.'

'Not long now,' she said grimly, as we neared a healthy bunch of youths who were standing joking at a corner.

'Press that button and all the doors will lock!' Sabrina gasped, as she closed the car windows.

'Surely you don't expect those boys will leap on a moving car?' I asked, as I obeyed.

'No, I know I'm silly, but I can't help it,' she blurted in terror.

The boys, who had ignored us before, saw what Sabrina was doing and began to jeer. A handful of gravel bounced off the rear window. If this were the Ghetto, mentioned in the school poem, then nobody looked very 'loved and free'.

Just then, as we left Enterprise Boulevard and made towards Church Street, three black horsemen on tall, mettlesome steeds, cantered by and rode off into the woods.

'Who were they?' I asked.

'I don't know! I've never seen anything like it before!'

Perhaps they were the Cowboys, 'some of the best', though in their pride they looked more like Spanish conquistadores. On the corner of Church Street, tottering plank cabins lurched towards the road. One of the most rickety ones had a sign painted on a board in wobbly writing: 'Apostolic Church'. Around the corner, a long wooden shed took up a lengthy stretch of roadside. Coloured men were leaning against the walls, amid heaps of broken television sets.

'Goldband Records. T.V. Repairs', read a sign over the door.

Sabrina parked the car, locked it in triplicate, and we went inside. An elderly white man in shirtsleeves and brown-rimmed spectacles welcomed us, his face wreathed in smiles. 'Hi, I'm Eddie Shuler, owner o' this here business concern,' he said, ushering us inside.

We found ourselves in a dark, barn-like interior, divided into several rooms and with steps up to an attic. Boxes of tapes, records and objects connected with record-making and telly repairs were stacked against the walls, reaching to the ceiling from which other devices were hanging. I rather fancy there was a hosepipe coiled up somewhere – certainly the whole place reminded me of the storage shed of Littlehampton Parks Department in Sussex.

'This used to be a Holiness Church and garage combined; now it's a studio, workshop and record store,' said Eddie. 'We also sell T-shirts.'

A rack along one of the plank walls contained an assortment of blues records, including several by Katie Webster, a local discovery of Eddie's who has performed in London.

Sabrina was not very interested in the recording business, so she sat mutely on a chair while I pestered Eddie Shuler with questions.

'You ask away. If you don't ask questions you run out of snuff,' he observed mildly.

Pieced together, Eddie Shuler's story went like this: 'I was born in 1913, and I'm a Texan! Came here to Lake Charles on Defence work in the forties, an' married a Cajun girl.'

I glanced around and saw a roster of musicians' photographs along the end wall. Almost every performer held an accordion. A large label read, 'Cajun Hall of Fame'.

'No, my wife never cared for Cajun music – she likes sentimental songs,' Eddie continued. 'When I came here from Texas, I liked country music an' sung with a local group, the Hackberry Ramblers. I played a saxophone, unknown in country music then, an' people would say, "What's that?" I always liked to be original. Jimmy Rodgers was my favourite back then, but the Hackberry Ramblers played some Cajun music. At that time, Cajuns played the fiddle more than they do now. These days, the accordion is *the* Cajun instrument, an' now the black blues singers play it – I recorded a number of them. There's Rocking Sidney (he's real big now) an' this new boy Bon Ton St Mary I've just signed up.'

He showed us a photograph of Bon Ton, a wild-looking dark-skinned young man with a touch of Red Indian about him. Clutching an accordion, he looked up defiantly.

'I started this recording studio just to plug our own band. Then one day I saw a ragged man, like a tramp, stumbling along, carrying something in a flour sack. He took it out, an' it was an accordion. The guy began demanding I make a record of him playing and singing. Iry Le June was his name, a real back-country Cajun. I was sorry for the feller, as he was half blind, so I agreed an' we shook hands. His records made a sensation, and Cajun music and Goldband Records took off right then and there! Let me show you round the place.'

He pointed out a drum kit in a dark nook, set up on a makeshift stage.

'I've cut a great many blues records up here, by guys like Hop Wilson an' Juke Boy Bonner. The key to black music is the rhythm. Blues with Cajun style accordion is called Zydeco, an' I've signed one feller called Highway Zydeco and his Highway Zydeco Band. Another thing I do now is make tapes of Catholic gospel songs by white singers, some of 'em in French or Spanish. I sell the heck out of those things! When a song doesn't need any work, I don't work on it. When all the great Cajun singers started out here, I left their music intact. I didn't know I was creating history! Now, since about four years ago, the younger musicians have begun fitting a modern beat to the music, all in the drum rhythm. The accordion is as popular as ever! Let me play you some tapes.'

A song by a Zydeco singer began as a rock and roll ditty with just a touch of accordion behind the drums. After the last chorus, the accordion spiralled away into a joyous madcap swirl of sound, as if played by a French peasant drunk on Southern moonshine.

'Notice he plays the fancy accordion towards the end, the commercial drumbeat at the beginning. That shows he's an Entertainer! Now listen to this! It's Love Bug Pellerin, one of our top accordion players. Here's his photo!'

I saw a burly white man with a curly teddy boy hairstyle and an engaging smile. His song was called 'Hey, John Pierre! Don't do that no more!' and concerned the activities of one John Pierre who visited Love Bug and rapidly ate up all the food in his house. ('You drank a gallon of milk – don't do that no more!')

Eddie seemed to love the music of Louisiana lounges, picnics and churches, and hopped spryly around waving tapes and photographs and talking rapidly. Sabrina seemed more bemused than I was, and murmured polite nothings from time to time.

'I recorded Dolly Parton when she was only thirteen,' Eddie continued, brandishing a photograph of a little girl who looked like Shirley Temple. 'She made a record in the fifties called "Puppy Love". I run a mail order business, an' I'm linked to Charlie Records in England.'

To the strains of a ditty called 'The Crawfish Song', he led Sabrina and myself into the offices at the rear of the building. Here I met a big man who greeted me in such a clear, bell-like accent that I asked him if he were an American.

'I'm French!' he said proudly. 'That is, Acadian or Cajun.'

A friendly office girl and a dainty little brown lady with old world manners, Mrs Shuler herself, seemed to be the only staff. Eddie took Sabrina and me to the other end of the barn, where amplifying machines poked from the entrance to the loft.

'That's a Studer Revox, the best recording machine on the market today!' he said, pointing at an oblong space age device that hung incongruously from the wall. 'It's Swedish, an' we're going to make some more records just as soon as we get the hang of it.'

Privately I doubted if anything good could come out of Sweden. Just then, Sabrina gave a cry as a red horsefly or stinging daddy-longlegs flew by.

'That's a wasp – they come in winter,' Eddie said. 'We had lots of 'em at one time, till I found their nest in the wall an' destroyed it. That's just a stray. I looked all over for their nest, an' I like to never found them. Then

I found a little old hole no bigger than my fingernail. You know, if those wasps saw me hanging about, they wouldn't go in or out o' their hole in case I found it.'

'How has the music here changed since you first started recording in the forties?' I enquired.

'Well the songs used to be all in French, but now they're a mixture of French and English verses. At one time the music was more important, now it's the song. People now like a strong story line.'

I noticed some pictures of coloured gospel singers on the wall, alongside men in cowboy hats with accordions. I described the West Indian gospel music of London to Eddie Shuler, and showed him my celebrated photographs of Mother Noël singing with the Mount Zion Spiritual Baptists. I even sang him a line or two of their Jubilee songs.

Mr Shuler stopped, with one leg on the ladder to the loft, and looked at me with keen interest. He appeared to want to sign Mother Noël to Goldband on the spot, and made several remarks that showed his deep understanding and respect for Negro music. I realised that here was a white Southerner who worked in a black district and admired his neighbours without ambivalence. Then he darted up the ladder and returned with a gospel tape and a record, which he pressed into my hands.

'That record was a real big hit out in Texas!' he assured me, as he waved goodbye. I looked at it in the car. It was called 'Don't Sell That Monkey', by Milton Landry and the Zydecos.

Sabrina cheered up as we reached the smarter end of Lake Charles. I praised her for her cleverness in finding me a black school *and* a recording studio.

'What kind of music do you like?' I asked her.

'Songs I can sing myself,' she replied gaily, and in a comic lilting voice she sang as she drove.

> 'Oh, I had a little chicken and she wouldn't lay an egg,
> I sprinkled hot water up and down her leg.
> She began to moan, and she began to beg,
> And then she went and laid me a hard-boiled egg!'

'Shoot, I nearly missed that light,' she added, as she swung the car round at the card-backed bridge and dropped me off at the Downtowner Hotel. There seemed to be more to Sabrina Sonnier than met the eye.

That afternoon, as arranged, Anne Hurley of the Calcasieu Preservation Society called for me in her car. I certainly hope that at least one or two tourists will go to Lake Charles, to justify the lavish hospitality I enjoyed. Anne was a well-dressed, dark-haired, middle-aged lady. She and her husband had restored one of the fine old plank mansions of Lake Charles, and they now lived in it.

'I'm going to tell you all about the Queen Anne houses of Lake Charles an' all the history round here, but first I've got to find Gaius,' she said.

As she continued talking about the elusive Gaius, I suddenly realised that she was not referring to a friend, but to gas – that is, petrol. A pity, for Gaius had sounded like an interesting person.

'Gaius' acquired, she told me about the early days at Lake Charles. 'There was competition among groups of settlers here over who could found the first town,' she said. 'Some people made a town called Marion, by erecting a log cabin courthouse. But the young men of Lake Charles went by night and *stole* the courthouse! They lifted it on to a barge an' brought it back here an' set it up. So that's why we now have the town of Lake Charles on this spot.

'At first the industry here was all lumbering. There was a timber boom, with sawmills everywhere. Lake Charles was famous for its long-leaf yellow pines. Many of the houses I'm going to show you are made from those pines. But finally the yellow pine was all cleaned out, and the lumber men started on the cypress trees. All the original forest has long been cleared. Lake Charles was discovered by the Spanish and settled in the French time, the eighteenth century. However, the architecture here has suffered a lot from fire and from the hurricane of 1918. Then a great deal was pulled down in the sixties. But I can promise to show you some delightful houses, even if they're not old by English standards.'

So saying, she drove me to a tree-lined neighbourhood where 'unrestored' wooden houses were now outnumbered by houses of Edwardian grandeur, with cast-iron lampposts outside and many other arty touches. Black men, looking rather cowed or sullen, walked rapidly in and out of the unrestored dwellings.

'Our house is in a mixed neighbourhood,' Mrs Hurley sighed. 'Still, I suppose the blacks here aren't too bad.'

Not only were they 'not too bad', but they were obviously not going to be around much longer, as their crowded lodging houses were being bought up and restored to their original beauty as white family homes. How dreadful to be an American 'black', forever spoken of as a calamity! I was glad that men like Eddie Shuler existed, even if most of white Lake Charles had never heard of him.

Anne Hurley parked outside her own house, but led me away from it into an avenue of bushy ilex trees and grandiose dwellings with gardens. I was reminded of Kingston Gorse, a private 1920ish housing estate in Sussex, and of the many similar leafy Millionaires' Rows of Surrey. An agreeable companion in most ways, Mrs Hurley began to expound upon the features of the Queen Anne houses.

'Most of the houses here were once the homes of lumber barons,' she said. As all of them were in an English style, I realised that little remained of French Lake Charles. Many houses seemed more Gothic than Queen Anne, with round turrets capped by pointed spires, and a general air of haunted-house weirdness. All were made from rows of planks, and some of the taller dwellings seemed top-heavy. They were painted white or pale green, colours that contrasted well with the dark oaks around them. The streets were very wide.

'That's our neighbour the professor's house,' Anne said admiringly. 'He's restoring it from an old lodging house. See his cast-iron nineteenth-century letter box? Now look there at that manhole cover on the sidewalk! There's the date, 1918, made into the ironwork. Many of the houses lost their roofs and porches during the hurricane, that's why they're not so uniform. The Lake Charles Queen Anne–Greek Revival style flourished from 1870 to about 1910. French-speaking carpenters, called *charpentiers*, built the houses from ready-made plans. There were no architects here at that time. See that lovely house? The contractor used an 1880 pattern book for that one. You could buy pattern books for houses that had been designed up North or somewhere, and have them built anywhere you liked.'

Well endowed with porches and delightfully named 'Juliet balconies', the Lumber Baronial Houses were indeed a pleasure to behold.

'Here we are back at my house!' Anne cried gaily, with the air of someone who saves the biggest treat till last. 'Sabrina told me how much you were interested in our Louisiana music, so I've arranged a surprise for you.'

Loud, harsh accordion music suddenly burst from the Hurley back door. We entered, and I gaped in surprise. In the hallway, on a wooden chair, sat a big tall man in blue dungarees and a creased brown face with a pop-eyed, bewildered expression. Awkwardly, all angular knees and elbows, he jerked the accordion to and fro, looking hideously un-comfortable. Obviously, he felt very ill-at-ease and out of place in such grand surroundings.

'My husband has found a Cajun Musician for you,' Anne Hurley said grandly. 'This is Jimmy!'

CHAPTER SEVENTEEN

Cajun Cooking

STRANGE POLKA-LIKE music jerked from the accordion of the tall brown-skinned Cajun in overalls. Anne Hurley, now joined by her husband, beamed approvingly. Jimmy the Cajun seemed to feel as incongruous as he looked, a garage handyman suddenly invited into the Big House to play for a foreigner from London. His music sounded rather mechanical, and I was more impressed by his accordion. It was not a button accordion, but closely resembled a melodeon or squeeze box. However, he could squeeze more notes out of it than can the average melodeon player. Both the squeezing-part and the polished wooden handles were dark red, with sundry ornaments resembling gypsy canal art.

'I'm French, and those are French tunes,' Jimmy blurted out when he had finished playing, still very ill at ease. 'I can't play so good without my band Country Kicks. You ought to hear me at night in Good Time Charlie's Lounge. Then I can really swing! I'm playing there tomorrow – if you wants to come, I'll play my best for you.'

'I'd love to!' I said. 'That's an unusual accordion you've got.'

'Yes, sir, it's a Mouton accordion, made in Crowley, not far from here. Mouton's the feller who makes 'em – he's still alive.'

Mr and Mrs Hurley invited us into the kitchen for coffee. Jimmy awkwardly fitted his long legs under the table. A successful-looking bearded businessman, Mr Hurley was connected with the Best Western Hotels chain. Jimmy worked in the garage next door to the Lake Charles Best Western.

'I stayed at one of your hotels at Meridian, Mississippi,' I told Mr Hurley. 'It had a coloured manager.'

'I know him. That's very unusual,' was the reply.

Jimmy had all the while been staring at me intensely. Suddenly a rapid volley of French burst from his lips. I started back in horror, reminded of school days, and asked him to translate.

'I said, "Are there many pretty French girls in London?" '

'Some come over in summer, I suppose.'

'How's that? Aren't you from France? I thought London was in France.'

When Mrs Hurley explained, Jimmy grew doubly abashed. I asked him if he had ever recorded at Goldband Studios.

'Eddie Shuler's place! Yes, I done a harmonica solo for 'im once. Some say he's a crook, 'cos he had a hit with a blues called "Sugar Bee" an' the blues singer says Eddie never gave 'im a cent. But I also heard tell the man got money but spent it all on drink an' fast cars. My record never took off, so I don't know. I'll see how Bon Ton St Mary gits on – he's one o' the new fellers just signed up. Rocking Sidney the Zydeco man lives here in Lake Charles, but he's away touring most o' the time, I guess.'

'What's your full name, so I can look out for you when you're famous?' I asked.

'Jimmy Le Beau, that's me. I can't write it down, 'cos I don't write so good. Now if all you folks will pardon me, I must be leaving. I sure have enjoyed your hospitality.'

Mr Hurley had to leave not long afterwards, and Anne Hurley offered to show me around their house. The tall, nineteenth-century dwelling was bursting with Victoriana. Life-size china dolls in bonnets and pinafores stared at me with piercing eyes. China dogs, much prized, looked crossly over their shoulders. I admired a bookshelf, which contained a copy of *Uncle Remus*, the book which had brought me to the South. It was now banned as 'racist'. I found a pirated copy of *Little Black Sambo* with the wrong pictures and no author's name. Mrs Hurley seemed interested to hear of the great Helen Bannerman, whose books are now in Remus-like disgrace in England. I was glad that the children at Molo, the black school, had enjoyed *Huckleberry Finn*, as that book is wobbling on the edge of banishment as I write. Huck Finn and Uncle Remus were my boyhood heroes.

Anne Hurley seemed particularly proud of some brightly and splodgily painted Bible scenes, the work of an old coloured lady who had lived nearby. 'She was born in slavery, an' when she got old, she just began to paint on doors and ironing boards in this mystic style,' I was told. 'See, there's a black Mary an' baby Jesus. All the black lady angels have got birds' feet an' beehive hayerdos [hairdos]. When someone asked her about the hayerstyles, she said they *must* have hayer like that, else it would all get in their eyes when they was flying. Isn't that something?'

It was, but I wasn't sure what. My hostess led me further upstairs.

'The great hurricane destroyed the Lake Charles jail, so the sheriff moved the prisoners to this house in chains,' Mrs Hurley continued. 'One o' them dived straight through a window to his death. So our house is haunted by the sound of breaking glass. We often hears it. At first we looked around to see if anything had broken, but now we're used to it. One of the neighbours was troubled by a ghost, an' she had the house blessed, an' it vanished.'

My favourite part of the house was the loft, which had been converted into a pioneer-cabin-like room for the Hurleys' twenty-six-year-old son. Heads of white-tailed deer frowned from the walls, for the highly Victorian craft of taxidermy thrives in the South today. On a dresser reposed a perfect wooden model of a Lumber Baronial house, complete with porch and pinnacles.

Every day, Sabrina Sonnier seemed different. Not only did she wear a different dress each time I saw her, but she also allowed a new facet of her personality to appear. No longer an English country girl, she was now Irish, innocent yet merry, crying 'Shoot!' at every disturbance and telling me about her husband Mark, the photocopy machine repairer. I was no longer 'sir', but seemed to be treated as a lifelong friend.

'Me and Mark live in a trailer home. He's six feet high so there isn't much room! We hope to build on a plot soon, but it's real expensive. A log cabin is the kind of house I'd like. Now it's a real shame, but my parents never liked me 'n Mark gettin' married. So I never see them now.'

'Oh dear. Where are you taking me today?'

'To see my grandma, and then to a bar I know.'

If this were tourism, I was all for it.

Sabrina parked beside a tiny wooden house half hidden by the trees. 'I call my grandma Mama Bear, 'cos our family name is Hebert,' she said. 'She's seventy-three years old, an' she keeps a real neat flower garden.'

We found Mama Bear talking to a man on a ladder. He was repairing damage caused by termites to the ceiling. Evidently a friend of the family, he shook all our hands and departed.

A cheery little brown woman with glasses, Mama Bear welcomed us in and sat me down at a table dominated by a bottle of Jack Daniel's whiskey. She offered me a glass, fussed over Sabrina in a grandmotherly way, and then cooked me a bowl of spicy jambalaya. Although her house was small, the windows were large, and semi-tropical plants grew all around.

'You ought to see my garden in summer – it's mighty colourful,' she said. 'Hummingbirds flying all round the touch-me-nots an' I don't know what else. Come out and see it now!'

To my surprise, cotton grew in a corner of the crowded garden, and she plucked me off a sprig. Sugar cane, tall with a blackish stem, and squash grew nearby. Ground near the garden shed had been neatly hoed and lily-like flowers were still in bloom.

'I don't suppose you've met poor people before,' Mama Bear said to me pleasantly. Perhaps she thought that all English people lived in castles. Lord Emsworth of Blandings Castle would have envied her garden.

Soon she had to go out to play cards with a friend. This happy mixture of merriment and domesticity seemed very Irish to me, but perhaps it is a Roman Catholic attribute. Throughout the South, people had told me that the Cajuns really enjoyed life, and it was true. But there was a dark side to Lake Charles life.

'Only across the way, a woman shot herself an' left her out-of-work husband to rear three children. I'm going to take them across a basket o' stuff. You see Roy, I left school early, an' I'm best at cooking an' trying to make people happy.' She gave me a hug as we parted, and her two cats purred goodbye.

'I'm takin' you to the Plantation House,' Sabrina told me. 'That's the only bar I go to in Lake Charles. It's a real historical place, and I sure hope you like it.'

A splendid mansion surrounded by trees, the Plantation House had been built in 1910. It had only recently been converted into a luxury inn, with a restaurant that served crawfish in eight different ways, to say nothing of shrimps, frog legs and catfish. I suppose that a crawfish must be the American cousin of the crayfish. Sabrina and I sat decorously at the bar. She drank something with a cherry in it, and waved gaily to friends across the room.

At the bar, I found a pamphlet that told the story of Lake Charles town. Apparently the district had been taken from the Indians by the Spanish, and called the Rio Hondo Territory. The first French settlers arrived in the 1770s. Slave traders and buccaneers later hid their ships in the swamps, sometimes pursued by 'the fledgling U.S. infantry'. One of these villains was Jean Lafitte, who commanded the *Pride*. He is an American hero, as he fought against the British at the Battle of New Orleans. Lake Charles had been named after an early French settler, Charles Sallier. The town came later, named after the lake. Americans (that is, sort of English) created most of the town and the surrounding farmland during the timber boom of the 1850s. Captain Goss, who flourished in the mid-nineteenth century, built the port. There was no canal at that time, but the wide Calcasieu River runs into Lake Charles.

Oddly enough, though I didn't point it out to Sabrina, the pamphlet told an entirely different version of her story of the Sallier Oak. Charles Sallier, the French pioneer, had lived with his wife in a cabin beside the tree. One day he shot both her and himself, in a fit of jealous French rage. She survived, and continued to live placidly beside the oak. That's all. There was no mention of Cajuns. How Irish of the Cajuns to invent a colourful myth around their cruel and callous expulsion from Nova Scotia by the British!

'Tomorrow, as it's your last day in Lake Charles, me and Mark are gonna cook you a real French gumbo dinner!' Sabrina promised me. 'Our trailer's kind of small, but you won't mind that, I reckon. Mark's parents will be coming over and all. Before that we're gonna take you round the swamps clear to the Gulf of Mexico, an' maybe find you a 'gator or two!'

She dropped me at the hotel. After a meal, I phoned for a taxi. The driver was a sarcastic coloured man in dark glasses.

'Take me to Good Time Charlie's Lounge,' I ordered.

He sneered but obeyed, and I found myself set down in a gaudy neon strip of pubs, clubs and take-away restaurants. Good Time Charlie's seemed a very small place. In I went.

I found myself in a crowded, smoky dark bar-room, with a pool table, a juke box, tables and chairs near a small dance floor, and a stage where drums had been set up and electric guitars plugged in. I could have been in an Irish pub in London. A tough beer-bellied giant of a man, with a bushy beard and a lumber shirt, looked at me in indolent amusement, twirling his billiard cue. I asked the blonde barmaid for a Budweiser.

'Jimmy's paying for it,' she said, as I fumbled for my money.

I turned and saw Jimmy Le Beau striding across the stage, clutching the lead guitar. Could this tall, proud, confident Red Indian chief of a man be the same awkward, humble person I had met at the Hurleys' house? He gave me a nod and then began whanging on his electric guitar like a good 'un. There seemed nothing incongruous about rock and roll as played by a brown, balding Cajun, as he stuck to the hillbilly blues of Memphis in the fifties, by now a Southern traditional style. The rest of Country Kicks consisted of the second guitarist, a scrubby-faced young man who also sang, and a drummer. Jimmy's Mouton accordion reposed in a corner.

Young men and girls in rough, casual wear crowded round the pool table, talking, laughing and shouting.

'Oowee, hot damn!' a shaggy blond youth cried, jumping in delight at a tricky shot at the pool table. All the pool players seemed very acrobatic, flinging their limbs around and moving rapidly round the table. I crossed the room and sat near the stage, next to a silent, grinning old man with a walking stick. He gave me a nod and grinned on. White men and women of all ages patronised Good Time Charlie's and some were very old indeed. All were enjoying themselves, and as all spoke English, it was impossible for me to tell who was a Cajun and who was not. Only one coloured man was there, a big man in a black stetson who looked like an oil tycoon. As Jimmy sang and played, Black Stetson danced energetically with a white girl in jeans. Almost every woman in the place, young or old, seemed to have dyed her hair peroxide blonde. When the dance floor was full, Jimmy laid down his guitar and produced a harmonica, on which he played a fast breakdown.

Seldom had I seen such innovative dancers, spinning, leaping and twirling to the rapid music. When Jimmy picked up his accordion and began to sing in French, along with the rest of the group, the character of the dancing changed. Couples performed a quick sideways dance, the Cajun Two Step. Jimmy's accordion playing was now fiery, swinging and free, quite unlike his stiff demonstration at the Hurleys'. One of the dancers, a young man, kneeled while his girl friend danced towards him, then sprang up and took her hand for a twirl once more. I wondered if this could have been a vestige of the Cushion Dance, an English country favourite in Restoration times. The hard floor was no kneeler's substitute for a cushion, yet the young man seemed as limber-legged as ever.

'Play "Daddy Crow!" ' someone shouted, and Jimmy obligingly swung into another tune. Then he picked up the guitar and began to play the blues, singing unconnected verses at random.

'Looky, looky yonder, down the railroad track . . .'

The dancers danced on, and the girl brought me a second Budweiser. Jimmy stepped down to the bar, and an old man who had been dancing picked up the harmonica and played a soft, plaintive tune.

'Thank you kindly!' said Jimmy on his return, and there was a patter of applause. 'Black Jack!' Jimmy announced, and launched into a lengthy harmonica solo, accompanied by the rest of the group. When it was over, he announced an interval, and the juke box was switched on. At once it began to play an accordion tune by Lake Charles's favourite son, Rocking Sidney.

'Let's Zydeco . . . my Zydeco shoes got the Zydeco blues,' sang the juke box, while Jimmy Le Beau fanned an imaginary harmonica. Everybody clapped and stamped.

Some say that the word Zydeco stems from *haricot*, the French for beans. Many Cajun songs are about food, so this is possible. But as Zydeco is the music of 'Black Cajuns', I prefer to think that the name comes from Africa. Unable to face a third Budweiser, I returned to my hotel in a Cajun taxi.

'I'm a hundred per cent French, from Lafayette,' the unshaven moustachioed driver told me. 'I speak French good, an' I'd like to go to France, but I t'ink I need one o' dem passport t'ings. How I get them, you know?'

At the Downtowner I had to push my way through the merry sixth-former-type football youths, who were singing 'Rah Rah Rah!' on my balcony. For some time I could hear them running up and down, white girls and boys among them, until they finally broke up to a cry of 'Everybody over to Room 37! Free beer, free party!'

I felt a bit headachy in the morning, but I cheered up at once at the sight of Sabrina stepping into the lounge, accompanied by her husband Mark. A big honest cheerful man with short curly hair and a moustache, he looked very French. So did Sabrina. However could I have thought her to be Irish? Just like young French visitors to the South of England, they both wore tight scarlet trousers. A true Frenchman seems impelled to wear tight trousers of pink or red. As Sabrina and Mark were both stout with very long thin legs, and as I am stout in a different way, we must have made a comical sight walking along to Mark's car – two lollipops and a pear. First of all we were going to call on Mark's parents.

Mark may have mended copying machines for a living, but he ought to have been a chef, for he talked about cooking the whole time. He and Sabrina spoke long and earnestly about the seafood supper they had planned. Mark and Sabrina seemed ideally suited, and I was sorry to recall that Sabrina's parents had withheld their blessing from the match. If they read this, I can assure them that Sabrina is in good hands.

Still talking about cooking, as if auditioning for the part of a Frenchman, Mark stopped his car outside a small suburban wooden house. Here his parents the Sonniers lived. Soon, after a glimpse into the highly ornamented front room, we all sat around the kitchen table drinking coffee and gossiping. Mrs Sonnier could have been an English housewife, but as for her big fat rascally husband, if I were in England I would have sworn that he was a Romany gypsy! A wicked grin on his round, battered brown face, he asked me if I had ever seen a 'Cajun microwave'. I had not, so he levered himself out of his chair and walked on bare feet to the back yard.

'Here she is,' he announced, and showed me a giant metal biscuit tin, the size of a water tank. A grating was raised about a foot from the bottom.

'We put the meat down on that tray,' Mr Sonnier said, 'an' then fit the charcoal grill on _top_ of the meat. Fire on top, meat in the middle, an' the gravy drips down below. Real tender, real tasty! You ever tasted Louisiana dried shrimp?'

Again I shook my head, so he took me indoors and opened an enormous freezer. It was stuffed from top to bottom with bags of small brown objects.

'Caught all these myself,' he mentioned, pulling out some dried shrimps and crunching them up like crisps. I tried some. They were quite nice. 'You want to see my boat?'

After showing me his small boat, Mr Sonnier beamed and led me back to the coffee table. The Sonniers would be coming to Sabrina and Mark's gumbo feast that night. So we wished them *au revoir* and set off for the swamp.

First of all we drove alongside a canal, where white egrets stood tall among the rushes. Soon we were out in the swamps, a flat eerie wilderness stretching on forever, our straight road a causeway with water on both sides. Swamps near New Orleans had been forested places of cypress trees and Spanish moss, but this was an open marsh. Islands of grass and shrubs rose from the lapping water at regular intervals, and spiky reeds showed that most of this floodland was shallow. Mark drove slowly, so I could see what was going on.

'Look at those pull-do!' he exclaimed, pointing.

Swimming among the reeds, nodding their heads vigorously, were small flocks of coots and moorhens, just as if I were in England. A typical countryman, Mark believed that the coots were male 'pull-do', the moorhens female. Mallards, pintail and shoveler ducks hurled through the air and splashed down with streams of ripples. Mark and Sabrina called the shoveler ducks 'spoonbills'. I was excited to see blue winged teal, which don't live in England. Each little teal had a white spot by its beak. A white pelican stood on an islet and spread its wings out to dry, and herons both blue and green fraternised with their cousins the egrets.

Mark and Sabrina seemed in high spirits, he joking into her ear and she giggling and crying, 'Oh shoot!' There was an undercurrent of bawdiness in their humour, and they seemed very fond of one another.

'He chased me till I caught him,' Sabrina told me.

Both were very proud of being French. 'I'm French through and through, with no other blood except Choctaw Indian,' Mark informed me.

Sabrina, very seriously, handed me a document full of exquisite French names. Her ancestry had been traced back to sixteenth-century France, before Nova Scotia had been settled. She didn't know anything about her French ancestors. It had been proven that they were French, and that was enough.

'Are you a Catholic, Roy?' Mark asked me, obviously hoping that I would say yes. He swallowed his disappointment as best as he could. A group of black people appeared on the bank, animatedly poking at the water with long-handled nets.

'They're crabbing!' Sabrina told me, her eyes aglow. 'I love to crab! I get up real early, Cajun-style, when I go fishing.'

Mark stopped the car next to a small group of white crabbers. Swamp waters lapped against the bank at the side of the road. The crabbers were friendly, and crabbed on while Mark explained their method to me. Each man sat expectantly beside a string, one end fastened on the bank, the other in the water.

'There's a chicken neck tied on the other end o' that string,' Mark said, 'an' when a crab grabs it, you haul 'im in. See, when he grips with his claw, he doesn't let go easy.'

Suddenly the string went taut, and the man pulled it out of the water, slowly and carefully. A big fresh-water crab was hanging on to the bait with one claw, his heavy body dangling. But not for long, for he was soon engulfed in the net, which was lowered beneath his scrabbling legs. In went the chicken neck, the string tightened, but the second crab was wiser. He sized up the situation in a moment, released his hold and fell back into the swamp with a splash.

'Shoot, you nearly had that sucker!' Sabrina cried.

'The old folk have a saying, and I do believe it's true,' observed Mark, 'that crabs caught by moonlight have more flesh on 'em and taste better, too.'

We drove on, while he described the local technique of catfish-fishing. American catfish are big rumbunctious fish-felines, quite unlike the little grey creatures sometimes sold in English pet shops as companions for goldfish.

'You stretch one line across the creek, fastened at each bank, an' this one line has rows of smaller lines dangling from it across the water. These small lines are baited with bluegill. You got to check on your line all night, 'cos the catfish comes out after dark, an' when it gets hooked, it puts up a heck of a fight.'

Creeks or bayous, natural canals with grassy banks, were covered with a thick mat of water-lily leaves. Mauve blossoms appeared here and there. 'Water hyacinths!' Mark commented. 'In Spanish times, a Governor's wife thought she'd like water lilies, so she sent for these, and now they're a plague.'

'It must be impossible for a boat to go through there,' I said.

'You'd think so, but the Coon-arse is a pretty clever fellow! He can skip through this stuff in a little boat with a propeller . . .'

'What was that word again? "Coon-arse"?'

'Is it possible you've never heard of a Coon-arse?' Mark shouted in surprise. 'A Coon-arse is the joke-name for a Cajun. Cajuns call each other Coon-arses, all in fun, like when niggers call each other niggers. I thought everyone had heard the name Coon-arse.'

I learned a new name in a moment, as a black cormorant flew by.

'That's a nigger goose!' Mark pointed out. 'See, the black people here eat all kind o' creatures. They cook an' eat those ol' black birds same as if they were geese, they eat possums and they like the tail an' ears of a pig. Black people round here fight pit-bulls, an' bet on cock fighting. Don't ever call them niggers – only they can do that. But the only name for that bird is nigger goose that I knows of. See those big mounds up there on the far bank? That's nutria.'

The nutria, or coypu rats, had thrown up heaps of earth like giant elongated molehills. Shortly afterwards, we left the swamps and found ourselves in a road not unlike an English country lane. Farmhouses, fields and trees appeared, but no hedges, only wire fences. Instead of shorthorns, great Zebu cattle grazed, enormous hump-backed creatures with lustrous black eyes and velvety hides of white rippled with grey. Sporadic clumps of prickly pear cacti took the place of bracken.

'Here's the place we want!' said Mark, and drove through a gateway marked 'Rockefeller Refuge'. 'There should be a game warden here somewhere,' he continued, as he parked and we climbed out. 'Let's see if he can show us some 'gators.'

Various closed-looking buildings were scattered about a concrete yard that baked in the sun. It did not look promising, but at last Mark found some steps that led up to a door which opened to reveal a friendly game warden. We explained our mission.

'Come in,' said the warden, and we found ourselves in a bare shed-like room furnished with old brown leather divans placed around a television set. Dirty and exhausted-looking young men slept heavily on the divans with boots on and mouths open. 'Fishermen and duck-hunters,' whispered the warden. 'They were up at three this morning. I'll join you outside and take you on a tour.'

A bright, boyish man, despite his white hair, the warden drove us around a corner of the Refuge devoted to alligator farming. 'We're breeding 'gators here as a nucleus for prospective 'gator farmers,' he told us. 'We give advice about rearing and harvesting alligators, an' if a man can prove he's capable o' running a 'gator farm, we start him off with a few of our 'gators.'

He drove along beside a series of large square-edged ponds. I was reminded of a trout farm, but the strong wire fences told a different story. No alligators were visible, for they had plenty of reeds and vegetation in which to hide. However, we saw an alligator nest, a heap of sticks and reeds made by a female 'gator on a small island. Inside, in an oven-like hollow, alligator eggs are incubated. Until recently, the Reserve had kept rare Chinese alligators with slit eyes.

Finally the warden pulled up beside two large metal tanks. We peered in, and Sabrina cried, 'Ahh!'

In the shallow water, scores of baby alligators skittered about, squeaking and yapping like puppies. Each little 'gator was about eighteen inches long. They did not like being disturbed, and splashed around in a panic, threshing the water with their sturdy little legs and sideways-flailing tails. Pale yellow below and banded above with black, they resembled strange water lizards. Smiling, the warden picked one up and gave it to Sabrina, who cooed with pleasure. At first the 'gator-baby uttered puppyish yaps, but soon it calmed down and looked up at Sabrina with round, green cat's eyes. These babies had short snouts and big eyes, with little trace of the long sly adult alligator head to come. With a final tickle, Sabrina returned her baby to his playmates and the warden led us back to the nest of sleeping duck-hunters.

In a back room, beyond the yawning, stretching men, he showed us bubbling tanks where prawns, crawfish and shrimps were being bred and observed. The prawns, like the crawfish, resembled lobsters. On the wall, a mounted head of a snarling wolf added a touch of drama. 'That's a Red Wolf,' said the warden. 'It was shot near here twenty years ago.'

Thanking the kind warden of the Rockefeller Refuge, we sped on towards the Gulf of Mexico. Soon intriguing flashes of silver ocean began to appear in the gaps of a lengthy mound of dunes. Mark drove off the road and along a sandy track between decrepit shanties of sun-bleached wood.

'These are camp houses,' Mark said. 'Camping', in Louisiana, meant 'weekending' far from town, and the shanties, some quite tall with wooden outdoor steps, were private chalets or weekend cottages. I was reminded more of a Western ghost town than of a resort, but a wooden Company Store-like shop was open, with a girl sitting on the porch.

'Here we are at Holly Beach!' Mark announced, driving straight on to the white sand. We emerged into eye-watering white sunshine on a white beach facing a radiant sea. Gulls stared at us coldly, and fork-tailed terns wheeled and dipped on swallow wings. I tried to feel awe at the sight of the Gulf of Mexico, a place much pondered over in my atlas-studying childhood. Instead I felt sun-stricken, and begged to be taken back to the soothing swamps. More Coon-arse than beachcomber, Mark and Sabrina readily agreed. Soon, we were beside the bayous once more.

'Creole Nature trail', a mock-rustic sign proclaimed, and once more we parked and climbed out to see what we could see.

'Animals and birds are protected here,' Mark said, 'so they should be pretty tame.'

A gravel car park, with an information centre, adjoined the swamps, where a path had been made between five-foot rushes and grasses on a solid peninsula of land. From the railing beside the car park, we could see wooden bridges, piers and walkways emerging from the reeds and connecting scattered swamp islands. To our surprise, a large grey alligator lay slumped across a mudbank as if it had been squirted out of a tube. Its fat wrinkled body tapered away to a tail-point, but its head could not be seen. Presumably it was beneath the water, the raised nostrils surfacing amid the reeds. The beast was completely immobile.

We followed the jungle path into the grasslands, where birds and crickets chirruped.

'See those tunnels in the reeds – it's either rabbit or nutria,' Mark pointed out.

'Look!' cried Sabrina, and we saw a big brindled rabbit with erect ears and staring eyes. It was the size of a fat hare, with snowshoe-rabbit spread-out toes.

'Swamp rabbit!' said Mark.

Taking its ease, the rabbit lolloped into one of the tunnels. Holes through various clumps of half-submerged grass suggested that the rabbit could walk on water. We emerged beside a stretch of open water, a lake within a flood, for the 'banks' were ribs of mud amid acres of rushes.

Flocks of colourful red-winged blackbirds flew from the reed jungles over the water. Dark heads of half-grown alligators crossed and re-crossed the open water, each a dark line with a lump at either end. One lump was the eye, the other the nostril. As no trail of knobbly back or sideways swishing tail could be seen, I think the 'gators were paddling along in deep water in a semi-upright position. Another big alligator lay on the mud beside the reeds. Again, its head was invisible and it refused to move.

Exasperated, Mark began to throw rocks at it. Some splashed within an inch of its scales, but it never stirred.

'I bet there's hundreds of laws against throwing rocks at alligators,' I warned.

'Let's break a few of them,' Mark suggested cheerfully.

It was no use. The alligator and subsequent alligators all refused to budge. A long walkway on wooden stilts led across the grassy waters. Coots and moorhens stayed near the reed beds, but glossy ibis waded by: these are dark velvet curlews with changing glints of green, purple and crimson in their plumage. Roseate spoonbills, extraordinary pink storks with bald wrinkles round their eyes and beaks shaped exactly like large flat wooden spoons, eyed us balefully.

A zigzag path led through the grasslands to a high wooden stand, which afforded a lengthy view out over the swamp. Wild, strange and dismal, like flooded pastureland, the swamp stretched on forever. Despite the flocks of birds who rose and settled, the endless marshes seemed mournful, eerie and haunted. I could imagine them at night, an awesome place of terror, filled with strange rustling, croaking and splashing, and glimpses of eyes illuminated in the torchlight. Perhaps out there where scrubby willows grew on none-too-solid islands, a few red wolves still lurked and sought for prey. It was evening now. Soon the dreary expanse of swamp would be blacker than night, a place of a thousand secrets, the sky a lighter, safer place above the dark menacing horizon.

We returned to the car park, finding the alligators as we had left them. Vivid black-and-white wading birds, with alert eyes and pointed beaks, jerked by on legs almost as long and fine, proportionally speaking, as those of a harvestman spider. Appropriately enough, they were called stilts. Another swamp rabbit scuttled past, then crouched in the grass, escaping just as Sabrina rushed to pick it up and stroke it.

Near Mark's car, on our return, I saw an old brown single-decker bus with small curtained windows. It looked exactly like the Peace Convoy buses seen at English pop festivals. A white cat eyed me attentively from between the curtains. To Mark and Sabrina's incredulity, I knocked at the door and was at once admitted by a pleasant bohemian girl with long dark hair and spectacles. Inside I found a cosy bookish mess, with pot plants, a bunk, a dog and a tame white rat named Morgan. Tina, as my hostess was named, placed Morgan on my shoulder. He was an old rat, half blind in one eye. Outside, through the window, I could see Mark and Sabrina looking stuffy, exactly like an English working-class couple might if confronted by hippies. Tina asked me to stay and meet her husband, but I feared that Mark and Sabrina might desert me, and galloped off.

'We've been living in a bus for quite some time,' Tina told me in cultured tones, before I left. 'The police sometimes search us for drugs, but they always let us go.'

She and her husband were Northerners. I remembered that in New Orleans I had seen shelves full of books through a half-open door on one of the most squalid floors of the Y.M.C.A. Perhaps a well-read intellectual class of American exists, poor, persecuted and forever on the move.

Forgiving my lapse into bohemianism, Mark drove swiftly towards Lake Charles. Leaving the swampland behind, we drove alongside a macabre, deserted fish-processing plant. Large wooden huts stood abandoned in the weeds.

'That's the "quarters", where the black workers used to live,' explained Mark.

We queued up, then drove on to the car ferry that carried us across the wide Intercoastal Waterway System, lakes and bayous linked by the canal that led into the port of Lake Charles.

It was dark by the time that we arrived at the caravan site (or 'trailer park') where Mark and Sabrina temporarily lived. They stepped up into their trailer, turned on the light and invited me in. Instead of an English egg-shaped caravan, Mark's trailer was shaped like a long prefab or school annexe. The brown interior faintly resembled a Saxon longhouse. Even the telly was in brown-and-white, not black-and-white, which gave it a rustic appearance. It nestled at one end of the dwelling, while the kitchen reposed at the other. Chairs and a bed-settee filled the middle.

Greatly concerned about the dinner, Mark and Sabrina flew into the kitchen, and became absolutely absorbed in preparing and cooking the food. I had never seen them so serious. Both conversed in stage whispers, and Mark looked more like a French chef than ever.

I dozed on the bed-settee, and looked at Sabrina's magazines. For some reason, she was mad about body-building and weightlifting for girls. Pictures showed the gruesome end results of such practices – hideous grinning girls with lumps of muscle all over them, linked by strips of stretched skin like an anatomist's drawing. A local paper showed a much more seemly maiden, Tracy Sheena Mudd, who had been crowned Miss Lake Charles. 'I owe my success to God,' she told reporters.

Mr and Mrs Sonnier arrived, the latter bearing a delicious home made cake. At last an anxious Mark and Sabrina served us a steaming rice stew, or gumbo, containing plentiful pieces of shrimps, oysters and crawfish. Hot potato salad was served on a separate dish. Old Mr Sonnier's battered gypsy face lit up as he saw the shrimps, his favourite food.

Finally I waved goodbye to my hosts, and the elder Sonniers drove me back to the Downtowner Hotel. Mr S. gripped the wheel with a bare brown arm well decorated with tattoos. 'This is the City of Lights,' he declared grandly, gesturing at the hell-like oil installations, which were illuminated. 'See the Perpetual Flame? It's oil-waste burning on top of a pole.'

I alighted at the Downtowner, where I found that the football youths had gone, but the bar was still open for a country and western dance. A group named Louisiana Express were playing as I entered the darkened crowded room. A big man pounded at the piano, while three young men in peaked white caps sang and played on guitar, drums and fiddle respectively. Sometimes the drums muffled the fiddle slightly, but apart from that I had no complaints. Beautiful Frenchified jazzy fiddle soared over the other instruments.

'Heard a fiddle laugh before?' the fiddler enquired, and with a few quick strokes of the bow, the instrument gave a silvery peal of merriment. Drinkers at the tables stamped and clapped in appreciation. The group had plenty of cheering local support, a giant in a stetson and another in a cap being the most vociferous. This was an all-white crowd.

'When I get the blues, I get me a rocking chair . . .' sang the pianist, while the fiddle player slurred his notes, with an echoey sound that would have gladdened the heart of master-fiddler Bob Wills. Country ballads alternated with Memphis rock and roll, and beneath dim red lights, the dancers swayed to the Creep or jumped to the Jive in the best 1950s coffee bar fashion.

'Accordion!' somebody shouted, but the musicians were not Cajuns and didn't have one. Never mind, the fun and frolic continued long after I had gone to bed, for distant yahooing and yelling drifted up to my room and intermingled with my dreams.

Next morning, on the seedy, deserted platform of Lake Charles railway station, I shook hands for the last time with Mark and Sabrina and pledged undying friendship. My red, white and blue bag had broken and they had given me a brown Cajun bag instead. In a moment they had gone, and the rain began spitting down.

The platform was in the middle of the run-down Negro quarter, and across the tracks, small bungalows stood in long grass beneath the trees. People walked dispiritedly to and fro, crossing the unfenced railway line, their heads bowed. Only the children seemed happy, and played chasing games until the storm broke. As usual, the train was an hour late, and I retired under the eaves of the boarded-up ticket office as white sheets of lightning and solid grey sheets of rain buffeted Lake Charles to the sound of thunder. A coloured woman who was meeting relatives from Houston joined me, and peered anxiously up the line.

'I sure hope that's not the freight train,' she said, as a distant whistle could be heard.

Oh happy day! It was the Amtrack train, and soon I was safely aboard. Sitting upstairs, I watched the Louisiana landscape glide by in the gloom. As the driver had decided to go no faster than five miles an hour, the journey back to New Orleans would take all day. Woods and streams gave way to rice fields. The storm ended, and we reached a delightful-looking town named New Iberia. Wooden houses faced the track, and children hurried out, all smiles, to wave at the train. In the distance, I saw a large neo-classical courthouse. Then we were among green cane fields, giant stalks of bunchy grass in rows, bent by the rain. Strips of woodland and a house or two divided the vast fields. Some of the cane had already been harvested.

Across the aisle, two white girls were loudly discussing a quiz in a magazine, as two smaller coloured girls, very neatly dressed, ran up and down the carriage. Whenever they passed the quizzical ones, they poked them, and all four girls laughed. I mistakenly asked two lady passengers if they were English, but was told most decisively that they were from Beddgelert in North Wales. Through a loudspeaker, a distant guard announced football results and pointed out items of scenic interest along the way.

Soon we were easing into New Orleans Station.

'Look, there's gran'fer!' a small boy shouted, pointing to a smiling man on the platform.

'We saved a room for you!' the one-armed man at the Y.M.C.A. desk greeted me cheerfully.

CHAPTER EIGHTEEN

Back in the Y.M.C.A.

WHERE WAS THE muggy, exciting, tropical New Orleans I had known? Now it was late November, and the city, the Y.M.C.A. and myself were enveloped in a grey cloud of gloom. Exhausted after my trip around the South, I slept most of the time. Hoping for a taste of luxury, I had taken one of the twenty-dollar rooms in the Y.M.C.A. but it was *still* full of cockroaches. The only difference was that now they scrambled over a yellow carpet instead of over lino.

The American holiday of Thanksgiving loomed ahead, apparently a kind of practice-Christmas, somehow linked with the landing of the Puritans in the *Mayflower*. Avis had gone from the breakfast café. Her replacement was a goofy-looking Chinese girl.

'Will you be open on Thanksgiving?' I asked, as I hoped for a cheap Y.M.C.A. breakfast. At once her face lit up in radiant happiness at the thought of her day off.

'No! Closed! Closed! Ha ha ha ha! Closed! Ha ha ha ha!'

Luckily the workmen's café round the corner would be staying open.

On Thanksgiving Eve, I gazed from my tiny window at midnight and saw a car pull up and two tall coloured men emerge, holding two white clubs. They switched on some music, and began to dance wildly, almost savagely, on the spot, tossing the white clubs from one to another without ever dropping one, and singing loudly all the while. Finally they lit cigarettes, smoked and talked for a few minutes, then hurled the cigarettes away in curves of fire, jumped into the car and departed. I went to sleep.

Thanksgiving Day dawned dull and cloudy. Everything was shut, and the city seemed deserted. I walked under a half-completed motorway bridge towards Magazine Street, the lively black district where I had met

Larry and Jessie in the Hamburger Grill. A coloured man walked towards me, head down and hands in pockets.

'Happy Thanksgiving,' he said as he passed.

Beneath a live oak tree, a woman brushed the grass with a handful of paper, evidently in search of acorns. She too wished me a Happy Thanksgiving. A lot of tramps seemed to be about, but all the colourful vivacity of Magazine Street had vanished with the sun and the open shops. Later I learned that tramps and strangers were given meals and hospitality on Thanksgiving, a Christian festival. As it was, I felt like a Christian visitor to North Africa during Ramadan.

Fortunately, in the good old workmen's café I was able to break my fast. Surrounded by lorry drivers and country music, Thanksgiving Day became a little less inscrutable to me, as I tucked into an enormous turkey dinner smothered in cranberry sauce.

At a nearby table, a fat policeman with a gun talked to a blonde girl about pickpockets. With an impassioned glance, she leaned forward and loudly whispered, 'I'm being investigated!'

I too had some investigating to do, for I was shortly to be joined by my sister Amina from England. A sophisticated girl of twenty-five, she would never stand for the Y.M.C.A. I remembered a delightful little hotel, surrounded by banana trees, that I had seen in the French Quarter. This was the Burgundy Inn in Burgundy Street. This Creole-French street formed a peaceful balconied backwater connected to Bourbon Street, Jackson Square and the Mississippi by myriad avenues with names such as Bienville, Toulouse, Dumaine and Ursuline. Two French-looking houses, one the grandiose Burgundy Inn Reception Hall, the other consisting only of bedrooms, faced the street. My bedroom window looked out through banana leaves on to old slave-quartery houses with wooden balconies grouped around an ancient courtyard and modern swimming pool. I explored the maze of old Burgundy Inn dwellings and found that it led eventually to an alley with a gateway to the street. Coffee in the morning was free, so I was satisfied.

How, you may ask, could I afford such luxury? You may well ask. I had spent almost all my traveller-cheque money and would soon be completely broke. Amina was a part-time blues singer and writer. She would provide. In return, I could show her New Orleans, as her previous visits to America had been to New York and California. With great difficulty, I found a bus that took me to the airport.

Daughter of my African stepfather, Amina had been born in England and brought up in a Sussex village. At the age of thirteen, she had very sensibly refused to attend her Comprehensive school, and continued her education as a strawberry picker, roving with gangs of gypsies. She got on very well with the gypsies, but fell foul of the Education Authorities, who kept sending a truant catcher after her. Amina named this hapless woman Minnie the Moocher, after the heroine of a jazz song.

Jazz became Amina's passion, and drew her to London. Her kind-hearted yet fiery nature had been shaped by the writings of P. G. Wodehouse, George Borrow and Dostoyevsky and by the music of Jelly Roll Morton and his Red Hot Peppers. For all I knew, Jelly Roll may have played the piano in the Burgundy Inn.

Trying to be as cool and natural as possible, as if meeting family members thousands of miles from home were an everyday occurrence, I greeted Amina at the airport. She was wearing a Parisian pill-box hat that made her look like a Chinese mandarin, and she seemed highly indignant at my so-called 'indifference'. Casually, as we rode back to the shuttle bus, I asked her how much money she had brought. To my horror, it was only a few hundred pounds. Laughing heartily, she spoke of all the unpaid bills she had left behind in London. This did not augur well for the future.

As we drove into the narrow streets of the French Quarter, Amina grew more and more animated. Glumly I watched her throw an enormous tip at the shuttle-bus-driver. I had chosen well, and she seemed delighted with her room. So after she had unpacked, I showed her Bourbon Street.

We were both very tired, and my chief memories of that evening are of blaring jazz at every corner, bright lights, restless, excited crowds and the mechanical feet jerking up and down in a strip-club window. Amina was entranced.

'It's like a dream! I can't believe it! I can't believe it!' she exclaimed.

In the morning, Amina admired the purple banana flower that hung from the tree beside her window like a red cabbage, and we set out on the town. In Jackson Square, she made the acquaintance of Mark Tuba Smith, and in a shop near Royal Street she tried on at least seven feathery hats without buying any. The milliner, who had designed all the hats himself, seemed enchanted with her, and waved goodbye.

I couldn't find the mule Jackson, so we settled for a buggy pulled by a she-mule called Sadie instead. A middle-aged Yankee couple sat behind us.

'From England, hey?' said the driver as he took up the reins and Sadie trotted off. 'This is where we fought your people, back in 1816.' With that, he broke into song.

'We took a little bacon and we took a little beans,
And we fought the bloody British at the town of New Orleens.'

'We kicked *their* butt!' commented the Northerner with immense satisfaction.

'Note the Cupid designs in the ironwork, the ship masts used as flagpoles,' our guide said expansively, flourishing a rolled-up whip at the balconies in the narrow streets. 'They call those spikes "Casanova catchers", as they prevented the young men from climbing up on to the balconies and getting into the brothels. Yes sir, most of these houses was brothels. See this big house yere? Back in the old times, the woman that lived yere once threw a slave girl to her death from that balcony. Neighbours would hear *screams* coming from in there. When they broke in, they found she had a torture chamber there, an' bought slaves just to torture them.'

The Northerner looked blandly at the building for a moment, then took a photograph.

After our day's sightseeing we both felt conscious of some peculiar glances, particularly in the residential streets. Here rich beer-can-swilling young people with depraved expressions had hired flats for long holidays in New Orleans. 'What's the matter, can't get a black dude? Why don't you pick your own colour?' they bawled at Amina, together with several obscenities. Their accents proclaimed them Northerners.

I realised how odd we must look, a scruffy middle-aged white man and a young coloured girl. People seemed to think we were a couple. The more innocent-minded assumed we were a married couple. Perhaps this had been the case in England too, but in England people minded their own business and didn't swear or bump into us. Complications seemed likely to ensue. I fretted over this, but Amina refused to let it bother her.

There was still one kind of American School I had not visited, and that was a High School, or secondary school for older pupils. While at the Y.M.C.A. I had arranged to see one, and now the time had come to do so.

'Don't tell the school we're brother and sister. Say I'm a fellow-author,' Amina told me. 'I can't bear it when you go into all that rigmarole about stepfathers.'

We took the rattling streetcar tram past Lee Circle and up the hill into the 'Garden District of Carrollton. White mansions sloped uphill in rows, each surrounded by a flowery garden. Once a separate city, Carrollton was now the wealthiest and most fashionable parish of New Orleans. Benjamin Franklin Senior High School stood surrounded by wooden annexes and a tall wire netting fence.

'Which is the way in?' we asked a group of pink, healthy-looking girls who were playing basketball. They ran up to the fence and eagerly showed us.

'We love your accent!' they added.

We soon found ourselves on the steps of a slightly dilapidated mansion. Built as Carrollton's courthouse in 1856, the mansion had been used by the occupying Northern troops as a stable during the Civil War. English cathedrals suffered the same fate during the *English* Civil War. After many vicissitudes, the building had become a High School in 1957.

Inside, a tall but narrow classroom-corridor led away from a grandiose hall where we sat on a bench outside the headmistress's room as if awaiting punishment. A full-size marble statue of Benjamin Franklin stood beside a case full of silver cups. He wore a mild, dreamy expression.

'The Principal can see you now,' a boy reported.

We introduced ourselves as writers from England.

'One of our teachers is English!' smiled the elegant headmistress. 'You will probably find a lot to talk about. This is a school for gifted children, chosen by an entrance examination. It is a public school, and offers a free education to all.'

In England, it would have been a grammar or Direct Grant School.

We were taken by the headmistress to a very English school annexe of creosoted planks. Inside, desks faced a table and blackboard, and we were introduced to Mr Veizer, who taught English to fourteen-year-olds. All the pupils of Ben Franklin seemed well-behaved, neatly dressed and eager to learn. Girls outnumbered boys, outdid them in confidence and set the tone for the school.

Mr Veizer was a wild-eyed bearded enthusiast, who resembled a burly lumberjack and was actually a Hungarian Jew. He sat us at the back of the class, while he continued to teach *King Lear*. This he did by showing a video film with Laurence Olivier in the title role. It was very hard to make sense of the rapidly moving story, and the class looked jaded and eye-strained from trying.

An endless fight seemed to be taking place on the small coloured screen with figures rolling and hurling themselves about. 'Ung! . . . Mmf! . . . Aghhh! . . . Ugh!' the Shakespearian dialogue ran.

Anxiously, a red-haired boy referred to the book to find out what was happening. A bell rang, and the class rushed out into the fresh air as if from prison.

Mr Veizer then took us to the staff room in the main building to meet the other English teacher, who really *was* English. I asked Mr Veizer about the subjects taught at Ben Franklin, and he reeled off an impressive list.

'You make no mention of Scripture,' I observed.

'In this country we emphasise the separation of Church and State,' he emphasised. 'Nothing that can offend anyone of any belief is allowed. No official Christian posters, concerning Easter or (in theory) Christmas are allowed in the street. A Moslem could see them and get offended.

Complaints have been made about cribs and Christmas displays. There is certainly no religion allowed in schools! I myself am a strong supporter of the separation of Church and State, and would never allow the mention of Christ in my class.'

His eyes gleamed in triumph. Persecution is notoriously good for Christians, and in America the churches are full, while in Christian England they are half-empty. However, with no mention of Christ allowed in school, no understanding of history or English literature can be possible. Then there is the matter of ethics. So I beg America to amend its Constitution.

A languid, well-spoken, tubby man with curly hair, the English-English teacher, greeted us affably. Henceforth I shall refer to him as 'E. E.' He reminded me of grammar school teachers I had known, and he came from Croydon.

'No, I didn't leave England because grammar schools were abolished,' he told us, over coffee. 'I just felt like a change. All the same, I hear that English schools have deteriorated rapidly. For instance, Birmingham, England, must be seventy per cent black by now, while New Orleans is only fifty per cent black. So we have only fifty per cent illiteracy among school leavers, whereas Birmingham must have seventy per cent.'

We both sat stunned, not only at his faulty statistics, or by his assumption that black people cannot learn to read and write (shared in secret by many white Southerners) but by the fact that he could say such a thing in a chatty tone when a coloured person was present.

'This is an unusually good school in a good neighbourhood,' E. E. continued. 'Most of the city high schools are unruly places. Violence is on the increase in New Orleans, with rising unemployment and a fifty per cent rate of . . .'

He trailed off without saying 'blackness', and passed the sugar. With a promise to allow us to sit in on one of his lessons later on, he handed us back to the hovering Mr Veizer.

That worthy led us to another annexe, where we met Mrs Simmons, a pleasant young lady who taught Journalism to sixteen-year-olds. In England, the idea of teaching a despised craft like journalism in a state school would seem absurd. Visions of children being taught how to drink whisky all day without falling over would come to mind. Together with politicians, journalists in England are all assumed to be liars. This may be a good thing, as it keeps reporters on their toes. In America, where no doubt there are Professors in News Theory, the papers are extremely dull.

We were allowed to address Mrs Simmons' class, thirty or so of Ben Franklin's brightest and best. Their eyes gleamed with intelligence. Fleet Street, not the Queen, was their interest, and many of them knew the names of English newspapers. Amina stood to one side and allowed me full honours. To her horror, I passed a glossy magazine with one of her stories in it around the class.

'In England, journalism is not a college subject in itself at all,' I told them, sowing seeds of subversion. 'Freelance journalism is the only sort I know anything about, and each piece of freelance work is judged by merit alone. No editor is remotely interested in whether you have passed an exam or not – he just looks at what you have written.

'Another thing – England is not so academically orientated as America. People are not automatically expected to go to college. In England, people don't ask a casual acquaintance, "What college did you go to?" as ten to one, he or she would never have been to any kind of college at all. What's more, a person who hasn't been to college is quite likely to be ten times as intelligent as someone who *has*.' My audience gaped. 'Many top Fleet Street staff reporters have begun by leaving school at fifteen or sixteen and then learning their craft on a local paper.'

I went on to explain how small England is, for in America nearly *all* papers are local papers. Then I got into a tangle, as I remembered that in English cities now, the young coloured people nearly all go to college straight from school in the American fashion. Places are found for them in Polytechnics, where they fool around in vague hopes that the job market might improve. Changing tack, I put in a plug for my forgotten novel, *Druid Madonna*.

'What is it about, sir?' asked a girl called Aditi Palit, whose parents had come from India.

'Iron Age Celts! I became very interested in the origins of the King Arthur stories, so I traced them backwards to the mythology of the pagan Celts who lived in England at the time of the Romans. When the Romans landed in Britain, they found a wild, warrior-like people similar to olden-day Red Indians . . .'

As I stumbled through the Celtic twilight and delved into Welsh legends, a coloured girl in the back row sat entranced, eyes shining as she hung on to every word. Celtic legends were in her blood, for Celts and Africans are the same people, in spirit if not in appearance.

Lesson-time ran out and I was sorry to see the last of Mrs Simmons' intelligent pupils. She gave me a magazine that they had written, printed on glossy paper in a most professional style.

Mr Veizer, who had been standing in a corner, took us down a tree-lined road to a former church, now used as yet another annexe to the scattered school. Here E. E. greeted us, and showed us to our desks in the back row of a class of fourteen-year-olds. They gave us friendly glances, then strained a trifle wearily to hear everything that Sir was saying. Naughtiness seemed unknown in this school.

The class had been reading *Robinson Crusoe*, and now E. E. was shooting questions at them about the book. We shrank in our seats, but luckily he missed us out. He lounged in his chair, and picked out victims in a soft-spoken relaxed fashion.

'Did anything unusual strike you about the book?' he asked a boy in the front row.

'Yes, sir. It was Crusoe's arrogance when he met Friday. The author and Crusoe both seemed to think that Friday had to be a kind of servant . . .'

'No, that's not it!' said E. E., who shared Defoe's enlightened views on race. (There was one coloured pupil in this class.) 'It's the initials of the central character – R. C. Was Defoe, a Protestant, consciously trying to make a statement about the Roman Catholics? Or was his statement unconscious? Then think of the name Friday. What does it suggest? Can it have a connection with the Roman Catholic fast day? Robinson Crusoe – R. C. Roman Catholic! Understand?'

The hard-working class uttered a cry that was half a gasp, half a groan. So reading books was not a straightforward matter of following a story! No, there were hidden subconscious clues, and no book could ever be understood again!

Privately, I thought that E. E. was flying too high, and applying theories in a school that would have made his reputation in a university. Perhaps, by driving his pupils mad, he was preparing them for higher education. At last, to the relief of almost all, the lesson came to an end.

So we said goodbye to Benjamin Franklin Senior High School and climbed into Mr E. E.'s car, for he had kindly offered to drive us around Lake Ponchartrain, brooking no refusal. School left behind, he became more agreeable, and gave us a horrifying description of his first hurricane.

'I thought it was all nonsense about a hurricane until I looked out of the window and saw oak trees flying through the air! All the lights went out, so I had the mad idea of going down to the shop to buy candles. When I opened the door, I was hurled against the wall. At last I managed to tie the doorhandle to the bannister rail, and shut it that way. When my neighbours had heard the warning, they'd simply left town. Very wise, too. So now I respect hurricanes. See that building? That's very unusual – a *black* university. A nun who inherited a fortune spent it on establishing a college for Red Indians and blacks. Now it's ninety per cent black, and they can't get white students to go there. Some parochial schools in this city are all-black. "Parochial" means they're run by the R.C.'s.'

He left Crusoe out of it this time. Amina looked as if she regretted accepting his invitation for a drive, but he had swept us into it. We saw some fine white and pink wooden houses beneath magnolias beside Lake Ponchartrain, and then E. E. dropped us at a huge university complex.

His adopted son, a Vietnamese boy, was there to meet him. With many thanks, we parted for the last time.

'Ugh! Academe! Get me out of here!' Amina cried, looking at all the students in horror. Quickly we ran for a nearby bus. To our delight, it was going to Jackson Square, near our hotel.

Before doing so, however, the bus passed through a delightful neighbourhood aptly named the Elysian Fields. Almost wholly a black district, it consisted of lawns beside a wide road, and rows of wooden houses, churches and lounges surrounded by trees. Soon the bus filled with schoolchildren.

'What nice children they were at Ben Franklin!' Amina exclaimed. 'They didn't laugh or sneer at our accents. Imagine the jeers that Americans would get in an English Comprehensive.'

'That one's laughing!' I said, as I suddenly noticed a fifteen-year-old girl beside me. She was absolutely convulsed, and shaking with laughter. A boy beside Amina was also in stitches.

'Are you laughing at me?' she asked severely.

'No! No!' the boy gulped, but as he got off, he shouted 'Jolly d.!'

No one had ever laughed at my accent, but Amina is better spoken than I. In a way it was a relief to see naughty children again.

We both brightened up at Jackson Square, and went to see about a coach tour of the countryside.

So, on the following day, we sat in a coach heading out of New Orleans for a day of sightseeing. Most of the holidaymakers on board were elderly couples. A young man who sat on his own proved to be an Australian. Our tour guide was a white Creole lady of striking appearance, with short hair, high cheekbones and green eyes. She took an instant liking to Amina, and seemed to read her every thought. Later she gave Amina her phone number, and said, 'Ring me if you get into any trouble.'

We sped out of town, beside the high Mississippi levee, and soon stopped at the gate of a house standing in a garden beside huge dome-like oil installations. This was San Francisco House, built as the Big House of an already thriving sugar plantation in 1856.

'Unfortunately this house lost its beautiful formal garden in 1930 when the levee was built,' the guide said. 'The plantation has gone, closed in 1974, and the oil plant has been built where the – er – servants' quarters used to be.'

Built, owned and decorated by various wealthy Louisiana French families, the house now belonged to a Foundation and existed only as a showcase. Elegant in the extreme, with balconies and dormer windows galore, it was flanked at either end by a detached tower crowned with a bright blue Oriental dome. These were water towers, connected to the house by gutter bridges. Inside, the rooms were small and square, with tall ceilings. Each of them was crammed with French furniture and ornaments, pictures in square frames, and everything square and box-like. All the doors were directly opposite one another, so if they had been left open, it would have been easy to chase someone round and round the house. It was easy to see that the previous owners had not been that kind of French. The house had the non-farcical atmosphere of a well-to-do nineteenth-century family of formal manners.

Upstairs, balconies extended round the corners of the house, overlooking great trees. A drive and private jetty had disappeared under the levee. I accidentally brushed against the Australian, and he said, 'Sorry, mate.'

Mate! It had been months since I had heard such an English (or Australian) word, and I felt homesick on the spot.

Outside, Amina posed for photographs, and we were on our way. The tall levee embankment shut out views of the Mississippi River. However, strange wigwam structures of logs began to appear on the levee top. One looked a little bit like a log version of Mr Sonnier's shrimp boat.

'You see those log structures on the levee top?' asked the guide. 'Those are the framework for unique Christmas decorations seen nowhere else in Louisiana. They will soon be decorated with dressed-up dummies and beautiful lights. The levee here looks just wonderful on a Christmas night. They call it Lighting the Way for the Christ-Child. People say that the Cajuns here are of German stock. Everyone in Cajun country wants to be French, and the descendants of German immigrants have taken French names.'

Cajun houses appeared by the roadside; sturdy wooden cabins of steep narrow Nova Scotian design. There seemed to be scarcely room to move inside them. Front doors resembled the rest of the house in shape – that of a pointy-topped Gothic church window. Cabins, shanties and wooden houses of every kind stood at angles amid sparse woodland and untidy fields. Both Cajuns and black people lived here, and their rickety fishing jetties poked out of the foliage over the waters of the creeks and bayous. Ghost cypress forests swathed in grey Spanish moss grew from muddy swampland. Open swamps such as I had seen near Lake Charles gave way to sugar-cane plantations. Amina scoffed at the mingy sugar cane, used as she was to the luxuriant growth of Africa and the West Indies.

Next we came to Houmas House, named after the Indians from whom the land was purchased in Spanish times. The present Houmas House, replete with white columns and balconies, had been built in 1840 by one John Smith Preston. It had been the centre of a flourishing cane plantation, now no more. Picturesque stone outbuildings, like giant gazebos, with bedrooms on top, were known as *garçonnières*. According to the guidebook, these had been built to accommodate the *garçons* or 'valets' who accompanied guests to the house.

Still privately owned, the house seemed to be run as a museum. All visitors were presumed to yearn for a dream-South of *Gone with the Wind* splendour. Instead of keepers, girls in Scarlett O'Hara costumes and fake accents showed us round. Probably they were drama students. Euphemisms such as 'servants' or *garçons* disguised the seamy side of the Southern dream, a dream believed in by most white Southerners for whom Houmas House represented an Ideal. Large red butterflies flapped over the flowers that bloomed in the December sun at beautiful Houmas House.

Our last stop on the way back to New Orleans was at the Cajun Cabin, a log-cabin seafood restaurant. Three Cajuns emerged as we entered; thin dishevelled brown men in overalls. Over a meal, Amina and I became friendly with the young Australian. 'Americans are so bland!' he exclaimed. 'All that talk about mansions and plantations, and no mention of slaves at all!'

In America, the Australian seemed as English as English, the only difference being that he swore with every other sentence, although obviously upon his best manners. Later that night we saw him with two coloured girls in Bourbon Street. He looked as if he was enjoying himself.

On Sunday morning, Amina flatly refused to go to church, saying that she was a Catholic. So I set off on my own to the Beecher Church, the one where the 'Vote·Aquarium' meeting had taken place. Not knowing the way, I walked to Jackson Square and hailed a taxi. A bald young man with a moustache and insane gleaming spectacles, the driver proved to have come from Philadelphia. I asked him to take me to the Beecher Church at North Miro, and at once he began to talk politics.

'I used to be a Liberal,' he said, 'but now I'm an ultra-right Conservative. God, I hate the poor! Like the old saying goes, you've got to know the poor to hate them. They're evil, decadent, parasitic, dirty, smelly leeches, particularly the *blacks*.'

'Well, it's a black church I'm going to.'

He said nothing, perhaps because he'd taken a wrong turning and got lost. Finally he piped up again. 'I came down here to New Orleans because I love jazz! You Europeans know more about jazz than we do here. I've met some really good Dutch musicians since I came here – big tall men! Danes and Swedes make brilliant jazz musicians! But one of the best in New Orleans, a living legend, is Chris Burke from England! He plays in the French Market – you ought to talk to him.'

'Stop! This is the place I want,' I said.

The driver goggled in amazement at the sight of dignified black people walking up the steps into church. 'Well, I'm damned!' he said.

Let this taxi driver's speech be a lesson to those English people who still think that the words 'Conservative' and 'right wing' have a world-wide meaning and international significance. Blanket words such as 'right' and 'left' distort rather than explain the differing political attitudes of the world. One man's right is another man's poison. The service was just beginning as I slipped in and was guided to a pew near the front.

Recognising me at once, the pastor greeted me from the rostrum. 'We come from England!' he added. 'That's where our church was born!'

With a flourish, the organist sent a surge of music swirling from the pipes, then rocked in his seat as he swung into a light jazzy tune. A drummer and guitarist, both young men, joined in. Up marched the choir, women dressed in flowing robes of cream and crimson. They took their places upon the stage, mouths wide open as a wordless chant poured from the pipe organ of their throats. This soon resolved itself into a song.

'Just gimme that Old Time Religion – it's good enough for me!'

After a short Bible reading, the service proceeded as a showcase of church talent. Men and women mounted the rostrum and recited poems with titles such as 'Don't Quit'. Some might have been their own compositions. The congregation looked on critically, and a child blew pink bubbles of gum and popped them. A big man sang 'Blessed Assurance' unaccompanied, in a deep brown voice. In a church such as this, the great Paul Robeson must have learned his craft. Applause broke out, growing louder and louder, as the Brother held the note of 'As*sure*' for at least four minutes before swooping down into '–ance' and drawing breath.

'Yeah!' girls cried, and there were screams and claps.

With a little wave and a foolish smile, the man stepped down and the choir began anew. They sang in the 'modern' gospel style this time, a wall of sound answering the screams of a solo vocalist. In England, this style of music is avidly imitated by the young Black British. Again, 'holding a note' was seen as the criterion of gospel success, and the girl who took the word 'Near' to the highest pitch accessible to the human ear and then kept it there was applauded mightily.

'I want to be near my Jesus!' answered the tidal wave of song.

Spontaneous prayers were launched by the pastor and then left to find their own courses. A stout woman uttered two piercing screams and then fainted. Other women galloped to her aid. A suave, self-possessed man, the tall light-skinned pastor calmed the church with a wave of his hand and began his sermon.

'My friends, I am going to talk to you about a Rocking Chair Religion. We need a Rocking Chair Religion, one that is calm and balanced, and serves us in good times and in bad. There are many kinds of chair, the electric chair and the executive's chair, but we are not allowed to sit in all of them. Not everyone should sit in the electric chair! Footnote, a lot of people should sit in it who don't do so. Not all of us can sit in the director's chair. But we can sit in the rocking chair. We sit and we rock and we sit and we rock and every now and then we hear a squeak. Every rocking chair has a squeak, but we don't mind the squeak, we used to it. We rock after a hard day's work.

'Now Jesus worked hard for us here below, working hard, working on the chain gang, on the *chain gang*. You know the Bible says He sits at the right hand of God the Almighty. I can just picture the angels leading Him to a golden rocking chair.'

Here the pastor sat down on an ordinary chair and began to rock in it.

'He sits and He rocks, He sits and He rocks, and He hears His people sing "Trying to Make Heaven My Home". But every now and then he hears a squeak. That squeak is the devil, trying to come between Him and His children. But He don't pay that ol' devil no mind, He just rocks. What does the song say? "Rock me, Lord! Rock me, Lord!" '

'Nice and easy!' a man called out from the audience.

With that, the pastor bowed and withdrew.

In that instant the choir began to sing, then they stopped and let the congregation take up the same refrain, then they began anew.

> 'Swing down, chariot, stop and let me ride,
> Swing down, chariot, stop and let me ri-i-ide,
> Rock me, Lord! Rock me Lord!
> Nice and easy
> I've got a home on the other side.'

A collection was taken up as the choir sang 'I Turn My Face to the Rising Sun'. Then, clapping hands and stopping to shake hands with friends in the pews, they paraded out down the aisle, singing 'This Little Light of Mine'.

The service was over, and Celestine, my church friend of long ago, ran up to me. She introduced me to another girl called Sheryl, who wore very light lipstick on her already light face. Both girls had a glossy, film-star quality about them.

'I live on the Creole side of town,' Sheryl said modestly. 'I must meet your sister and take her shopping some time. Y'all got to come round and eat up all my red beans and rice. I can cook in the old Louisiana style – my folks still live on the same piece o' land near Lafayette as was given to their family after the Civil War. God has really blessed me, I'm so humble. Did you know I have my own T.V. show?'

I never saw Sheryl again, but Celestine told me to bring Amina to Jackson Square next afternoon, where she would be singing.

When we arrived at Jackson Square, the centre of the French Quarter, we found Celestine competing with the other buskers as she sang 'Just a Closer Walk With Thee', a cardboard box at her feet. She danced as she sang, watched appreciatively by her husband Dulaney. A good-natured, unassuming man who 'taught school', Dulaney was not of the same Creole background as his wife. Her song over, Celestine attached herself firmly to Amina, and began to talk enthusiastically.

'My sister's a gineacologist – that's someone who studies the science of hairdressing,' I heard her say.

'There's a place here you can pay the man an' cut a record in a recording booth,' Dulaney told me, as we walked into Decatur Street. 'That's where we're going now.'

When we arrived, we found that a family party occupied the booth, visible through a glass door. Their song echoed through a loudspeaker together with a pre-recorded musical backing.

A tall coloured girl, her mother and her devil-may-care boyfriend, were falling about laughing as they sang a soul ditty, 'I Heard It Through the Grapevine'. They too danced as they sang, in a parody of a show-biz style, screeching with merriment, doubling up and holding their sides. Celestine looked very prim, and coolly took her place next for 'Amazing Grace'. But Dulaney brought the house down with 'Georgia on My Mind', passers-by from the street stopping to applaud.

Before Amina could think of an excuse, Celestine had swept us both back to the French Market, where a friend of hers would be singing in a club called Storyville.

Normally a jazz club for Danes, Dutchmen and so on, Storyville that day was devoted to rhythm and blues. Rows of trestle tables, every seat packed, filled a large dingy hall. Up on stage, a coloured group made merry with piano, guitar, drums and saxophone. We managed to squeeze into a space near the stage. White and coloured people mixed easily, the latter predominating. I was now beginning to make sense of the colour lines of New Orleans. Here in the Quarter, and in the wooden suburbs beyond, many of the people are Creoles of a Roman Catholic background. Beecher Church, though Protestant, recruited from this class. Hence the easy-going tolerance of hedonism, so unusual in Negro churches.

There are white Creoles, or New Orleans French, and coloured Creoles. Coloured Creoles are not only of mixed French and African blood, evident by their lighter skin, but have been merged in the past with mulatto immigrants from Toussaint L'Ouverture's Haiti.

In the late eighteenth century, the time of the French Revolution, the slaves on the island of Haiti had rebelled against their French masters. As the French fled in terror, the erstwhile slaves turned their murderous wrath upon the 'free men of colour', the mulattos. A caste who had arisen through French dalliance among the slaves, the free mulattos had been accused of siding with the white masters. Both sorts of French refugees, white and coloured, had been welcomed to New Orleans and absorbed into the French Quarter. West Indian rhythms began to penetrate the music of the Quarter.

Canal Street, that wide thoroughfare, has always been the borderline between Creoles and Americans. Beyond Canal Street, the black people are *black*, somewhat scorned by mulatto Creoles now as in the eighteenth century.

Colour snobbery and Creole-black boundaries had relaxed since then, as witness Celestine and Dulaney's marriage and the 'mixed' congregation at their church, but they still existed. Jazz belonged with the Creoles, now shared among Nordic newcomers, and gospel puritanism with the darker skins across Canal Street. A lazy, Latin atmosphere suffused the French side of the Canal Street border. Combined with tourism, this made the French Quarter seem unreal. Amina felt as if she were living in a film-set.

Celestine introduced us to her singer friend, a friendly, buxom Creole named Wanda Roussin. She had Creole-green eyes and dyed-blonde hair falling over brown skin. She too 'taught school', but I would not have thought so, seeing her on stage a moment later shouting the blues. A woman sitting near us, who looked just like a Jamaican church lady, held her little daughter up to hear the blues. A few songs later, the child fell asleep in her arms.

Suddenly a Mardi Gras rhythm broke loose, with Caribbean-style maracas clicking away, and Wanda broke into an impassioned dance, leaping all over the stage.

'Quick! A kerchief!' cried Celestine, grabbing a white hanky. 'Now I'll show you how we dance the Second Line at the Mardi Gras carnival!'

Jazz bands apparently form the First Line at the Mardi Gras and other New Orleans processions, and the dancing followers are known as the Second Line. Celestine held a white handkerchief, like a morris dancer, and she and Dulaney took to the floor. Here all resemblance to a morris dance vanished.

Waving a white cloth in the air with her right hand, Celestine lifted her red skirt and shimmered her whole body, moving backwards and forwards in front of Dulaney. Had the Spanish flamenco left its mark on New Orleans? Dulaney did a blues dance, arms hanging loosely, then a stand-up shuffle on the spot. As we left, Dulaney and Celestine were flinging their arms and legs about, jiving without touching one another, Celestine's hanky still high up in the air. Wanda waved goodbye to us from the stage.

Somehow, we had to find a cheaper place to stay. My money had gone long ago, and Amina's was rapidly vanishing. I remembered that the workmen's café near the Y.M.C.A. let out rooms upstairs to lorry drivers and their wives.

'It's a nice clean café, so the rooms are sure to be nice,' I told my crestfallen sister. 'Failing that, it's the Y.M.C.A. We can stay at the Burgundy Inn for another week, then stay at a cheap place for our final five or six days.'

Leaving the French Quarter, we emerged into Canal Street, where modern America began. Most of the well-dressed shoppers, shop girls and noisy, shouting schoolchildren were *American* black people, hurrying at a brisk American pace. Instead of bright, tropical colours, they dressed with businesslike severity. We took the St Charles streetcar to the workmen's café.

Eagerly, a tousle-haired young man who worked there took us upstairs to show us the rooms.

Our heart sank at the sight of the dark narrow musty stairway we would have to climb each night if we stayed there. We emerged on to a broken, wooden, higgledy piggledy balcony facing a sheer drop between blank walls. Proudly, the man showed us the rooms, but his face dropped as he saw our faces drop. Hideous, brown and peeling, smelling of things unspeakable, these were the worst rooms I had yet seen in America or anywhere else. Oh, for the bright, clean lorry driver dormitory I once knew, in the annexe behind the transport caff at Ely, Cambridgeshire!

'England must be a great country – I'd like to go there,' the youth mumbled, as we hurried out.

I booked two twenty-dollar rooms at the Y.M.C.A., then took Amina to the Confederate Museum to cheer her up. Instead it horrified her, as the glorification of the Old South made her feel she was among people who wished to restore slavery and then whip her.

'Oh my God! Look!' she cried.

Walking towards us, looking down at the showcases, were two young men impeccably dressed in the uniform of the South in the Civil War.

'There's a society that dresses up and re-enacts the battles of the Civil War, like the Sealed Knot in England. They must belong to it,' I whispered.

'Go and talk to them – I dare you!'

I knew that they were not Ku Klux Klan members, as Amina seemed to suppose, so I went across and introduced myself. Amina followed and stood by my side.

One of the young men was short and saturnine, and wore a grey cloak. I addressed the other, a big, beefy, innocent-looking youth with a deer-hunter's beard around his mouth and chin. Pleased to meet people from England, he told us about his exciting life, fighting battles as a proud member of the Nineteenth Louisiana Infantry. He greeted Amina politely.

'Yes, I come from this city and my name is Joseph Faciane,' he continued. 'Me and my buddy re-enact battles with our Infantry just whenever we can. All of us Confederate soldiers go out in the country an' pitch tents in long lines, just like before the real battles. We do everything like it was done in the War Between the States. Look, I'll show you some pictures.'

We admired photographs of the Louisiana Infantry posing outside long lines of white tents. Huge black cannons stood with muzzles at the ready, and Joseph Faciane and comrades prepared for war in what looked like scarlet knee-length bathing trunks. Pine trees in the background made an authentic setting.

'We got over forty cannons,' Joseph said, 'and some o' them were used in the actual war. On that exercise, we dressed in red 'cos we were supposed to be cut-throats shanghaied from the waterfront. It's good to wake up in a tent real early in the morning an' smell bacon and coffee on the fire outside.'

I admired Joseph Faciane's uniform, which gave me some idea of the appearance of a Confederate trooper. Many of the soldiers must have been well-meaning young men such as Joseph. He wore a battered peaked cap, its flat top crumpled forwards, a gold bugle embossed on the grey material. Two white straps criss-crossed his grey uniform, and a tin water canteen with a cork hung at his belt. The illusion stopped at his feet, as he wore ordinary shoes instead of boots. Nevertheless he made an impressive sight. We parted cordially.

Soon Amina and I were in the equally unreal world of the French Quarter, where time had stood still long before the Civil War.

'Come on,' she urged me. 'Let's go and hear some jazz.'

CHAPTER NINETEEN

New Orleans Jazz

MARK TUBA SMITH'S tuba, black with a red open maw, gaped like a whale but emitted sweet music whenever its owner's cheeks ballooned outwards. A drummer peppered his horizontal drumskin with rapid shots and a saxophone player bent double in imitation of his instrument. It was a sunny day, and we were in Jackson Square listening to the music. So were a school party of six-year-old children, boys and girls, who danced joyously. I left Amina there, enraptured, and hurried through the palmy square to the banks of the Mississippi. There, at anchor beside the quay, stood the great white paddle steamer, the *Natchez*. High on the upper deck, leaning over a rail, Captain Hawley surveyed the swirling brown waters.

Ten minutes later, he was sitting opposite me in the lengthy bar-room and trying to answer my questions. He was a short good-natured man in naval dress, and he regarded me with keen dark eyes.

'My great interest in life is playing the steam calliope,' he said. 'That's the great organ you have probably heard playing on the *Natchez*. I started out working on a steamer at the age of fifteen, following in the footsteps of my great-uncle and his brother. They were both steamboat captains. When I was fifteen, I sailed on seven different rivers in one year, playing the steam calliope and working in the food department. The rivers were, let's see, the Ohio, the Mississippi, the Tennessee River, the Kanawha in West Virginia, the Missouri, the St Croix (a tributary of the Mississippi) and the Arkansas River.'

I forgot to ask the Captain about it, but at some time or other, the title 'River' must have moved. In England, the title goes *before* the river, as in River Mississippi.

'Yes, I've always been on pleasure boats,' the Captain continued. 'The heyday of paddle steamers as everyday working vessels was between 1850 and 1880. Little paddle-wheel pushboats lasted till the 1950s. They pushed barges down the river, but now diesel pushboats are used. Just over a hundred years ago, there would be seventy-five to eighty paddle steamers a day, stopping right here at New Orleans. Sailing vessels went out around 1910. Before that, the ships that came here carried rocks as ballast, and most of the courtyard flagstones in the French Quarter served as ballast on the voyage over.

'I served ten years on the pleasure boat *Delta Queen*. First I was mate, then pilot and finally captain. I've done the coastguard exams, but I've had no experience at sea. The Mississippi is a difficult river, and you have to put up with snow, rain and fog in winter and stifling heat in summer. This ship is the ninth *Natchez*, modelled after the one before. It's one of only five steam-powered vessels left on the Mississippi. Our navigation aids and our lights are electric now, of course, and the boat is made of steel, not wood. In Mark Twain's day, the steamers were of wood, very combustible and only lasted four years. This boat's twelve years old, and her engines are sixty-two!

'So you like Mark Twain, hey? D'you know what the name means? Two fathoms! There was a Captain Isaiah Sellars who wrote a gossip column for the *New Orleans Picayune* using the name "Mark Twain". When he died, Samuel Clemens took over and used the same name, and stayed Mark Twain ever since. Nowadays the paper's called the *Times Picayune* – a picayune was a French coin.'

Pleased with my questions and with his own answers, Captain Hawley gave me two free tickets for a ride on the *Natchez*. We parted on the best of terms.

Back at the hotel, I found Amina to be jubilant, as she had followed a Jackson Square jazz band in procession down to the banks of the river and back, dancing in the Second Line. We compared notes, for we had reached the nerve-racking stage of rationing out a certain amount of dollars to spend a day.

'Look, I've got free steamboat tickets for interviewing a captain!' I said. 'I'll phone up and fix an interview with the head of that jazz museum you saw near the French Market. Then we won't have to pay to go in.'

So, a few minutes later, I announced that I had successfully arranged an interview with Don Marquis, the curator of jazz archives for the Louisiana State Museum. After that, we went out for a night on the town. At a café, Amina poured scorn on my passion for hominy grits, the triumph of Southern civilisation, and ordered exotic-sounding French Creole dishes with aplomb.

Soon we were wandering up and down Bourbon Street, window shopping for jazz. We actually went inside one club, called The Famous Door, where an excellent blues singer was shouting 'Going to Kansas

City', to the fiery music of honking saxophones. But when we saw the price of the cheapest soft drink on sale, we too had to go. Mischievously, Amina peeped into a male strip show and shouted 'Shocking!' to the surprised tout.

White jazz bands, no doubt composed of Dutchmen, played technically, as if following mental sheet music dated 1922. 'They're good in their way, but too wooden,' Amina exclaimed.

She was too young to remember the English 'trad jazz' craze that swept the grammar schools and art colleges of the early sixties. However, she had suffered its effects, for English jazz had settled down as white boozy bohemian music. Pub musicians groaned or sneered at the sight of a coloured person, looking on black people as the treacherous race who had invented 'pure, true jazz', and then deserted it for other styles. In New Orleans, probably spurred on by England, jazz snobbery had reached a crescendo. Tourist guides urged everyone to go to Preservation Hall, where the true, real jazz was upheld for the benefit of true, real believers.

Amina and I tried to get into Preservation Hall, but the queues were too great. We peeped through the window, which opened on to the back of the stage. An old coloured man, presumably a treasured relic of the twenties, sat on a wooden chair holding a trumpet and looking benignly at the tootling white musicians around him. There were no chairs, and fresh, pink-faced young people, mostly girls in bright dresses, sat on the floor, enraptured. I was reminded of pictures I had seen of idealistic young Communists in New York in the forties, sitting on floors listening to Southern musicians imported by John and Alan Lomax. It was quite a touching scene, but it did not please Amina.

'It isn't fair!' cried Amina. 'Mark Tuba Smith told me that he plays with a band who still play at funerals along Rampart Street. Yet because they have a saxophone and play modern tunes as well as old ones, they can't make a living in the French Quarter at all! All the good jobs in clubs go to the "true" jazz musicians, that is, the white ones. How can it be "true jazz" if it isn't allowed to change? The old tunes are still there, so why can't new ones be added? Mark Tuba Smith and his friends *love* the old tunes!'

Jackson Square musicians, who played beside open hats or cardboard boxes, had apprenticed themselves to jazz as small children. Despite their enormous talents, they saw themselves as beggars, and felt too humble to push themselves forwards. However, few of the coloured musicians who *did* play in Bourbon Street clubs seemed to be doing very well.

In the After Hours club, where we settled down at last with a drink apiece, a big coloured man, all smiles and gold rings, sang rhythm and blues songs from a high pulpit. He could imitate various singers, and sang word-for-word versions of famous New Orleans songs of the fifties and early sixties. Only when he switched to his own electrifying blues voice did I recognise him as Blues Boy Benjamen.

Beaming, he swept his twenty-carat hands up and down the keyboard. When his eyes fell on Amina, they twinkled wickedly and went on looking straight *at* her. He sang blues verses apparently at random.

> 'See that girl all dressed in red?
> If you don't look out, she's gonna mess up your head!'

'Why *you're* dressed in red!' I said to Amina, but she did not reply. 'Hey!' I called out, as the Blues Boy finished his set of songs and dashed out towards his next venue.

'I remember you!' he said, delighted. 'I'm singing at the Rising Sun next – why don't you two come over?'

'That's the name – Rising Sun!' Amina cried. 'Do you know a jazz band who play there with Mark Tuba Smith?'

'Oh, they play outside on the Rising Sun Patio,' he said dismissively. 'I play *in* the house. I sure hope I can count on seeing y'all there.'

With that he was off, and we soon followed. After traipsing up and down gaudy Bourbon Street for a while, we turned our faces to the Rising Sun. It was a muggy, tropical night, for a New Orleans December was allowed to enjoy two or three hot summer days every week. Or so it appeared. Three fat, drunk, white men, two with beards and glasses, fell out of a doorway, fighting ineffectually, and rolled on the pavement.

As usual, black crowds stood outside the Rising Sun and white crowds danced and roared inside. A slim, dark jitterbugging waiter-tout flung himself around in the doorway, doing the cross-leg wimble wamble dance. When his face occasionally relaxed, it took on a contemptuous, ironic expression. We peeped around this waiter, to see what was going on.

Blues Boy Benjamen was not singing, but trying to persuade a friend of his to sing. A middle-aged coloured man with a cap, glasses and a self-effacing smile, the man was wryly refusing to do so. I didn't blame him, for the audience looked as stupid a bunch of white rock fans as one could hope to see anywhere, all bare arms and smear-on moustaches.

'This is Tommy Ridgely, a well-known musician here in New Orleans,' the Blues Boy explained. 'I hoped he would sing for y'all, but it seems he's just passing through. So now a little rock and roll number, called "Flip, Flop and . . . *Fly*".'

'Ugh, look at the mad way they're dancing,' Amina shuddered, pulling me away. 'I hate Caucs!'

'Caucs', short for 'Caucasians', was her pet name for young white Bourbon Street revellers, of the sort who surged from club to club and only behaved themselves if the band was composed of white people. They seemed to be very rich, and all Bourbon Street was Cauc-conscious. Girls in jeans and ringlets, red-faced with drink, shrieked and hung on to their conga dancing menfolk.

Just round the corner from the Rising Sun, an alley with an open wrought-iron gateway led straight into a little flagstoned courtyard with scattered chairs and tables. A small shed-like bar had been erected in a corner, and a sign read 'Rising Sun Patio'.

We just had time to see all this, when there was a whirring sound, and a stout young coloured man in spectacles appeared miraculously before us. He had an air of beaming, convivial respectability about him, resembling half an accountant, half a Creole Mr Pickwick.

'Welcome to N'Awlins, y'all!' he cried, ushering us in with frantic joviality. 'We havin' a party, y'all, and *y'all's* invited! You don't have to come in, it's not mandatory, but we'd be sure glad if y'all joined us.'

We took our seats and looked round to see six white tourists sipping drinks, and Mark Tuba Smith and his friends the drummer and saxophonist. Mark gave us a shy look of recognition. A loudspeaker had been rigged up to amplify their music. A tall shabby waiter came forward and took our order. Although a young man, his face seemed prematurely lined with tragedy. From this worn-out face, two small brown eyes, tinged with kindness, sympathy and wry self-deprecating humour, looked out at the world. His long brown overcoat was torn and raggy, with holes in places. He returned and lowered our drinks on to our table with half a bow.

'He looks exactly like Jelly Roll Morton!' Amina whispered excitedly.

This was high praise, for the original Jelly Roll Morton had been the self-proclaimed Inventor of Jazz. The modern Jelly seemed a far more humble man, but when the music started, he performed a rapid winding dance in the gateway to attract more customers. No matter how absurdly his body behaved, his face always kept its dignity.

Meanwhile, the bespectacled man had produced a gleaming trumpet. 'Now, here's a song for *y'all* about our favourite football team, the Saints!' he announced. 'Y'all should go and see them play at the Superdome. They don't always win, but we still love them just the same. This is real N'Awlins jazz, y'all, just as it was played in the old days, absolutely genuine!'

With that, his cheeks bulged outwards and he and the band began to play 'When the Saints Go Marching In'. They played with great verve, and the saxophone player turned the well-worn theme into a new song altogether. When the tune was over, Amina congratulated the trumpeter and asked his name.

'Surreal,' he answered, wiping away the sweat. 'It must be a French name – I look French, don't I? Ha ha!'

Surreal led his band, the New Orleans Jazz Quartet, into number after number, each one surpassing the tune before. Amina looked very happy, and Jelly Roll Morton jitterbugged. A good rough-voiced blues singer, Surreal played and sang in turn. He explained that his band 'did funerals', and sang an extraordinary unfuneral song, 'Didn't He Ramble?' as a demonstration. Introducing each member of the band in turn, he allowed the saxophonist a lengthy solo on 'Blue Monk'. Whenever a group of tourists paused at the gateway, he rushed towards them and began shouting 'It's not mandatory!'

It was a pity, for Surreal's sake, that drinking at the Rising Sun Patio was not mandatory. Perhaps the legislature ought to do something about it, for poor Surreal and his friends were not being paid a wage for their efforts.

'Don't forget the tip-kitty, y'all!' he would say.

A bulky, grumpy fifty-year-old Nordic hippie, the bar owner, glared out at the band and the customers in gloomy satisfaction. How kind he was to allow them to play there! On good nights the band could earn thirty dollars between them, but if it rained they were lucky to get five. Possibly Jelly Roll Morton was allowed to sleep there. Whenever a new customer came in, Surreal would play the 'Saints', the New Orleans anthem, and then make a speech telling everyone how authentic the music was.

'It spoils it all when he does that!' Amina complained. 'He makes it *less* authentic.'

'You know what Americans are,' I said, 'you've seen tourists in England. What they like are bogus things, so something *real* has to be disguised as bogus before it can be accepted as real.'

With a final verse of 'Down By the Riverside', Surreal announced a break, and joined the band in the bar. When they returned, to find that no new customers required the 'Saints', they began to play modern rhythm and blues numbers. These sounded wonderfully fresh and jaunty played with a jazz line-up.

'If you're going to New Orleans, you ought to see the Mardi Gras,' Surreal wailed, before blowing fiery zigzags of sound from his trumpet, the Latin American blues. Insistent Haitian drum beats and sizzling calypso cymbals showed that little of New Orleans' Caribbean influence had escaped the drummer. Mark Tuba Smith blared solemnly, as Surreal sang.

'Got my ticket in my hand, down on Rampart and Dumaine.
Got my ticket in my ha-and, down on Rampart and Dumaine,
And if you stay right there, you're sure to see the Zulu Queen.'

'Now another song by the late, great Professor Longhair – "Big Chief"!' shouted Surreal.

Grinding saxophone and a blare of brass came to a halt now and again, as Surreal announced in heavy Redskin tones: 'Big Chief like fire water!'

As a tribute to Fats Domino, the living rhythm and blues King of New Orleans, Surreal played 'I'm Walkin'', a fast and furious tune that did credit to his magical trumpet. Then Blues Boy Benjamen walked in, half raising a hand in recognition of one and all, before sitting at our table. Pleased to see him, I began to prattle of this and that, and told him of our proposed trip down the river on the *Natchez*. Bonhomie, mischief and good nature shone from his Barbadian features – high cheekbones on a full face.

'Down on Bour-bon Street,' sang Surreal, before sighting an inquisitive tourist and galloping off to assure her that coming in and placing an enormous donation in the tip-kitty was not mandatory, but nevertheless desirable. She came in and brought her husband, so it was the 'Saints' once more.

It seemed like a dream sitting there beneath a warm velvety sky. Sometimes a mule in a red hat trotted by the open gateway, pulling a landau with a fringe on top. Ice cream vendors rolled their wagons along the lively street. Friends and relations of the band stopped and waved. A big coloured man in a smart suit danced past the doorway, bending backwards and raising his feet high in the air. His girlfriend followed behind, her head resting on his shoulder.

With a word or two in Amina's ear, Blues Boy Benjamen melted away into the night.

'He's got a nerve!' she said, on the way to the hotel. 'He thought we were married, and said, "Slip away from your husband, and come along with me." Apparently he's got a girlfriend at home, but he doesn't like her. He got a surprise when I said that we were brother and sister.'

'Did you say that you'd see him again?'

'No, but I've got a feeling that I will.'

Don Marquis, Curator of Jazz Archives, welcomed us to his office at the Jazz Museum. This was housed in a huge brick building at the edge of the French Quarter, The Old Mint. It looked more like a courthouse than a Mint, and had once been used as a prison.

Instead of the dashing Spanish aristocrat we had expected, Don Marquis proved to be middle-aged and tweed-jacketed, with spectacles. In appearance, he was the very epitome of an English ex-grammar school jazz fan. Don was short for Donald. We introduced ourselves as two writers, not as brother and sister, as Amina so hated my lengthy explanations. Drawing our chairs up to his desk, we admired a book he had written, *In Search of Buddy Bolden, First Man of Jazz* (Louisiana University Press). Another contender for the title of Inventor of Jazz,

Bolden had been a hairdresser and trumpet player. Don Marquis also gave us a jazz magazine called *Second Line*.

'This jazz museum was founded by a bunch of enthusiasts in 1962, when it was housed in a cottage on Dumaine Street,' he said. 'It grew until the point came when it was turned over to the city and housed here in the Old Mint, in '77. I came here a year later, and first of all catalogued the exhibits, mostly instruments, and then designed the exhibition showcases. I laid out the museum from five hundred boxes of trumpets and stuff, old photographs and rare gramophone records.

'I come from Northern Indiana, and I loved jazz ever since I heard my first Louis Armstrong record. I listened to jazz programmes on the radio, and subscribed to *Second Line* magazine. At that time, bands from Preservation Hall would come up and play at Cleveland, Ohio. My first job was Ideas Man to a greeting card company. Finally I was freelancing for twenty card companies. I first came to this city to work on the New Orleans *Times Picayune*. Then, in 1973, I began researching Buddy Bolden, talking to old black people who might have known him. I met old women who had danced to his music, and I reunited two old ladies who used to go dancing together in 1920 and now lived a few blocks apart, each not realising the other was still alive . . .'

I could see Amina stifling a yawn, but she sat up with a jerk when he mentioned Jelly Roll Morton.

'People say that Jelly Roll was a liar, but his stories about shootings and killings in New Orleans, that he told to Alan Lomax, have been confirmed by the city homicide reports of the day. He lived just near here, at Frenchman Street – the house is still standing.'

'Could you give me the number?' Amina asked, trying to stay calm.

'Sure. Now I'll take you on a tour of the museum.'

Walking around rapidly, and talking all the time, Don Marquis hustled us past stands of old photographs, antique instruments and waxworks in Mardi Gras costume. Amina looked wistfully over her shoulder.

'My colleagues have stabbed me in the back, stabbed me in the back,' he cried petulantly. 'Why is there no piped jazz music here as I requested? Penny-pinching officialdom is ruining the museum. Why, we're only open two days a week, as we can't afford the security guards for a full week! Then why are there no exhibits on the Old Mint? People interested in coins come here all the time, and they get furious when they see no trace of the Mint here.'

Still talking about his colleagues, Don Marquis led us upstairs where he showed us ghastly iron-barred cages where convicts had been housed within living memory. Then he took us to the Amistad Room, not a part of the Museum, where we met a very pleasant coloured lady director. A frieze on the wall showed the story of the cargo ship *Amistad*.

One day, in 1839, two Spanish slave traders hired the *Amistad* to transport fifty-three slaves from Havana, Cuba to another Cuban port, Guanaja. All the slaves, members of the Mende tribe, had been captured illegally in the same part of Sierra Leone. Consequently, they formed a united force, and once at sea they seized the ship with much bloodshed. The surviving Spanish crewmen were ordered by the slaves to steer the vessel back to Africa. Pretending to obey, they headed for America instead, and were stopped by an American vessel at Long Island. Charged with piracy and murder, the slaves were confined in a local jail. Meanwhile a legal battle over the hapless Africans took place between the Spaniards and the captain of the American ship. The Spaniards wanted 'their' slaves back, but the captain claimed them as salvage!

However, Christian abolitionists from New York heard of the matter and formed the Amistad Committee to free the prisoners. After many lawsuits, the U.S. Supreme Court declared that the slaves were free. The Amistad-lady did not tell me what happened to them, but I hope they were taken back to Africa. The original Amistad Committee continued to work for the freedom of slaves and the wellbeing of black people. Now, renamed the American Missionary Association, and largely run by the educated descendants of slaves, it had established the Amistad Room as a centre for historical research.

As we were saying goodbye to the friendly Amistad-lady, we were hustled out by Don Marquis, who wanted his lunch. 'There's a very good restaurant just across the road from here,' the hungry Don urged us. 'I'll join you for lunch. I don't eat out often, so it'll be a treat for me.'

This was awkward, as we had worked out that our money could last out if we had only two meals a day, breakfast and supper.

'We have no money on us, only travellers' cheques,' I said hastily.

'No matter, no matter, I know a hotel that will change them.'

So saying, he almost ran to an hotel. Mercifully it was closed. However, the persistent Don rang the bell until a bearded young man appeared. At once Don launched into an urgent request for cheque-changing. Then he looked at us triumphantly, expecting broken thanks. Slowly Amina pulled her last travellers' cheque out of her handbag, one that we had promised ourselves would remain inviolate till Friday.

Drooping, we followed the ebullient Don back to the restaurant, a spacious palmy place where we were the only customers. He seemed mildly surprised at our lack of appetite. I toyed miserably with my one bowl of clear soup, while he ordered oysters and various things with French names.

'You writers get expenses, don't you? Good, good! Now I'll tell you what I can about jazz. True jazz flourished from 1915 to 1922. Most of the jazz you hear in New Orleans is not authentic. Young boys play jazz instruments, but not in the authentic New Orleans style. Some use electric amplification, others might use saxophones, and all these non-authentic groups of black performers play tunes that were composed after 1922. No, to hear *real* jazz, you must either go to Preservation Hall, or seek out some of the European musicians. You *must* talk to Chris Burke, he's an Englishman, and he's one of the most authentic musicians in New Orleans today.

'One band, all Africans, were formed in Zimbabwe by an Englishman who only allowed the musicians to hear records from the early twenties. That way their music had to be authentic! When they came to New Orleans, everyone was surprised how loud they could play without amplification.'

It was a good thing that the Don hadn't been around in Jelly Roll Morton or Buddy Bolden's day, or jazz would never have been invented. *Second Line*, a semi-literate fan magazine, also regarded the use of electricity in any form as 'disqualifying' a band. Writers deplored that so many New Orleans clubs had gone over to rhythm and blues, without realising that rhythm and blues was the current form of jazz, a popular Negro music.

'When I was at grammar school, in the fifties, a book that made a big impact was *Really the Blues* by Mezz Mezzrow,' I said. 'I think it had a bad influence on everyone who read it. A white American, Mezzrow seemed to revel in Negro low-life too much, and he boasted in a silly way about being sent to prison as a drug pedlar.'

'I've been to prison!' Don Marquis cried gleefully, startling the waiter, who approached with an enormous bill on a plate. 'I was locked up for one night on a charge of S. and D. That's Suspicious and Dangerous! A cop saw me talking to these black musicians, and ran me in. He told the judge I'd been following a black woman on Bourbon Street, but the judge threw the whole case out of court. So I spent a night in a cell! Here's your check. Well, it's certainly been a pleasure meeting you both! As I said, I don't usually eat here.'

With that, the Suspicious and Dangerous Don took his leave. Feeling faint and frantically trying to do mental arithmetic, we tottered along Frenchman Street in search of Jelly Roll Morton's house.

Stretching far out of the French Quarter, Frenchman Street was a pleasant neighbourhood of small wooden houses, some with doors facing the brick pavement, others with porches. Most of them telescoped out at the back, with pieces of house stuck on in rows, one behind the other. Such long wooden houses were known as 'shotgun houses', perhaps from their length. Whether shotgun or pistol, the houses all had green lawns and trees at their rear. Only coloured people seemed to live here, and there was a lazy Creole atmosphere. Passers-by nodded and said hello.

Perhaps Frenchman Street had not changed greatly since Jelly Roll Morton's day.

We found his house, which had been divided into two since Jelly's time. Steps led up to a porch, with two front doors. One half of the house was empty, the other had Catholic ornaments in the window. A corner house, it stretched back quite a way, with a green lawn and a high wire netting fence. It was a plank house, painted white, and there was no plaque.

Amina at once began to photograph it. I refused to touch the camera, claiming that every machine broke as soon as it saw me. So she stopped two teenage girls who were walking along the road and asked them to take a photo of her in front of Jelly Roll Morton's house.

The girls, who were very dark and had been conversing animatedly in French, switched to English and smilingly agreed. They appeared to have heard of Morton, so the request had not seemed an unusual one.

We walked back towards the Quarter, when suddenly Amina cried, 'I feel giddy! Something's swimming round in my head!'

She tried to walk on, but couldn't.

'It's Jelly Roll Morton!' I told her. 'He's trying to tell you to go back to his house. We were so stunned by Don Marquis that we've been acting like Americans, photoing something and then just walking off! We haven't really seen his house at all.'

'You're right,' said Amina, and she found that when she walked *back* to Jelly's house, she felt perfectly all right. We stood looking at the house and imagining it as it might have been when it was new, a hundred years ago. Eventually we were all satisfied, even Jelly Roll Morton's spirit, and we walked back into town in a more cheerful frame of mind. As if with a click, our Don-induced daze had vanished, and we were in our right minds once more. I noticed a drawing of a marijuana cigarette on a fence, labelled 'Bo Weed'. Teenage gangs here were called 'Crews', not 'Posses' as in England.

At Jackson Square, I consulted Amina, who held the purse strings, and then invested in a shoe shine. The coloured shoe-shiner looked sceptically at my winkle-pickers for a moment and then set to work.

'You got good taste in women, but bad taste in shoes,' he remarked.

'She's my sister, actually,' I said. 'We come from England.'

'Your sister?' the man repeated ruminatively. 'Hmm. If I may mention a technicality, she is a mite darker than you.'

'Well, her father comes from Nigeria.'

Here he pulled a face of comic surprise. 'They pull that stunt there too? Claim their folks just come over from Africa when they got "Mississippi" written all *over* them . . .'

'Come on!' Amina cried furiously, so the man gave my pointed shoes a final wipe and I escaped.

'Never tell people anything!' she commanded fiercely.

'Well, I was only going to say there's no Mississippi in England . . .'

Just then we saw the clock on the St Louis Cathedral and realised that we would have to run if we were to catch the *Natchez* paddle steamer. To our relief, the great three-decker ship had not left port, and we could hear Captain Hawley playing loud tunes on the mighty calliope, or steam organ.

'Look who that is, up on the deck!' I cried. 'It's Blues Boy Benjamen.'

'Hi there!' called the Blues Boy, with a wicked grin. He was dressed in a nautical shirt and wore sunglasses.

We compared notes, and found that he too had not bought a ticket. A friend on the crew had smuggled him on board. Amina seemed a little shy at first, but soon she and Blues Boy were the best of friends. Like passengers on a great liner, we sat three in a row on deck seats and looked out over the river. Now and again, Amina and Blues Boy disappeared to the bar and returned. He spoke earnestly about his career and the blues and soul singers he admired. His ambition was to leave the tourist dives of Bourbon Street and play for club bookings. He spoke wistfully of Malaco Records, and I wished that I could help him.

Our conversation was punctuated by siren blasts from the steamboat whistle and undecipherable comments by Captain Hawley in loudspeaker-language. Amina was disappointed in the Mississippi. The dreary closed docks and the strike-bound ships reminded her all too clearly of Liverpool.

Without strong sunshine, the Mississippi mud looked as uninspiring as mud anywhere else. A dry dock had been out of action for a year thanks to a strike, and two Liberian-registered ships, the *African Hyacinth* and the *African Dahlia* reposed there sullenly. Industrial wastelands lined the banks of the river, with scrubby woods in the distance.

'We are now passing Marie Laveau's park,' crackled the unseen Captain. 'She bought the estate with wealth gained from her voodoo practice, and when she died, nobody claimed the house. It became a ruin, and until a few weeks ago, people would go inside and walk around. The mansion was noted for its great tower. Unfortunately, the whole place burnt down in a recent fire.'

'It was a firebug!' said a passing deckhand, who walked by holding a broom. 'I hope they find that sucker and hang him.'

A chill wind blew over the Mississippi, and Blues Boy shivered in his thin shirt. We passed the site of the Battle of New Orleans, another stretch of waste ground. Apparently the battle had been fought by mistake, as no one knew that the war between England and America had ended.

On our return (for the trip had been a short one) the Captain, now speaking very clearly, pointed out the Algiers Landing Restaurant. It was a leaning heap of wooden shanties resting on a spider's web of criss-cross wooden piles. Corrugated iron patches had been stuck on here and there, some new and silvery, others red with rust.

'That restaurant is completely new!' announced the Captain, to our amazement. 'It has been made like a crazy old heap of fishermen's huts on purpose. Inside it's a real swell eating joint.'

I noticed that in spite of their ramshackledness, the heap of shanties all had shining glass windows. Nearby warehouses were being converted into luxury flats, just as at Wapping on London's river.

Captain Hawley appeared in person and gave us a cheerful wave as we walked down the gangplank. Blues Boy had to go, but arranged to call on us at the Y.M.C.A., which was destined to be our home.

On our last evening at the Burgundy Inn, we walked down to the Rising Sun Patio to hear Surreal and his friends play. We were stopped by a mad old lady we had often seen before, who tried to sell us 'magic beads', and later by tipsy youths who urged us to stick to our respective colours. Crowds of tourists and sightseers thronged the narrow fern-hung streets, loud disco music poured from the souvenir shops. Ill, shrivelled coloured women in doorways occasionally whispered 'Please', and held shaking hands out for alms. At last we reached the Patio, and found Surreal in fine form, singing: 'I went to the Audubon Zoo – and they all asked after you!'

'Here's our mascots!' he cried, when he saw Amina and myself, and he showed us to a seat near the bar. Jelly Roll Morton II served us courteously, his eyes momentarily meeting ours as if he hoped for a secret message.

'We're moving out of the French Quarter, to the Y.M.C.A., so we may not see you so often,' I told Surreal. 'At the end of next week we go home to London.'

'You can move into *my* house, if you can't afford a hotel,' he offered, looking shocked and concerned. 'Then perhaps you can stay in New Orleans a little longer.'

'Surreal, how kind!' cried Amina. 'But we have to be home for Christmas.'

Mark Tuba Smith sounded an exploratory blare on his tuba, and the band swung into 'Bill Baily', with Surreal singing the verses.

A ridiculous tourist with a fixed red-faced grin sat next to us, clapping and jerking about. 'I'm a Dane,' he said as he tried to put his arm round Amina. Drunk or mad he may have been, but he was sane or sober enough to shrink back from the shaft of pure disdain that flashed from her eyes. Then he danced like a lunatic up to the band and tried to put his arms round them while they were playing. Finally, to our relief, he danced out of the alley-way, ignoring the tip-kitty, and danced off down the road.

Surreal dashed over to us and apologised about the Dane, then waved his trumpet in the air and gave a big bespectacled grin as young tipsy customers began to dance.

'We're having a party, y'all!' he cried, as usual. '*Y'all's* welcome, and if you want, we can play for y'all all night long! We're just so happy to have y'all here! Why if I could, I'd buy y'all drinks and even *pay* y'all to stay here and enjoy yourselves! If you *must* leave, y'all don't forget the tip-kitty.'

Unfortunately more customers drifted out than drifted in. Surreal began to look frantic, his smile grew broader and his eyes grew glassier. Breaking off from a brilliant trumpet solo, he dashed out to the road, where a line of young drunk white girls were dancing past. As the music swirled out towards the girls, they began to fling their arms and legs about in a parody of black dance. Surreal grabbed a girl's hand and led them all into the Patio, a leg-kicking centipede of female Caucs. Then he grabbed his trumpet and tried to Pied Piperise them into staying. With wild shrieks of laughter, the girls paraded four times round the courtyard and then out into the street again, ignoring the tip-kitty.

'Well, it was a good try!' he told us. We were his confidants.

Surreal and his friends were master jazz-craftsmen, who took their music very seriously, and it distressed Amina to see them wasting their talents in this way. Luckily, most of the white customers were not Caucs in Amina's definition (young, drunk and half-jeering) but middle-aged couples who sat sedately at the tables.

For some reason, the big hulking manager of the Patio lumbered out, a seventeen-stone hippie with long blond hair and a raggedy thatched upper lip. He walked across the courtyard, then turned round abruptly. His behind swept two full glasses from a table and alarmed the middle-aged couple who sat there.

Growling apologies, he called for the waiter, Jelly Roll Morton II, who cleared up the mess and brought fresh drinks in the twinkling of an eye.

'Goddammit, you ***!' roared the hippie at poor Jelly Roll. 'Why don't you arrange the tables right! Get out here and move that table!'

Without a word, the waiter complied, and the Nordic hippie stalked back to his lair, fuming. Still the band played on. Two noisy young men, labelled Caucs by Amina, performed a lurching dance, bumping into the band. The attitude of Caucs to coloured musicians seemed a combination of admiration and condescension. Were they trying too hard to behave like black people, or were they consciously parodying them? Being drunk, they could not tell us. When the Dane returned, his fixed grin wider than ever, jerking and jumping and making 'hepcat' noises, Amina rose to leave. Surreal was sorry to see us go, but he gave the Dane the full 'mandatory' treatment none the less. Mark Tuba Smith blew on impassively.

In crowded Bourbon Street I paused wistfully at the door of a large dancefloor-pub where a Cajun group was playing, the fiddle player stamping and the audience galloping up and down holding hands on high. Amina steered me onwards, and we ended up in a little club, or pub, with a piano.

At the piano sat the merriest old coloured man I had ever seen. His eyes formed the centres of webs of smile-creases, and he shook and almost wept with suppressed laughter as he played. Each of his hands seemed possessed of a merry devil of its own, both working in harmony to create some of the finest blues and boogie woogie music that we had ever heard. Every now and then, the rolling rhythms would cease as he leaned towards the door and shouted, 'This is New Orleans, y'all!' as if there could be any doubt. In a corner near the piano sat a little old wrinkled white lady, her head in a shawl. She listened intently to the piano player, devouring him with piercing eyes. After every number, she clapped energetically.

Amina and I sat beside the piano player, who gave us one of his cards. 'Al Broussard, Human Trumpet,' it read. He didn't look very trumpet-shaped, but in a moment we saw what he meant. While singing and playing a number called 'Boogie Woogie Gal', he suddenly pursed his lips and began playing pure rooty-tooty trumpet music with his mouth. The old lady seemed beside herself with excitement. We were then treated to an engaging little ditty called 'I Aint Gonna Give Nobody None of My Jelly Roll'. I studied the old lady. That hawk-like nose, those features – surely she was upper-class English! I moved over and sat beside her.

'Excuse me, are you from England the same as me?' I asked.

At once she flew into a terrible rage, jumped up and darted out both hands to scratch me. I dodged her and hurried back to Amina. The old lady climbed off her chair, glaring, but climbed back on again when the manager appeared and gave her a talking to. Finally she wrote a message on a piece of paper and handed it to me with outraged dignity. Then she returned to her seat.

'I'm Welsh, from Cardiff,' the note said.

I shouted it to Amina, who smiled soothingly at the glowering old lady.

'Yacky dar!' Amina said. The effect was magical. With tears in her eyes, the lady jumped up and embraced Amina, hugging her and repeating 'Yacky dar.'

Al Broussard smiled warmly at this sentimental scene. 'I'm eighty years old, and she's seventy-three,' he said. 'She's the only person I allow to play on my piano.'

With a flourish he rose and helped her on to the piano stool. Frowning severely, the old lady played not 'Men of Harlech' but 'Loch Lomond'. Al Broussard clapped her with an air of great gallantry when she finished, and then went back to work.

'See See Rider, see what you done done,' he sang. 'You made me love you, now your man done come.'

This is a very old blues. 'Rider' is a sexual metaphor, and 'See See' is usually taken to be a corruption of 'Easy'. However, there is a modern blues called 'Searching for my See See', which suggests otherwise.

Al Broussard, still suffused with merriment, sang the words and then added explanations in a speaking voice, with great emphasis. Other customers sat on high stools at the bar, listening indolently.

> 'Gonna buy me a pistol – *he's gonna shoot her!* – long as I am tall.
> Buy me a pistol, long as I am tall.
> Gonna shoot that woman, catch the *Cannonball*.'

'Now that's a train. He says he's gonna shoot her, but he won't shoot her; shall I tell you why? 'Cos he still loves her, that's why. But she's got another man, an' she won't take him back. He's tried pleading, but now he's too proud to plead no more. Only thing to do is to leave town and forget her! But he can't forget her, no matter what he do.

> 'Going away, baby, won't be back till fall – *he's leaving*!
> Going away, baby, won't be back till fall.
> If I can't love you, I won't love no one at all.'

'Who wrote that song?' I asked, when Mr Broussard had finished.

'My Uncle Jimmy,' he replied calmly. 'He lived in a shotgun house not far from yere, an' he used to always sing this song as a duet with his girlfriend. But one day, she jilted him and left, and he married another girl a week later on the rebound. After they been married a while, my Uncle Jimmy calls on his old sweetheart to try an' make peace with her. She greets him as friendly as anything, an' fixes him a drink.

' "Why don't we sing that song 'See See Rider', same like we used to do?" he says. "Sure," she says, so they begins to sing. When he gets up to the line, "If I can't love you, I won't love no one at all", she says to his face, "You're right! You won't love no one at all, 'cos I've just poisoned you! It's an old African recipe an' the doctor won't find *nothin'*. In about an hour, you'll get cramp and then you'll die."

'An' so it happened. Now he's in the fifth grave in one o' the rows in the St Louis Cemetery. My Uncle Jimmy was only thirty years old when he died.'

We finished our drinks in pensive mood. The old lady wished us goodbye in upper-class English tones, and Al Broussard called out to the next group of incoming customers, 'This is New Orleans, y'all! Home of jazz!'

'What does "Yacky dar" mean?' I asked Amina, as we hurried along Dumaine Street to our hotel.

'I haven't the faintest idea.'

'Went to the Rising Sun Patio,' Amina wrote in her diary that night. 'Korky the Cauc was in evidence, so we left.'

CHAPTER TWENTY

A Social Whirl

'I CAN MAKE MYSELF at home anywhere,' said Amina, in a small, shaky voice, as I showed her to her room in the Y.M.C.A. She winced and backed away as cockroaches scrambled across the room in all directions. They weren't even very big cockroaches, by Y.M.C.A. standards. 'As long as they don't have any poisonous spiders here,' she continued.

'No, no,' I soothed her, though in fact I had been told of two local species, the Black Widow and the Brown Sojourner, whose very names suggested New Orleans.

Half an hour later, we were sitting in the Y.M.C.A. Washeteria, as Amina's dresses spun round and round in a hopeless attempt at drying. An earnest coloured youth with glasses spoke to us rapidly.

'My navy career was marred by the way I fooled around with drugs,' he admitted sadly. 'This led to a spell in a mental institution, and right now I'm paying for my keep by doing odd jobs here at the Y. My aim in life is to teach school. I would like to be a German teacher.'

'Can you speak German?' asked Amina.

'Yeah, I can say *auf Wiedersehen*. My favourite poet is Kipling. Would you like me to recite "If"?'

Amina was too broken-spirited to say 'No,' so he went ahead and recited it. Seeing her sitting there in a corner, half crouched in a rumpled red dress that seemed too big for her, I would have supposed her to be a waif from a children's home, if I hadn't known she was my sister. She seemed to be shrinking and growing paler before my eyes.

I spent a feverish night, tossing and scratching. Outside, police sirens screamed 'wow wow wow!' in a computerised style now copied in England. In the morning, my hands and legs were covered in red spots that itched abominably. Amina had suffered in the same way.

'This place is swarming with bedbugs!' she told me crossly. 'At night I could hear them rustling inside my pillow case. We *can't* stay here!'

'It's only a few more days,' I said dismally. I had previously been quite content in the Y.M.C.A. but now I could see it through Amina's eyes and I could barely stand it.

My sister took one look at the Chinese girl wiping her nose on the back of her hand before serving breakfast and swept out of the cafeteria. We took the St Charles' streetcar to Canal Street.

'I wonder if I could use my Barclaycard here in New Orleans?' I said idly.

'What! You've got a Barclaycard! No! I don't believe you!'

'Yes, here it is, look.'

'Why didn't you use it? You can use those anywhere! Our troubles might be over!'

To test my magic card, we entered a grand hotel and approached the lady at Reception. I asked her if a Barclaycard were valid in America.

'No, I've never heard of a card of that name. We can't give you credit on them here,' she said shortly.

'Well, it was a good try,' I said, as we straggled out into the street.

After window shopping for a while, we retraced our steps, for I had not yet introduced Amina to the delights of Magazine Street. Away from the French Quarter, across the Canal Street divide, this was a black rather than a Creole neighbourhood, with a vital atmosphere of its own. But now that winter was approaching and the weather was dull and gloomy, the streets were nearly empty.

We entered a dark little bar near the Orphans' Home, and all eyes turned sardonically towards us. The other customers seemed all to be pimps in superbly cut clothes, waistcoats, suits and snap-brimmed hats.

'Good afternoon,' I said politely.

'Good morning,' was the sarcastic reply.

Zydeco music poured from the juke box. We drank up and left.

At Davy Jones's Locker, the small but picturesque seamen's hostel, we asked for cheap beds in vain.

'Sorry, seamen only,' a gruff Dutch sea dog told us.

Finally, after straying to and fro, we arrived at the Hamburger Grill, the café where Fat Larry from Honduras reigned supreme. He had been very kind to me on my first visit to New Orleans.

'Larry's not here right now,' the stout blonde serving-lady told us, when we had climbed up on to stools at the counter and ordered coffee. Many of the customers remembered me, and reminisced of old times, two months before, when I had blundered into the café.

'Have you seen that girl called Jessie Bee whom I met in here?' I asked.

'That's her, right there!' was the reply.

I had been looking at a tall, slim girl wondering if she were Jessie B. Scott, the tough no-nonsense woman who had seemed so touched when I had given her an English penny. The girl had shown no sign of recognition, so I thought I must have made a mistake.

'Jessie!' I called out, and she gladly came over.

'I figured that if you don't know me, then I don't know you,' she explained. 'If you had walked out 'thout recognisin' me, I was not gonna say one word, just walk on by and hand you back your English penny.'

Jessie and Amina took to one another immediately. Each fell in love with the other's accent. Soon Jessie was talking animatedly about her two children, aged twelve and thirteen, and her job serving drinks in a club at night. She lived in the Project, the tenement 'council estate' behind the café.

'When I get home, they just 'bout be's gettin' up, so we sits and talk, an' then I git some sleep,' she told us. 'I got 'em trained so good, that I can give 'em a hundred dollars to pay a bill an' bring back the change an' they do it. They can look after 'emselves, but I sleep real light, so's if they want sump'n, I can git it.'

'I've never heard anyone talk like you before,' Amina said, admiringly. 'You talk so slow and so deep. Let me have a try: Well, Ah declare, Ah be's goin' down the road to buy a whole heap o' black eyed peas an' molasses . . .'

'You're talkin' like you come from the plantation!' Jessie laughed. 'Now I wants you to meet one or two friends o' mine.'

Dickie and Smitty, a brown-skinned Cajun and a coloured man, two shirtsleeved friends who sat together, greeted us enthusiastically. Another Mediterranean-looking Cajun listened to our tale of Y.M.C.A. woe with interest, then asked to see my Barclaycard.

'I work as a cook in the Hilton, so I know all about cards,' he said. 'Yes, this one's all right, it's got "Visa" written in one corner. Your mistake was to call it a Barclaycard and not Visa. You can get anything you want with this.'

Great was our jubilation, and I thanked him fervently. It had been our lucky day when we had decided to visit Larry's café.

'I'll take you to where Larry's at right now!' said Jessie with spirit. 'I know he'll be real pleased to see you.'

So saying, she led us along a few hundred yards of pavement and into a long, dark, shabby-looking pub, where white and coloured people sat up at the bar drinking. As Jessie had predicted, Larry was effusively pleased to see us, and at once ordered beers all round. We perched by his side, Jessie included, and listened to the oft-told tale of his travels in Europe. A barmaid opened a fridge and revealed a long row of glasses of ice-cold beer, frost settling on the froth. She selected four, and we drank cold beer from round narrow-stemmed glasses of a shape usually reserved for jellies and cream.

'I sure am pleased to see you, Roy and Amina, my English friends,' Larry chuckled.

Again, Zydeco music rampaged from the juke box, blues verses sung in French with an accordion taking the place of the usual harmonica.

'There you are, Amina, you didn't know people could get the blues in French,' I said.

Most of the songs on the juke box were by Fats Domino, a local boy made good. Larry claimed to know him. 'Fats Domino, he lives near me, in a house painted all in orchid and gold,' he said. 'He's real friendly to everybody in my neighbourhood. Listen, you two be sure to be at my Grill tomorrow morning, as I'm playing Santa Claus for all the kids round here, handing out presents. Don't let me down now.'

As we made ready to leave, Jessie handed Amina a card with an address on it, and a name that simply read 'The Club'. 'I'm lookin' to see you both there next Friday night,' she announced firmly.

Now radiantly restored, Amina drew cries of admiration from the young men hanging around in the streets. One even composed a blues in her honour.

'Miss World went walkin' by, oh me oh me oh my . . .'

We tested the Barclaycard at a luxurious Chinese restaurant in the Jax building near Jackson Square.

'Visa is good anywhere,' said the head waiter with hushed respect in his voice. Bowing and grovelling, he led us to a seat by the window, overlooking the Mississippi. Steam whistle blowing, the good ship *Natchez* chugged by. I had never used a credit card before, but Amina showed me what to do. A life-size giant panda toy sat at the restaurant piano, perpetually playing 'Jingle Bells' (no doubt by means of a mechanical device). So we dined in splendour, entertained by a panda, and without apparently spending any money. I was very surprised.

Next morning, we hurried to the Hamburger Grill in Magazine Street.

'He's up there, getting dressed,' the blonde lady told us. She was Larry's girlfriend.

A loud jingling sound could now be heard, and Larry was in our midst. Bells hung from the tops of his boots, and his round brown face seemed lost in an enormous combination of fluffy beard and mane of curly white hair.

'Ho, ho ho,' he said, rather flatly, in his speaking voice.

Our novelty had worn off, for he barely nodded to us in his preoccupation with the Christmassy matter in hand. His friends gathered around, admiring the fine costume. Jessie was not there that day.

'There's my elf!' Larry suddenly shouted, looking up.

A big white swag-bellied workman in a pick-up truck, the man honking outside looked most un-elf-like. He was dressed in his ordinary clothes, his lumber jacket hanging open to give his stomach room to breathe. Larry hurried outside.

Half an hour later we discovered Larry sitting in a makeshift grotto on a small lawn at a crossroads, further down Magazine Street. Children of all colours crowded round him, and he handed out sweets and deadpan 'ho ho hos'.

'Don't the people here look poor and shabby!' Amina exclaimed.

'Yes, but at least the men are fat,' I said, trying to distinguish the Elf in the crowd.

An assistant Elf, a skinny man, appeared and gave us each a 'stick of candy', a sweet walking stick with stripes.

Now began a Social Whirl, as, with the aid of our magic card, we could listen to jazz, soul and blues in Bourbon Street until the small hours of the morning. Such a life suited Amina better than it did myself. As I didn't dare to let her roam Bourbon Street on her own, I tagged along at all times, almost hallucinating with want of sleep. Fortunately, after a few days, big avuncular Blues Boy Benjamen took over my job as escort, once his night's singing-stint at the Rising Sun was over.

In a dreamlike haze, I saw the same characters appear again and again in different settings, their affairs entwined in a kaleidoscope of musical hustling, a musicians' world within a world. We would begin the evening at the Rising Sun Patio, the courtyard where Surreal, Mark Tuba Smith and the New Orleans Jazz Quartet played out of doors at the whim of the unpredictable manager. Jelly Roll Morton II would dance wildly in the doorway to attract custom, until I thought he would fall to bits. Sometimes Blues Boy Benjamen would glide into the courtyard for a whispered word with Jelly Roll. Outside in the tourist-crowded street, Miss Yacky Dar, the old Welsh lady, sat on a stool and sold newspapers.

Later we would be in the Rising Sun itself, indoors, listening to Blues Boy Benjamen. Jelly Roll II would appear, elaborately sneaking past rows of tourists to locate a friend. In other clubs, such as the After Hours, Papa Joe's or Krazy Korner, the Blues Boy would step in to sing while the band had a drink. Jelly Roll II would inexplicably appear as a waiter and Miss Yacky Dar would alternate as resident eccentric with the mad old lady who sold magic beans and beads.

Was it real or was it a dream? Did Blues Boy Benjamen urge me to return to Malaco Records at Jackson and get him a contract? Or was that the occasion when one of the Rising Sun musicians grew desperate for heroin and tried to borrow money from everybody in the mystic circle?

Sometimes jealous and evasive, sometimes open-hearted and generous, the scuffling musicians of Bourbon Street and neighbourhood seemed linked one to another in a never-ending circle or Wheel of Fate. Happy laughter aimed at the tourists might conceal aching hearts and unpaid rent.

Amazing talent was thrown away each night for oafish Caucs to snigger at. Much has been made of the gruelling 'chitling circuit' of one night tours of black concert halls and clubs throughout the South, the initiation of many a blues and soul singer. Bourbon Street musicians were on a rung *below* the chitling circuit, and most yearned to play in black clubs where they would not have to be happy all the time ('This is New Orleans, y'all!'). One day that contract would come, one day . . .

As soon as I had learned how to use my magic card, we left the Y.M.C.A. and moved into stately Morrell House, a survivor of Magazine Street's grander days, and very handy for Larry's café. Amina had gone for a drive with Blues Boy Benjamen on the day I discovered Morrell House. The Blues Boy had called at the Y.M.C.A. that morning, exuding lazy charm and producing a neat, big-eyed one-year-old girl whom he introduced with pride as his daughter Nicolette.

'I figured if I brought Nicolette along, you wouldn't be scared I'd kidnap you,' he explained.

Very fond of children, except for the few she classifies as 'brats', Amina seemed pleased by this arrangement. I waved them goodbye, and then set out for Magazine Street.

Morrell House, which I had noticed before, stood a pearl among shanties, a white antebellum house with red ribbons tied to the rails and pillars of the porch doorway. A Christmas holly wreath hung from the door itself. Inside, a jolly dark-haired lady showed me from room to chandeliered room. Her husband, an antiques collector, had furnished the town mansion in stately-home style, with wall-high mirrors. Amina's room faced a balcony that spanned the first floor, here overlooking the tree-lined street, there commanding a view of a brick courtyard where a fountain played.

'We serve breakfast in the kitchen every morning, and we want you to feel as if you're our personal guests here,' the landlady told me, doing clever things with my magic card on a piece of paper. 'There's nothing here to remind you of an hotel.'

Indeed, the vast front room, with flasks of sherry and whiskey on a small rosewood table, seemed to await a grand family Christmas party. A dark fifteen-foot spruce tree, aglow with fairy lights and crystal balls, stood in a tub surrounded by boxes wrapped with ribbons and bows. Among these stood a model church with a spire and lit-up windows. Nearby, a dolls' four-poster bed, complete with sheets and counterpane, mimicked the gigantic curtain-hung beds upstairs. I could hardly wait to show Amina.

I was asleep in my Y.M.C.A. room when she knocked, and excitedly told me of her day with Blues Boy.

'He's ever so fond of his little girl! She's sweet. We went to a soul food café run by a big, tough woman called Mama Riley. All the other customers were *most* respectful of her. Nicolette sat on my knee the whole time, and everyone thought she was mine. We had chitlings [chitterlings] and all kind of spicy food, and the juke box played nothing but blues.'

'It sounds exactly like Annie Mae's Café, the place in the Little Milton song I heard at Malaco Records.'

'Oh yes, and then he drove us to Seasaint Records, where he does session work, and he played piano for me and sang soul and blues, including his own compositions. I met the owner, Allen Touissaint, and he gave us a sarcastic look.'

'Was Blues Boy a perfect gentleman?'

'Not *perfect*, as he talked about Nicolette's mother a lot, and kept marijuana gear in his car. But he's all right.'

I then told her about Morrell House, and we began to pack. When we arrived, Amina was as impressed as I had hoped. The door was opened by a smiling coloured girl called Debra, who was soon talking to us as if we three were old friends.

'Do you live here in this house?' I asked her.

'No, just two blocks down the road, that's where I lives at. I get to come here most days to help the family out.'

When Amina opened her bag, in her palatial room, five very active Y.M.C.A. cockroaches jumped out and rushed off in all directions. They must have felt as if they were in Paradise. Despite all that soap and water could do, a few bedbugs survived the journey, as they were later to survive the flight to England. But the English climate was soon to kill them. Despite all these distractions, we sank on to our respective four-poster beds with cries of luxury.

On our way down the stairs, we encountered the landlord, a tall anguished-looking man who gave a great start and then reeled away from us with a look of horror. Bleating pathetically, he rushed off in search of his wife, who no doubt told him not to be so silly. Soon we were sitting in the front room, sipping sherry and waiting for the taxi to come and take us to Jessie's club.

'It's not like staying in a hotel here!' Amina remarked happily. 'It's more like being a guest in a private house where the owner doesn't like you.'

Outside, when the taxi honked, we stood transfixed, for the whole of Magazine Street had become pink. A pink sunset shone so strongly that it could not be contained by the sky. The road, trees and houses stood suffused in a gentle glow of pink. By the time we neared Jessie's club, however, a sultry New Orleans night had fallen, and our headlights spotlighted small plank houses as our car dived beneath bridges and overpasses.

A plank house like all the others, Jessie's club stood at the corner. Inside, a bright bar beckoned across a long, highly-polished and dimly-lit room, with scattered tables, a wide dance floor and a juke box.

Here the pink lights were artificial. Few customers had arrived as yet. At once, with a cry of gladness, Jessie ran from behind the bar to greet us. Tall and slim, she was dressed in red, with her hair combed up and her brown eyes beaming friendliness. After Santa Larry's cold shoulder, this came as a great relief.

'*Uh-huh*! You don't need to buy *no* drinks when *I* invites you. Uh-*huh*!' she repeated emphatically.

Soon we were sitting cosily round a table near the juke box. Jessie Bee showed us photographs of her children, Touissaint and Anitra. She spoke animatedly, in her vigorous 'uh huh' language.

'. . . So he had the nerve to say that to *me*, an' I just goes "Uh-huh"! So he asked me what *I* thought, an' I goes "*Uh-huh*!" . . . Yeah, an' all the time, Amina, I be thinkin' "*Uh-huh*!" Finally he said would I run off with him an' I said "Nope".'

Every now and then, fresh customers drifted in: groups of coloured men in open-neck shirts, or smartly dressed couples who made for the dance floor, where speckly disco-lights were now swirling.

'Hey, you turkey!' Jessie would yell at men she knew, before springing up to serve their drinks and then hurrying back to our table. She seemed to be in sole charge of the place.

'There sometimes be a band,' Jessie told us, 'but tonight it just be the juke box. Sam Cooke, he's the singer I like.'

Couples swayed slowly on the floor, and men lined the bar drinking slowly and watching explicit scenes of nude cavorting on the television. Most of the juke box songs were old ones, by Ray Charles or Lowell Fulson. Jessie served a couple of 'turkeys', then hot-footed it back to our table again. I told her of the pimps' pub we had found on Magazine Street.

'There be some bad places there, Roy. I tell you, some o' them bars an' lounges there don't have an open door, they have a buzzer. I never press that buzzer, no ways, 'cos to me that buzzer signifies they don't want black people in there. So when I see that buzzer, I goes "Uh-*huh*"!'

Just then a new and haunting tune, with rippling piano and guitar, rang out from the juke box.

'That's them old sassy *blues*,' Jessie said appreciatively.

At that moment, Jessie gave a yelp of joy, and welcomed two newcomers to our table. They were Dickie and Smitty from Larry's café, and both seemed pleased to see us. Dickie's face lit up with boyish candour, and Smitty smiled broadly.

'My real name is Leonard Smith, but everyone jus' calls me Smitty,' the latter explained. He was a big round-headed man with an innocent expression, and he worked at the Superdome indoor football stadium, maintaining the air conditioning. Amina and I tried to describe London to him, and he showed great interest in our description of the Underground trains. 'I sure would like to go on that Tube,' he confessed yearningly.

Dickie, his best friend, was a wiry brown-skinned Cajun, a shirtsleeved Mediterranean Red Indian with black curly hair, a moustache and a merry, pixyish face that sometimes flashed a glance of innocent, childish wonder and earnestness our way. He too was an air conditioner repairer, and a sometime chauffeur and handyman for a wealthy businessman named Mr Gamble. Like Jessie Bee, he was fascinated by our English money.

'You mean these coins can really *buy* things, when they don't be's dollars or nickels or dimes or nothin'?' he asked incredulously, his first glimpse of a world outside America.

So we sat there chattering merrily over our free drinks (in my case orange juice) till two in the morning. Amina was the centre of attraction, but at last even she grew sleepy. Dickie slipped out and returned resplendent in a chauffeur's uniform and cap.

'Well, look at *that*!' Jessie Bee enthused, as she waved us goodbye.

With a smile of pure pleasure, Dickie escorted us to the door of his boss's enormous silver-grey limousine, a car fit for an Arab prince. The huge streamlined car looked out of place among the tottering streets of shanties. We rode back to Morrell House in style.

On the following evening, Dickie called for us at Morrell House, complete with cap and limousine. We sank back in the comfortable seats and looked out at New Orleans through tinted windows.

After driving along Basin Street for a time, Dickie parked beside an ugly concrete building and took out a bunch of keys. 'One o' my jobs be's takin' care o' the Carnival costumes,' he said. 'Here's where they stored at. It's a fine sight to see all o' those tings.'

'You've got three jobs, *and* you stay up nearly all night enjoying yourself!' exclaimed Amina. 'When do you sleep?'

'Sleep? Ha ha, I don' need no sleep! Maybe I have a little nap ever' three days or so.'

Delighted with the treat he had in store for us, Dickie opened a gate and then a door, and we found ourselves in a strange treasure house.

Gigantic floats used at the New Orleans Mardi Gras loomed over us in the gloomy half-light. New Orleanians, apparently, usually refer to Mardi Gras as 'the Carnival'. Gazing around, I felt as if I had stumbled into a vault of an Egyptian pyramid or into the Assyrian Bulls' room in the British Museum.

'That's the Famous Cow,' Dickie said, pointing upwards at a rampant white cow with staring eyes, a figurehead on a hundred-foot-high float. Other decorated floats, all of immense size, included a leering, manic Jester with thick black eyelashes and a bunch of smaller human-size jesters growing out of each hand. Bright paint and giant ornamental clothes adorned the magnificent garish and semi-classical figures. Craning our necks upward, for the floats towered to the roof of the immense hangar in which we found ourselves, we stared at a herd of galloping white horses, a massive elephant, a gold reclining Buddha, an Aztec sun chariot and a gang of cherubs with a battery of golden trumpets. All the floats were crammed in together, forming a maze through which we stepped carefully, climbing over the great iron bars that would connect the floats to the lorries.

In another part of the hangar, we admired a half-finished float, a huge scarlet and yellow dragon-bird with rapacious eyes and a protruding tongue, half-hidden in the shadows.

Dickie switched on a corridor light, and we saw rows and rows of crudely coloured sketches of floats and costumes pinned on the walls, the work of the Carnival's Arts and Ideas department.

'The Carnival societies who make all o' these tings are called "Krewes",' Dickie told us. 'Now more an' more Krewes are bein' started, even in the outskirts. Everyone wants to be in a Krewe; black, white, all the peoples. Carnival time be's so crowded, you can't walk down the streets.'

Costumes of purple, gold and green velvet hung upon tailor-shop rows of hangers, and boxes of Krewe badges filled the cupboards. Scattered about the smaller rooms that opened off the corridor, we saw half-made costumes and rough pastel sketches that had since led to the construction of enormous floats. Surfeited with wonders at last, we allowed Dickie to lead us to his car. He drove us around Lake Ponchartrain, past Christmas lights in mansion windows and white yachts at the water's edge.

'That's my boss's yacht, over there!' he exclaimed proudly. 'I make good money here in New Awlins, but I miss my house an' peoples Down Home on the bayou. We lives way out on the swamp, an' I goes out with my fishin' pole to catch my breakfast. We goes huntin' a lot, an' before I come here to N'awlins, I useter breed worms for bait to sell. Come my birthday, I get some liquor, get real happy, oh yes! Las' birthday I got up an' I dance, dance on the table! My grandmother say "Come down from there, boy," but I say "Oh no, grandmother, I stay here an' dance, 'cos I be's *happy*!" Amina, I wisht you could come, meet my folks Down Home in the country . . .'

Dickie turned the limousine around, and Amina directed him to the Rising Sun Patio, where Surreal and his jazz quartet were playing.

'That's my kind o' music!' Dickie shouted, as the New Orleans Jazz Quartet began the Mardi Gras theme always accredited to 'the late great Professor Longhair'.

'I see that you're from the bayou,' Surreal said, when he heard Dickie's accent. 'Are you a friend of our two mascots, Roy and Amina?'

'Naw, I jus' be's the chauffeur!' Dickie suddenly snapped like a sulky boy.

Amina enjoyed the music, but the atmosphere felt a little strained. Before long, Dickie jumped up, ran outside the Patio and bought Amina a rose from a nearby vendor. A beefy young man, this vendor had berated me night upon night for not buying 'my wife' a rose.

'You're a nasty, nasty man!' he had shouted last time, not realising I was filled with brotherly embarrassment. So when Amina at last clutched a freshly-cut rose, the vendor crowed in triumph.

'Come with me, I'll show you something good!' Dickie cried, now full of boyish glee. We followed him into a large souvenir shop where we had our photographs taken staring through the rubber-barred window of a mock 'Bourbon Street Jail'. Evidently in an elated mood, he drove us back to the house he shared with Smitty.

'I've been friends with Smitty for the longest time,' he told us. 'We met each other in a bar.'

Plank cabin-like houses, raised on blocks of stone, looked strange in the greenish-glow of the lamp-light; avenue upon avenue of white-painted garden sheds and summer house-like homes. Teenage boys jostled one another playfully at one corner, a very English touch. At last we stopped in front of a long shotgun house, a former cabin with rows of plank annexe-rooms boarded on at the back.

The door opened to reveal a mosquito-net awning which opened in turn, and we stepped into a front room where Smitty and his three-year-old nephew Kevin sat watching television. Soon we were sitting beside them on the long brown settee, while Dickie ran through to the kitchen to pop open some Cokes. Kevin was a tiny, quiet little boy, who stared solemnly at the screen.

Above the television, shelves with cheap plaster knick-knacks adorned the painted hardboard wall, along with family photographs and a large mirror. Every door inside the house was open, and most of the furniture was arranged to leave an uninterrupted passage from the front door to the telescoped-out back, five rooms away. All the doors stood in alignment, so

I could stare straight through the house. Each room represented an extra tacked-on bit of house, all of different sizes. A more apt name than shotgun house might be 'telescope house'. Our settee was on one side of the room, the television on another. The nearest door opened on to a bedroom, and I admired the majestic bed, huge and heavy, with a towering, curved headpiece like the top of a Royal throne. It was a cosy house.

Smitty's sister, Kevin's mother, arrived a moment later, a plump, cheerful young lady who seemed pleased to meet us. Dickie was in high spirits, handing out beer and Coke and chattering away to Amina. A far cry from the programme shown in Jessie's club (which may have been a porn video), the film that engrossed the Smitty household was *Swiss Family Robinson*.

'We've got them on the run!' Father Robinson shouted in triumph, as he and his Swiss Family hurled sticks of dynamite at a gang of Chinese pirates, chased them into pits full of man-eating tigers and levered half a mountain's worth of avalanche on top of them.

'Got them on the run? He's killed them!' Dickie cried, leaning forward on his seat. When the film ended, he drove us back to Morrell House. 'So you came here from the Y.M.C.A.? Be a bit different, don't they? I 'member I installed some air conditioning to the Y.M.C.A. last year, an' I was shocked by all them 'roaches.'

Our last full day in New Orleans, in the South and in America began in a peculiar way by Smitty phoning my room at eight in the morning, when I was fast asleep. 'If you come to the Superdome today, I can get you cheap football souvenirs!' he said keenly.

'I'll think about it,' I promised, before going back to sleep.

An hour later, Amina and I sat at the kitchen table eating hot croissants and drinking orange juice. With a smile, Debra showed us where everything was, as we had to make coffee by ourselves.

'I'm going out with Blues Boy this morning and Dickie this afternoon,' Amina told me. 'Then we'll go to the Rising Sun tonight for the last time. Dear old New Orleans! I'm going to miss you! Nobody here ever seems to get any sleep. I think that's why you can't talk ideas with New Orleanians. All their mental energy must be needed just to stay awake. Even then, I don't believe they can tell what is a dream and what's real.'

Before I had finished my breakfast, Blues Boy honked outside and Amina dashed off, telling me to meet her in Jackson Square. When I finally set off, the sky grew overcast. I heard *another* honk, and there was Dickie, all smiles, in his shirtsleeves at the wheel of a small pick-up truck.

'Amina's just gone out with a friend,' I told him. 'We'll see you this afternoon at Jackson Square.'

With a wave, he was on his way. I wandered down to the Y.M.C.A. to see if any letters awaited me, and then went to the workmen's café for a hot peach pie and ice cream. Outside, a torrent of rain began to fall. A man in a yellow oilskin lurched into the room and climbed up on a counter stool beside me. We did not speak, but every now and then he burst into disconcerting laughter, perhaps at my accent, perhaps at my table manners. Finally I strugged out into the rain and walked head-down towards Magazine Street once more. Outside the Y.M.C.A. I hesitated, dreading the maelstrom of rubble, road building and looming overpass that I would have to cross to reach my hotel for a nap.

'Hello,' said a voice. I recognised the yellow oilskin and grey hair of my café companion, seen dimly through the pouring rain.

'Ah, you remember me? Like you, I am not American. I am from Italy. I used to stay here in the Y.M.C.A. but it got too expensive, so I took to rabbing people.'

Surely he couldn't mean 'robbing'? I asked my new friend if he knew of a short cut to Magazine Street, one that didn't involve slithering about on a torn-up road in the blinding rain. Eagerly, he led me to a side street and then urged me to follow him down an alley.

'Anyway, why go to Magazine?' he reasoned. 'Come and stay in my room.'

Suddenly, I decided that 'rabbing' *did* mean robbing, and ran away very quickly, ignoring his shouts. Slithering and gasping, I reached Morrell House, where I dried myself and dived into bed.

Bright sunshine winked in the puddles by the time I met Amina in Jackson Square. She roared with laughter over my Italian adventure. Dickie seemed to be rather late, so we sat and watched a party of charming six-year-old schoolgirls dancing and clapping around the teenage boys' jazz band. The children imitated each musician, sliding imaginary trombones and beating imaginary drums.

Still no Dickie, so we read a Black Moslem newspaper that somebody had left on a bench. It showed pictures of Black Moslem prophets dressed as wizards in robes embroidered with stars and moons. One such prophet, said to be a reincarnation of Moses, also wore a fez, dark glasses and a bow tie. 'Moslem gospel songs' were advertised, and the Black Moslem faith (like its Rastafarian counterpart in England and Jamaica) seemed to be a twisted offshoot of Christianity.

'Our Saviour, Silis Mohammed, was born in Marlin, Texas, on June 21st, 1938,' I read. 'Do not believe the devil (Caucasian Race). What the Moslems want: We want separation from the slavemasters' children in America. After giving America four hundred years of our blood, sweat and tears, we want to return home. Oh Africa! Hear our cry!'

I folded the paper and looked up at the arches of the Cabildo, where, according to Desita, the newly landed slaves had been led in chains to be roughly examined by prospective buyers.

Still no Dickie, so I tried to phone him up. After many unsuccessful attempts (for the American phone system was the inspiration for British Telecom) I at last got through and spoke to Smitty.

'Dickie is asleep in bed!' he snapped angrily. 'Goodbye!'

'Whatever can be the matter?' Amina wondered in surprise, when I returned. 'Perhaps he followed Blues Boy's car and spied on us eating at Mama Riley's café. Or perhaps his need for sleep has caught up on him, and he dreamed I did something awful and thought it was real.'

Whatever the case, we heard no more of Dickie until he and Jessie phoned us up in England with a friendly message. Jessie began a correspondence, but Dickie, like so many Cajuns, had to admit that 'he didn't write so good'.

So Amina and I spent a few nostalgic hours saying goodbye to the French Quarter.

That night in the Rising Sun club, Blues Boy Benjamen surpassed himself, singing nothing but blues. He seemed to glow with mischievous energy, and winked and waved at us, his gold rings sparkling. Two country-looking Negroes in vests and slacks sat just below Blues Boy's keyboard, looking admiringly up at him as they clapped and swayed along with the music.

> 'If you got a good woman, don't leave her on her own!
> If you got a good woman, don't leave her on her own!
> First thing you know is Jody took your girl and gone!'

'Jody' is the archetypical adulterer, a back-door man who first found his way into the G.I. Blues of marching black troops in Europe. Now Jody songs were back in fashion, with a reply-song from a girl blues singer, 'I Don't Need No Jody,' as heard on the juke box in Jessie's club.

'These two visitors are from the state of Mississippi!' Blues Boy announced, pointing at the two men. 'I believe one of 'em's gonna sing for you all!'

'I'll do anything, baby, anything you want me to . . .' the man crooned sentimentally.

We suddenly noticed Jelly Roll Morton II slumped in a chair in a corner with his old coat thrown over him. He shivered in his sleep. As Blues Boy took the microphone once more, the growing Cauc element in the audience yelled, roared and danced with their bellies flopping about. The owner of the Rising Sun sat near Jelly Roll II, a big sinister Texan in a stetson hat and dark glasses. He seemed to approve of the rowdy young men, who were all big spenders.

Blues Boy brought his song to an end with a roll of the drum machine. 'Nobody wants the blues!' he announced. 'But the blues is something you just can't lose. That's a very old music, the blues. There's always been the blues and there always will be the blues.'

'Play something psychedelic!' yelled a depraved-looking young man with a smear of moustache on the corners of his mouth.

With an obliging grin, Blue Boy played a zany jumble of notes on his keyboard and then turned to the tough proprietor. 'What you say, Big Boss Man, shall I stop now or go on?'

'If you go on, there's a bottle of Jack in it for you,' said the boss, indicating the brand name 'Jack Daniel's' on the bottle of whiskey.

Making an heroic effort, Blues Boy sang 'The Thrill is Gone' and 'Mustang Sally'.

'Run outside to the Patio and see if Surreal and the others are playing out there,' Amina whispered to me. 'If it's wet, they might go home before I can say goodbye. Tell them to hang on till I get there.'

So I dashed out and found the New Orleans Jazz Quartet setting up their instruments and plugging in the loudspeakers.

'My sister's just listening to Blues Boy Benjamen, and she'll be here in twenty minutes,' I told Surreal. 'She wants to say goodbye to you.'

His Pickwickian beam vanished, and he looked utterly amazed and anguish-stricken. 'Your *sister?*' he wailed. 'I thought she was your wife! If I had known, I would have invited her to go out with me.'

'Didn't Mark Tuba Smith tell you? I told him all about our family.'

But Mark Tuba Smith could not have understood me. He came over and consoled Surreal. The self-effacing genius of the trumpet had showed greater self control than Blues Boy Benjamen, who had simply told my sister, Jody-style, to 'slip away from your husband for a while'. All the band gathered round me.

'Do they have black people in England?' asked the drummer in surprise.

'Yes, of course – thousands of them.'

'I'm sorry you an' Amina won't be comin' here no more,' said Mark Tuba Smith in the soft, shy voice that sounded so strange coming from such a big man. 'This is my wife Catallia here.'

A sweet-looking woman, Catallia unwrapped an arm from her husband's shoulder and shook my hand. I had not thought of Mark Tuba Smith as a family man before, yet from her handbag Catallia produced photographs of their two little girls, Janet and Tina.

Despite the noise, I managed to phone Jessie and wish her goodbye. 'I love the way you say "Uh-huh",' I told her.

'Uh-*huh*!' she replied.

Back inside the Rising Sun club, I found the Blues Boy reduced to singing minstrel songs:

'Oh, Li'l Liza! Little Liza Jane!
Oh, Li'l Liza! She died on the train!'

At last his set was finished. Benignly, the Blues Boy collected his bottle of whiskey and strolled over to our table. After a drink together, Amina suggested a visit to the Patio. There we found the band in disarray, and the customers bewildered. Luckily the Nordic-hippie boss was absent.

'Surreal jus' ran off an' left us!' explained the open-mouthed saxophone player.

Without a singer and trumpet player, the band seemed at a loss. Blues Boy Benjamen laughed rather scornfully, for he considered *his* sort of music to be far superior to jazz. After many false starts, a young white trumpeter was somehow found, and the Quartet began to play.

Who should walk in at that moment, all weary smiles and rubbery legs, but Jelly Roll Morton II, the sometime waiter. Now utterly transformed from his previous comatose state, he danced, clapped and sang, the life and soul of the evening. A mysterious man, Jelly Roll II had a secret understanding with Blues Boy Benjamen, and sometimes caught his eye, sometimes avoided it.

When the show was over, and farewells had been made, Amina and I left with the Blues Boy, who was going to drive us back to Magazine Street. Like a liner among fishing boats, he glided his shiny-suited way through the flotsam and jetsam of Bourbon Street. All of a sudden, we heard a shout and Surreal ran towards us, glasses awry and forehead beaded with sweat. Without a word, he handed Amina a rose, and then vanished.

In the car park, Jelly Roll Morton II appeared, and ingratiatingly helped the Blues Boy to find his car. Hardly speaking, the strange waiter stared long and hard at my sister, as if impressing her features on his mind. He seemed to want to say something, but remained dumb and waved us out of sight.

Now with wistful memories, I am in England once more, still dreaming about the South. There is the White South, so hospitable to strangers, so tied to Confederate memories. And there is the Black South, home of the abandoned subjects of deposed King Cotton, a harsh monarch in his day, yet one who taught his people how to sing them old sassy blues. Somewhere between the two, I had travelled for too short a while, wondering what to make of it all. What did Gladstone say in 1862?

There is no doubt that Jefferson Davis and other leaders of the South have made an army; they are making, it appears, a navy; and they have made what is more than either, they have made a nation.

In Georgia, the setting of so many of Erskine Caldwell's stories, I had asked a white member of the Southern nation his opinion of that author. I wanted to see how far the South could take friendly criticism.

'Anyone who portrays the South as dirty, ignorant and poverty-stricken, is okay with me!' he replied with spirit. 'That's the kind of writing that keeps the Yankees away!'

Walton Guest House
Walton Street
Oxford: 1987

Index

Trinity River, 217, 231
truck drivers, 129–30
Tuscaloosa (Alabama), 62–4, 130; County
  Jail, 63; First African Baptist Church,
  62, 63; First Episcopal Church, 63;
  Ramada hostel, 62
Twain, Mark, 1, 300
'Tyrone', 121, 122, 123, 129

unemployment, 18–19, 259, 269
United Church of Christ, New Orleans,
  36–40

Vaca, Felipe Cebeza de, 220
Vaden, Mr and Mrs, of Oak Ridge, 89, 90,
  91–4, 95, 98, 99
Veizer, Mr, English teacher, 286–7, 288
Vicksburg (Mississippi), 140, 145–6,
  156–7, 163–4, 184, 186; Catfish Row,
  145; downtown, 145–6; National
  Military Park, 146

waffles, 77
Walker, W. A., painter, 151
Washington, Booker T., 4, 205; *Up From
  Slavery*, 4, 5, 186–7
Western Swing, 226, 228
Wharton, Larry, 212
whistle pig (woodchuck), 82
'Wilkinson, Michelle', Probate Judge,
  106, 116
Williams Brothers, 166, 167, 168
Wills, Bob and Mrs, 226–7
Wilson, Lincoln, 212
Wincherterter, Paul and Mary, 159–60,
  171
Wright, Dr Benny, 182

Yazoo River, 146, 147

Zebu (Brahma cattle), 245, 275
Zydeco, 248, 261–3, 267, 271, 317,
  319

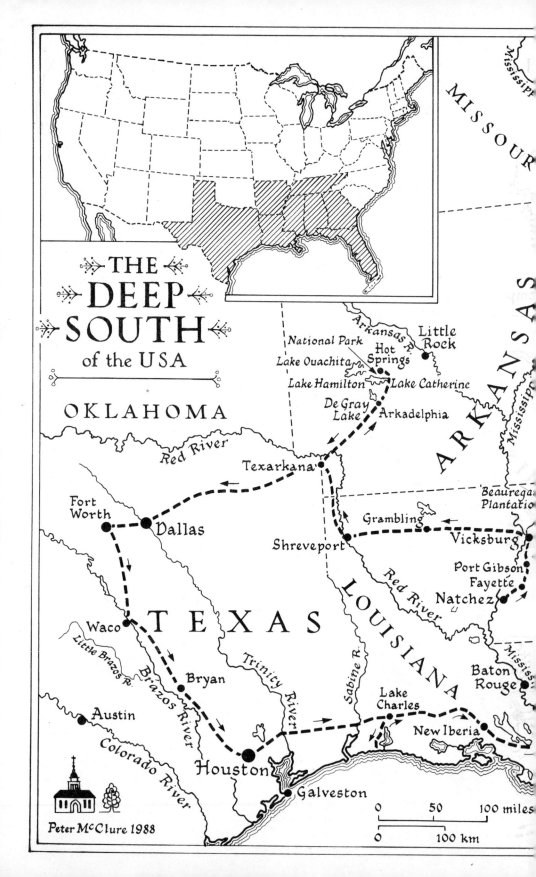

THE DEEP SOUTH
of the USA

MISSOURI

OKLAHOMA

ARKANSAS

Arkansas R.

Little Rock

National Park
Lake Ouachita

Hot Springs

Lake Hamilton · Lake Catherine

De Gray Lake · Arkadelphia

Red River

Texarkana

Beauregard Plantation

Fort Worth

Dallas

Grambling

Vicksburg

Shreveport

Port Gibson
Fayette
Natchez

Waco

TEXAS

Little Brazos R.

Brazos River

Bryan

Trinity River

LOUISIANA

Red River

Sabine R.

Mississippi

Baton Rouge

Austin

Colorado River

Lake Charles

New Iberia

Houston

Galveston

Peter McClure 1988

| 0 | 50 | 100 miles |
| 0 | | 100 km |